SCENES FROM A VARIED LIFE

Scenes from a Varied Life

Copyright © 2021 Tom Siewert

All rights reserved. No part of this book may be reproduced by any means without permission.

Cover photo courtesy the late David Thompson
Photos on pages 272 and 344 © Alan Laurie

ISBN 978-1-945824-42-5
First Left Fork Edition: 2021

10 9 8 7 6 5 4 3 2 1

Left Fork
PO Box 110
O'Brien, OR 97534
www.leftforkbooks.com

Scenes from a Varied Life

Tom Siewert

Contents

Introduction	vii
Beginnings	1
Ranger Tales	17
On a Clear Day You Can See the Brocken	111
Working for the MLC	180
Thailand, December 1996	192
Telling Tales	206
Weddings	223
Bigfoot Serenade	238
Travels With Pedro	271
A Few Odds and Ends	321
China	332
Searching	363
Afterthoughts and Acknowledgements	380
Appendix	385

Introduction

One night while working at the Grand Canyon, I was helping out my colleague Kirk in the dispatch office when a call came in from a traffic stop. A law enforcement ranger had pulled over a car for going a little too fast and ran a check on the license. Then he called in for another check on the driver, which we ran through the computer. It all came back with no wants or warrants, nothing unusual to get worried about, no reason to take him in, so he let the guy go with a warning. Then the ranger, who had a permanent job with the National Park Service, radioed to us that he just thought it seemed a little strange that the guy had a driver's license in one state, the car license in another, and was living in a third state. Kirk, who had been seasonal ranger (sort of like part time) like me until recently, responded, "Maybe he was a seasonal park ranger." Kirk and I just laughed, since that description could have been either one of us. In those days seasonal rangers tended to be vagabonds, wandering from park to park, state to state, region to region.

    I don't consider myself an exceptional person, but I would say I've had some exceptional experiences during my time on this Earth thus far. I hope you will agree after reading this, my life has been nothing if not full of variety, though there have been certain areas of focus, themes if you will. For some silly reason, through most of my life I have often chosen to cast stability to the wind and follow wherever that wind led me. In my life I have "moved" more than 45 times. I've lost count. Most of those moves were more like travels, though often loaded down with more stuff, and with the necessity of filling out a good many "Change of

Address" forms for the U.S. Postal Service. It's more amazing considering I predominantly started out living with my parents in the same house for 28 years before I even started most of that wandering. Many of those moves were prompted by working as a seasonal ranger for the National Park Service, but certainly not all of them. Each of us has had interesting things happen in our lives and most of us could write fascinating books about them, but often we like to read about things that are different from our own day to day existence. Since most people don't move so much and haven't had quite the variety that I have had in these last 60-odd years, I thought it might be interesting to share these stories with you. Also, I like to write.

To give you an idea of what kind of variety I mean, let's look at a few facts about my life. Besides my home state of Wisconsin, I've lived in the states of Virginia, North Carolina, Florida, Alaska, Oregon, California, Arizona, and Colorado, and traveled to all of the other states except North Dakota and Hawaii. I've also visited Canada and Mexico. I lived in Germany and have visited eleven other countries in Europe. I currently live in China and also in Asia I have visited Japan, Thailand, Indonesia, the Maldives, and Singapore. As for work, I've been a brickyard worker, paint and wallpaper salesman, cashier, musician, storyteller, information clerk, sales manager, English as a Second Language teacher, middle school teacher, janitor, grocery store clerk, delivery man, police and ambulance dispatcher, temp on construction projects, and park ranger, which also included doing educational programs, library work, law enforcement, fire fighting, and emergency medicine. I've done light construction and worked on a farm helping raise chickens, ducks, geese, Guinea fowl, goats, vegetables, fruits, nuts and medicinal herbs. Not all of these places or vocations will be explained further in the following pages, but you'll find stories about most of them. Rather than one, continuous narrative, I will tell you tales of some interesting and amusing things that have happened in my life as I've wandered here and there, as well as some of the meanderings of my mind and the interesting and odd people I've met along the way. Therefore it is not completely chronological, so if the book seems a bit disjointed at times, then that's why. If you want the short, chronological version, there is a timeline in the appendix at the end of the book.

Now you know a little of what to expect in the rest of the book. What should you not expect? You're not going to read about my love life with a few brief exceptions. I'm not one to kiss and tell, even though I know that's a popular trend today. I personally can't justify sharing intimate details of people I mostly still care about too much to embarrass them or reveal intimate details about their lives. If you're perceptive you'll notice that there are a number of names of girlfriends mentioned in the stories, however, so there's variety in this aspect of my life as well. You'll also not read much about my personal problems, depression, anxiety, and such, though it's hard to avoid that completely, just like my love life. At times it was serious, very serious. I've already started another book about it because if it were in this one, it would be way too long and complicated. I will say a bit more about it towards the end of the book. I think even without these items, there will still be plenty to amuse and interest you.

Throughout the book I mostly use just the first names of people, and even those have sometimes been changed, in order to protect privacy. With the variety of places I've lived and the numbers of people I've known in my life, there is no way I can go back and get approval from these people to use their full names and have them add details to the stories I may have missed or forgotten. You may notice that I capitalize some words that we don't usually capitalize in English, in particular Earth and Nature (Nature in the big sense). I view those as proper names. If you don't like it, sorry, but that's your problem. I just ask you to consider the possibility. All of the following stories, unless otherwise noted, happened as written to the best of my knowledge.

BEGINNINGS

In the early morning hours of Sunday, June 8, 1958, Arline M. Siewert went into labour, and before too long gave birth to a little boy. She and her husband Willard already had two girls, and this was their first and only boy. They named him Thomas Almond. That's me. Why Thomas? No idea, and nobody living knows. All I can say about the name is that it is Aramaic and means "twin." Couple that with the fact that I was born under the sign of Gemini, the twins, and if there is anything to such portents, well, I would be a person who could see two sides of an issue well, thereby making it nigh unto impossible for me to make decisions. I'd say that's true to this day, though maybe not for those reasons. I can walk into a grocery store, spend a half an hour, only to walk out with two things. Why Almond? That was my paternal grandfather's given name and also my father's middle name. It's an odd, nutty sort of name, but as far as I can tell I wasn't named after a nut. The name is German, and the nut "almond" is called "Mandel" in the aforementioned language, so it's not likely the source of the name. The best I can tell from my reading is that the name came from some Germanic dialect and refers to the Alemanni, which was a coalition of Germanic tribes way back in the early days of the land that became Germany. At least that sounds more distinguished than being named after a nut, much as I do love to eat them. My ancestors came from northern Germany and Denmark, Siewert being German meaning "Peace in victory," "Victorious guardian," or some such thing, and my mother's maiden name was Petersen, a good Danish name whose meaning should be rather evident.

My early life was not particularly notable. I grew up in Racine, Wisconsin, an industrial town in a farming state along the shores of Lake Michigan. I was a skinny little boy, fairly smart, but not particularly gifted physically. I got picked on and made fun of a lot, beaten up often enough, mostly by my "friends" and classmates. I have two older sisters, Nancy and Pat. My parents were Lutherans, so we were too. We went to church most Sundays, Sunday Bible School when we were little as well, and went to religious schools from first grade through twelfth. All three of us were good students, though none of us were great athletes, though Nancy and I enjoyed sports. Our parents didn't put much emphasis on extracurricular activities, and we were expected to study hard and get good grades. I spent a lot of time at the library following my interests, which were Native American history, Vikings (my distant ancestors), and Nature. As a child I wanted to be a herpetologist focusing on salamanders. That was a point of fascination for my parents, because they often asked me to tell people what I wanted to be when I grew up. None of them knew what a herpetologist was until I explained it. They study reptiles and amphibians. The looks on people's faces when I told them were varied and endlessly amusing.

I went to a public school near my home for kindergarten, then

Me as a little guy when I still had a little fat on my bones. I soon began to grow much thinner.

in first grade moved to a religious school connected to my church where I stayed through 8th grade. They were good at teaching the three Rs, Reading wRiting and aRithmetic, but lacked in nearly all other subjects. Of course there were Bible studies as well, and the teachers were fond of telling us how "Every time you sin you're driving another nail into Jesus' hands." I was a visually-oriented imaginative boy and that haunted me for many years. There was no physical education class at this school, though we did have softball, basketball and flag football teams in which I participated. During my 7th and 8th grade years we never won a single game in anything. Of course we had about 6 kids in my grade level in the whole school and the other grades weren't too much bigger, not exactly enough for making a good team. I graduated with honors from Racine Lutheran High School with nearly as many science credits as I could get from a conservative Lutheran school. I played on the basketball team my first year, then intramural basketball for another year or two. I got drunk a number of times, high on a few occasions, but otherwise didn't do much naughty stuff. While I had some good friends there, most of my high school days I would rather forget. So that's all. Don't look for any more.

Before we leave the early days, there is a question which requires an answer, that of how a simple, skinny, little middle class boy from a not very big midwestern industrial town ended up following such a diverse and unusual path? Without getting into the psychological aspects of the question, I can point to 3 things that helped me along toward that end. The first is my dad's lifetime subscription to *National Geographic* magazine. He stored them all in the attic of our home. As we were growing up, I would spend hours up there looking at those magazines, and not only the pictures of naked native women, and wondering about what it would be like to travel there, sometimes imagining where I would live, what work I would do. That was a huge influence on me in appreciating the variety of the world, fostering a love for the natural world, and to eventually becoming a geography teacher. I still read the magazine today.

The second item was our yearly trips to northern Wisconsin, a place called Blue Lake Resort. We would spend a week there every year in July, although one year my dad splurged and we lived in that little cabin for 2 weeks! We'd go fishing, walking in the woods, visiting the nearby Indian reservation, watching the boat show in Minocqua, and play in the water. That's where I nearly drowned one day. I was little, maybe 9 years old, and I decided to try swimming out past the end of the pier in front of our place. I dove under the water and my foot caught on one of the weeds as I reached time and again for the pier I couldn't quite grasp, my head just under the water level. Finally I pushed down with my foot, loosed the weed, and was able to surface and gasp for air. My sisters sitting on the pier hadn't noticed anything and never believed me, at least not for many years. Anyhow, traveling there, being in nature, and feeling the new environment all helped me to develop a taste for the feast we call wanderlust and a love for the natural world around me.

In 1964, when I was just 6 years old, we didn't go to our cabin in northern Wisconsin, but instead our parents took us out of school early to go on a much longer trip. We loaded our family into the old Plymouth station wagon and headed for the East Coast, across the flat lands of northern Indiana and Ohio, winding around the hills of Pennsylvania, our ultimate goals being Washington DC and the New York World's Fair, all done when the Interstate Highway System was still in its infancy. The magnificent buildings of the national capital, the interesting, intricate world of the Smithsonian Museum, and the plethora of international exhibits at the World's Fair, these, without a doubt, inspired me to aspire to see and experience it all. Trips like this were rare among the people that I knew in my youth; it was a very different society back then. We were lucky to have had the experience. I almost didn't include this last one in the book, since I was so young when it all happened, but I was reminded of it recently here in China. In Jinghong City there are trucks that drive around spraying the streets with water to keep down the dust because of the constant construction. As they slowly meander around the neighborhoods, they all have music playing. One of the trucks plays "It's a Small World" over, and over, and over again, just like they did at one of the exhibits at the fair, reminding how mind-numbing it was.

The Music Years

Though I didn't have much formal training or experience in music other than the church youth choir and listening to the radio, my interests began to shift during high school, and by the time I graduated I wanted to be a rock star. I'd attend concerts or watch them on TV, imaging myself on stage performing. To try and make this a reality I studied guitar with a jazz player and later voice with a classical singer, while working my way through high school and part of college in my dad's brickyard and building materials store. More on that brickyard stuff later. Music became my thing. I played in a few garage bands for several years, mostly as a bass guitarist and occasional singer. I worked hard at learning to play the bass and my most memorable compliment on my abilities came from one of the area's best rock guitarists, a guy named Tony, who played in a band that mostly covered Jethro Tull songs. Jethro Tull was my favorite band, and in high school my nickname was "Jethro." Anyhow, Tony's day job was painting houses and he occasionally came into the store where I worked to buy paint. I had told him I played bass. Once he saw me perform at a free concert in town, and the next time he came into the store he told me, "I know you said you played bass, but I did't know you were really good at it!" I glowed for a while.

I took a year off of my studies after high school to play music, make some money working for dad, and figure out what I should do next. Then I began formal music study in college focusing on classical guitar and composing. As it turns out I should have stuck to playing bass. As a bass player I was getting respect, but I never got many compliments playing classical guitar. I did a little better at composing, though not brilliantly. I studied first at the University of Wisconsin - Parkside, then after a year transferred to the Wisconsin Conservatory of Music, which was in an old, drafty mansion on Milwaukee's East Side near Lake Michigan. I got an apartment near the school and my first girlfriend soon after, though that didn't last too long.

My first night in the apartment was a rather shocking lesson in living away from home. When I signed the lease the apartment manager, a middle aged woman who looked like she had seen a lot of life, lectured another new tenant and me about how how careful we needed to be living in that area, how there were bad people to watch out for. I rented an apartment at the back end of the building near the parking lot. After I made dinner that first warm, early September evening, I listened to the sounds of the rock band Styx performing an outdoor rock concert at the lakefront nearby. As it got dark the sounds of people arguing at the other end of the building vibrated through the walls and down the halls. A man and a woman were having it out with each other, and soon they began screaming at the tops of their lungs. That progressed to sounds of breaking beer bottles and a physical altercation, and soon after another man's voice entered the fight. The two men ended up outside my window shouting at each other, one obviously drunk and the other more clear headed, the drunk one accusing the other of sleeping with his woman, which he denied. "And how is she your woman when she just kicked you out," he shouted. "Just leave." And finally the drunk man did. Didn't I call the police? No phone. Cell phones didn't exist and they hadn't gotten around to hooking up my land line yet. Apparently nobody else called either. In the midst of all that came a knock at my door. It turned out to be a young woman who knew the former resident and wanted to call someone about the fight, but was shocked at finding me there. She later became my girlfriend for a time, a lovely, though somewhat neurotic lass from New Jersey. As it turned out

Playing my Rickenbocker bass guitar and singing at a gig in a Milwaukee, WI, bar

the woman in the fight was the apartment manager, and these little bouts became regular Friday and Saturday entertainment for a while until the owners found a new manager. It was in that apartment I also had my first experiences with thieves. First one came in through the window and stole a handful of change and some nuts and bolts I had for a prepared piano piece I was working on, though oddly left my guitars and my TV, the only valuable things I had. Then one cold winter day I went out to start my car and found it was dead. I popped the hood to check the battery … but it had disappeared. Welcome to the big city!

Music school went alright for me, but I never developed into the kind of guitarist or musician I had envisioned. To paraphrase an old joke, I had a good musical education, but never let it go to my hands. I knew a lot about music, but was not a very gifted guitarist. My hands just couldn't seem to keep up with what I wanted them to do no matter how much I practiced. There was another problem that reared its ugly head as well. Part of music school involved what we called "juries," basically mini-performances for a select group of teachers held in a small room with no windows, which were often nerve-wracking experiences. It was how they graded you on your instruments. You sit in front of the teachers and they tell you "Play a 3 octave phrygian mode starting on C." You would play it and they would give you another to play, then another, and another. Then you would perform one or more pieces of music for them. One thing we had to study besides our main instrument was basic piano, and that entailed doing a jury for some of the faculty members. I chose to do a Chopin prelude as my main piece, which went pretty well at first, but then my right leg began to shake rather noticeably as I played, vibrating up and down like a pile driver on steroids. I passed the exam, but one of the teachers said she did so partly because she felt bad for me being so nervous. I told her that I didn't think it was nerves so much as the pedals were at a different height than I was used to and my leg felt uncomfortable. "Ah," she said, "That was it." She gave me a look like she didn't quite believe me, but left it at that. I passed either way and my playing, while not concert level, at least reached satisfactory competence for the program. Haven't played much piano since. With me moving so much, it's hard to carry one around.

I was also supposed to do an open performance on guitar as well, two actually, to get a grade for my classical guitar lessons prior to graduation, one each during my junior and senior years. I never did get around to doing those concerts as my playing didn't develop as well as I had hoped. I did OK at the faculty exams, but playing for master classes when famous guitarists came to our school I had some real disasters. When I had played bass guitar in rock bands I didn't seem to have that problem, even when doing solos, but with classical guitar it was completely different. I guess I should have stayed with the bass. The real problem at hand was anxiety. Maybe after I had performed a few hundred, or a few thousand times it would have dissipated, but the demon follows me still today in various aspects of my life.

I left the conservatory after 5 semesters and took more time off from school, during which I got involved in music in a different way. I had seen a local rock band I really liked, called Arroyo. After the gigs I talked with the musicians and helped them break down their gear and load it into their truck. They offered me a job as a roadie traveling with the band and I accepted. When they weren't active I still worked at my dad's store, but for about a year I was one of their full-time roadies, running the lights and stage monitors and taking care of the guitars as they traveled around the midwest. The summer saw us play a couple of times at several stages for Summerfest on Milwaukee's lakefront. At the time it was the world's largest annual music festival in terms of the numbers of people in attendance, and lots of both local and national musicians performed. Most of the time we played in bars to fairly intoxicated clientele, or at least they were that way by the end of the night. We would load our equipment into the clubs at roughly dinner time, tap directly into their often scary looking electrical systems, then get the stage set up and the sound checked. At some point the musicians arrived to get ready and make adjustments, started playing around 8 or 9 p.m., and then finished usually between midnight and 2 a.m. After that the roadies, normally 3 of us, would take things down, load them into the truck, and either head home, to a motel, or drive to the next town. Many times I was going to sleep as the sun began to rise. It was an often fun, but not very healthy lifestyle. We ate copious amounts of fast food, drank a lot, smoked, and kept crazy hours. Though I was never much into drugs other than alcohol, they were around, even though the band members were not as heavily into them as others I've seen. At one gig at a county fair in northern Wisconsin we had another band play before us. We worked with their roadies to collaborate equipment, and they were all taking "speeders," so they offered me one. I was useless for most of the gig, my hands shaking and unable to focus. Good thing it was a short set, although I drove to the next town in the darkness after the gig with no problem, talking the whole time, on and on and on…

That winter we went through an incredible cold spell in Wisconsin. I recall loading our gear out of clubs at 3 a.m. two Saturdays in a row where the air temperature was colder than -20 degrees F, and the windchill more than 50 degrees below zero. I had grown a beard and even being out for less than a minute the beard would freeze solid from the moisture in my breath hitting the frigid air. Driving home from one gig I discovered my break lines had frozen because they exploded when I put my foot on the break pedal. I could barely stop my car making creative use of the snow banks along the city streets. Luckily it was 5 a.m. so not many cars were around and I got it to a parking lot near my apartment. My dad drove up the next day and helped me to get the car to a garage to have it repaired. Then Arroyo went to Florida. We had four weeks of work booked in 4 different clubs there and after our freezing experiences, we were ever so happy to feel warm again. Going down and coming back we drove straight through more than 20 hours between Milwaukee and the Sunshine State, with each of us taking turns driving and sleeping, or trying to sleep. The second summer I worked with them the band split up and later I returned to college, deciding to pursue my interest in nature and study geology. I continued to work occasionally as a sound technician, both at college and with sound companies and rock bands, and part time at my dad's store. At one more Summerfest gig, the stage manager from DB Sound in Chicago, one of the largest sound and light companies in the US at the time, asked me if I wanted a job with them. I declined telling him I wanted to focus on my studies. The next summer I was told they did the sound and lights at the 1984 Olympic Games in Los Angeles. I've always wanted to go to the Olympics. It was not to be.

Just to finish the education story, I eventually graduated Magna cum laude from the University of Wisconsin - Parkside with a Bachelor degree in geology and a minor in music in 1986. Our geology studies often involved field trips, usually just one day to a long weekend around places in Wisconsin, but several times we took longer trips, including one out west to the northern Rocky Mountains focusing on Yellowstone, Grand Teton, and Devil's Tower National Parks (well, actually the latter is a national monument), and one to Florida during Spring Break week. Yes, I went to Florida during Spring Break, but I mostly looked at rocks ... mostly. I also attended Indiana University's prestigious Geology Field Camp in 1985, again traveling to the northern Rockies, but this time all the way up to magnificent Glacier N.P. On all of those trips I used my experience on long drives from my roadie days to help drive the vehicles for the groups. On the Florida trip we had gone down all the way to Key West. On the way back I was driving the lead of two vans with all of my passengers asleep, several having spent their free time sucking down beers at Sloppy Joe's Bar, as we headed over the famous Seven Mile Bridge, which traverses 7 miles over open water between keys. At the time there were only two lanes: one heading in either direction. Up ahead I could see a large truck trying to pass a car, the truck, of course, coming at me in my lane. Neither of them wanted to give way and they got into a race with each other. I watched in disbelief as the two of them sped toward me, and I didn't have a shoulder wide enough to pull over onto to get completely out of the way. I slowed down and hoped they would settle their contest before reaching my van. The truck looked larger and larger as it approached. I moved over as far as I could, and the truck pulled into the other lane just before reaching me. My driving to the side shook the passengers who awoke and told me to drive better. None of them, nor anyone in the van behind me, had seen what had happened. None of them believed me, but it was true. I hope you believe me. Anyhow, after undergraduate school I then attended a semester of graduate school studying geology at the University of South Florida in Tampa. Those geology field trips to national parks put me in contact with park rangers for the first time. I decided I wanted to do that for a living, so I left grad school to become a park ranger, which you can read about soon.

The Brickyard

Meanwhile back at the old homestead in Racine, I also worked off and on for about 15 years in my dad's business called, J.H. Haumersen & Sons. The business dated back to the later years of the 19th century when the Haumersen family started a coal and brick selling company. My grandfather had worked there since the 1920s, and my dad, who started out in banking, eventually went to work there and bought controlling interest in the company. Then came me. I started working there the summer after I graduated from grade school, which in my case was 8th grade, 1972. My sister Nancy had also worked at the store before me. When I started there one of the original buildings was still standing and Hank the brickyard worker told me how when he started at the company, he used to come in early and feed the horses everyday in that shed. They delivered bricks and coal by horse-drawn carts in those days. We no longer sold coal, but had expanded to selling not only bricks and cement, but other building items such as paint, wallpaper, tools, etc. The place had a lot of stories, many of which I wish I had written down when I heard them, but most went with the people who lived them. Between the employees and customers Haumersen's had a cast of characters that would have made a good TV sitcom.

The only Haumersen still working during my tenure was the bookkeeper, Irene. She looked about the same when as a child I first saw her, as she did when she passed on at the age of 90+: always old. Her dad had started the company and she admired him with a nearly religious fervor. My grandfather had worked there about as long as she, and the dynamic between the two of them was antagonistic in a relatively passive sort of way, and rather humorous, except when my dad needed work done. Irene was a strict Methodist and believed in not touching alcohol. She would tell customers how her dad never touched a drop of drink, but if my grandpa heard her say that he would pipe in with, "Oh, nonsense, he used to go down to the pub and have a poke with us every now and then." Irene would get upset and exclaim, "I have to go t'the bank," her old shoe soles scraping on the floor, and just leave to drive around for a while until she calmed down. Meanwhile my dad would come in and say

"Where's Irene?" Gramps would respond, "Oh I don't know, she said she's goin' to the bank," and dad would scowl, knowing what had happened. This was a common occurrence. A friend of Irene's went to the doctor and the doctor said all she needed was to relax and maybe have a beer once in a while. She didn't drive, so she asked Irene to pick up a six pack for her. Irene required a prescription from the doctor before she would do it. When she worked she was a good, if old fashioned bookkeeper, clanging away on her historic accounting machine. Like all of us, though, her mind got less and less sharp as the years wore on, and my dad's frustrations grew along with the numbers of accounting errors.

Willard, my father, was a responsible manager, who, it seemed to me, always worked to do right for the customers as well as the store, and the company had quite a good reputation in town. He tried to keep the business working well, though it was quite a challenge at times, especially as larger chain building centers began moving into town later. He knew a lot of firemen in town, and since their schedule was such that they worked 24 hours on and had several days off, a number of them came to work part time during those days. They were an interesting bunch and generally did a good job. We usually had two brickyard workers, three when the things got really busy for a couple of years. There was Hank, previously mentioned, whose experience on the job gave him a wisdom other yard workers just didn't have, and could find the simplest ways to get things accomplished. One day after I had worked there a couple of years, the union, whose office was right next door, forced Hank to retire. He had worked so long he didn't know what to do with himself. He began drinking a lot, and one, cold winter day they found him in a snow bank with massive frostbite. He died soon after. Curmudgeonly ole Joe was also there when I started and still there when I left. He could be hot headed at times and liked complaining about the equipment never being good enough, though while he was often right, he never saw what the accountants saw. Bud replaced Hank a year or so after the old man passed away, a slow talking, slow walking sort of guy. The customers were quite a mixed bag of folks, from the crusty old brick layers, painters, always in a hurry, weekend do-it-yourselfers, and prim ladies wearing high heels coming in to look at wallpaper samples or pick out paint colors for their pantries, or wherever.

The masons (bricklayers), in particular, seemed quite a colorful bunch. Bob used to come in to the office to have a seat and chat with us, no matter how busy we were. If my dad wasn't at his desk, Bob would sit there and hold conversations with us as we went by him dealing with this or that customer, then after a half hour of this my dad would finally come in and say, "Bob, can I sit at my desk so I can get some work done?" "Oh, I guess so," he'd reply, and slowly get up to mosey out to his truck. Giuseppe was an old Sicilian mason who was always talking about his uncle, who seemed to have been some sort of mafia godfather, and he was always on the lookout for deals on things, even if he had to create his own discounts. He came in once and asked Bud if he could just take some broken pieces of cement blocks if he found them in the yard. Bud consented and went about his work. A couple of minutes later he saw Giuseppe with some perfectly good cement blocks using his hammer to break them into pieces he needed. Giuseppe didn't get away with it that time. Once he came in to get some cement and started telling me about the colonoscopy he just had. "Holy fuckina shit Tom, I'm a tellin' you. They took this big fuckin' hose," he picked up a piece of wood, "about this fuckin' big, and they shoved this cocksucker up my fuckin' ass. I'm a tellin' you..." Just what I wanted to hear about that day at work. Curtis was another old mason who, like Bob, was good at pacing himself. One day I was mixing concrete for him and next in line was Serge, a recent Serbian immigrant. I don't know if Curtis, who was black, and Serge had known each other before that day, but as I was mixing the cement they began talking. Serge asked, "Have heard black mens got big vons, is true?" Curtis, without batting an eye, just said "Yep, that's true," and continued chewing his tobacco. Their conversation continued after that, but I was just so flabbergasted at what I'd heard, I was too busy suppressing laughter to comprehend it.

I worked in this comedy/drama with its cast of characters for 15 years. When I started out, making $1.25 per hour, I cleaned and stocked the shelves, mopped the floors, cleaned windows and the like. Soon after I began working in the brickyard as well. One of my first duties there was when we got in two enclosed train cars full of bricks. Normally we would just take the forklift, drive into the car, lift up a stack of bricks, and drive out again. We could stack them in the warehouse or load them right onto the truck to go out to the job site. Normally. These, however, had mostly broken the metal bands that held them together and were spread all over the car, so my job was to sit in the car which sat under the hot summer sun, and stack all of those bricks by hand onto wooden pallets that we could then move with the forklift, hour after hour, day after day, until they were all unloaded. In the following months and years I began waiting on customers, handling money, then mixing paint, mixing concrete, making deliveries, balancing the day's cash drawers, calculating cement or paint jobs for customers, figuring out the payroll, and basically whatever needed to be done. When my dad went on vacation, I was the operational boss.

Dad had hopes that I would take over the business someday, but though I hated to disappoint him, I just didn't have a mind for business. I was focused on music, science, environmental causes, and not economics. I could live very frugally and manage my own finances, such that they were, I was good with numbers, but making money was not my forte by a long shot. Even today I can understand economics pretty well, but I'm no businessman and never made much money. Eventually I left there and my dad grew older. He didn't want to be tied to the business nearly until the day he died like his father had, so he sold his share of the company to Irene's nephews and it became a Haumersen family business once again. Dad stayed on to do the books for them until one day when he came in to work they told him his services were no longer needed. He got in his car and drove home. Within a year they had driven the business into the ground and gone bankrupt. In a "last laugh" scenario, the accountants paid my dad to liquidate all of the assets of the company to get back whatever money he could from the ashes of the venerable old store.

Mom

I was the youngest child in our family and over the years grew very fond of my mother. Most kids love their mothers, but she and I had developed a particularly close relationship. During my time studying music, she apparently loved hearing me play the classical guitar, and especially flute, but oddly enough she never said as much. My dad told me one day that he wished I would play more often because Mom loved it so much, though, knowing my dad, he might also have liked it and said it that way because he couldn't say that he liked it. My parents were funny that way. If they wanted you to do something, they would say it as if the other parent were the one who wanted it, whether it was my playing music or not doing something that troubled them.

Anyhow, one Sunday in August of 1984 we went to Milwaukee for a picnic with Nancy and her husband Dennis. I drove my own car, and my parents and grandparents drove in Grandpa's big Oldsmobile. Nancy and Dennis lived in Milwaukee near the park. It was a lovely summer day for Wisconsin, the food was delicious, and company pleasant. I drove home, while the four elders drove back to my grandparents' house. I was out shooting buckets, trying to imagine myself as Kareem Abdul Jabbar or the "up and coming" Michael Jordan, when the neighbor lady came running over and said that my dad had been trying to call me. Couldn't hear the phone ringing, apparently. She said I needed to go to St. Mary's hospital emergency room ASAP. I asked for details, but she said she didn't know. I figured Grandma or Grandpa were ill. When I arrived, I went to the waiting room where Dad met me and said, "It's mother, and it doesn't look good." I asked, "Your mother?" "No, yours," came the reply. A ton of bricks just slammed into my heart. I sat down in shock and asked what had happened.

In typical fashion, Dad and Grandpa had ridden up front with Mom and Grandma riding in the back. Mom had fallen asleep, though it was only a half hour drive. Dad looked in the rear view mirror at her and thought, "She doesn't look right." They were nearly to the house at the time, so he decided to wait until they arrived before saying something. When he parked the car, they tried to awaken Mom, but to no avail. He felt for a pulse and said she had one. That's possible, but with my own medical training I can say that it's also possible that his adrenaline might have kicked in and the pulse he felt was his own in his fingertips. They called for an ambulance and took her to the hospital.

We waited for a while, during which time Nancy arrived. Pat was living in North Carolina then, as now, so we waited to call her until we knew something for certain. The doctor came out and told us she didn't make it, that there was nothing they could have done, though they tried. We waited a little longer so they could clean her up, then we went in to see her. She lay cold and still on the metal table, drops of blood in a few spatters in contrast to the formerly clean, white sheet that covered most of her body. I burst into tears and hugged her, sobbing.

That evening at home, dad and I sat in shock as the house began to darken with the growing night. He just looked down and said, "This house is going to feel awfully lonely." I agreed. Within a couple of years he remarried and moved out. That day mom had just gotten the house cleaned, all of the laundry done, and they had gone shopping on Friday, so there wasn't much that needed to be done. Just to feel.

My mother was the kind of person that everyone seemed to like. Her funeral was very well-attended. She had worked at the local Sears Department Store, and I'm not sure how they were able to stay open during that time as it looked like the whole store was there. Everyone was helpful and comforting, not the least of which were our neighbors, the Overmans. They had lost their mother several years earlier to cancer. Whether you lose someone suddenly, or to a long, drawn-out illness, it doesn't matter to the amount of grief, but the quality is different. I'm not saying better or worse. It's just different. Either way, it hurts.

This was only the beginning…

Ranger Tales

Waking up every morning on the high plateau of the Grand Canyon, or in the taiga forests of Denali, is a privilege not to be overlooked. Feeling the crisp air on your face and looking out your window to see a moose toying with the volleyball net, watching the sun rise and cast a glow on clouds floating below you among the red rocks, breathing clean, fresh air filled with the scent of pine, these are experiences that decorate a rich life. Starting in 1986 and continuing until I moved to China in 2010 I mostly worked as a park ranger for the National Park Service (NPS), with scattered forays into other venues. I worked at 6 different NPS sites: Shenandoah, Grand Canyon, Saguaro, Mesa Verde, Denali, and Oregon Caves. Each place had their stories to tell, their special beauties to make your heart glow, and their frustrations and difficulties to overcome, but each experience is dear to me.

There are many people who work in national parks and not all of them for the NPS, people such as cashiers, hotel employees, store clerks, pumping gas, etc. I worked in a store during my first year at the Grand Canyon. Working for the NPS itself can also take many forms. Some have permanent jobs with benefits and a pension, but others are seasonal, with few benefits, usually working 3-6 months at a time, and others may be volunteers or interns. I mostly worked as a seasonal because permanent, full time employment was usually hard to get. The main two divisions that visitors to the parks see are the rangers and the maintenance people, though there of course are important behind-the-scenes employees as well. I worked in the ranger division in the following capacities:

Interpretive rangers: This is where I'd spent most of my time in the NPS both as a paid ranger and as a volunteer. Interpretive rangers work in visitor centers or other information facilities and research, prepare and present interpretive programs. "Interpretive" doesn't mean translating languages in this case, though some rangers do that as an additional duty. Basically these are educational programs that help people understand the places in terms of their natural and cultural histories. As someone trained in geology I focused a lot on that subject, but I also gave programs on various other topics from trees, to wolves, to native peoples, etc.

In the depths of the Grand Canyon.

Law enforcement rangers: There are primarily two types of these, but basically both act as policemen in the NPS sites giving citations for breaking laws, arresting people when needed, and responding to various emergencies. Many are trained in such things as emergency medicine, fighting fires, and doing search and rescue operations when people are missing, sick or injured in areas that are hard to get to. Backcountry rangers hike the trails, maybe work at remote ranger stations like the bottom of the Grand Canyon. Frontcountry rangers are more like typical policemen, riding in cars or on horses in the more developed areas of the parks. While I worked much more as an interpretive ranger, I must admit that most of my good stories from my ranger days occurred during my time in law enforcement. Education, while vital, is generally not as exciting as when people do bad or stupid things, or just in general get themselves into trouble.

In emergencies rangers or other NPS employees may be called on to help out in whatever ways they can. Because of the remote locations of many of these places, plus the large numbers of people that often visit them, people who live and work there have to be ready to handle whatever happens, so the more skills you have the better. I was certified as a law enforcement officer, an emergency medical technician, a wildfire fighter, a level 1 structural (building) fire fighter, and was trained in cave rescue, rope rescue, river rescue, and search management. That was in addition to my knowledge of natural and cultural history. So if needed I could arrest you for damaging park resources, bandage your wounds after having pulled you out of a cave using ropes and pulleys, all the while telling you that the rocks beneath you were Permian limestones and how native people used chert nodules from them to make spear heads, then dig a line around you to keep the oncoming forest fire from burning you up before we got you to jail.

I'm not alone in this, though I may have had more diverse training than many. This is just what rangers do. Often we could be called "jacks of all trades, but masters of none", although I had coworkers who I felt were truly masters at some of those activities. I'm proud of the work I did as a ranger. We saved lives. We provided the best information available. We helped a lot of people. We took care of the resources in our parks. And compared to many people, we didn't get paid all that much for it, often living in old trailers and even tents, though some now have pretty nice park-supplied houses, and some live in private homes out of the park. It's because we loved the places and loved what we did that we stuck with it in spite of the pay or conditions. I'd probably still be doing it had I not fallen in love, gotten married, and moved to China, but that's another story.

As of this writing, there are about 417 units of the National Park System (the land of the NPS), and about 61 of those are called "national parks". The rest may be called national monuments, preserves, recreation areas, battlefields, military parks, historic sites, etc. If you want to know more, go to the NPS website or find a good book about it … or Wikipedia.

Shenandoah National Park, Virginia

Shenandoah is a beautiful forested area in the northern reaches of the Blue Ridge Mountains in central Virginia. I worked 3 months there in the fall of 1986 as a volunteer, my first experience working for the NPS. I spent a lot of time answering phones in the visitor center especially people asking the question "When's the peak?" Shenandoah is a great place to see the changing of leaf color in the fall, so people would call throughout September and October wondering when the best time to see the color was, the "peak," as they called it. It was hard not to get cynical with so many people asking the exact same question over and over and over again, but we always tried to be civil. Occasionally we'd joke with people and say something like "It will be on October 17th at 2:08 a.m.," but we'd always then give them our usual narrative of when it could happen.

Shenandoah is also a place teeming with wildlife, both big and small, including a great habitat for black bears. I had the opportunity to go out bear tracking a couple of times with the park's bear researcher. The first occasion we went to set up traps to catch bears so we could put radio collars on them for study. Bears are incredibly smart, and trying to get them to step in the right place is not at all easy, so I learned a bit about bear habits and psychology from that experience. Dan the Bear Man told me a story of his trying to trap a grizzly in Montana one time. The bear was especially smart, so he put a dead deer in a stream at the base of a cliff and put traps in the water all around it. The grizzly not only carried away the meat, but apparently used a bone to spring all of his traps as well. Never did catch her. Anyhow, I set one of the traps on this trip in the park. I didn't have a chance to go check the traps with him later as I was working at the visitor center, but he said my trap caught a bear. The next time out we tracked a few collared bears to see where they were going, and I finally had a chance to see my first black bear up close. He was eating acorns. We watched him for a while, then tried to get closer and inadvertently rattled some dry leaves, causing him to make a hasty retreat deeper into the forest. Since then I've seen a good number of both black and grizzly bears and it's always been a joy, even if sometimes a bit anxious.

Bears weren't the only animals of interest there, and visitors actually seldom saw them. People were enthralled with seeing the whitetail deer. I worked at Big Meadows Visitor Center, and every evening the deer came to the Big Meadow to feed. Of course the tourists came there to gawk and photograph them, which is what we do as tourists, isn't it. We saw the deer all the time, and while we appreciated their beauty, it just became common everyday activity, like making dinner or getting on the subway to go to work, so we always enjoyed the odd sightings. One of the deer commonly seen and reported had an arrow through his head (cue Steve Martin). One year a local poacher shot him with a crossbow, but he ran off and survived. I guess the arrow didn't go through his brain. The end of the arrow had broken off, but if you got close enough or had binoculars you could see the stubs sticking out. They tell me he was there for quite a few years, not as robust as many of similar age, but apparently not in poor health considering the situation.

One animal people didn't specifically come to see was the skunk, but we had plenty of those as well. You had to be careful walking in the dark. One evening after work I thought I'd try to develop my very limited musculature, so I had gone to a workroom where we kept some exercise equipment to do some weight lifting. Two rather aromatic law enforcement rangers came in. Actually, they reeked so bad from across the room it made my eyes water. They had been on patrol along the park road when a visitor flagged them down to point out a skunk that was stuck in a drainage pipe in the wall along the road. Normally they would just leave it alone and after a while the skunk would probably get out of it all by herself. In this case, however, tourists were watching and expecting something to be done about it. The front end of a skunk is nothing to mess with. Sharp teeth and claws can do some serious damage to your hands. Of course, the back end can also be dangerous, but it's not as bad as being bitten and possibly getting rabies. The one ranger took his night stick and shoved the skunk through the hole from behind. In payment from the skunk his arm and night stick got sprayed with that awful smelling liquid. At such close range, the smell was intensely pungent. The other ranger didn't get hit so directly. Luckily not much was on their flesh, so they'd come back for clean clothes and a new pair of gloves before going back out on patrol to see what other excitement the evening would bring.

Roving interpretation means walking around and talking to people, answering questions, and generally just trying to be helpful. One night while roving in the campground I came across a couple of well-muscled tough guys from New Jersey. They said, "Hey, this place is beautiful. We're really looking forward to spending a couple of days here." "That's great, welcome!" I responded. We talked a bit more, then I went on to chat with others. On my way back I saw the New Jersey guys packing up in haste. "What's up? I thought you guys were staying a while. Something wrong?" "We just saw a wild animal. This place is scary, man, we're getting outa here." Their description indicated it had been a skunk. The animal obviously had not sprayed them. Had it charged them or bared its teeth? "No," they said, "but we're not waiting for that to happen." We all have our vulnerabilities.

Grand Canyon National Park, Arizona

It's easy to miss the Grand Canyon (GC). Yes, you can see it from space, and from an airplane she just gapes at you while you gape back at her. But when you're driving along or riding on a bus, you climb up some steep roads, then drive along relatively flat landscapes until suddenly the road just disappears into what could be the world's largest pothole. There's this forest, and then suddenly the land just drops off before you. If you went parallel to her, though not far away, you could easily not see her at all. This large plateau was uplifted mostly flat, then a river carved down through it creating one of the most amazing pieces of sculpture the world has ever seen. The South Rim, where most of the people visit, sits at 6000-7500 feet above sea level and the North Rim 7500-9000 feet in the main tourist area. The upper reaches, the rim area, is covered with forests, but much of the inner Canyon is a desert, a place of incredible diversity. GC is not the largest canyon in the world, but she's damn big: 278 miles long, up to one mile or so deep and through much of it 5-10 miles across. The weather can be very diverse in a short distance. You could start on the rim in the morning freezing, then descend to the bottom and swelter in afternoon heat.

There are plenty of lodges on the South Rim and one big one on the North Rim. Both rims have campgrounds. Phantom Ranch sits along the Colorado River at the bottom of the Canyon and it is generally accessed by 3 trails: Bright Angel Trail, South Kaibab Trail, and North Kaibab trail. Phantom Ranch is a lodging area along Bright Angel Creek on the north side of the Colorado River that was first built in the 1920s. To get there you either have to hike or take a mule down from the rim. Bright Angel Campground is close by and there are two ranger stations: Phantom and River. That's the simplified version of Canyon basics, good enough for our purposes. Plenty has been written about GC and much more will be, I'm sure.

I first worked at the Grand Canyon for the Fred Harvey Company on the South Rim in 1987 at a rock shop known as the Lookout Studio. It's illegal to remove rocks from the Canyon without special permission, so we sold rocks from other places around the world, though tour guides and others who came in to the shop trying to impress their friends told people they were all from the Canyon. I started in April and continued through the fall while also volunteering on my off days for the NPS. I got hired on as a seasonal interpretive ranger on the South Rim working at Yavapai Geology Museum, then I came back for a second season in 1989 at the same place. I volunteered briefly at the Backcountry Reservation Office helping give out hiking permits, before going to law enforcement training in California in the fall of that year. I got my first LE ranger job working at the Phantom Ranch Ranger Station at the bottom of the Canyon in 1990. After working at Saguaro N.M. in the fall, I came back to work a few months at the Indian Garden Ranger Station in winter/spring of 1991. After spending that summer in Alaska I returned to work 3 months as an evening shift frontcountry LE ranger on the South Rim, then spent the summer as an interpretive ranger on the North Rim for two summers, 1992 & 1993. I worked on the South Rim at the main visitor center during the winter and spring of 1994 before leaving the NPS and moving to Flagstaff, AZ, to work in their visitor center just to try something different.

I'll never forget my first trip into the Canyon by helicopter on official business. The pilot knew it was my first time and thought he would shake me up a little, though not in any dangerous way. We flew just above the forest on the South Rim, then when we reached the steep drop off that makes its way toward the Colorado River at the bottom, he let the helicopter plunge quickly into the abyss. My stomach stayed up at the rim as we suddenly descended, but when he looked over at me, I was all smiles. Best flight of any kind I've ever had. At the time I worked there, Grand Canyon National Park leased its own Bell 206 Jet Ranger helicopter to be used for emergency, maintenance, and administrative purposes. The pilots were mostly former military men who had flown in the Vietnam War, so I was confident of their abilities. I used the helicopter many times on search and rescue activities. They're dangerous, as aircraft go, but fun and incredibly useful as long as you're careful. Airplane and helicopter crashes have caused more fatalities than any other cause of death at the Canyon, including car crashes, heart attacks, heat stroke, etc., but as of when I was there, none of those was the park helicopter. In the summer we used the helicopter often for people with really serious heat illness or dehydration.

Most people really don't know how to behave in raw Nature. The Canyon was no exception to that. The inner Canyon being mostly desert, which could reach well over 100F in the summer, we constantly had problems with people who just didn't know how to hike in such a situation, despite all the warnings. Of course most people made it alright, but a significant number who went far into the Canyon developed some sort of problem, mostly caused by the heat and/or dryness. Basic dehydration was often an hourly issue in the summer. Beyond simple dehydration, people sometime got into higher level heat exhaustion, where they were in serious need of water or salts or both. Occasionally they got to the point of not being able to drink anymore, and just would take a drink and throw it all back up. That's getting pretty serious and usually needs an IV for treatment. That's when we would try to get them out ASAP by helicopter or mule or carrying them. Heat stroke is often fatal and happens when the body completely stops being able to cool itself off. People look red and can't sweat. Luckily, because it was a desert, people didn't often get that far unless they didn't drink at all for a while in extreme heat. I tell you all this because it's important info if you go there. Learn how to take care of yourself and do it. I also tell you this because it plays into some of the stories that follow.

As stated before, most of the stories about my time at the GC were from time spent working as a law enforcement ranger. Ironically, one of the best nights I had when I did evening shift road patrol work on the South Rim, I can't recall enough details to really make a good story out of. I guess we were just too busy to stop and think about it. New Year's Eve can usually keep any on duty policeman busy, and this was no exception. There were four of us working that night, whereas most nights we had two or, at most, three. I just remember that everything clicked so well that we just kept moving from one thing to another for the entire shift. There would be a drunk and disorderly call at the residence area, so two of us headed over there to settle things down, while two others responded to a medical at the lodge. Then we would meet up for a disturbance at the bar in Maswick Lodge. Then split up again as two of us take the "disturber" to the holding cell, while others responded to traffic incidents. Again, I don't recall the details, but it went something like that all night. I may have had prouder moments doing other ranger duties, but as for the whole package of working as a patrol ranger, this was one of my proudest days … nights. I just wish I could remember more of it.

No, It Is the Heat

There's an old saying, "It's not the heat, it's the humidity." While it's true, hot, humid weather can be more oppressive than when the humidity is very low, but 122° F is just plain hot and difficult anyway you look at it, no matter how dry. We had a day like that at Phantom Ranch while I worked there. The average high temperature at Phantom in July is 106F, so it's usually pretty hot, but this was an exceptional day. The entire state of Arizona sweltered in the heat, and the airport in Phoenix had to close down for a while because of it. Aircraft of any kind have limits on how much weight they can carry, and those limits are dependent on the air temperature. None of their calculations went high enough to account for the temperatures that day, so they had to get engineers to figure out how much the planes could carry before they would let them take off. That's hot!

We had three LE rangers at Phantom that day, due to a quirk of scheduling, so we divided up the work in the heat. I took the early shift doing the morning campground check and hiking around the area to look for illegal campers, people having difficulties, or other things out of the ordinary. Bryan set to work about mid-morning digging a ditch in the campground for drainage. Patti staffed the ranger station and did the late campground shift. It could have been an awful day for people with heat exhaustion, but it turned out to be so hot that people actually realized they had to drink lots of water, and others decided to forego the hike altogether, so medical responses weren't too much in need, thank goodness.

Late in the afternoon, Bryan was finishing up his digging activities and Patti and I were out checking on hikers, when we all happened to end up in the campground together. As we chatted, I smelled smoke. Campfires there are illegal and this was definitely plant material burning. Patti and Bryan took a whiff in the air and also smelled it, so we began following our noses to find the source. The last thing we needed on such a hot day was to deal with a wildfire. Bryan had gone along the campground checking, and Patti and I crossed Bright Angel Creek to check the other side. Our noses led us to the mule corral and we saw a little smoke rising from just outside the fence. There we found several little smoldering circles of dry grass. How had it started? There were no matches or cigarette butts, no broken pieces of glass that could have focused the light and started a fire, nothing but a small amount of mule dung and the hot sun. We surmised that the tiny fires started by spontaneous combustion in the dried grass, with dung as a possible catalyst. It was truly a hot day.

Patti returned to the ranger station and she asked me to extinguish the fire, which I did. Didn't take me long. I headed to the ranger station where she called it in as an official fire in the fire crew's log book. They asked her several questions about the fire such as who discovered it, the time, how it started, and then they asked "How was it extinguished?" Patti looked at me and asked. I blushed a little, and then told her, "I peed on it." Patti laughed and then scrambled for an answer to give them. She put the phone to her mouth and said, "Pumper." (A pumper is a fire truck with a big hose that pumps water on the fire.). They understood. When we finished laughing, I went back outside and made sure the fire was, indeed, out. It was. I felt satisfied.

Rim to Rim to Rim

The North Rim of the Grand Canyon had a record snowfall, with layers of white burying the houses to roof level and higher. It was the winter of 1992-93, and at the time I was working as an interpretive ranger at the main visitor center on the South Rim, where we also had a good snowfall, but nothing like the North Rim had. Snow in this part of Arizona is not rare due to the high elevations in many places. Usually the snow is quite dry, with a 10 inches of snow to one inch of water type ratio. Back in Wisconsin where I was born it was more like 5 or 6 to 1, much wetter snow. That winter we had plenty of the very fluffy dry stuff, but we also had some unusually wet snow.

The wet snow proved to be a real problem for the mules on the trails. Once a week or so, Stan, the mule packer for the NPS, would pack up supplies for the ranger stations at Indian Garden and Phantom Ranch and deliver them, taking out garbage and other unneeded items on his return to the rim. He was scheduled to go down the trail on the day after the wet snow had fallen, but he wasn't used to this kind of snow and neither were the mules. As he started down the Bright Angel Trail, that wet snow balled up under the hooves of the mules, causing the normally sure-footed animals to slip on the trail. He had about 8 mules in his pack train, with him riding the front mule. The last mule slipped off of the trail and fell over the cliff, and since the mules are tied together, they all began to go over like dominoes. It happened so fast that Stan barely had time to pull his knife and cut the rope that tied him to the mule behind, thus saving himself, but the others all plunged to their deaths. All, that is, except the most stubborn, nastiest one of them all. He sustained some cuts and bruises, but walked out and lived to pack again.

Stan was obviously very shaken by this turn of events, as we all were to some degree. The park administration closed the trail until we got it all cleaned up. Because they're so big, the trail crew had to go in with saws to cut the mules into pieces so they could be flown to the rim by helicopter. I was stationed at the top of the trail to keep people from going down until they got it cleaned up, so I saw as all the pieces being flown out. Not one of my more pleasant experiences working at the Canyon.

Nonetheless, when I heard about the big snow on the North Rim, and knowing my supervisor Dale and his wife Katie were staying there for the winter, I decided to hike across on my weekend. Of course MY weekend, was not THE weekend. Few of us on the NPS front lines had Saturday and Sunday off, as those are very busy days in national parks. My Friday was a Wednesday. I called ahead to let them know I'd be coming over. They were looking forward to seeing a new and friendly face, since on the North Rim it gets pretty lonely in the winter, being closed for half of the year and all, and it was already March, so they had been cooped up in their house for most of the winter. Then I talked to the folks working at Phantom Ranger Station so that I could stay there for a night on my way across. All was in order.

On Wednesday after work I grabbed the items I needed for the hike, changed into my handy dandy trail clothes, drove to the parking area for the South Kaibab Trail, and headed down into the abyss. It was still light when I left, and I didn't need to carry much except clothes, water and some snacks, so I made it down to the ranger station in a few hours before it got really dark. I chatted with old friends at Phantom Ranch and at the ranger station. Sjors, the perennial NPS volunteer down there, told me I should grab a pair of snowshoes for going up to the North Rim and detailed exactly where they were at the Roaring Springs Pump House, 4.5 miles below the North Rim. All of the water for the North Rim, South Rim developed area, and Inner Canyon ranger stations comes from a spring there, and normally a maintenance person stays in the cabin while the North Rim is open for visitors. In the off season, the Phantom Ranch maintenance people hike up to Roaring Springs when they need to check on the system or make repairs. No one else would be using the snowshoes and I just had to make sure I put them back on my return.

The next day I started early because it's a long haul up to the North Rim: a 14 mile hike, all uphill, climbing 5800 feet from the Phantom Ranger Station to the top, and from all the reports I had heard about the condition of the trail, it would be quite a challenge. I made it to Roaring Springs without a problem just after lunchtime. I grabbed the snowshoes, attached them to my pack and continued up the trail. It wasn't long before I needed them, so I stopped and strapped them on. They worked pretty well, but the day had warmed up nicely and the top of the snow had become soft, so each time I stepped, the snowshoes sunk into the snow and I pulled up a pile of what looked like a snow cone each time I lifted a foot. Also, the snow in the sunny spots had completely melted, causing me to stop and take off the snowshoes if it was more than a short distance. In some spots the trail had been nearly washed away by landslides, and snow and rocks would fall on the trail or across it periodically as I walked. None of the falling material came close to hitting me, but it made passing on the trail quite a chore and very precarious, with steep drop offs commonplace in parts of the trail. After a while I no longer had to take off the snowshoes, but standing 4-6 feet above the trail on top of the snow and with the cliffs below me, it tried my nerves in a few spots. My legs were getting sore from the heavy snow on the snowshoes, but I kept moving.

I finally reached the top of the trail as the sunlight began to wane. I still had a ways to go, but at least it was more level ground and I could walk across the top of the snow much easier, it being more solid in the cold North Rim air. The first building I saw took me by surprise; all I saw was a little "A" sticking above the white horizon and a stairway cut in the snow down to the doorway. In the dim evening light with an afterglow in the west, I arrived at my destination, Dale and Katie's house. I took off the snowshoes, went down the white steps, and knocked on the door. They greeted me with warm smiles and welcomed me into their home. They immediately ran a hot bath for me and finished preparing dinner while I soaked my aching muscles. We ate and talked and talked and talked about our adventures since we last met. They told me about the unusually heavy snow, and how when they finally got it cleared off of Judy's roof (North Rim District Ranger), the walls of the house creaked and groaned as they went straight again. Scary. A little more snow on her roof and it might have collapsed on top of her. It had been beautiful, but also difficult both physically and mentally, in a sense trapped on the rim for much of the winter. They had managed to get out for a short trip to visit relatives. It didn't take long before I started fading, given my strenuous day, and I had another big day ahead of me, so they let me float into the world of dreams.

The next morning we ate a quick breakfast, and they walked me out to the trailhead. I said my farewells and dropped over the rim to the Canyon below. It was a glorious morning, with clear skies, crisp air, and a cheerful glow on the red rocks. The snow had once again stiffened, so using the snowshoes wasn't quite so difficult as it had been with the soft snow. This time, when I got to the section where the day before I'd had to take the snowshoes off and on and off and on to deal with snowy parts and dry parts, I was able to just keep the snowshoes off because the snow was hard enough to just walk on top of it. Roaring Springs by mid-morning to put away the snowshoes, Cottonwood Ranger Station an hour later, and Phantom Ranch by mid-afternoon. Then it was time for the long climb up to the South Rim. The trail was clear and inviting, so the hike out, while exhausting after the previous 48 hours, went by quickly and without incident. I reached my car, took a deep breath, and headed for home.

The next day I reported for work as usual. They had me scheduled for a rim walk, where we gathered visitors by the main lodge area and walked with them along the rim discussing the sights and history on the way.

About two thirds of the way into the walk, I suddenly felt my knee give way and I went down in pain. The visitors were concerned and helped me back to the lodge area. I used my radio to call for assistance, and a patrol car gave me a ride to the clinic. After exams and X-rays, they determined it had been nothing serious, just over stressed and a pinched nerve. I was on crutches for a few days, then gently back to normal. After all, I had just hiked 46 miles in two days descending a total of two vertical miles and ascending the same under some difficult conditions. I think the heavy snow on the snowshoes going up to the North Rim really did it. I guess it had been a bit much, but there's no doubt in my mind that it was worth it.

Phantom Folderol

A belief is not the same as a fact. Both are good in their own ways, but when it comes to arguments, facts work better. I spent part of the summer of 1989 working as an interpretive ranger at Phantom Ranch Ranger Station. The job entailed helping out with whatever needed to be done in this remote location, and of course doing a few interpretive programs, that summer including an afternoon talk and an evening campfire program after Phantom Ranch Lodge finished their dinner. One of my afternoon talks was to be a fossil program, which worked well, me being a geologist and all.

One afternoon I started the fossil talk, which was well-attended, and quickly realized that some members of my audience had no real intention of learning anything from me, they wanted to be the teachers. I used the phrase "simple, single-celled organism," to which they raised the point that no organism, even those with only one cell, is truly simple. In a way they were correct, but it's relative. I didn't indicate simple to imply a value judgment, rather to be a relative term. If you have many cells working together, it's just more complex than if you have only one, even if that one cell can perform most of the functions of the many. Anyhow, I made a brief statement conceding the point to keep the peace, and moved on. Moments later, another interruption, soon another, then another, etc. The entire program became a series of responding to their objections to what

I said, and they wouldn't have it any other way. The other participants began to look disturbed by this and some left the program. I finally made it through and the thorns in my side introduced themselves as members of a field trip from the "Institute for Creation Research (ICR)." I felt peeved, but tried to remain civil with them. That's my job, after all.

The truth is I did answer most of the objections they posed with fact-based reasoning, and there are legitimate questions yet to be posed. We don't know it all. My program was based on hard data, on thorough research, though I respect everyone's right to have a different opinion. I know that mainstream science doesn't have all of the answers, but they do have a lot of them, and the scientific method, when applied with an open mind, is tried and true for coming up with such answers, like it or not. I felt disturbed by the incident and decided to find arguments I could use to diffuse their objections more effectively. I came upon the name of a geologist in California who specialized in geologic dating methods and had had some experience dealing with people from the ICR, so I gave him a call. He told me that many members of the ICR were well-educated and raised good questions, but that from his experience they refused to listen to evidence, facts, that proved them wrong. When he attended a conference with them, at some point they just told him he was wrong, crossed their arms, and stopped the conversation once he had shown them the errors in their arguments.

A few days after the incident at Phantom Ranch, when I was back on the Rim for my days off, one of the law enforcement rangers told me he had heard of my difficulties and informed me that what had happened constituted "interfering with a government official in the course of their lawful duties," and that next time it happened I should notify LE rangers so they could deal with it. Yet a few more weeks later I received a book promoting creationist viewpoints from the folks at my program. I put the book in the park's library. After all, I'm not closed to their questions or ideas. Then I wrote them a letter explaining what the LE ranger had told me. Next year when they came for the field trip, I was the LE ranger at Phantom Ranch. They didn't say a word, except "Hello." There are myriad different ways for people to present their message to the world, so why do they feel they need to do that during my talk?!

The Rolling Code "W"*

The Grand Canyon is a difficult place to hike. Unlike hiking in the mountains, you start out at the top, go down first when all seems fairly easy, then have to hike up at the end when you're already tired to some degree. The elevation at the rim ranges from 7000 to 9000 feet, which can make breathing hard if you're not used to it. It's a desert inside the canyon, so water is not often readily available, until you get to the Colorado River at the bottom. The name "Colorado" basically means "colored red" due to the amount of red dirt it can often carry, so even that water isn't easy to make drinkable sometimes. Most people come in summer when, in spite of the cool mornings on the rim, at the bottom the temperature can reach well over 100F on a regular basis, and the highest I saw when I was there was just over 120F, as mentioned earlier. The heat and dryness can suck the water out of you faster than you can replace it. All of the trails going into the Canyon are steep and rocky, so anyone who is going to hike it for more than a couple of hours has to be in good shape.

Plenty of people run into problems while hiking the Canyon, be it the heat, the cold the dryness, the steepness, or whatever combination of factors that led to their not being able to finish the hike on their own. A lot of those people are just not in shape for it, either mentally, physically, or both, and many also don't know their limitations. A significant number have no idea about the difficulties of hiking in the desert. As park rangers we did our best to inform them of the rigors of the trail, but often enough our words fell on deaf ears. Part of our job was to get people out of the trouble they got themselves into. Rangers who regularly hiked the trails were also not immune to the problems, though we generally knew how to deal with them. Still, we occasionally got ourselves into trouble as well. More on that later.

One quick example of many, was the man who wanted to hike to the Colorado River on the Bright Angel Trail. He got down to Indian Garden Ranger Station, then continued on toward the river, but instead of staying on the Bright Angel Trail, he made the mistake of taking off on the Tonto

---

* Wimp.

Trail, which contours along the Tonto Plateau and doesn't go into the Inner Canyon. About a half mile out the Tonto Trail he realized he'd probably made a mistake, and feeling lost (the trail can be hard to see in places if you're not familiar with it), he sat down and waited for someone to come past. Nobody did. He sat there for nearly 2 days, running out of water and drinking his own urine to stay alive. Finally a ranger happened by as his family had called and told us he was missing, so we sent some people out to check on him. He survived.

I worked at Phantom Ranger Station during the summer of 1990. My job, like that of any backcountry ranger, was to hike the trails to make certain people were obeying the rules and were safe and healthy. I was both a law enforcement officer carrying a gun and a book of citations (tickets) and an EMT, a medical response person. I stayed at the Phantom Ranger Station, typically working for 9 days in a row, each day about 9-10 hours long, then hiking out to the rim of the Canyon for 5 days off.

After my 5 day weekend, I prepared to head back to work down at Phantom Ranch. Typically we would work a late schedule on that day, starting around 11 and finishing at 9. As I was getting ready to go, I received a call from the dispatcher that there was a couple on their way to Phantom Ranch on the South Kaibab trail, which I would take to work, who were having problems and they wanted me to go down the trail and evaluate the situation. This sort of thing is a daily situation somewhere on the main trails in the summer at Grand Canyon, but indications were that this was maybe a little more worrisome than normal. I went in to the office first to take care of paperwork and get more info on our hikers in distress, then started hiking as noon approached. On my way down I frequently encountered people who informed me of the difficult situation these people were in. This trail is one of the most heavily used hiking trails in the US, so I had lots of people talk to me about it. I helped several people along the way in various stages of difficulty. I encountered some folks about an hour into my hike who were in more serious distress and I figured I had met my targets. This couple, in early middle age, was obviously in low stage heat exhaustion, as well as just plain tired and not feeling too well. I spent some time with them, gave them water, had them rest, and when they were ready I had them hike back up the trail. It seemed they would be OK. Mission accomplished.

Or so I thought. I spoke to some other folks coming up the trail a few minutes after I left them and they told me of a couple having difficulty, they didn't think they were going to make it. I said I had just encountered them, but was informed that, no, these people were still a bit ahead of me. I continued down the trail and before long I found the people who I knew were the ones in question. They were in their early 50s and neither of them was in shape for this kind of hike. Let's just say they were almost as big around as they were tall. I gave them some water with electrolytes (we carry a lot on such hikes) and began talking with them. I used my old Motorola radio and called in to dispatch that I had encountered the people in question and would get back with them when I had more information.

As I talked with them I checked their blood pressure and pulse, and evaluated them for heat illness, checking their skin for "tenting" and capillary refill, checked their mental awareness, etc. I did the usual things we did for people in such distress. They were in early stage heat exhaustion, but not serious. They were just slow and very tired. The man, Hal, was in good spirits and just complained about being thirsty. He kept telling me how wonderful it all was and how he had been planning this hike for years. It was his dream to hike to the bottom of the Grand Canyon. He smiled and chatted in obvious enthusiasm. His wife Norma didn't say much at all. She just looked at me like she was not happy and was trying not to show it too much, a good dutiful wife.

I discovered that they had started hiking at 6 a.m. It was now about 2:00 in the afternoon. Normally it takes a hiker 3-4 hours to hike the 6.5 miles to Phantom Ranch on that trail. I usually did it in a little over 2 hours. They had been on the trail for 8 hours, and were barely half way there. This was not looking good. There was no elevator. There was no ambulance. There were mules that could take people out, but they were not going to take people this large. The helicopter had limited landing ability in the Canyon. I considered going back up with them, but I knew that would not work because if they had this much trouble with exhaustion going down, going up was not going to be any better. People hiking down such a steep trail normally have trouble with muscle and joint problems due to the jarring of their weight as it descended. Going up people usually had trouble with exhaustion and over-exertion. That's when they usually got the effects of dehydration as well. They had all of these issues, though were not yet seriously dehydrated, and were only going down.

I told them that I would hike with them and make sure they got to Phantom Ranch OK, and we began walking together towards that goal. At first they could go 100 yards or more before having to stop and rest, especially in the more gentle areas. In the steeper sections they had to stop more frequently. As I talked with Hal, I asked him how he had gotten himself in shape for this hike, one he had been planning and dreaming of much of his life. They went walking regularly at their local shipping mall. The Grand Canyon is not at all like a shopping mall. Being from the flat Midwest, they had possibly never hiked in real mountains, let alone desert canyons.

We made a short stop at a place called the Tipoff, which is 4.5 miles down the trail. This spot has an emergency phone and a water cache for emergencies. We still had plenty of water with us, so I didn't need the cache, but I used the phone to contact dispatch and tell them to contact Phantom Ranch to say that Hal and Norma would not be in time for dinner. At this point we were moving slowly, but moving nonetheless. That didn't last long.

Soon after the Tipoff is the descent through the old, very hard PreCambrian rocks and is much more steep than what we had just hiked. The distance we could cover between resting on the trail was getting shorter, and before long had reached the point of only being able to go 30 feet without a rest. Oddly, it was Hal who needed to rest the most. Norma was still not looking too happy and not saying much, but she was moving along better than he. Hal's spirits were starting to wane. Another few hundred yards down the trail, and Hal began periodically throwing up, a sign of moderate to serious heat exhaustion. I tried calling in to dispatch or directly to Patty, the other ranger at Phantom Ranch who was awaiting my arrival, but my radio died. The sun was setting on another sweltering day inside the Canyon, I had two people having great difficulty, and now I had no communication with the outside world.

Our ordeal continued with them walking 20 or 30 feet then having to rest, me encouraging them as much as possible, Hal's spirits waning, and Norma, now trying to be as upbeat as possible, considering that it was obvious she wanted absolutely nothing to do with this experience. When the sun sets inside the Canyon, it get's dark quickly. Those old, black rocks just tend to exacerbate the problem, and what's more is that they hold the day's heat quite well, so it wasn't really cooling off much. We would walk a short ways. Hal would throw up. Then he would stop and ask "Can't I just sleep here for the night?" "No Hal, it's not a good place to stop and sleep. We need water soon and it's not too much farther." Over and over and over again it went like this. In retrospect, it might have been a decent idea to have them sleep there. I could have gone down the trail to get water and some padding for the rocks and I could have stayed with them for the night and watched over them. There were worse concerns than him getting his blue knit shirt and plaid shorts full of red canyon dust, however. I was worried about Hal's vomiting and the possibility of them falling asleep and rolling off of the trail and down the rocks. Also, twilight is the time for all good rattlesnakes and scorpions to come out and play. Though they generally don't cause problems, I didn't want that to contribute any more stress to the situation. I tried to keep them moving, slow though it was.

Finally we neared the point just above the river where we could nearly see our destination. I had already turned on my headlamp, though the starlight did brighten things enough that you could see a little, and I could tell the bridge across the river was not far below us. I said, "Look, we're almost there! I can see the bridge across the Colorado River." At this point, Norma, who had mostly kept her composure, came unhinged. "A bridge? We have to cross a bridge? I'm terrified of bridges!" "Look," I said firmly, "we are not there yet. Don't panic. We'll deal with that when we get there." She apparently calmed enough, but I figured she was still thinking about it.

We hobbled down to the tunnel just before the bridge. I walked Norma through with my headlamp and had her wait while I got Hal to the bridge. Then it was time for the crossing. Norma was obviously distraught about the situation, but I told her that we had no other choice but to cross the bridge. A bed, water, food, and help lay on the other side. She grew increasingly agitated. "But I'm terrified of bridges. I'm scared of heights!"

This went on for a moment when finally I shouted "Listen. We HAVE to cross the bridge. There is no other way. It's totally black outside and you can't see anything below you. Just cross the damn bridge!" She took off in a sort of half jog, half shuffle, all the while screaming and made it across in a flash, so to speak. Hal had to stop several times on his way across, but eventually we made it. Just then I saw a headlamp coming my way and a familiar voice called out from behind it "Tom, what happened? We've been worried about you. Why didn't you call us?" I explained to Patti that my radio had died and that these two people were totally exhausted. She told me to go up to the ranger station to have dinner, that she would walk them the easy mile to Phantom Ranch. I made haste to the ranger station, which is nearly to Phantom Ranch, cleaned up a bit, made a quick dinner, washed the dishes, and came back out. Patti, Hal, and Norma had not yet reached the ranger station. I went down and assisted them getting to the Ranch. Phantom Ranch has bunk beds in the hiker dormitories. Hal, thank goodness, had a lower bunk available. He drank some water, undressed to his underwear, and collapsed into the oblivion of sleep. Patti and Norma weren't so lucky. Only a top bunk was available, and Norma sure wasn't getting up there herself. Patti got under her and shoved with all her might, Norma doing what she could to help, and together they got her into the bunk.

Patti and I went out and sat on a bench by the campfire circle used for evening programs that sits between the Ranch and the ranger station. We looked at each other, shook our heads, smiled, laughed, chatted for a few minutes, then went back to our respective rooms. Patti took another shower to wash off Norma's sweat. I took a shower to wash off the dust of the trail and went to bed. It was after 11 p.m.

Sunrise comes early to the Grand Canyon in summer as most of Arizona is not on daylight savings time (only the Navajo reservation changes their clocks). I was up before dawn and ready to get the day going. It was already heating up and the predicted high was about 110F. That meant in order to fly our couple out they needed to get going right away. Helicopters, or any aircraft besides rockets, have less lift, less ability to carry weight, when the temperature rises. The combined weight of our two passengers was about 600 pounds, so to have enough lift to get out of the Canyon we'd have to fly them before 7, preferably by 6 a.m. They didn't want to get out of bed, didn't want to move at all, but when informed of the situation, that after it got hot they would have to walk out, they realized they would have to leave quickly, though they had hardly seen anything of Phantom Ranch. They had a quick snack, grabbed their bags, and off they went.

Boomer the pilot flew down with another ranger, a paramedic, and they hurried us all to the landing zone. We put Hal and Norma both in the back seats to balance the load. A Bell 206 Jet Ranger helicopter is pretty dependable, but not as strong with loads as some other helicopters. The chopper struggled a bit as it tried to ascend, but caught the ground effect enough to get above the cottonwood trees and rise into the blue.

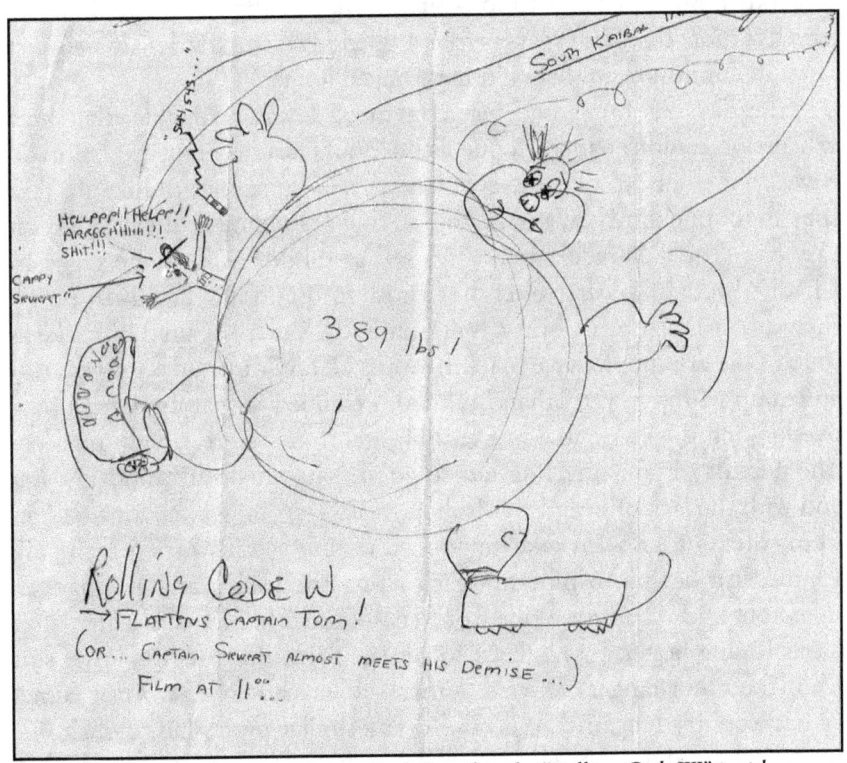

A drawing by dispatcher Brian Rutledge after the "Rolling Code W" incident

Epilogue to the Rolling Code W

It's easy to laugh and say these people were far too out of shape to go hiking in the Canyon and to wonder how they could deceive themselves into believing they could do it, but in reality, most all of us do that to some degree, often more than we will ever admit to. I had my own experience with self-deceit later that summer. I was scheduled to hike down the Grandview Trail, along the Tonto Trail to the east, then up the New Hance Trail, for a total time of 3 days. Chris, one of my colleagues, came with me down the Grandview and camped with me the first night, then hiked back up the same trail. I continued on, feeling pretty good in spite of a bad night's sleep. I stopped along a creek where there is a spring of good, fresh water and to look at carvings in the rocks left by other travelers more than 100 years before. I filled my water bottles after a short rest and continued on. I should have stayed longer.

The day was hot, but I was convinced I was invincible, that heat exhaustion couldn't happen to me. I chose not to camp along the Colorado River at the bottom of the New Hance Trail, but rather to hike up to a spot about one third way up the trail so that I could make the next day an easy one. The Colorado River water was as muddy as its name suggests. I hadn't brought a water filter, but chose to use iodine tablets to purify the water, which don't work as well in muddy water. I again didn't take as much time as I should have to let the water sit and the mud settle out, so I ended up with less water than I needed. I camped for the night on a rock overlooking the lower part of the trail. Again, not a great night of sleep. The next day I got to feeling not so good. I hadn't drunk enough water and with the lack of sleep I was feeling weak. I've done much longer hikes in my life, but it doesn't take long to get feeling bad if you're dehydrated. I ended up having to hide my pack along the trail near the top, then hiked out and called for a ride from one of the other rangers. Later, after I was feeling better, I went back to get the pack, but I took a lot of shit from the other rangers for that – there's a "macho code" when it comes to backcountry rangers, like people in any similar profession, though one ranger admitted they had all done the same thing at one time or another. So I had my own code W. Self-deceit comes in big packages and skinny ones.

Hell Week at Phantom Ranch

Patti and Bryan, my esteemed fellow backcountry rangers at Phantom Ranch that summer, had to leave the park for a couple of weeks, so I ended up working a double stint of 18 days in a row down in the bottom of the Canyon, most of it without the benefit of our usual two person team. There were other employees with me, an interpretive ranger, a volunteer, and a maintenance worker for NPS employees, and then, of course, the lodging area had a handful of people working there at any one time, so I wasn't alone. However, in case of emergency, I was the person in charge, and I would have to do all of the campground checks, morning, noon and night. If need be they could send someone else down in an emergency, by helicopter during the day if conditions allowed, or by hiking 5-7 miles from elsewhere. No problem.

The first couple days of that long stint, Bryan was still with me. After I hiked in we spent the first evening doing what we often did for entertainment. With no TV, no radio, and in those days no computer to speak of, we were left with the bats. After it got dark and when the lights were on in the ranger station, moths would come and dance outside of the big picture window in the kitchen. Bats love to eat moths, so they would come and pick off the moths one by one and we would sit amazed watching them. All outside was dark, and just the moths would be illuminated by the kitchen lights. Then, suddenly you'd see the spread wings of a bat and his little body, and in a flash he'd be gone ... and so would the moth. This could go on for a long time. So we'd sit and converse, or just sit, and periodically we would shout like people watching fireworks as the bats came by for a meal. Who needs TV?!

That day we had a couple of men hike down, and stay at one of the hiker dorms. We got called to their cabin because the one man wasn't feeling so well. They had just eaten dinner at the Ranch, so maybe the food didn't sit well with him, although few people ever complained about their wonderful stew, but when we checked him out, he did seem a bit dehydrated. We told him to drink more water (drink until you pee clear), and told him to check with us in the morning. As I recall they were to stay for two nights.

The next day he still complained about feeling ill and was having a hard time eating. We still didn't find much in the way of physical signs, but it was obvious he was in some distress. Later that day we found out that he suffered from serious depression and had previously tried killing himself by threatening to jump off of a bridge. Of course, to leave Phantom Ranch and go back to the South Rim he would have to cross the bridge. This concerned us, because it obviously concerned him. We learned that he was taking Prozac for his depression. Prozac was relatively new at the time and we didn't know much about it, so we looked it up in our copy of the Physicians Desk Reference, which is the definitive book of reference material on prescription drugs in the US. The list of possible side effects for the drug amazed us, and they would amaze you too if you ever read them. Of course most of those are rare, but still ... Anyhow, we started a conversation with doctors and nurses at the South Rim Clinic. They recommended we be patient and supportive, which we already were, but also be very careful and keep an eye on him. The next day when he was scheduled to hike out, he still claimed to be feeling very ill. There had been a cancellation, so he could stay another night, and he did. The next day he seemed to be even worse, pale and weak and ridden with anxiety. He was supposed to hike out, but he became terrified at the prospect of doing so. He had run out of his medication the day before, only expecting to stay two nights. We called the clinic and our dispatch office and together we devised a plan. Even though we usually only flew people out of the Canyon due to extreme physical illness, we felt this was just as serious. A ranger went to their car on the South Rim, broke into it with their permission, and retrieved the medicine. I asked the nurse on the rim how long it needed to take effect. She responded, "As soon as he has it in his hand." She was right. When the helicopter landed with a paramedic, she handed him the medicine, and he looked much better before it hit his lips. I remembered that several years later when I was prescribed the same medicine. We flew him to the rim, and a possible tragedy was averted. There were a couple more to go. Bryan hiked out and left me in charge of the ranger station.

   The next day in the evening as I was getting ready for a check of the campground, I saw an unlikely site walking along the trail toward

Phantom Ranch. A short woman with permed hair, carrying a purse, wearing jewelry, and walking in dress shoes with medium heals went past the ranger station not looking too happy. The trails to Phantom Ranch are hard enough in hiking boots or athletic shoes, but medium heals on dress shoes? I thought, "This could be trouble," but I did my campground check without issue and returned to the ranger station for dinner. I got a call on the radio to go to the Ranch to check on a woman having difficulty. I responded immediately and they directed me to her cabin. I found a 40+ aged woman from New York City, who had never been out of the city in her adult life, the same one I had seen earlier. She had been brought there by her nephew and his family who wanted to take her on a hike in the Canyon. They planned to stay two nights, then hike out, but Auntie was not happy at all. She refused to eat or drink anything, which is not too healthy considering where she was, what she had already done, and what she needed to do soon when she hiked out. She said that she was terrified that the Canyon would swallow her. I told her that it had never really swallowed anyone (at least that I knew of), so why would it swallow her. "I don't know, I just know that it will." I tried to get her to drink something, but she wouldn't. A brief physical exam showed no signs other than a little dehydration. She was on no major medication. Whew! I told her to drink something, get some sleep, and she would likely feel better in the morning. I asked her family to be as helpful and understanding as possible. They said nothing.

The next day she still didn't want to drink anything and wouldn't listen to anything I said about taking care of herself. She hadn't slept at all and broke down in tears often. She still wouldn't eat or drink. I thought, "Maybe she needs a woman's tender viewpoint," so I asked Bonnie, the interpretive ranger who was at the ranger station, to come see her with me. The woman still wouldn't eat or drink. When asked what her favorite food was she replied, "Beans and rice." Bonnie asked, "So do you want some beans and rice?" "No I don't want no beans and rice, I want to get out of here!" The conversation went on for some time, always with the same result: she wanted to leave. When Bonnie and I were out of the cabin I asked her opinion. She said, "The woman is a basket case. Get her out of here!" So much for the gentle woman's touch. The crying and refusal to eat or drink went on all evening when I checked on her. Her family had little to say on the matter. I talked it over with the doctors on the South Rim and they agreed that she needed to be flown out of the Canyon. Two days of not eating or drinking would make such a hike extremely difficult, even if she weren't so upset, so we made plans to fly her out at first light while it was still relatively cool. It's better for the helicopter that way. I instructed her family to wait until I arrived in the morning before they left on their hike out of the Canyon. We could fly her and her bag out, but no one else and no other bags than hers.

The next morning I arrived at their cabin and Auntie was there, but the rest of the family was gone. They did, however, leave behind all the things they didn't need for their hike. So much for listening to instructions. The helicopter landed and the paramedic got out to prepare Auntie for her flight out of the Canyon. The first thing she did was give Auntie some Valium, prescribed by the South Rim doctor. They said this should relax her. The paramedic, Melanie, I believe, got her into a flight suit, which was too large for her. The pilot had once had an anxiety patient try to crash his helicopter, so they wanted to make certain it didn't happen again. I loaded the gear on the chopper and after a short time Melanie and Auntie came out of her cabin. The woman was so relaxed she just floated to the helicopter. It was the only time I had seen her smile. They sat her in the back seat and Melanie got in with her. They tied the extra-long arms of the flight suit together so she couldn't grab at anything in the helicopter. I don't think she could have grabbed anything in her state anyhow. Two days without food or water and then Valium? She was feeling no pain. They lifted off and up into the big blue above. They arrived at the South Rim without incident. I seriously doubt that she ever returned.

A day or two later I was checking out the situation of people arriving at the Ranch on yet another hot, dry early evening. I saw a couple arriving and the man motioned to me to come over. He said his wife was having some problems due to the heat, but didn't say much else. She seemed quite disoriented, although she did know what day it was, her name, and vaguely where she was. Her balance wasn't good, so we helped her walk to the ranger station. She was middle aged and hadn't drunk enough water, according to their account. Her skin was red and mostly dry. In the ranger station I checked her armpits and they were also dry. It could be she had been holding her arms up a lot, so in the desert air they had dried out. However, when someone is getting to heat stroke from heat exhaustion, they stop sweating, their skin often turns red, they get hot, they become disoriented and, if coherent at all, they may start talking jibberish, nonsense. She was talking, but much of it seemed to make little sense. I looked at her husband and he looked worried, but said little. She seemed to be getting into heat stroke and her temperature was definitely high when I checked it. I talked with Sjors, our volunteer. Even though he had no formal medical training, he had been at the Ranger Station for years and had seen many cases of heat illness in varying degrees. We agreed she needed to cool down quickly. She didn't feel like drinking, though we got some water into her, some of which she had vomited.

The cold shower brought her around a bit, and she wanted out, but we insisted on getting her cooled down as much as possible. She wasn't happy about it, though. I called the clinic and they seemed to think it would be good to get her out of the Canyon. The sun was beginning to set and we couldn't fly her out after dark, so we made the decision to fly her. The chopper headed down with a medic on board. We began trying to get her to the landing site along the river. In the growing darkness we couldn't use the closer site. We did a two person carry, but she was heavy and it wasn't going as quickly as we needed. Dave, our ever trusty maintenance man, brought the wheelbarrow and we put her in, moving as quickly as possible to the helipad as the woman talked, and cackled, and complained of the bumps. The chopper landed and the medic, Gibson, came to hurry us along. Near the helicopter we had to stop using the wheelbarrow, so Gibson and I did a carry. He tripped on the rocks and we went down, but was up in a second and we got her to the helicopter. The pilot and husband in the front, the medic and patient in the back, they lifted off.

Shortly thereafter I received a call from the clinic as to why we had flown her out. I told them all I could, all that was on my report, but they said her temperature was below normal. Had I done the right thing? Was she just dehydrated and could have done alright with some rest and more water? Vomiting wasn't a good sign, and there were indications she could have been going into heat stroke. She was quite hot when I took her temperature. Some days later I was still doubting myself when I talked with a nurse from the clinic. I asked about that patient. She seemed surprised I had asked. "Well, the clinic person I talked to said she was below normal temperature and seemed to think we had overreacted." "I talked with her husband. You know he's a doctor? He told me he had been very, very worried as her behavior was so unusual. He seemed to think you did the right thing." I felt better. Maybe he was only a foot doctor. I don't know. I had little time and I had to make the call. Err on the side of taking best care of the patient. Life goes on.

A few days later I was awakened at sunrise by a phone call from the dispatcher. A woman at the emergency phone by the unstaffed River Ranger Station was reporting a fatality … her husband. I got dressed and woke up Kathy, the interpretive ranger who had just hiked in, asked her to get ready and meet me shortly, and headed for the River Ranger Station. The woman looked exhausted, dehydrated, and very distraught. There's a water spigot by the phone, which is near the public restrooms along the river, and she was drinking water to try and get herself back to a reasonable level of hydration, which was the right thing to do. I introduced myself, told her I had been sent to help, offered my sympathies, and asked her to go to the River Ranger Station with me so we could talk. I radioed to Kathy, told her where we were and asked her to join us as soon as she could. She arrived in a few minutes. We checked her over physically and found her dehydrated, but apparently OK. Emotions were another matter. Over the next couple of hours Kathy and I sat with her and, with all the patience and understanding we could possibly give her, listened to her tell her story. She waxed and waned in her emotional state, sometimes lucid and coherent, telling us her story, then would plunge into tears and sobs that shook her whole body, and us with it, though we didn't show it.

She was in her mid-twenties and was from Pennsylvania. She had recently been married, her husband of similar age and origin, and he was about to enter graduate school, the medical field as I recall. They had decided to come to the Canyon and do a multi-day hike. They had hiked down the Grandview Trail, across the Tonto Trail to the South Kaibab Trail, and had planned to hike out via the Corridor (Kaibab or Bright

Angel Trails). The Grandview Trail is steep, but in very good condition, the Kaibab trail a highway as backcountry trails go, but that section of the Tonto Trail is much more difficult than people expect, with limited water available and sometimes hard to find. They did alright for the first couple of days, but on the Tonto Trail they were running out of water. They found some, but it had algae in it and they chose not to make use of it. This was their first experience hiking in the desert and didn't know that algae in the water is a good sign: it means there is likely nothing poisonous in the water, which can happen in some springs. They continued on, but found no other water sources. He gave her the last of their water as he continued to decline. Around dark they neared the intersection with the South Kaibab Trail and could see people on the trail. They tried shouting to them, but it's a big place, and the people apparently couldn't hear them. His lips were cracked and dry and he was losing consciousness. She lay down next to him and tried to rest. Just before dawn she realized that he had passed away. She had walked to the edge of the Inner Gorge, the steep area that leads down to the Colorado River below, and thought of throwing herself over the edge, but stepped back. At first light she went to the Kaibab Trail, and thinking it much easier to go down than up, made haste to the river where she found water and the phone. That's when I had been called.

While we were getting the story from her, a helicopter with rangers had headed to the site where her husband lay still. They declared him dead, investigated the area, did their report and prepared to have him and their gear taken up to the rim. The biggest tragedy was that he had died nearly within sight of the emergency phone at the Tipoff and a cache of bout 30 gallons of water. They just didn't know it was there. After we had been with our lady for a few hours, the helicopter arrived with a paramedic, who spent some time with her doing a more thorough physical exam and probably a little counseling. We walked them to the helicopter landing site, they got inside, and flew up and away. As soon as the helicopter took off, Kathy and I turned to look at each other, then fell into each other's arms, and sobbed our eyes out. After composing ourselves sometime later, we walked to Phantom Ranch to tell the employees there about the incident. They had heard little bits, but we filled in what details we were allowed to, and they made us breakfast. Good people. Then, somehow, we went on with the day.

So that was my Hell Week at Phantom Ranch. If you add up all the days, it was more than a week, though it was all one long tour of duty. This, to the best of my memory, is how it all went. The rest of my time on that back-to-back was less eventful, thank goodness. For a few days they sent another ranger from the rim to help out. I guess they figured I'd had enough.

Going on a Manhunt

One morning I slept soundly in my little cabin on the North Rim of the Grand Canyon, when an urgent knock resounded on my door at about 4 a.m.. I staggered on over rubbing a crust of sleep from my eyes and opened it to find Dale, my supervisor, standing on my porch in the dark before the dawn. He informed me that a serious law enforcement incident had taken place on the South Rim, and my assistance was required. He said to pack some clothes and meet at the helibase (where the helicopter lands) at dawn to ride the chopper over to the South Rim.

It was the summer of 1992 and I lived on the North Rim where I worked as an interpretive ranger, though I still had my law enforcement commission from recent work as an LE ranger. They apparently needed every hand they could get, so they sent for me. For several weeks in June we had received reports of an escaped convict named Danny who had snuck out of prison just east of Phoenix, AZ, and led the officers on a wild goose chase, eventually to the northwest towards Flagstaff. Before he came to Grand Canyon, Danny had been on the run for more than 5 weeks.

Sitting at the helibase, as is typical of such events, it became a case of "hurry up and wait." I appeared at the appointed time, but the helicopter did not. It seems that we expected the imminent arrival of two other rangers driving down from Zion National Park in Utah. In most places that would be considered a long drive, but in Arizona it's just a quick jaunt of several hours, so we waited. It gave me a chance to eat breakfast.

When they finally arrived, we waited for the helicopter while the

North Rim district ranger filled us in on the details. Danny had taken two hostages at gunpoint in Flagstaff and forced them to drive to the Grand Canyon. Hey, everybody wants to go there, whether just on vacation from work, or vacation from prison! They got a room at the El Tovar Hotel on the South Rim where they spent the night, ordered room service, and enjoyed the view. Well, at least Danny probably enjoyed the view. His hostages were likely too scared to do much enjoying of anything.

The next day in the parking lot of Babbitt's General Store on the South Rim, Danny tried taking a family in an RV hostage. One of our rangers tried to confront him and, after a face off with guns pointed, Danny drove off at high speed in the car he had already stolen, with the two hostages in the back seat. He shot at two of our rangers during the chase, then drove out the West Rim Drive, which dead ends about 8 miles from the South Rim Village. He ran the car off of the road, got out, and took off by foot into the forest.

When I arrived at the South Rim, I found that just about every available law enforcement officer from the state and the region was there, including, but not limited to, several different national parks, the U.S. Forest Service, Bureau of Land Management, Arizona Department of Corrections, with their bloodhounds, at least one swat team from Phoenix, the Arizona State Patrol, the Coconino County Sheriffs, the Navajo Tribal Police, and the FBI, including their Hostage Rescue Team. There were more guns in the South Rim Village than I had seen in my life, from pistols, to shotguns, to high powered rifles, to assault rifles.

In total I spent about 10 days on the incident, including the Fourth of July weekend. I spent most of my time at road blocks, searching cars as they drove out of the park. It amazed me that, on numerous occasions, I stopped cars and searched their trunks at gunpoint, while people talked and acted as if this were perfectly normal. I don't know where they lived, but there were cops carrying assault rifles and dressed in camouflage walking all over the village, and these people seemed to think it was life as usual. Hmmm.

One day after I had spent about 11 hours at a roadblock in an area which had not been very busy, other than a few elk, a badger, and lots of Steller's jays, the dispatcher asked me to go to the Yavapai Museum and escort the cashier to the Visitor Center with the money from the Museum's bookstore. At the time, the main focus of the search centered near the museum. Just as night settled upon us, my partner from the roadblock dropped me off at the museum turnoff. I walked with my shotgun through the parking lot to the museum and knocked on the back door of the building. I didn't hear anything. I knocked again. Still no response. I began to consider my situation: I stood under the only light in the area, in the middle of the search focus, and the person I was supposed to meet did not answer. I thought "Why is the cashier not answering? Danny could be in the museum holding her at gunpoint. Or…he could be out here by me and I'm under the only light around." I also recalled that Danny had already shot at my colleagues.

I pointed the shotgun at the darkness and stepped out of the light. I began walking down toward the parking lot, all the while thinking "I'm on the path and there's just enough light to see me if he were nearby hiding among the trees." I decided to increase my speed, thereby making myself a more difficult target to hit. I jogged down the path, and just as I reached the parking lot, lights flashed on all around me, the sound of guns clicking as they moved to the ready position filled my ears, and a voice called out "Who goes there?!"

A strained, high pitched voice responded from somewhere inside of me "Park Ranger?"

The response came back in a loud growl "Walk!!"

Again the strained voice replied "OK."

And as every sphincter in my body tried to relax again, I walked past the FBI Hostage Rescue Team to the road, where my ride took me back to the Command Post at the Ranger Office. There I discovered that somebody else had driven the cashier to Park Headquarters, and nobody had bothered to inform me of the fact. Ah, the importance of good communication!

I took part in another incident of note during the manhunt, when I escorted a woman to her house at a place called "Supai Camp, which is a series of cabins in varying states of disrepair just west of Grand Canyon Village and a half mile or so south of the canyon rim. The residents are members of the Havasupai tribe. Supai Camp had previously been evacuated and searched, and the residents intended to stay away until Danny was either caught or left the area. As the search had gone on for so long, one of the residents needed to return for some extra clothes from her house.

I drove her to Supai Camp where we got out of the car and walked to her cabin. The dry Arizona wind blew through pinyon and juniper trees and caused loose shutters on the buildings around to slap back and forth. With each "Whack" I grew a little more nervous, holding the shotgun firmly in my hands. I followed the lady up the stairs to the door, where she turned and said, "The door's unlocked."

I asked "Had it been locked when you left the building?"

"Yes," came the reply, "and my grandfather's shotgun and rifle are inside." I asked her to step back and I approached the door. I pushed the door open and darted to one side, holding my shotgun in the ready position. I saw nobody. I crept into the building and searched both rooms, but found no Danny waiting for me. The lady entered and looked for her grandfather's guns, but could not find them.

I carefully walked her to the patrol car, put her inside, called for assistance, and stood guard from behind the vehicle. After a few minutes a SWAT team arrived to search the buildings once again. Dressed in black combat gear and brandishing assault rifles, they went from cabin to cabin in a methodical search for the escaped convict. With each slap of the shutters, each opening of a door, the tension grew.

All of the buildings but one utility shed had been searched, and all attention focused on the sliding doors of the small, green aluminum building. Two SWAT team members moved forward and took positions on either side of the doors, while others stood back under cover, rifles pointed at the shed. The two forward men reached out, put their hands on the door handles, and counted in silence to one another. "One." "Two." On "Three" they slid the doors back and stepped aside, as a black cat leaped from the shed's interior. All guns took aim…but remained silent. The cat landed on all fours and took off behind one of the cabins. There it stopped, looked around, and with typical feline nonchalance began grooming itself, while the entire SWAT team and I had ourselves a good laugh, releasing the tension that then blew away with the dry Arizona breeze.

So what happened to the guns? And why was the door unlocked? Grandfather had gone back to the cabin several days earlier to retrieve the guns and that information had not been passed on to his granddaughter. Communication ... again.

The manhunt ended a few days later as Danny escaped from the park, hijacked another car and headed south with more hostages along the way. Eventually a state patrol officer spotted him near Flagstaff and followed at high speed. Danny drove off the interstate, ditched the car, and headed into the high desert. A few hours later officers caught him huddled in a gazebo in the yard of a house near Sedona. How had Danny survived with so many people looking for him on the South Rim of the Grand Canyon? Simple. He hid within sight of one of the road blocks. Occasionally, due to miscommunication, the roadblocks remained unstaffed for short periods during the shift changes, and he snuck down to grab food and drinks left by the departing officers.

Throughout this ordeal, from the time he escaped until his recapture, a growing number of people came to view him as a sort of cult hero. "The wild man running from the cops outsmarts the best officers in the country!" I can understand why, because so many people dislike or fear law enforcement officers, or any authority figures, for that matter. Danny, however, was not truly hero material in my book. True, his survival and evasion skills are admirable, but he had been in prison for sexually molesting his own five year old daughter, he had robbed at least 4 banks, and later the state of California convicted him of murder and dismemberment of a man that he and his brother had previously robbed. Not exactly someone I would choose to emulate.

My goal here was to present a couple of my stories from this manhunt. If you want more information, there's an interesting article at this website: https://www.territorysupply.com/danny-ray-horning . I don't know how accurate it is, but there are a lot of details that I didn't know, and it has a reference list, so I suspect it's a pretty good account. I know that my stories are accurate, because I was there.

Littering, etc.

When I used to tell people that I worked as a law enforcement ranger in national parks, a common response was to ask, "What did you do, bust people for littering?" Of course by now you know that this is far from the truth. While generally not as intense as working as a big city policeman, it had its share of danger and conflict. Still, when I worked as a naturalist before doing law enforcement, it was common to find people littering and my colleagues and I would talk to them, usually with some sort of repentant response and subsequent picking up of the offending items. Sometimes, however, people laughed in our faces and walked away. We had no legal recourse other than to call an LE ranger, who likely would be too busy or too far away to get there in time. On top of that, picking up litter when I saw it was part of my job and there was enough of it from accidental sources, let alone that which they cast aside on purpose. There were other offenses that we also saw and had little recourse other than talking, things such as people camping illegally, feeding deer, throwing rocks over the rim of the Grand Canyon, or as I saw one time, three guys took a huge slingshot, fired a series of water balloons over the rim of the Canyon, then quickly ran away. As an LE ranger I almost never saw this kind of behavior, either due to being too busy with other things or because people behaved when they saw me there carrying a gun.

What, you may ask, difference does it make? Who cares about littering? Well, we cared. And the general public cared. People don't come to national parks to see other people's trash, and the law reflected that ... it's illegal. People who hike into the Canyon are required by law to carry out all of their trash, whatever it may be. There are no garbage trucks, or trucks of any kind in the Canyon, and there are just too damn many people and too few park employees to be able to clean the place up just because of the laziness of some. But also, the NPS has a purpose to help people understand the importance and integrity of the resources, be they natural or cultural. Let's face it, people often have, and still do, view Nature as one big toilet. We pump tons and tons of pollution into the natural world and Mother Nature handles it until she can't anymore. Then we get stuck with situations where it not only looks bad, but can become unhealthy or even deadly. One of our goals as interpreters/naturalists was to help the public see things like dumping their take out containers on the side of the road, smashing their beer bottles on the rocks of a beautiful mountain, or mindlessly tossing away their ever-present cigarette butts were part of the larger continuum of soiling that which sustains us: the natural world. It may sound preachy, but we really believed that, and the logic makes sense when you sit down and ponder it.

So did I ever get a chance to catch people littering or write tickets for it as an LE ranger? A few times. The first happened early one morning as I conducted my patrol on the lower reaches of the Bright Angel Trail in Grand Canyon. As I turned from the River Trail onto the Bright Angel, I began seeing little cards left along the way saying things like "Jesus loves you" or "Have you talked with God today?" along with a message on the other side and the name of the group that made the cards. I could tell that they had been left there very recently, and I also knew that a religious group had stayed at Bright Angel Campground the night before. I picked up my pace, though still collected the cards, as I made my way up the trail. Ten minutes later I caught up to the group that had stayed at the campground the night before and just remained quietly a short distance behind them observing. It didn't take long before I saw the last person in line drop a couple of the cards on the side of the trail. I grabbed the cards as I passed and caught up in seconds.

We had a little chat. I showed them the cards I had collected and they admitted to having left them there. I talked about littering in national parks and then asked if their intent was to mar God's beauty here in the park. Best to reach people on their own terms. "Well, we hadn't thought of it that way," they responded. I debated giving them a ticket, but seeing the looks on their faces, I knew the message had hit home. I asked them to inform the rest of their group up ahead of the situation, then took their hiking permit information so I could write a ticket later if need be. I told them that if we found any more of their cards defacing the magnificent Grand Canyon, that they would hear from us. Then, with them still there, I radioed to my colleagues further up the trail and informed them of the incident, asking them to look out for the group and their cards. We never found any more of them. There's an old adage they told us in law enforcement training: use the minimum of enforcement required to gain compliance. Mission accomplished.

The next incident proved ever more satisfying. I was working at Indian Garden Ranger Station, half way up the Bright Angel Trail from Phantom Ranch. My colleague Brian was working at the Phantom Ranch Ranger Station down at the bottom. He radioed me early one morning to ask me to check the trail for a group he had encountered at the campground the night before. It seems that when he entered their campsite, he had found a bag of trash sitting in a corner of their site, sort of hidden by the bushes, and asked them if they were going to carry the bag out with them the next morning. They said they knew they had to do so and would definitely have it with them the next day on the trail. Brian wasn't quite convinced by the tone of their voices, so he found out which trail they would use, and, when they weren't looking, he wrote his initials on the bag.

Brian had returned early the next morning, only to find the campers gone and the bag of trash still sitting there in the corner by the shrubs. He gave me the name of the permit holder, a description of the group, and asked me to go to the 3 Mile Rest House to look for them. I made it there in short order and waited for a group meeting their description to arrive. In the meantime I had some wonderful conversations with hikers who stopped in for a rest and a drink, helping many with hiking advice and suggestions. After about an hour of chatting and watching I saw a group of guys meeting the description pull into the rest house and drop their packs. I asked to see their camping permit and the permit holder, who was just putting his pack down, complied. It was them, alright. I then asked to see some identification and informed them that they were being cited for depositing litter in the Canyon. One of the guys got in my face and started to argue that they hadn't done anything wrong. I just stepped back and informed him that Brian had written his initials on their garbage bag the night before, and that it was still in the campsite this morning. He wouldn't back down, but the permit holder pulled him away and said, "Stop it man, he's got us dead to rights." The guy reluctantly backed off. Given the fact that Brian had already discussed this with them and they still didn't carry out their trash, and the fact that there were four of them, big strong guys who could easily have complied, we decided to write them for the more serious littering offense carrying twice the fine. The argumentative one told the permit holder not to pay it, so I just gently reminded them that it was not a local citation, but one from the national government that would show up on the NCIC, a federal crime computer network. That shut him up. I just handed them the ticket and recommended that next time, they do the right thing and we would all be happier. That last sentence wasn't quite true. I really was happy to finally catch someone littering and be able to really do something about it after five years as a ranger.

Now that I live in China I take a slightly different view of littering. Picking up litter provides thousands, maybe millions of jobs for people in this country, so in many places there's always someone to pick up your trash. I still don't like to see people deliberately throwing things on the ground, especially when there may be a trash can within two steps, but I have learned to tolerate it. Where it REALLY bugs me is in the beautiful natural areas I've gone and seen people throwing their garbage on the ground, even in the most scenic spots. In truth, most people do use the trash cans along the trails, which are often provided, though with so many people there's always someone who doesn't realize that there aren't so many trash pickers to clean up after them in remote places. Unfortunately having an in depth discussion of proper trash management is beyond the scope of my language skills, so occasionally I will pick up their trash and deposit it properly. Part of me will always be a ranger.

Saguaro National Park (formerly national monument), Arizona

Saguaros are those statuesque and stately cacti that can grow as tall as eight times my height with many branching arms, and Saguaro National Park was created to preserve some magnificent groves of them as well as prime Sonoran Desert landscape. The park has two sections, the smaller one west of Tucson, Arizona, and the larger east of the city, that goes from the relatively flat desert areas the cacti love up to the moderately high Rincon Mountains. If you think deserts are boring, then this is a place that can change your mind, just like the Grand Canyon, but in a different way. The flowers blooming in springtime can be absolutely magnificent, though I only actually worked there from September until early January (1990-1). I was a frontcountry law enforcement ranger there, and it's where I made my first arrest. In our patrol cars we not only carried shotguns, but also high powered rifles, because those were what drug smugglers used, or so they told us. We didn't want to be outgunned. Glad I never had to use it.

First Arrest

My first arrest happened when I was getting to know the ropes, riding with another ranger around the park perimeter. Driving down one of the many roller coaster roads in the area with the radar on, I tagged someone speeding. Roller coaster roads are those built across a series of small arroyos (natural drainage ditches that fill up when it rains) and they do a fairly rapid up and down and up and down and ... you get the idea. Like a roller coaster. The Tucson area has many of these, one even formally called "Roller Coaster Road."

Anyhow, on this Sunday afternoon, the old Chevy station wagon was going a little too fast, so I put on the lights and siren, turned around, and chased after the car. Before we made the stop, my colleague Chris and I discussed it and agreed that if everything was OK we'd just give them a warning and let it go at that. The car had a couple of adults and a handful of children inside. The driver, a rather burly man in a sleeveless shirt and arms bigger than my thighs, calmly handed us his driver's license. I asked for the car registration as well, and he complied. The kids in the back were starting to whimper. I told him he was going too fast and that he needed to slow down on the park roads. He explained that he and the children's mother wanted to give the kids some fun and drive fast over the roller coaster part of the road, but that they were otherwise not driving quickly. I went back to the patrol car and ran a check on his license. Expired. I returned and told him and he said he was sorry. I told him he couldn't drive the car and asked if there was another licensed driver in the car. Unfortunately they had none. I guess the six year old hadn't had time to take his driver's exam. Then dispatch came back with a check on the car registration. Expired. What's more is that the Tucson Police Department had a warrant out for his arrest. As calmly as possible I told him he was under arrest and to please step out of the car. He looked even bigger and stronger out of the car and I must admit, my skinny little frame would have broken in half had he decided to play rough, but he was very civil and came along quietly. I somehow managed to get the handcuffs on him, but they were tight. We put him in back of the patrol car. By this time the children were crying at the tops of their little lungs on the side of the road under the Arizona sun. With no licensed driver and the car expired, what would we do with it? There were no cell phones at that time, so we called dispatch and gave them a number of a family member to call to come and get the passengers. We would also allow them to drive the car home, as long as they promised to leave it there until it was registered. Dispatch succeeded after a while, and with screaming children we waited until they arrived.

We took our man to the ranger office and filled out some paperwork. When we were finally finished, we headed to the jail to turn him over to the city police. Neither Chris nor I had ever been there, so we followed the directions they gave us, but the directions weren't too helpful. Hell, the directions were crap, written by someone who never went there. "Where are you guys taking me?" asked our prisoner. We told him and he said, "Oh, turn right up ahead. I'll get you there. This place has a great snack bar." He told us that he was wanted for assaulting a man in a bar, but that the other guy started it. As a profession he made high quality bows and arrows, something I can greatly respect. From all appearances, a very nice guy, though we were not in a bar and he hadn't been drinking. I was sad to have to turn him over, but it was my job and he had several strikes against him. I shook his hand, wished him well, and walked away.

Stake-Out

Saguaro National Park was named for a cactus, so as you might guess, removing them from the park is strictly forbidden, whether they are living or dead. People often really like these stately succulents and many locals want to have them in their yards. They're not always easy to cultivate, and if you're successful they still take a long time to grow. People don't want to wait that long, so they try to get them already growing, whether by purchase or theft. There's actually quite a big business in snatching these big cacti from public lands and selling them for good money to people in the area, most of whom don't know they are actually buying stolen goods. Of course, not everyone loves them, which is why there is also a problem with people taking their guns out to some remote spot with saguaros and shooting them down like so many political prisoners on a firing squad. One infamous man met his end by shooting down a saguaro, which then fell right on top of him. Not an auspicious way to die. Condolences to his family, and that of the cactus.

When saguaros die the living flesh dries and rots away, leaving a skeleton of the woody fibers underneath. These are pretty neat looking and make lovely decorations, but as I said, they're also protected in a national park. One sunny afternoon (we had a lot of those) I was out on patrol, when I came across two saguaro skeletons in the park propped against the barbed wire fence along the road. I got out to investigate and found where they had been dragged from within the fence out to near the road. Someone was obviously going to return and pick them up at a later time. I called Paula, my supervisor, who met me shortly thereafter, and I showed her the drag marks and probable points of origin of the long dead saguaros. What to do? Do we sit out here and wait all day for someone to come by and pick them up, or just put them back? We figured that whoever was coming for them wouldn't get them in broad daylight, though now that I think about it, they probably dragged them there in broad daylight figuring it wasn't likely they would get caught in such an out of the way place. Well, it sounded good at the time. We returned the skeletons to their points of origin and decided to come back in the evening and wait out of sight to see if someone would return to snatch these woody remains. Time for a stake out.

We returned to headquarters and grabbed something to eat, then just before sunset we parked out of sight and put the skeletons back on the fence to see if someone would return to pick them up. We found a comfy spot beneath a couple of mesquite trees within sight and easy response to the contraband, and settled in to watch. We each had our revolvers, our high-powered rifles, and some warm clothes. Gets cold in the desert at night. It was my first, and ended up being my last stake out in my law enforcement career.

Not much activity out on that road. We kept our eyes glued to the skeletons watching for car lights to slow down by them. One hour. Two hours. The time just flew by... not. Paula and I watched the stars come out and dance across the clear desert sky. We chatted a bit ... quietly. I wrote a poem or two while we were waiting. A car slowed down near the skeletons, then drove off into the chilly night. We chatted some more. Another car, that just drove by. About midnight we figured that if anyone was going to come they would already have done so. Possibly they had seen us earlier near the skeletons and decided it wasn't worth getting arrested. We returned the saguaro skeletons to where they had originally fallen and made our way back to the office. Tomorrow would be good enough for filling out the paperwork.

We did follow up on that stake out by going to some local garden shops and questioning them about their saguaro skeletons in stock (there are legal sources) and if anyone had approached them about supplying them more, but nothing came of it. All in all, it had been a nice night under the stars and a good chat.

Tracker

I was trained to track people in my search and rescue training at the Grand Canyon, but didn't have much chance to use it in my work until I went to Saguaro. Hunting is illegal in most NPS areas, and Saguaro was no exception. One day during deer hunting season Paula and I were on patrol checking out some of the more remote parts of the monument, when we received a call that someone saw a man walking into the park with a hunting rifle. When we arrived we found a car near the area in question. At first glance we couldn't see anyone in the area, so we started walking into the park and I began tracking his footsteps, watching for footprints in the dirt, broken twigs, things out of place and other signs. A short ways in she suggested she head back to the car in case he returned there by another route. I continued tracking him. Areas where he walked over bare rock were hard to tell, so I had to look for signs when he went back to softer ground. I believe I did pretty well for a while, but it got harder as I continued tracking. At a particularly frustrating spot I got a call from Paula that the hunter had returned. He hadn't shot any deer, so she questioned him for a while and let him off with a warning. He answered all of her questions well and seemed to really believe he was on legal hunting ground. Before he left she asked him about his route through the park. When I returned he was already gone, but when she described where he went, it seemed I had been right on his trail. Never did that again, but it was fun while it lasted.

While I'm on the subject of deer, the only time I actually had to shoot my gun while at work (besides practice) was shooting an injured deer. Night had fallen and the dry desert air felt crisp and clear on my skin. I drove along the public road through the park when I spotted a group of people along the side of the road in the park. I stopped to see what had happened, and found they were gathered around a deer that had been hit by a car. One woman was seated on the ground with the head of the deer resting in her lap, drops of blood smearing her coat and pants. They told me what had happened and asked what we could do for the deer.

I love animals and would like to have helped the deer, but I knew that if she couldn't move, there was little anyone could do to help her. They were undaunted in their desire to help the deer. I called our dispatch office to ask if there was anyplace we could take injured wildlife for rehabilitation. The dispatcher humored me and looked it up, but found nothing. The people insisted we try the Human Society, who usually deals with pets or farm animals. I asked the dispatcher, but there was no answer at the Humane Society when he called. Several of the people were crying. It took some discussion, but I convinced them that we could not help the deer and that I would have to shoot her to end her pain. More tears ensued. People headed back to their cars. The woman with the deer in her lap was the last to go, reluctantly heading back to her car. The other cars drove off, but hers did not. She waited. I took my gun and put a couple of bullets into the deer. Then I dragged her body across the road to a low spot out of sight. Certainly the coyotes would have a feast tonight. The woman's car drove off, and shortly thereafter, so did I.

An odd ending to that story came the next day. I went to my taiji class in the evening. The instructor chose me to use to demonstrate a move and how it is used in self-defence. He always told us never to try to change what he asks us to do as he would just react. I was feeling playful and tried something different. Instantly I found myself falling as if in slow motion and landed face down on the mat. I sat up dazed, then began laughing as blood began to spurt out of my mouth. The instructor freaked out, thinking he had really knocked me silly. His wife knew better and laughed with me. It was just some release of emotion and I have no idea where it came from. I calmed him down and he took me to his home for the night so I could go to the dentist the next day. I needed a root canal. I didn't blame him and knew it was as much my fault as his. I doubt there's a connection, but it occurred exactly 24 hours after I shot the deer. Hmmm, sort of a cosmic occurrence.

Firsts

Saguaro had a lot of firsts for me: first tracking experience, first frontcountry law enforcement, first stake out, first arrest. One thing that wasn't a first was seeing the desert in snow, but it was one of the most special times experiencing the white stuff in this environment and my first in that particularly place. Most people don't expect to find snow in the desert when they come to a place like Saguaro or Tucson, but in a dry climate there are extremes of temperatures, from some of the highest highs, to some bitter cold lows. The last time I was in Tucson before moving to China, during the winter of 2009, we had near whiteout conditions where it got hard to see past a few hundred yards. The snow piled up to where even I had some trouble driving, and I've lived in snowy places much of my life. I had intended to camp, but the hotel proved much more comfortable.

On this particular occasion in the winter of 1990-91, I had gone into Tucson in the evening and was driving back out to the park after dark. What started as light rain, almost mist, in my headlights, began turning to flakes as I drove up the mountains to the pass. Coming down the other side the flakes continued and got bigger and more abundant, until I could start to see small amounts of snow gracing the rocks on the side of the road. When I arrived back at my trailer I spent a few minutes walking in the flying fluff, catching a few on my tongue as I twirled around. Then I got into my trailer, turned on the heat, and got ready for bed.

The next morning was a magical scene graced by tall, stately saguaros capped with white, like odd colored match sticks. The clear morning sky turned pink by the sunrise had cast a shimmer over the desert shrubs in their finery. I went into work and Paula had decided to close the park roads until the snow melted a bit. Some of the dirt roads were hazardous when wet, so we closed the gates to those, although the paved roads stayed open. A few hours later we went out to check on the roads as the sun began to melt the night sky's handiwork. I was driving the Ford Bronco and Paula was riding shotgun. The roads seemed in pretty good shape.

As an LE ranger at Saguaro N.P. in 1990

Then we happened upon a coyote crossing the road. We heard them frequently, but didn't often see them. When they're not in the park, they aren't protected and some of the local people take joy in shooting them whenever and wherever they can. It's understandable why they aren't crazy about humans. We saw this one go into the brush and as we drove forwarded, we stopped at that spot. He was sitting behind a bush on the side of the road on Paula's side of the car. We just watched for a moment as the coyote looked at us, then looked around briefly, then turned his eyes back to us. I opened the car door, then stepped outside keeping my eyes on our friend. He looked at me with an appraising glance, looked at Paula in the truck, checked the sides, then back to me. I said something to him, though for the life of me can't recall what, not that it matters. Probably something silly like "Hi, how are ya?" He gave me a deep look. A moment later he trotted off into the brush and we continued on. Without the winter storm, I don't think that would have happened. The snow slid off of the saguaros and plopped on the rocks below.

A few days later I took the horse out to patrol the park for the last time before I left to go back to the Grand Canyon. He had a lesson to teach me. Before working at Saguaro I had not ridden horses very much, and riding as part of my duty as a ranger was another first for me.. They taught me how to prepare the horse for riding, putting the bit in the mouth (the horses, not mine!), securing the saddle, etc., and how to care for the horse afterwards, brushing him down, checking his hooves, and such. I claim no great expertise in all of this, but it was a good experience to learn and to spend time with the horses. Like all of the animals I've met, they have much to teach us.

My previous trips through the park on horseback were pleasant and uneventful, but for the park visitors who enjoyed seeing and talking with us. On this particular morning, the snow had mostly melted, but it was still quite cold for Tucson. I got everything ready they way I usually did, except that he didn't seem to want to take the bit in his mouth. I tried several times before I finally got it situated in its proper place.

When we left the stable, he immediately began giving me hell. He ran like crazy a short distance, then stopped, nearly sending me flying over his head. We headed for the arroyo, a rocky dry stream bed, to check out an area I liked, but hadn't spent much time in. He continually would run like mad, then slow and try to rub me up against the rocks or the cacti. He ran under tree limbs that would have knocked me off had I not been paying attention. He fought me when I tried to turn him, didn't want to move when I wanted him to, then bolted when I wasn't expecting it. Finally, I managed to get him back to the stable, my clothes soiled and torn, my legs bruised, and covered with leaves and twigs, a few cactus needles poking out of my jacket. If you're a horse person, you probably already know why all this happened.

I got him in the stable, took off the saddle and pulled the bit from his mouth. Then he seemed to calm down. I felt the bit, how much warmer it was than when we had started and realized what I had done. On a cold morning you need to warm the bit before you put it in the horses mouth. I had just taken a piece of ice and shoved it into his mouth, propping against the tender flesh of his gums. No wonder he was angry with me. I apologized, though I'm not sure he understood that. He didn't seem to hold it against me, though. Once the bit left his mouth, he seemed to have forgiven me. I gave him a good brushing, cleaned his hooves well, fed him, and spent a little time with him. Sorry ole boy.

Soon after that I finished my contract with Saguaro, then headed back north to work at Indian Garden Ranger Station for the rest of the winter and the spring. Saguaro was an eventful time, with a lot of lessons learned and a wealth of experience in just 4 short months.

Denali National Park, Alaska

Denali is a huge park in central Alaska, about the size of the state of Massachusetts. Formerly it was known as Mt. McKinley National Park, even though President McKinley never stepped a foot in it. People mostly go there to see the wildlife: grizzly bears, Dall sheep, moose, caribou, and wolves, to mention the most famous charismatic mega-fauna. People also want to see the highest peak in North America, Mt. McKinley, known as Denali (The High One) to the native people, though it seems that few people get a good view of the mountain, mostly due to the weather during the main tourist season. The main part of the park has one road that takes people into its depths. For about 15 miles it's paved and accessible to all, but beyond that are 76 miles of graded dirt road where cars are generally prohibited unless you have a permit to camp there. Most people take bus rides into the park on that road, either those run by the NPS or formal tours by the concession company. I worked as an interpreter so my job consisted partly of working in the visitor center helping people arrange bus rides and hikes, doing formal ranger programs, including dog sled demonstrations, and riding the buses to talk with the visitors, answer their questions, and try to keep them from doing stupid things around animals like bears, moose, and wolves. I just worked there during the summer of 1991 between seasons at the Grand Canyon. My friend Tom had worked in Denali and thought it would be a good idea for me to go there and work in the same park with him, though he was in a different part of it. More on that later. I also just happened to have a girlfriend at the time from Arizona who was heading back to Alaska to finish some things for school at the University of Alaska in Fairbanks. Quite the coincidence.

Denali has a short season, being in Alaska with a long winter and all. I arrived in Fairbanks in late April and then went down to the park in May to start seasonal training. Most other seasonal rangers left the park at the end of August, but I stayed on until the end of September and helped get things ready for winter. It gets extremely cold there and the audio-visual equipment we used for our programs would get destroyed if just left in the unheated visitor center, which would get down to -40F. It's too expensive and wasteful to heat the whole building, so we gathered up the electronic equipment, put it in a small storage room with a space heater plugged in and set to low, then sealed up the door. As long as the power didn't go out or the heater cause a fire, it would be in workable shape come springtime. We also spent time stocking the ranger cabins along the park road with food, fuel and anything else they might need when rangers took dog sleds there on patrol in the biting cold and snow. Then there were the sled dogs to attend to. They can tell when mushing season is getting close and excitement runs so high you can practically cut it with a knife.

Missing Rangers

Denali National Park is home to some of the highest mountains in North America. Denali/Mt. McKinley is the highest at 20,310 feet with Mount Foraker at 17,342, both I n the Alaska Range. Why do people climb mountains? Because they are there, is the oft given response. In August of 1991, two of our rangers set out to climb one of the lesser peaks close to Denali. They were experienced hikers and had all the gear they needed. They intended to be out for about 3 days. Unfortunately it's hard to predict the weather in a place like Denali, not that it's easy anywhere, but a storm came in bringing with it high winds, though not a lot of precipitation, some rain in the lower areas, but snow in the high country.

The rangers at Eielson Visitor Center, which sits across the valley from where they were hiking and in direct view of Denali, could see their tent during those 3 days, but on the fourth day as the wind increased they could see the tent flapping in the breeze. Obviously, there was a problem. The park mobilized for a search, and I was included in the people who would go to the glacier and assist in looking for them. There were several teams, each going in at different places to try to locate our colleagues. Climbing specialists from the mountaineering center in the southern part of the park would handle the higher elevations, and I was part of the team that went straight to the tent site to investigate and begin searching for them, or evidence of them, which is what we mostly do in searches. Yes, we want to find THEM, but we can't overlook the clues, or we may not end up finding our targets at all.

The winds on the glacier were fierce, precluding the possibility of searching by air which would have been more efficient for a start. The ground search was our only option. When we arrived at our campsite by their tent, we began by setting up our own tents to have protection from the elements. Pounding stakes into the ice and snow to hold our tents in position proved an exercise in futility, as they just pulled out and our tents began blowing away. We found rocks, big rocks, that we placed inside of them to hold them down and decided while we were searching that we should just lay the tent poles inside of the tents, otherwise the wind could destroy them. Hopefully the wind would die down at night so we wouldn't end up with them getting shredded while we were sleeping. Once the tents were secured we organized and began examining what evidence we had. There was some food in their tent and most of their sleeping gear, which is what helped to anchor the tent so it didn't blow away. That, and a few footprints, was all we had to start with. We then set to work searching the crevices in the glacier and making our way up the glacier to look for signs of our friends, but nothing really came to light. The wind made our progress like pouring molasses in January, even made walking difficult. Your foot often landed someplace other than where you had intended it.

Back in camp we exchanged info, and based on our day's work things didn't look too promising. My good friend Tom and I cooked dinner inside of our tent to keep the wind from blowing out our camp stove, and after we finished we bedded down for the night, trying to sleep with the howling of the wind in our ears. The next day, after a quick breakfast, we headed out to search again. Like the day before we had little luck, but the winds definitely calmed a bit. Further up on the glacier we encountered the mountaineering group, who also hadn't had much luck. One of their members did tell us that higher up the winds got so fierce, that when he put his arms out it had picked him up off of his feet for a moment. We ate a quick lunch, and the consensus was that they seemed to have disappeared without trace. It was then we heard on the radio that they had been found and were alright. Shouts for joy went up all around and we headed back to camp to pack up and return to the visitor center, our starting point.

It turns out they had only camped one night in their tent on that north side of the mountains. The next day they had taken off to try and summit Scott peak, but that's when the weather had changed and they got into a white out, couldn't see more than a few meters or less. They began heading down slope to get below the snow, and ended up on the wrong side of the ridge ... they went to the south side of the mountains. They had brought a sleeping bag with them in case they got into trouble, which proved very useful. They got down to the lowland and tried to find things to eat, but there wasn't much available. Their main sustenance was soapberries, which are called that because they taste like ...well, you guessed right. Yuck! They're also small and require a lot of picking to get enough to fill the void in your hungry stomach. Bears eating them to put on fat for the winter just strip them from the branches in bunches and literally eat tens of thousands of them per day. At one point they saw a caribou and the one boy, a lifelong vegetarian, chased it with his ice axe to try to kill it for food. That didn't work too well, something for which he was later very grateful. Finally when the winds died down a little, the park airplane went out and spotted them that morning, and rangers went to their location to bring them in. We were reunited at the park headquarters where stories, pizza, and laughter ended a long couple of days.

Mushing

Dog sled are usually more dependable than snow machines. If you have a dog sled and one of the dogs has a problem, you toss him in the sled and keep going. If your snow machine has a problem, you're stuck, possibly many miles from help and likely in bitter, life threatening cold. Denali National Park keeps a team of 20-30 sled dogs which they use for patrolling the park in the winter time. During the summer they still need to keep in shape and be ready for "mushing season", as it's called, so they enlist the aid of willing seasonal rangers. I was willing and eager, much like the dogs when it comes to pulling sleds. Our job was to regularly, at least several times per week, go to the kennels and carefully take our dog out for a walk. We also spent time with the dogs to make sure they had enough love, though some of the dogs made that difficult. They all have their own personalities.

The dog that was assigned to me had the name of "Havoc", which I think is a great name for a sled dog. He was a big boy, and usually operated as a "wheel dog," which are the dogs closest to the sled that take the brunt of the weight of the sled. In front of those are the "team dogs" who add speed and pulling power. In front, of course, are the "lead dogs", usually one or two, who take commands such as "gee" for right, "haw" for left, "hike" to go, and "whoa" for stop, at least these are some of the most common commands. Havoc could also operate well as a lead dog, but his size kept him mostly at the wheel position. Such a large, strong dog did prove to be a challenge at times walking him. On warm summer days he wasn't so eager and didn't pull as much, but on cool days, especially when it got close to autumn, he would drag me up and down the roads. That brings me to another point: we stuck to the park roads on our walks and didn't go off into the brush, the fields, the forests, so as to minimize difficult encounters with wildlife, such a wolves, bears, wolverines, or moose.

One of our duties as interpretive rangers in Denali was to present Dog Sled Demonstrations, which were very popular with the park visitors. Since most of us had never mushed before, we spent time at the beginning of the season learning about mushing, the dogs, the history, and what it was like to run a sled in the winter. Our training was conducted by a musher who had run well in both the Iditarod, the world's most famous sled dog race, and the Yukon Quest, not as well known, but likely more grueling and difficult.

The Dog Sled Demos started with visitors wandering around the kennels, looking at the dogs, and NPS people making sure visitors behaved around them, providing information about the dogs and their work in the park. At the appointed time we would gather the crowd together in front of the kennel office, then ask people not to move away from the circle we had made together. The dogs really, REALLY love to pull sleds, and the dog sled demos were a big adrenaline rush for them. The dogs see the demonstrations every day and know that when people start moving away from the circle, five of them are going to be chosen for pulling the sled, and that makes them so excited that their barking, yowling, and howling would put an end to the talk, even if we weren't ready for it. For my talk I generally chose to discuss the dogs themselves and the properties which make a good sled dog. After our talk we gave instructions on where they should go and what was going to happen, then moved them to the side of the track. The dogs then went absolutely crazy, jumping all over, running around their pens, and making so much noise you couldn't hear yourself think. Then we went out and got one dog at a time starting with the lead dog. The sled itself, a wheeled one in the summertime, was attached with one chain in front and one in back to keep the dogs from running off with it. The kennels manager gave us a list of the dogs we would use for each demo. We had to be very careful when opening the doors of each kennel, because the excitement of the dogs made them hard to hold onto. Luckily I only had one dog get away from me during my summer in Denali, and the kennels manager had to go chase him while his assistant continued helping us hook up the dogs. We lifted the dogs off of their front legs to make them easier to control, and they typically jumped hard with their back legs as we walked them over to the sled and hooked them into their harnesses. As soon as each dog got hooked up to the sled, they would usually start jumping into their harnesses, causing the front end of the sled to fly up, then slap down on the dirt. When we had all of the dogs hooked up we got on the back of the sled, with the kennels manager by the lead dog making sure the path was clear before he gave you the thumbs up and unhooked the lead dog. Then we would reach back and unhook the chain holding onto the back of the sled, at which time the sled would jerk forward and off you would go into the forest. We would be out of sight from the visitors for a minute, then make a turn and come back to where we started on a path that took us right in front of the line of onlookers. The kennels manager would then stop the sled and secure it while we would get off and answer questions the people might have.

The main tourist season is short in Alaskan national parks. By the middle of August, tourism slowed down considerably and by American Labor Day in early September, the place was quiet but for a few ranger parties and the occasional howl of wolves. The tourists that did come in late August still crowded in for the dogsled demonstrations. My friend Tom and I decided to give them an extra special show. Tom, as you may recall, was the main reason I had gone to work in Denali, that and my girlfriend Marianne. Tom and I had been good friends ever since I began working at the Grand Canyon, where we met. We had spent several years at GRCA together, but he had spent one summer in Denali already and suggested I join him. We had worked in separate locations for the summer, but as September neared they closed the other visitor center and we had the chance to spend some time together. At the time we not only had a given name in common, but were about the same height, had nearly identical beards, and were both, as Tom liked to say, pencil necked geeks: skinny guys.

During one of my last dog sled demos I started as usual, gathering people, giving the talk, then setting up the sled. The dogs chosen were all the biggest and fastest ones we had, with Havoc as the lead dog. The sled took off like a shot, faster than I had experienced before, and it almost left me sitting on my butt at the start. We sped through the forest like a blur, where Tom (the other one) was waiting. He yelled for me to hop off, which I did, nearly slamming into a spruce tree while I tried to keep my feet beneath me, and he ran as fast as he could, grabbed onto the handle and pulled himself onto the sled, all in the forest where the visitors couldn't see us. The sled left my sight and made the turn toward the finish line. I caught my breath and slowly made my way to where Tom was answering questions. Through the trees I could see their confused looks and the smile on Gary's face. Our beloved kennel manager hadn't known about the switch Tom and I had pulled, and had a hard time keeping from bursting out laughing as visitors struggled to figure out what had happened: "He looks like our ranger, his name tag says he' Tom, but something's not quite right." Ah, the world of illusion!

One quick note: Some people think it's cruel to use dogs for transportation and to keep them outside in these conditions. I have been around dogs nearly all my life, and I can say that these were some of the most happy and engaged dogs I've ever seen. Some mushers, I've heard, are abusive to their dogs, but most realize that the dogs are their lifeline when they are out in the cold, so the care taken for them is like that of high caliber athletes. It's just like humans, in a way. If we have nothing to do, no real purpose, it seldom, if ever, leads to us becoming better humans. Sitting on the beach or in the lap of luxury are fine for a while, but far from the pinnacle of humanity. The dogs know what is expected of them and from what I saw they respond wholeheartedly, even love it. They're made for the cold and handle it without batting an eye. I wish I could say the same, but the cold is the main reason I left Denali.

Fun With Wolves

Wolves have captured my interest for a long time. In Wisconsin during my college years and thereafter I volunteered for an organization called the Timberwolf Preservation Society, which had a captive pack of wolves that they kept in runs (large cages) with one one to three wolves in each. I'm not sure what drew me to wolves, other than the fact that I've always loved dogs, but for whatever reason, after high school I did a lot of reading about wolves and when I heard about the organization I joined up. I would often go there on weekends to help care for the wolves, giving them food, hosing down their runs, and providing tours for visitors to the facility in southern Milwaukee county.

At first I just stayed outside of the cages and watched the wolves. Once they got used to me being there they sometimes would put their bodies up against the fences and I would come over and scratch their backs ... carefully. They liked it, but also recognized their captive state and one in particular, Ivan, would occasionally try to catch my fingers, I think just to keep me on my toes. He never got them, but one time I did end up with his saliva on my fingers, which led me to believe he wasn't that serious about biting them off. Ivan was fairly old when I first got to know him and I volunteered there for more than 5 years. He passed away during that time, and was donated to the Milwaukee County Historical Museum. When I last checked, his preserved body was still in one of their exhibits.

One bitter cold winter morning I went there right after working all night doing sound for a rock band at a local club. I knew Jim, the proprietor, got up early, so I thought I'd surprise him. He offered me coffee and we sat and chatted, when suddenly we heard a single, plaintive call rising from the wolf pens. Soon it was joined by others softly sending their howls into the crisp, clear sunrise. I'll never forget that feeling, the privilege of listening to their music that morning. Wolves have a couple of different howls, and that soft, gentle call was one you usually only heard in the morning or evening if you happened to be there at the right time. A more common call was the excited, "let's have a party" type of call, where they howled, barked, and whined while running and jumping around, nipping at each other (a sign of affection) and generally having wolf fun.

After I had gotten to know the wolves pretty well, and more importantly, they got to know me, I would go into the cages with a few of them on a fairly regular basis to clean up and give them water and food. On a nice summer's day I though I would go in and clean the pens of Boltar, a young male, and Cinnamon, a slightly older, very dominant female. They were in separate , but connected runs, and to enter Cinnamon's domain you had to go through Boltar's. I calmly, slowly entered Boltar's run and gave him a few scratches behind the ear. Then I carefully opened the gate and went in with Cinnamon. She jumped up on her house, like she often did, and gave me that look like she expected me to pet her a while, which I did. Then I began cleaning up her run a bit, when I heard one of those active howls rising from across the way. The wolves began getting excited, running around, and joining in with the howl. I knew it would be best for me to get out of there. I didn't think Cinnamon would hurt me on purpose, but she would relate to me as she would with other wolves. I wasn't another wolf. She began trotting in circles inside her run, howling, and when she passed me she would jump up on me and nip at my shirt, her long nails also scratching it as her feet hit my chest. I tried to stay calm as my shirt began coming apart. Each time after she left me to run around, I snuck closer to the gate. Then she would come back and jump on me again, tearing my shirt more, then leave and I would go for the gate. Finally, with my shirt mostly ripped apart and scratches on my chest and arms, I got out of the gate. That meant I was in with Boltar, who was larger, though not as dominant, and therefore a little more timid. He jumped up on me with his feet on my shoulders and his mouth in front of mine. I gave him a cuff with my partly opened hand over his muzzle and he put his feet back on the ground to continue his trotting around. I made for the gate and got out. I stood there for a moment, my knees shaking a bit, catching my breath. The howl began to subside and the activity level declined. I turned and looked at Cinnamon. She gave me a look that felt like "Where did you go? We were just starting to have fun!"

When I went to Alaska to work in Denali National Park in 1991 I brought those experiences with me to a place where wild wolves are still common. I talked with the wolf researchers there, read everything I could, and developed a program that involved stories, anecdotes and facts about wolves and how people have perceived them over time. Normally ranger evening programs involved slide shows, now power points, but this program was just me talking, telling stories. One visitor complained after my program by telling me that usually, when rangers shut off the lights and started their slide shows, he went right to sleep, but he had to stay awake for the entire program. He also said he was glad he stayed awake. I continued to do this program when I returned to the Grand Canyon. Ellis, our Chief of Interpretation told me it was "possibly the best ranger program I have ever seen." Maybe my best compliment came one night when I performed it on the North Rim. Ranchers in the western US have often had a difficult relationship with wolves over time, which is a nice way of saying they've usually killed them at every opportunity. This night after I finished a woman jumped out of her seat and hurried up to the stage to tell me "You know, I come from a long line of ranching people." I immediately thought she was going to tell me I was full of shit talking about wolves like that, but she continued, "You've really given me something to think about. Thank you." With that, she turned and walked away. It was the best compliment I think I could ever receive. This is the same program that ended up brining me to Germany to work in a national park there after one of their employees saw me perform it on the South Rim. I felt very proud of the presentation, one of the high points in my generally rewarding NPS career.

Having said all that about this program, when I began performing it in Denali, and for most of my summer there, I had not seen a wolf in the park. I briefly saw one in Canada while driving to Alaska, but none in the park. People would come up and tell me their stories of seeing wolves, and I'd smile and say "That's great!" while thinking of how much I wanted to have experiences like that. Finally, one day while doing roving interpretation on the buses going into the park, I had my chance.

The day had dawned overcast and I stepped aboard the bus heading for the park interior. At one of the broad river valleys we saw a couple of buses stopped on the bridge over the river. We pulled up and stopped to see what they were looking at, and on a gravel bar in the braided stream at a distance of maybe a quarter of a mile from us we saw some wolves near a caribou they had killed. A grizzly bear had come up and was trying to chase the wolves off so he could eat his fill. The wolves were taunting him, trying to keep him from eating their meal. The dance between them kept going back and forth, grizzly chasing the wolves off, and the wolves keeping the bear from getting much food. Just then a silver fox came up from behind the bus, walked along side of it, but when she got near the front of the bus she paused and trotted off the roadside and into the brush. A moment later, a wolf popped out of the brush in front of the bus. He paused to look around and evaluate the situation, then turned and started trotting down the road, our bus following him at a short distance. Based on my limited first-hand knowledge of wild wolves, this one appeared to be a young male.

The wolf moved along at a comfortable pace, stopping now and then to sniff the cool Alaskan air, occasionally chasing ground squirrels, without too much success. After a time we could see a couple of hikers coming towards us, still quite a distance away. So we had the bus moving towards the hikers, and a wolf trotting along towards them in between. A woman sitting near the front of the bus began to get worried, "What if the wolf charges them?" she asked in a quite anxious tone of voice. "Don't worry, it's not going to do that," I offered. "But what if it does?" As the wolf and bus drew closer to the hikers, she got more worked up, eventually frothing into a frenzy, yelling "Oh, my gosh it's going to attack them, can't we do something?" I tried to calm her down by saying that nobody, and I mean nobody, has ever been killed by a wolf in the park (that anybody knows of). My words fell on deaf ears as the tension built. Then, just as the hikers got within about 50 feet of the wolf, they walked off the side of the road about 15 feet, shooting pictures as the wolf trotted up the road past them. When the bus got to their location we stopped, and the couple climbed aboard. They had smiles a mile wide and as they walked down the aisle they said "That was SO cool!!" Yes, it certainly was. For me, there was more to come.

Havoc and the Wolf

It was September 30, 1991, my last day of work at Denali National Park. Havoc, the sled dog assigned to me, and I had become close friends during the season, and during my last day I decided to take him out for a good walk along the park road. As we walked, him pulling me up the road, I noticed that a large flock of ravens and magpies had gathered in a grove of white spruce trees about 100 feet off of the road. I had not seen that many of these scavengers gathered in one place all summer, and I figured something was going on, so I periodically glanced up to the trees as Havoc dragged me down the road. At one point, a voice inside of me said, "Tom, Stop!" I froze. Havoc was carving a counterclockwise circle on the pavement in front of me. He knew something was up, but he couldn't see because of the tall grass.

I peered through the grass and saw that, 75 feet away, looking right back at me, stood a wolf. I had studied quite a bit about wolves and was not truly afraid, but from somewhere deep inside came a twinge of primal fear. We made eye contact for 15-20 seconds; it seemed like much longer.

Me with Havoc the sled dog in Denali, 1991 (Such a handsome boy... him, not me)

Then he turned and sought the cover of the trees. I thought to myself, "All those scavengers and a wolf, it must be a kill site." Whenever there was a kill in the park, the area would be closed off so that the wolves could eat in peace. Also, it was common for grizzlies to come in and feed on the carcass, like in the previous story. If a person went in there with wolves feeding they would most likely just back off, but the last place a person would want to be is between a grizzly and fresh meat.

I finished my walk with Havoc and notified one of the law enforcement rangers of my suspicion. We grabbed some 'Police Line, Do Not Cross' tape and 2 shotguns, just in case. We headed out to where I had seen the wolf where we separated and began walking through the spruce grove. I turned a corner around a tree and looked to my left. There I saw it: a yearling moose that was not going to get any older. It lie on its back, split down the middle, with entrails pulled here and there, and blood pooling in the body cavity. The hair on the back of my neck stood up and I knew the wolves were watching me.

That may seem like a gruesome picture, but for me to be there, where moments before, a drama between moose and wolves had been lived out in the same place that it had occurred for thousands, maybe millions of years, was one of the most powerful experiences of my life. It was there that I really felt the meaning of the terms 'wildness' and 'wilderness.' After checking the scene we flagged the area off and went back to the office.

The next day I was leaving the park and heading back to Arizona, but before I left, I went to the place along the road where I had seen the wolf. I saw two wolves this time, probably a mated pair, playing and chasing after one another, their backs and heads barely visible above the grass.

An old, white Ford Ranchero in fine condition pulled up behind me, and the man inside asked, "D'ya see anything?" I had been pointing things out to visitors for the last 5 months and was no longer employed as a ranger. I looked at the wolves and said, "Nope. Saw a wolf up there yesterday though." "But you don't see anything now?" "Nope." He drove off. Some things you just have to savor for yourself.

I left the park that day and haven't been back since. Maybe I will go back sometime, but whether I do or not, I know that the story, and the feeling, will always be with me.

Wonders at Wonder Lake

Fall comes early to Denali National Park, bringing with it the tundra's wine red colors, clear days, and ripe wild blueberries. By late August you could tell the light had changed along with colors of leaves, and the sun began going down below the horizon long enough to have something we could call night for a short time. I had done a lot of day hiking in the park, but not much backpacking, so I decided to take one of my weekends and hike with three of my colleagues to the area around Wonder Lake, at the far end of the park road. We got our permit, our Bear Resistant Food Containers, and hopped on the bus around noon to spend a night in the inner reaches of the park.

Denali has few trails and people mostly spread out and go cross-country. When we got off of the bus at our appointed stop, we checked the map and started hiking over the hills near the lake. We began to notice our boots taking on a dark, blue dye, and realized it was the juice of blueberries that burst on our boots as we walked, so we started grabbing the little azure globes and popping them into our mouths every few steps. I've never experienced a sweeter, more delicious hike in my life. A fox was also out enjoying the berries, and she danced around before us, leading us on through the tundra, her silken, red, gray, and white fur flowing and catching the daylight. After a time she left us and we stopped for a break overlooking a pond where a large antlered moose waded into the cold water, thrusting his head into the drink to pull up water plants and chew on them. In the distance stood the High One, Denali, Mt. McKinley, dressed in more snow than we had seen in many months. Eventually, after only about 1.5 miles of hiking, we found a spot to spend the night, such that it is. We were judging night more by our watches than the sky, since it still never got really dark. We made a quick dinner and settled in to get some sleep.

Sometime after midnight I awoke to go out and pee some of that blueberry juice from earlier in the day. When I emerged from the tent, I could tell the sky colors had faded to near night shades, but looking around the heavens were illuminated. Sitting on the horizon, just above the snow-covered peaks, sat the moon in a crescent shape with what's called "Earth shine" outlining her dark remainder. Also sitting on the horizon, spreading out from the moon in both directions almost completely encircling me were norther lights, greens, blues, purples, reds, dancing and shimmering with a lively vibrance unlike I had ever seen. I watched for a while, taking in a show that only Nature can provide.

The return hike was beautiful, yet uneventful, and somewhat anti-climactic after the night's activities. The bus ride back I can't even recall. Yet the trip was unforgettable.

Mesa Verde National Park, Colorado

"Mesa Verde" means "Green Table" in Spanish, and it stands in the high desert area of southwestern Colorado at elevations of 6000 to over 8000 feet, much of it covered in forest of pine and juniper trees, oddly enough, like a big, green table. The main attraction is the incredible number of ancient dwellings of Puebloan Indians, mostly occupied from 800 to 1200 A.D. thereabouts. A fair number of these dwellings are tucked into alcoves in the sandstone and are known as cliff dwellings. My friends on the Hopi Reservation in Arizona tell me their ancestors lived there a long, long time ago. I worked at Mesa Verde National Park during the winter of 2001-2002, and I can tell you that in this high, dry place it can get colder than a polar bear's butt. It's magnificent. It's beautiful. But in winter, when the sun dips below the western horizon, it's cold. I worked there as an interpretive ranger leading tours of the cliff dwellings, particularly Spruce Tree House, and working in the Chapin Mesa Archeological Museum. Toward the end of my season there I also had a taste of the summer activities, giving tours of Cliff Palace, the most famous of the cliff dwellings, Balcony House, and Long House. I left just as things began really warming up, heading back to Oregon Caves.

Mesa Verde, in its own way, is one of the most mystical places I've been. Spending time there you can feel the lives of the ancient ones as they go about their daily chores in the crisp, clear air. Of course, maybe that's just the power of suggestion, but the place is truly beautiful and special. As the witching hour of midnight on New Years Eve loomed, I wanted to have a special experience of Mesa Verde, even a mystical one, if possible. I got a permit to spend part of the night in a kiva in Spruce Tree House. Kivas are usually, though not always, circular structures built into the ground that serve as religious centers for the Pueblo people. Somewhere in every kiva is a small hole that represents the origin point of people who emerged from previous worlds into this one. Dances and other ceremonies are often held there. In preparation I asked Gerald, one of my Hopi friends, what things I should or should not do while in the kiva. The main thing he told me was I should take with me some Bear Root, a plant others know as Osha Root, in the wild carrot family. He said it would help protect me from bad spirits. I had some Osha because I used it to soothe my throat when I had colds or talked too much in cold, dry weather, a common thing in my profession. It has a very strong flavor, but works well. Gerald also told me to bring something as a gift to the spirits.

As I prepared for my experience, I brought the Osha, some items as gifts, candles, sage incense, and wore lots of warm clothing. Well after darkness had settled over the mesa and the stars began dancing across the sky, I took these items and my permit and went to the gate. I unlocked it and walked by moonlight to Spruce Tree House on this beautiful, clear, cold night, turned on my flashlight, and climbed down the wooden ladder into the kiva. The usual musty smell greeted my nostrils and it was quiet, deafeningly quiet. I lit the candles and incense then extinguished the flashlight and settled in to meditate. I alternated deep breathing exercises, quiet meditation, singing, and moving around to keep warm during my 4 hours or so in the kiva.

I wish I could tell you I had some amazing visions, some great revelations, or some sort of awakening during my time in the kiva that night, but in truth there was none of that. Meditation and deep breathing have their benefits and those I definitely experienced, but none was particularly mystical. Did spirits came to visit me? Only a few mice that poked their heads in to see just what the hell was going on in their kiva. Were they the spirits? Maybe. Or maybe not. So was it a wasted time? Not at all. I've spent so many New Years Eves getting drunk, going to parties, which were fun in their way, but for me not usually very healthy or fulfilling. It may not have been the mystical experience I had hoped for, but it also didn't give me a hangover, not even a little headache. It didn't leave me disappointed that I hadn't found the woman of my dreams, not even the woman of the moment, or make me regret my actions. It was peaceful and in its own oddly simple way enjoyable. I hiked back to the gate, then got in my car and drove back to my little residence. I had a snack and went to bed.

I like the place very much, but since I was there during the slow season and for just a few months, not too much else happened to tell about.

Oregon Caves National Monument, Oregon

This little gem of a national monument is small, less than a square mile when I worked there, sitting in the Siskiyou Mountains of southern Oregon at an elevation of about 4000 feet, surrounded by national forest. More recently it was expanded to just over 7 square miles, the 'new' land just transferred from the U.S. Forest Service to the NPS. Above ground is a beautiful forest with some magnificent Douglas fir trees, rare plants, and steep hillsides. Below ground is a marble cave of nearly 3 miles of total passageways. My job when I started there in 2001 was working as an interpretive ranger, leading cave tours, doing other programs and working in the visitor center. I worked one summer, then went to Mesa Verde for the winter. After that I returned and later in 2002 got my first and only permanent job with the NPS as the head guide. I stayed in that position for nearly 4 years before getting burned out and needing a break. I was also going through a difficult personal period during that time. After a hiatus I returned to work as a seasonal, which was much less stressful. Every year the NPS does a survey to rate how they are doing with the park visitors in every one of the 400 plus sites they operate around the country. During my time as Head Guide we achieved the highest rating in the NPS for customer service, which was one of the proudest accomplishments in my working life.

In total I lived in this area for more than 8 years. Prior to starting at Oregon Caves (ORCA for short), I had been working for Whole Foods Market in North Carolina and I left ORCA when I moved to China in

2010. When I first arrived in 2001 I lived in the dormitory, which is the in the same building as the visitor center. It had been built in the 1920s as the original hotel and had lots of character, but was rather drafty when it got cold. When I came back from Mesa Verde I needed housing outside the monument, so I first shared a house in Cave Junction for a time with another ranger. When she moved out I couldn't afford to stay in the house, so I rented a small, nice, but poorly insulated trailer from a delightful old couple in Kerby, OR, nearby. Later I moved into a much more comfortable cabin in Cave Junction, which is where I stayed for the next 3 years, a sweet little place near the Illinois River. During the last couple of years I worked at ORCA I lived in an even smaller cabin at the Frog Farm in Takilma, OR, where my friends who own the farm raise medicinal herbs, fruit trees, vegetables, chickens, ducks, geese and goats. Ranger by day, and farmer by night, so to speak.

My first day in training at the Caves was spent learning about the natural resources and human history there. Since my degree is in geology and I had done some extra coursework studying the chemistry of groundwater, I knew quite a lot about caves. I understood how the slightly acidified rainwater, soil acids, or other sources of acidic water dissolved the carbonate rocks to create these holes in the ground, at least in most cases. Most of my colleagues in the ORCA training sessions had limited knowledge of geology. The afternoon of that first day we went to the Resource Management Office of the park, a little cabin on the steep slope above the visitor center. John, the Chief Scientist for the park and Chief of Resources Management, gave us our talk on cave geology, which I was really looking forward to. The session began and before long I found myself getting totally confused, not sure what exactly he was talking about. I listened intently and knew the language, the words, the ideas, but the pieces just didn't seem to fit together. Suddenly about three fourths of the way through the talk it dawned on me that John had started sort of in the middle of the talk. He had left out lots of preliminary information that would have helped us get a handle on the complex subject. It's funny, because I later learned that he was quite good at leading cave tours for the general public. I'm not sure if the visitors really understood most of what he was saying, but they came away with an appreciation of the beauty, the wonder, the magic of the place, and in most cases that's really the most we can ask of them or ourselves as rangers. I guess he just thought we already had the basics and that he didn't need to go over them. We've been friends ever since that day, going on 20 years as of this writing, but he's never given me a clear explanation of his thoughts behind the presentation. After our session I checked with my colleagues, and as I suspected they understood pretty much nothing of that session, so we found time that evening and I explained it to them. They were greatly appreciative. The next day, Roger, the Chief Naturalist, also gave us some more geology info that we could understand. Ever since then during my time at the Caves, I ended up sort of interpreting for John with the seasonal, and some of the permanent employees. He's a wonderful man, brilliant in many ways, but yet like many such people it didn't always come across in conversation just what he wanted to say when it came to science matters. Obviously my main focus was geology there as it had been at the Grand Canyon, but another thing really sparked my interest that set me on a course which I hadn't expected.

I never had a history class in college, other than historical geology, but working as a ranger for the NPS you have the chance to explore a wide variety of subjects. Ever since I started working for them at Shenandoah in 1986, I learned about and developed talks on many subjects, not the least of which was history. I generally have read much more about Native American history than I did about other aspects of history of the United States, but for some reason that changed when I came to the Oregon Caves. The park has an official historian who works out of Crater Lake National Park not too far away, and John, our chief scientist also has a strong knowledge of the history of the place, but I became the unofficial resident historian for ORCA.

Elijah Davidson was the first known person to have discovered Oregon Caves in 1874, or 73, or 75, or whenever, depending on which account you refer to, though the official date is that first one (Later we found evidence of Native Americans in the Cave, but there was none when I started there in 2001). Maybe it was the dog in the story, maybe that he was born so close to my hometown, maybe it was that I just came to like the place so much or that I felt it was the best way I could contribute to the operation, but I became fascinated with the discovery story and chose to spend a lot of my work and free time researching this man and his life. One day while giving a talk outside the cave, I met Babe Fields who had known Elijah Davidson and had heard him tell the story of the discovery first hand. I traveled to his home nearby and did an oral history report. Later I learned of another woman who had met Elijah, who also lived near Babe, though she had only faint recollections of him. In the years to follow we had some of Elijah's descendants visit the Caves and I learned of other people, relatives who knew him or had info about him. I traveled to Stockton, CA, to interview Elijah's granddaughter, then to Vancouver, WA, to interview another. I gathered the stories wherever I could find them and recorded them for the park's historical archives.

During the busy summer season we were scheduled to do either an off-trail cave tour involving crawling through hight spaces, or an historical candlelight tour. We chose one or the other, not both. I chose the candlelight tour and decided I would do it in the person of Elijah Davidson. When Irma, the granddaughter in Stockton, saw me standing at her door, she just started laughing. "YOU, portray MY grandfather? But he was just a little guy! He was strong as an ox, but short." I'm a bit over 6 feet tall, and not too strong. Well, the audience generally didn't know all that, except when his relatives came to see me perform. Elijah had found the Cave while out hunting and his dog chased a bear into it, or so the story goes. I started the tour in my ranger uniform, then went off before we entered the Cave and changed into clothes more like Elijah would have worn. I started shouting for my dog, then came running out chasing after him. "Have you seen my dog?" I asked the visitors, then began telling them how I must have come from the "Great Beyond" because someone was thinking about who had discovered the Cave. I kept in the character of "the Ghost of Elijah Davidson" throughout the tour, even finding ways to deal with issues that had happened after Elijah passed away. It became a very popular tour and was always an adrenaline rush for me, none more so than when I did the program for some of Elijah's descendants. One of these days maybe I'll publish the info I've collected into a small book about Elijah to be sold at the Caves, but now that I live in China it sits in the historical archives of the Caves and I hope someone else is using the information to develop their own programs. People in China have generally never heard of the Oregon Caves.

2002

2002 proved to be a very trying year for Oregon Caves. Actually it may have started with the fall of 2001. I had a day off and was planning to go on a long drive with Samantha (Sam), our Australian volunteer, to show her some of southern Oregon, some of which I hadn't seen yet either. We set off going down the hill and I realized I needed some gas urgently, so I stopped at the maintenance garage to buy a gallon to get me down the hill to the gas station. The maintenance crew was all in the office watching TV and told me I needed to see what was happening. The date was September 11. There was chaos all over the TV, no matter what station you checked, as the twin towers collapsed. We had one seasonal from New York City, so after I got my gasoline I drove back up to the dormitory and we awoke her and told her what had happened. She immediately turned on the TV in shock. We sat with her for a while, then when others had awakened and discovered the news, they stayed with her and we set off on our journey. Along the way we stopped in restaurants or convenience stores and checked the TV for the latest news. It ended up being a beautiful day on the West Coast … not so nice on the East Coast.

The 2002 season started as usual in March when new seasonal guides arrived and went through training. Cave tours started when the schools were on spring break in April. I was in Mesa Verde at the time and considered staying in that area for the summer, but when the Caves offered me a lead guide position, one of 4 they gave out that year, I decided to return, arriving back in Cave Junction in June. It wasn't a permanent job, but it wasn't seasonal either: a four year position. In my first couple of weeks I had heard rumors of some bad behavior taking place in the dorm, mostly during the night: too much alcohol and too few inhibitions. Some of the guides were reportedly still drunk when they came to work in the morning, and others were hung over. It came to a head when some of the seasonals decided to go swimming in the fish pond in front of the lodge in the wee hours of the morning, making enough noise to wake up paying guests. In the midst of that I got promoted to the permanent position of Head Guide, and my first order from the superintendent directly was to get a handle on discipline among the staff. The guides didn't take it very well when they showed up in bad condition for work and I sent them to their rooms without pay until they were in a better frame of mind for work. Some became resentful, thinking I was letting power go to my head, but I was under pressure to get things under control. Eventually things mellowed. Then came the fire.

People often think of Oregon as a wet state, being close to the ocean and all. It's true that the coastal area has some rainforests and the western part of the state can get quite a lot of rain and snow, but southern Oregon has a Mediterranean climate, which means the summers are hot and dry and winters are cool and wet. The record high summer temperature is 114F/46C. The summer of 2002 was a particularly dry one, going 80 days without a single drop of rain in Cave Junction. Thunder clouds moved in at times and brought some light rain to the mountains, but the valleys stayed hot and dry. Oregon Caves sits at 4000 feet in the mountains, but even there we had no rain for the entire summer.

On the night of July 13, lightening started 5 fires in the Kalmiopsis Wilderness area west of my home, 15-20 miles from ORCA as the crow flies, and with the dryness and winds those 5 fires eventually merged into one big fire that burned nearly 500,000 acres, or more than 2000 km2 of forest. Even though I was trained as a forest fire fighter, I had other duties to attend to so I didn't go to work fighting the fire. As the fire began building, smoke enveloped Cave Junction and the Oregon Caves, and nights never got very dark as a constant reddish glow lit up the western sky. After about 2 weeks the fire looked like it was heading for Cave Junction. In one night, when fires are usually not moving as fast, it advanced nearly 20 miles and we could see flames from the road that passed by my house. The little town of less than 2000 people suddenly took on an air of the apocalyptic with billowing smoke above us, glowing skies to the west, and people either leaving to stay with family members elsewhere or buying up food and bottled water for the pending tragedy, spraying down their homes to try to keep them safe. Military and fire trucks darted through town. I figured that Oregon Caves, since it lay east of Cave Junction more than 10 miles and therefore away from the fire, would be a safer place for my belongings, so I packed up my most valuable things and transported them to a corner of a maintenance garage in the monument. There I stored my guitar, my desktop computer, my favorite books, my journals, some of my clothes, and various memorabilia, though some stayed in my car. In the evening after work I would drive down to my home in the valley and try to get some rest, all the while knowing the fire raged just to the west. During the days a few visitors straggled up to the Caves to find respite from the smoke and heat in the dark underground. Mostly we just watched and waited.

In the midst of all of the fire chaos, we developed phone problems at the Caves. Seasonal employees living there had a payphone they could use to make calls to friends or relatives, and they kept that phone pretty busy, especially after the fire started. The fire was on national news and family members were terribly worried about their loved ones. At the time, cell phones were mostly useless there, though if the weather was just perfect, the stars were aligned properly, you chanced to find the right spot, and you did the proper dance to appease the gods of cell phone service, you might just get a signal for a few minutes. So the pay phone was the only consistent option. After the fire had been burning for a few weeks, the payphone developed problems and began working only intermittently. Eventually the company that operated the phone, after sending up folks to fix it several times, decided to cancel the account, and the employees were left without any phone service. The official park business phones still worked, but government rules prohibit their use for personal purposes, especially long distance calls. After a couple of heated meetings, I helped convince the administration to make some concession for the extenuating circumstances, and the seasonals could once again talk to their families.

The danger to Cave Junction passed as the winds made an adjustment and the fire headed more south and west. Firefighters continued to work on it, but the difficult, steep terrain, dryness, and winds created a fire that would not be tamed. Luckily not many houses were burned by the fire, and those lay on the north end in a remote community in the mountains. As the fire kept moving away from the Caves, some more visitors found their way up the mountain to keep our seasonal tour guides occupied, some taking forest roads over the mountains, which in itself provided them with adventure and tested their route finding skills. The fire died down a bit as conditions cooled in the fall, but was not fully contained until November. Finally on December 31st as the winter rains and snows had started in earnest a month earlier, the fire was declared out, five months and 18 days after it had begun.

The problems of 2002 bled over a bit into 2003. We started out with 13 seasonal tour guides in March, mostly paid guides, but a couple of volunteers as well, then ended up with 8 of them leaving by June. For the most part it had nothing to do with the job. The seasonal guides mostly lived, like I had, in the dormitory above the visitor center, and for some reason, some of them just couldn't get along with each other. One couple that split up also decided to split with their work. One left due to contracting what he thought was an illness called SARS to check himself into the VA Hospital. It ended up not being SARS, but he still didn't return. One left because part of the job was collecting fees for tours and selling books. Even though he had said on his application that he had lots of experience running a cash register, he ended up not figuring out ours and couldn't count money worth a damn. That spring I spent all my time training new people and covering cave tours for the people who had left. Finally, when we did get a staff that would stay and do the job, we ended up with a great group of people, many of whom returned for another season or two. A few also ended up with permanent jobs at the Caves, one of them even replacing me when I left.

I continued to work at the Caves in the Head Guide position until 2006. There were other events that I could write about, but the main thing that took place in 2003 is that it started another chapter in my life, the Pedro chapter.

He'd Had a Bad Day

It had been a very long and busy first day of the summer season at Oregon Caves. As I got off of work at about 8:45 p.m., one of my employees, Robert, stopped me as I walked down the stairs from the Visitor Center to the parking lot. He told me that he had just driven up the hill from Cave Junction on a quick trip for groceries, and along the way he picked up a hitchhiker. The hitchhiker wanted to be dropped off at Takilma Road, so my friend had told him to ride in the back of his pick-up truck and to knock on the window when they neared the correct spot for him to hop out. Takilma sits about 7 miles south of Cave Junction, so not really on the way to the Caves from Cave Junction, but Robert was new and didn't know that.

Robert passed a number of intersections and called back to ask his passenger if one of them had been his. The reply came as a negative. Robert continued driving. After a few more minutes they neared the spot where the road began the steep climb up the mountain to the caves (it rises almost 3000 ft./900 meters), beyond which nobody lives except some of those who work at Oregon Caves National Monument. Robert stopped to ask his guest what was up, and the individual promptly told him just to keep driving because he didn't want to get out of the truck.

Upon their arrival, Robert parked his vehicle and grabbed his groceries. The other man stated his desire to sleep in the back of the pick-up truck. Camping overnight, even in a car, is not allowed in NPS units except in campgrounds or with special permits. We didn't have a campground. I met Robert in the parking lot and he told me what had happened. I walked through the parking lot towards the far end where our employees park their vehicles. When still about 100 ft./30 m. away from Robert's pick-up, I saw the back of the head and shoulders of a man just above the shrubs in front of Robert's truck. He wore a tie-dyed shirt and a floppy hat. I glanced away momentarily and when I looked back I no longer saw the man, and heard a rumbling sound, as of someone running or falling down a steep slope. I made haste to where I had last seen him.

When I arrived at the end of the lot, I looked down the hill through the Douglas fir trees, but could see no human at first due to the shrubs in my way. I stepped to the side and saw the lower body of a man lying on his back. The figure moved and groaned a bit. I surmised that he had attempted to pee, but had lost his balance and fallen down about 10 ft./3m. to a slightly level place in the otherwise very steep slope. I called out "Are you OK?" The reply came "Well…I have my penis out." "Yes, I can see that," I said, "but can you get up?" The man pulled up his shorts and attempted to stand, but the steepness, and his obvious disorientation, caused him to begin tumbling backwards. He dropped to all fours and I advised him to crawl. He did so with great difficulty, so I found a relatively safe place to step down and assisted him from behind to ensure that he wouldn't fall backwards again, possibly to death or serious injury. During my first close encounter with the gentleman I got a whiff of what I had suspected, the distinct odor of intoxication. It wasn't just the odor of alcohol, but rather that of LOTS of alcohol.

Once again on level ground I informed him that we would have to leave the monument and told him that I would drive him back down the hill. In slurred speech, this man, probably in his mid-40s with shaggy, neck length brown hair and similar stature to mine, told me he wanted to stay where he was and sleep in the woods. In a firm voice I told him that he could not do so, that it is illegal, and that I would call the Sheriff should he protest. He reluctantly agreed. You have to be firm and clear with drunken people. I learned that from my years working as a roadie for rock groups, as well as my law enforcement years with the NPS. I've also been drunk out of my gourd enough times to know, though not for many years, now, thank goodness.

I lifted his small backpack out of Robert's truck and walked to my car parked a stone's throw away. I asked the man's name and he said it was Rick. I opened the door of my Honda and tossed his pack inside. Rick walked to within a few feet of my car, then turned and paused. "My brother died yesterday," he told me. What could I say but "I'm sorry for your loss." I paused by my car door and listened patiently to his gentle sobs. After a couple of minutes during which his sobs quieted I suggested he get into the car and tell me about it on the way. He stepped over, climbed inside, and I closed the door for him.

During the ride down the mountain he told me that his brother Matt had Multiple Sclerosis, which had finally consumed him. He cried some, to which I just put my hand on his shoulder and listened. Then he would stop to expound upon the beauty of the forest and the sun setting over the mountains. I agreed, it was really beautiful. He also remarked on what a great fall he had taken, the word "great" indicating "well done." I have to admit he was right; I certainly could not have survived such a fall as well as he did, but then I wasn't drunk. Rick said he was a cook and that he wanted to work in the lodge at the caves. I recommended he wait until a better day before filling out an application. He agreed.

About half way in our drive Rick mentioned his dog. I asked the dog's name and he said it was Henry. About 10 minutes later he again mentioned his dog, to which I responded "You mean Henry?" "Yeah, how did you know my dog's name?!" "I just know these things." "Naw, you musta picked me up hitchin' a ride before." I left the matter alone and smiled. Rick had had better days. The last time he had seen his brother was a year before. His family lives in Michigan, which is a long ways from here. I know…most of my family of birth also lives near there. I know how that separation feels. In spite of the lateness and my lack of dinner, I drove Rick to his place in Takilma. I didn't have the heart to do any less. When he exited I wished him well, told him to get some rest, and to take care of his dog. He wished me the same.

I don't know if Rick made a regular habit of drinking to such an extent and his brother's death was just an added reason, or if this episode was entirely precipitated by his loss, but either way I felt he needed a kind ear and a friendly ride to his door. Maybe I'll see him again, or maybe not, but I wish him a full and fruitful grieving process. As I drove home to my own dog and a late dinner, I couldn't help but think about how first appearances can deceive. I first looked at him as just another drunken partier, which he may be, but if it took the liquor to loosen his tears, then so be it. I know one thing for certain: after the liquor wore off, he would know that he had fallen.

Seeing Rick made me think of the days of my youth when I got rip-roaring drunk more times than I care to remember. Oh, the wasted time, the deceased brain cells I could really use now as I get older, and older. Getting drunk is mostly a human thing, but not exclusively. My teacher

Martin talked about how anteaters in Guatemala would climb trees and get into beehives to devour the honey. They would get drunk on all that sugar, fall to the ground, sleep it off, and awaken in a terrible mood, all hungover. Apparently you really don't want to encounter a hungover anteater.

We also had a situation at Oregon Caves like the anteaters, but instead with ravens, my favorite birds. One spring while the ground was still covered with heavy snow up in the high country of the Caves, our ravens began stealing the rubber blades off of the windshield wipers of cars in the parking lot. That completely amazed me, because I've tried replacing my wiper blades before, and it can often drive you crazy. There's usually a trick known only to the initiated that makes it easy, but if you don't know that you can waste a lot of time trying to figure it out. Somehow these ravens were so good at it that they were able to pop the wiper blades off in less time than it took to run to your car and chase them away. That wasn't the only odd behavior by our ravens. The lodge at the Caves still had not opened, but our maintenance crew sometimes went inside to do work. On several occasions they saw ravens banging their beaks on the windows to the point where the ravens were bleeding. They even cracked one of the windows!

We were all puzzled by this, even our Chief Scientist, who seemed to have an answer to almost any question. I made a point of discussing it during a meeting with our new seasonal rangers and one of them said a similar thing had happened in a park in which he had worked, but with crows, the raven's closest relatives. They investigated the issue and discovered that the crows were eating lots of berries. Remember that berries usually don't ripen in the spring, they ripen in the fall. It seems the berries had hung on the branches all winter fermenting. Basically they had developed into an alcohol like wine. So the birds were eating the berries, getting drunk, and doing things they wouldn't normally do. It made perfect sense.

The problem waned through the springtime, and once the snow melted, the tourists returned, and the ravens had other food sources, the problem disappeared completely. Drunken ravens ... who would have thought!

Doing CPR

National parks are often far from hospitals, and Grand Canyon was no exception. From the South Rim to the nearest full medical facility is about 90 miles. The park does have a clinic with doctors and nurses, but caring for people in the field and getting them to the clinic or the hospital in Flagstaff was the job of the park rangers. When I first went to work at the Grand Canyon for the concession company, I also spent some time volunteering at Yavapai Museum on my off days. Paula, my supervisor there, told me that they had a class coming up on being an Emergency Medical Technician (EMT) and asked if I was interested. She knew my goal was to become a ranger and this was a skill that would help me to that end, as well as make me more useful to the park. I had already done basic first aid and CPR (Cardio-Pulmonary Resuscitation) classes in the past, probably influenced by my dad's obsession with all things to do with fire departments and his own first aid training as part of a fire department auxiliary. I went to the person who would be teaching the class, Sherry, one of the park's paramedics and head of Emergency Medical Services, and asked her if I could join the class. The park usually did not offer the training to volunteers, but the fact that I intended to become a ranger impressed her enough to try to get me into it. She asked the administrative people in charge and they agreed, so by the time I got my first ranger position I was already certified as an EMT.

After my first year at the Grand Canyon, I returned to Wisconsin for the off season, where I worked as a third shift dispatcher for a private ambulance company. Normally a dispatcher takes emergency calls and sends out the ambulance to the address in question, which can be pretty exciting stuff. This company normally did transportation between hospitals and nursing home s, because the city ran its own ambulances for emergencies. I was working 11 p.m. until 7 a.m., so I didn't see much action. Not much action? Hell, it was like watching a snail race! Mostly I filled out insurance forms and tried to stay awake. We maybe had 10 calls during the few months I worked there, those almost all just before the dayshift guy took over. I leapt at my first chance to return to the Canyon, so I left my job at the ambulance company after a month and headed down the interstate highway to the Great Southwest.

As I passed through New Mexico one cold afternoon, I came upon a nasty car accident. A drunk driver had tried to enter the highway by driving down the off ramp, and hit a car carrying a mother, grandmother and a couple of children head-on. I stopped to see if I could help, eager to use my new EMT skills. The mother and children were not too bad off, but grandmother was lying on the road, still and quiet. In class they always told us to check our own pulse before the patient's, because our adrenaline would be pumped up and it would be hard to feel another's pulse, so that's what I did. I put my face by hers to check if she was breathing, but couldn't detect any breath. I checked her pulse, but I couldn't get one no matter what I tried. I looked at her lying there, face an ashen color. This was the reality of what I had gotten myself into. It was not the first dead body I had seen, but it was the first dead stranger, for which felt I had a duty to respond, and it shook me.

When you come on a trauma situation, like a car accident, and you find someone without breath or a pulse, you could start CPR, but your priority is to tend to people who were still alive. For emergency medical purposes, anyone needing CPR is already dead. We first need to take care of the living. Other people were caring for the mother and children, who still seemed shocked, but ok. I went to the man trapped in the car. He was unconscious, bleeding and his feet were stuck under the steering wheel, but when I checked, he seemed to have a pulse. Shortly thereafter the local ambulance arrived along with the fire department. I told them what I had found and they set to work trying to get the man out of the car with the jaws of life. They put a sheet over the grandmother. When they got the door open and freed the man we started CPR as his pulse had disappeared. I helped until he got into the ambulance and they took off for the hospital. I offered my sympathies to the mother and her children, went to my car, and just sat for a while. There was still daylight and I could have kept driving, but, feeling rather shaken, I decided to find a motel, take a shower, and get some rest. There I checked the TV and discovered how the accident had happened, and that the man had died. Apparently his blood alcohol level was way above the legal limit. I had guessed that to be the case. People who aren't drunk don't usually try to enter the highway by driving head-on into exiting traffic.

A couple of days later I arrived back at the Canyon and got settled into my job as an interpretive ranger at Yavapai Museum. One afternoon on the South Rim I set out for a run. I happened to jog past the garage where they kept some of our emergency vehicles and saw a patrol ranger checking the ambulance to make sure everything was stocked and working properly. I stopped to chat for a bit and just then we got a call of someone having a heart attack at Supai Camp. He asked if I was ready to go and I said I was, so we hopped in, turned on lights and siren, and headed for the scene. Supai Camp is a place where some Havasupai Indians lived a few miles from the rim and from Grand Canyon Villlage (it's not the famous place with the waterfalls). As we sped down the road more details came in. A 40 something year old Havasupai man had been digging a ditch with a few others when he collapsed. They called the Fred Harvey Company security people who were already on scene doing CPR. We picked up two other rangers on the way and when we arrived, we took out the litter and the backboard, scooped him up quickly so we didn't disturb the CPR rhythm, put him in the ambulance and took off for the clinic.

I set to work in the ambulance doing chest compressions on the man and Ken was using a bag valve mask to assist his breathing. The man had a barrel chest and I was pumping hard to try and get enough blood moving to bring him around. I had my feet planted with a wide stance for balance as the ambulance jostled on the bumpy gravel road. My head was wedged up against the cabinets on the wall of the van and when we hit bumps or curves, of which there were plenty, it banged against the cabinets or slid along them, causing the doors of the cabinets to pinch the hair on my head, pulling a few out with each pinch. I just kept on pumping. "Hey Marty, drive better," Ken shouted, as we bumped along. "I"m trying!" came the reply. It's always a delicate balance between hurrying and trying to do a good job for the patient. You want both, but there's often a compromise.

About a half mile from the clinic Ken must have decided that my thin frame was inadequate to move this guy's big chest, so he slid over and started throwing all his more ample weight and muscle into chest compressions. Maybe I just looked tired…CPR is hard work. I took over the bag valve mask and we continued to work on him. We arrived at the clinic soon after and the staff there were ready and waiting. Marty and I unloaded the litter with Ken still pumping the man's chest as we wheeled him into the emergency room. The clinic people took over and we finally had a chance to catch our breath. I checked to see if I had any hair remaining on the top of my head. I'm lucky that lack of hair up there has never been a problem, so I still had some, but I did have a nasty bump and bruise. We waited to see if our patient would make it, but as with nearly all CPR, he did not. Even when you do it perfectly, at best about 1 in 12 might pull through.

A few years later I was working night shift road patrol on the South Rim when I got a call of an 80 year old man who had stopped breathing at one of the lodges, the Thunderbird, as I recall. He was there with his family and after dinner had collapsed in their room. His daughter was doing rescue breathing on him, but said he had a pulse. I turned on the flashing lights and siren and headed with all haste to the lodge. On a blind curve the car in front of me refused to pull over in spite of me flashing lights at them and shouting over the loud speaker to pull over. When the road straightened I passed them and made it to the lodge ASAP. I grabbed my medical gear and ran to their room. The family stood crowded around the door and I firmly asked them to make way for me to get through. I told the woman doing rescue breathing to continue while I checked his pulse. He had none. I called dispatch that I was starting CPR. I opened his shirt and, in contrast to the previous CPR case, on my first chest compression I felt his ribs crack. That's common, especially for someone this old. I got a bad feeling in the pit of my stomach, but kept going.

The ambulance arrived just a few minutes later and someone took over the breathing part with a bag valve mask. I kept up my rhythm "One and two and three and four and one and two and ..." A ranger gently cleared the family from the room so we could work. Two more rangers arrived. They set to putting a tube in his throat to facilitate breathing, started an IV, then set up the defibrillator. They had me stop and they shocked the man. Someone took over for me doing chest compressions, and I caught my breath while I went to the door to assure the family we were doing all we could. They didn't have a pulse yet, so shocked him again. We got the litter ready to load him into the ambulance and, as quickly as possible, placed him onto it. I returned to doing CPR as we wheeled him out the door. Lucky for my head, the roads to the clinic from there were all paved with only a few curves. We kept up our work as we wheeled him into the emergency room, where the doctors took over. The man was stronger than he looked. When we stopped CPR so the doctor could check his heartbeat, there was still a faint one, after 3 defibrillations and me breaking his ribs. They worked on him a while longer, but like most such situations, a short time later they declared that he had passed away.

It's an odd thing. People come up to the Canyon and don't realize the elevation, don't think about how much harder it is to breathe. For healthy people, it's not a big impact, but for anyone whose body already is having a hard time just keeping up with day to day life, that can really cause problems. An old man with weakened heart or lungs eats a big meal, goes to his room, and the combination of that and the elevation turn a vacation into a tragedy. Of course, who's to say it wouldn't have happened elsewhere. And he did get to see the Grand Canyon.

More than the other CPR I've done, this one was hard for me. Yes, the man was old, had outlived most people. I didn't know him or his family. But the fact that they were all there watching was hard. We tried and couldn't save him. We did well, but it didn't matter. And then there was the fact that I had been the first to arrive and my first chest compression had broken his ribs. That's a pretty creepy feeling. But would I do it again? Yes, of course I would.

As an EMT, most of the medical emergencies didn't involve CPR, but rather what's called "environmental illness", which is stuff like problems with heat, cold, water, etc. Working at a place like the inner Grand Canyon you get so you can recognize heat and dehydration problems from 100 paces, though it's important to always make certain there isn't something else going on as well. I recall seeing an older man accompanied by several younger men walking up to the Phantom Ranger Station one hot summer's day. I knew at once he was dehydrated, and in the early stages of heat exhaustion. The man was dazed and unsteady on his feet, and his friends were holding his hands, helping him to walk. At one point, he stopped along the path to Phantom Ranch, with lots of people within sight, and decided to take a pee. He began to unzip his pants when his friends and I stopped him and I said he should wait for just another hundred feet where he could use the toilet in the ranger station.

When we arrived there and after he used the restroom, I sat him down and began a preliminary exam, checking his vital signs, asking questions about his activities that day and the day previous. I also offered him some water and he began drinking. He said he was a doctor and that he knew something serious was going on. He said needed a full blood test. I told him he wasn't going to get one at Phantom Ranger Station. He drank another glass of water. I asked if he had had anything to drink during the day. "Yes, espresso," he replied. "How much espresso?" I asked. "Nine cups this morning," he said. "Any water?" "A little on the trail. Look, I know I'm having something more serious going on. Can you fly me out?" Another glass of water. "Yeah, but let's just see how you feel once you have some water in you and have rested." Before he left the ranger station he had drunk 5 big glasses of water. Really big glasses. Like a half liter per glass. After I finished my exam I had him go to his room at Phantom Ranch to rest, and told him to come back in little while or send for me to go to his room and then we would see how he was doing. He agreed and one of his friends helped him to his room. About 4 hours later he walked back to the ranger station. He appeared much healthier, not as pale and was certainly more coherent. He looked at me somewhat sheepishly and said, "You were right: dehydration. Good diagnosis doctor." I just smiled and said "Thanks. Glad you're feeling better." Stuff like this happens a lot there.

I worked in the desert a lot at the Canyon, Saguaro, Mesa Verde, and when people hear that they often ask about things like snake bites, scorpion stings, and the like. I never saw a case of snakebite, never heard of one in the Canyon, though I'm sure it must have happened a few times. I know of some people bitten by spiders, but they were rangers who encountered them in the line of duty. We had some scorpion stings, but the only serious ones usually were people who had developed allergies to them, which was rare. The only case I know of was one ranger who may have been more emotional about it than allergic, but I never saw him after a sting. The worst case I have personal knowledge of was a boatman on the Colorado River who had a scorpion crawl into his shorts and sting him multiple times in a very tender place ... a VERY tender place. YOW!!! He was not a happy person for several days, the neurotoxin making his whole body not want to be touched, but by the time his boat made it to Phantom Ranch where I was working, he was feeling much better. Not great, but better. A friend and coworker once had a case where he was sitting on the toilet with his pants at his ankles, and a scorpion crawled in and sat in his underwear. Lucky for him he saw it and just waited until the scorpion left. He felt glad he had brought reading material. Scorpions were very common at Phantom Ranch, a daily occurrence. I'd get up in the morning, walk to the kitchen, grab a bowl for breakfast, throw out the scorpion, and sit down to eat. Well, maybe not every day, but often enough. As far as larger animals are concerned, we had coyotes, bears, various types of deer, and in Denali NP, wolves, but of those the only problems we usually had were the deer. Actually, it wasn't the deer, but people with the deer. They aren't pets, but people think of them that way. One family at the Canyon's rim saw a large buck with antlers and wanted a picture of him with their boy. They told the boy to go hug the big deer. The buck turned his head away, and his antlers caught on the boy's gold neck chain. The deer turned his head toward the boy to get loose, and an antler point stabbed the boy in his neck, causing deadly bleeding. We had paramedics there in a few minutes and they saved his life. Don't mess with the animals. They're wild.

We did have some trauma incidents, such as broken limbs, sprains, and strains. Most of those weren't too serious. One patient of mine, who had hiked down to Phantom Ranch, was complaining that his knee hurt. He was already wearing a knee brace, so I asked what his history of knee problems was, and he said he had torn his anterior cruciate ligament twice and had surgery both times. The doctor told him that if he tore it again it could not be repaired. Carrying weight downhill is hard on your joints. I asked him what he was doing at the bottom of the Grand Canyon carrying a heavy pack (he carried his girlfriend's things as well) considering his history and he just looked at me. Fortunately at the Canyon, the hard part for the joints comes first. If you start having serious pain on the way down, just turn around and go back up. I gave the man a knee exam, then put an ice pack on it to keep the swelling down. I told him to take some inflammatory medication and said that he would not likely have much problem on the way up other than tiredness. I heard nothing more about it, so I guess he got out of the Canyon alright.

An older woman on the South Rim wasn't so lucky. I was working at Yavapai Museum giving a geology talk when someone interrupted to say a woman had fallen in the parking lot and couldn't get up due to horrible pain. I apologized to the visitors, ended the talk, grabbed a radio and medical pack, and ran down to the parking lot. She had gotten out of the car on the side where there was a moderate gravel slope and had slid on the gravel. When I found her she was lying on her back, her left leg out straight. Her right leg was bent and her foot should have been under her right buttock. However, it stuck out at an odd angle to her right side. Didn't look at all nice. I called for an ambulance immediately, but they were on another call. A patrol ranger would come by to help. I began talking to the woman and her family and doing a basic exam. Where did it hurt? Could she feel her foot? How bad would she rate the pain? She rated it near childbirth, so I knew it was serious.

Brian arrived shortly and we discuss what to do. I said she needed to get the leg straightened out to minimize the pain and get her ready for transport to the clinic. He understood me to mean we needed to set her fracture. Nice idea, but beyond our training. I explained what I really meant, and he agreed. We got the long, wooden backboard from the museum and had some people help us. I carefully held her broken leg as they turned her onto her left side, "On the count of 3." I carefully moved her leg back into its natural position, which brought a blood curdling scream of pain. We shoved the backboard onto her back and laid her down. Straightening her leg and getting her laying flat eased her pain, well, after the initial pain of moving it. We strapped her on so she wouldn't fall off, then carried her over to flat ground. The ambulance arrived shortly thereafter. They loaded her in and set off for the clinic. Glad it wasn't my leg. I went back to the museum to see what else the day would bring.

In January 1991, after some time away, I returned to the Canyon to work as a backcountry ranger at Indian Garden Ranger Station, which is located 4.5 miles down from the South Rim along the Bright Angel Trail.

The winter and spring were not all that busy, so most of the time it was rather peaceful. One day a man with his two young boys showed up to stay at the campground. They had already hiked down the South Kaibab Trail and stayed a couple of nights at Bright Angel Campground near Phantom Ranch. Then they hiked up to Indian Garden for a couple of nights before intending to hike back to the South Rim. My first encounter with the man was when he lost his plate as he was dumping his food waste into the composting toilets. The NPS had installed some wonderful composting toilets at the Indian Garden Campground, which would turn human waste into soil that could be used to nourish plants. There was plenty of human waste at the busy campground, so we didn't need any extra, and park rules say that people needed to hike out all of their trash, including food waste. So I talked with him about that, then contacted Jerry, the current maintenance man, to unlock the back of the toilet area and retrieve his plate. As I chatted with him he mentioned that one of his boys wasn't feeling well, so I asked him to bring him up to the ranger station and I would give him a quick medical exam and see if I could help.

The boys and their father came up shortly thereafter, and I began checking his vital signs and asking some questions. As I recall, the boy was about 8 years old. Let's call him Bobby. In doing my exam it became apparent that he was likely dehydrated. He could also have had something else going on like a stomach bug or flu, but the immediate problem was dehydration. He had drunk very little that day or the day before, was weak, nauseous, pale, and even his skin was "tenting" a bit. That's when you pinch a little skin on the hand and if it doesn't quickly go back to normal, it's a safe bet the person doesn't have enough liquid in them. While tenting is common in older people, in someone this young it just shouldn't happen. I told the father to re-hydrate him, make him drink until he could pee, and the next day we would see how he was doing.

The following day dawned with a change in the weather. Clouds began moving in and the forecast called for rain or snow. Bobby was still not doing too well. He had tried drinking, but had vomited a couple of times. He couldn't eat much of anything and was getting weaker and more pale. They had one more day at the campground, but I recommended that they get out as quickly as possible. The people at the South Rim Clinic agreed. If I were a paramedic I could have given him an IV, which likely would have made a big difference, but as a basic EMT, that was not an option.

The Canyon, by this time, had gotten completely filled in with clouds. Light rain began to fall at Indian Garden and winds began blowing. The helicopter couldn't fly in this weather. We decided that they should hike out. Bobby couldn't go on his own power, so his father and I would take turns carrying him. I put my medical pack on my front, and him on my back, and we began hiking.

It was getting colder and the rain began turning to snow not too far above the ranger station. From Indian Garden to the South Rim is a steep 3000 foot climb. We moved up slowly. When I tired, the boy's father carried him and I carried his father's pack and my medical pack. Bobby began holding some water down as we got up above the 3 Mile Resthouse (3 miles from the rim). As we got close to the 1.5 Mile Resthouse, Bobby was able to walk a bit on his own. One of the other backcountry rangers hiked down from the rim and met us about a half mile from the top. He walked Bobby and his family to the rim, and I went back down to Indian Garden, where I took a good hot shower and had a rest.

A few weeks later a letter came for me from Bobby and his father. The boy had drawn a picture of me carrying him and had written a nice note thanking me for helping him. He said the doctor told him he had the flu. That doesn't surprise me at all, and was likely contributing to his dehydration. I had that letter and picture for a long time, but moving as much as I did I must have lost it somewhere. I hope he came back again and hiked the Canyon when he was feeling better.

There have been many other cases over the years that I could write about, and a few of them are in the stories about Phantom Ranch. Had I remained there as a backcountry ranger I'd have so many stories they would be uncountable, and had I worked on an ambulance in a big city they would become a blur, but for me these are some of the cases that stand out. Once I left park ranger work, I had little use for my EMT skills except with my family and friends, but since I was no longer wearing a uniform, they mostly didn't listen to my advice anyhow. Funny how that works.

A picture drawn by Geoff as I carried him out of the Canyon, 1991

Fighting Fires

Yellowstone National Park was burning the summer of 1988, along with many other places in the West. I didn't work in Yellowstone, I was at the Grand Canyon, but when there's a big fire season, all people available with the proper training get sent out to help with those fires, and many of our experienced firefighters were already out of the park doing just that. Having never gone to a big fire, but trained to do so, I was eager to go and experience one. While working at Yavapai Museum one day I got notice from my supervisor that I was being sent out on a fire with a crew made up of some of my coworkers and some people from the Kaibab National Forest that bordered the park. I was told to go back to my residence, get my personal gear ready, and go to the fire office to get my fire clothing and gear and await further instructions. They told us the fire we would go to was likely somewhere in the Yellowstone area.

So what's it like to work on a big fire? My initial response, like for many big incidents, is it's a lot of "hurry up and wait." This one started off as no exception. I packed everything I would need for the fire, including some warm clothing, as it can get quite cold in the northern Rocky Mountains. Cotton or wool are usually best, as many synthetic fabrics, if subjected to the heat of a fire, can start to melt on your skin. Not fun. I did take some synthetic long underwear for sleeping at night. I arrived at the fire office and was given other gear that I would need: fire pack, helmet, gloves, emergency food (MREs), outer clothing (made of a fire-resistant fabric called Nomex), and utility belt, including water bottles and fire shelter. A fire shelter is like a small tent made of fire-resistant material that looks like aluminum foil, and if it appears a fire is going to overtake you and you can't escape, you wrap it over your back and collapse on the ground face down. Hopefully the fire will burn over you, but you'll survive in your little aluminum foil-looking pup tent like a turkey in the oven for Thanksgiving. Sometimes they work. Sometimes. Nobody wants to have to use one, but everyone needs to be able to use it.

Hurry up and wait. Once we were all assembled in the fire office, the coordinator told us to just wait until we got word to set off. There were about 5 of us. We would be driven to the Kaibab National Forest office at some point, where a bus would take us to Phoenix, AZ, then we all would catch a plane for northwestern Montana. We were going to work on the Dry Fork Fire, near the Canadian border. We sat there, waiting and chatting. Chatting and waiting. We got hungry, so he let us go home to have a quick dinner. Then we returned to the office for chatting and ... finally after dark we got word to set off. We loaded into his car and headed for the National Forest office. There we met the rest of our crew, as well as some other crews from the area, got on the bus, after some chatting and waiting, and headed for Phoenix.

Above: On fire duty in Montana in 1988, an overview of the fire camp as we all arrived and found our patch of grassland on which to sleep. Next page: Our swarthy crew during a break.

Once in Phoenix, the bus drove around until it found our staging area in a gymnasium. From there they would take us to the airport, but seeing as it was around midnight, we had to wait until morning for that. We were told to get some sleep. The excitement was a bit much, but I managed to get a little rest. Early in the morning they fed us some eggs, bacon, toast, and coffee and, after some chatting and waiting, we boarded buses for the airport. They took us to a separate part of the airport than that used for regular flights, and boarded a plane specially chartered for the fire crews. There would be no in-flight movies or alcohol, though we did have snacks and soft drinks. The flight to Kalispell, MT, was beautiful, though uneventful, and they took us by bus out to the fire from the airport, which took a couple of hours. Another fire was burning in Glacier National Park, near Kalispell, and we saw a bit of that on the way.

The fire camp was in a broad, open valley with a large meadow that was already covered with tents, both store-bought and makeshift, and had a haze of smoke settled nicely into it. My friend Tom and I hadn't brought a tent, so we got a few wooden pallets, lashed them together, and covered the whole thing with black plastic. We had sleeping bags, but were informed that it would be getting near freezing at night, so we picked up some of the cheap "paper sleeping bags" they provided as well. These were white sleeping bags with a fluffy, cotton-like stuffing covered by a flexible paper-like material to hold it together. We made quite a cozy little cave out of this. They had a central canteen set up where we would eat breakfast and dinner (hopefully) and could prepare lunch before we set out in the morning for the fire. There was a shower area and they even had a little store set up to sell things we had forgotten or just plain needed.

The little town of Libby, MT, was supplying the store, and the retailers in town did their best business ever. There was also a medical tent, of course.

It turned out we had planted our tent in the exact spot where they started in the morning to wake up the whole camp. We were lucky enough to be the first every day to hear the shout of "It's 5 a.m. and there's hot coffee." It was still dark. The first day wasn't so bad, but by the 10th day, Tom and I were ready to take him and dump him in the hot coffee and go back to bed. The cold made getting out of bed not at all easy. This did make us among the first to eat breakfast, which was nice because the food was often still nearly warm. The metal folding chairs, however, had been sitting in the cold all night, so when you sat on them it just drained whatever heat your body had right out of you. The food wasn't bad considering the situation and was abundant. We ate, made our lunches, then stood around the fire drinking coffee and waiting. Since we were the first up, we also had the longest wait. Once everyone had eaten, our crew leaders had a general briefing to get our assignments, then we would find our bus and head out to the fire.

When you see people fighting forest fires in movies or on TV you generally see the water drops from airplanes, fire fighters jumping out of planes near the fire and firemen engaging the raging torrent directly. Those are initial attack crews with extensive training and experience. Our crew was a rookie group, so we did what they call "mop up." That means we would go through areas that had already burnt and look for spots still burning or smoldering to make sure they wouldn't spread and start things up again. Typically a forest fire burns along the ground, sometimes through the trees, and often after it passes there is still much unburnt material. If it got going again, it could sneak up behind a crew and create a threat. While not the exciting, highly dangerous life of initial attack crews, mop up came with its own hazards. Often the areas were very smoky and you couldn't see far at all. Some of the big trees around us looked good and strong, but their roots would slowly smolder. You could be walking along and suddenly a tree would come crashing down, often taking other trees with it. Just before we arrived a firefighter lost his life to one of these falling trees in Glacier National Park nearby. It was common for us to be walking through the smokey forest and hear big trees, 100 foot tall larches and firs, falling down like a crack of thunder.

One day on the fire I was asked to go to an area where a large number of small trees had not burnt. It's an area that had been clear cut (all the trees cut down) and replanted. All the trees were about my height, on average. I walked through the little forest looking for areas smoldering and I spotted one. The small trees surrounded me, all about 3 feet away, and the burning area on the ground was about 2 inches in diameter. I started digging down to get to the bottom of it, and as I dug the smoldering area got bigger, and bigger, and bigger, until it was more than 18" in diameter. I was using my shovel to expose it too the air to burn itself out or to whack it and snuff it out, when suddenly all the trees around me just burst into flames. I made a hasty exit between two burning trees and got a coworker with a backpack pump (known as a piss pump) to put some water on the area and cool it down. It was then I noticed that the soles on my work boots, were not the recommended brand, as they had partly melted. No wonder my feet were so warm!

Most days on the fire were not so exciting, just grunge work putting out little smoldering embers hour after hour, stopping for the occasional snack or a brief chat with my colleagues. One occasion they asked me to help lay hose up a steep, heavily forested hillside so they could get more water on a particularly nasty area. Water can be a luxury on a forest fire, and much of our work was done with little or no water, but this area needed it. Our handful of people carried sections of hose up the hills and attached them one at a time. At one spot we put in some connections so we could run 3 or 4 other hoses off of the main hose line. We ran the hoses out from there, but only one could be used at a time due to the limited water pressure. They had me then wait with my radio at the connections so I could switch the hoses when they called. Generally they would work on one hose for 15-20 minutes or more, so I just sat and waited. It had been a tough morning hauling more than a mile of hose up this steep hillside, and after I had a snack I started nodding off. Just then I heard a loud "Thwack" that rattled my helmet. I looked around, but could see nobody, nothing that could have caused it. I figured it was a pine cone that had fallen from the tree. A couple of minutes later the same thing happened. I got up and looked more closely, only to be scolded by a red squirrel high up above in the branch of a fir tree, who promptly threw down a few more cones before he set off for another part of the forest.

We did see some more directly burning areas on the fire. We spent one morning cutting line on the fire: as a long line of firefighters we would each dig a little with our respective tools as we walked along slowly, so that by the time the last person finished there would be space without burnable materials so that a ground fire couldn't cross it. Near the end of our time on the fire they also asked us to help with a back burn. This is where you go to an area where the fire is advancing and start it on fire to burn out the materials so it would stop an advancing fire. This has to be done very carefully so as not to create more of a problem, but when done well it's very effective. As a rookie crew we didn't use the torches to start the fire, but were there to watch for spot fires, little fires that start out of area we wanted them. It was the most flame we had seen since arriving at the fire. It went well and helped us to contain the fire almost completely at that point.

A couple of days later, after 16 days on the fire, we packed up and headed home. It had been a good learning experience for me, where I finally got to use skills I had trained for. At Grand Canyon I had only one other experience with wildfire, this one working in the administrative end of it, the supply section to be exact. Not so exciting, but still part of the team. Not until going to work at Oregon Caves some 18 or so years later did I have the chance to use firefighting skills again, though I continued my training and certification. By that time I had gotten out of the mode of being an "adrenaline junkie", as we called it, but as I mentioned before, when you live in a park or any remote area like that, you get used to doing whatever needs to be done. We had a couple of small fires start during a lightning storm one afternoon, and since I was one of the only trained firefighters in the park I helped lead the crew of rank amateurs to do what we could to keep our beautiful Douglas fir forest from becoming a raging inferno in the hot, dry southern Oregon summer. We got the fires subdued and nobody got hurt. Mission accomplished.

ON A CLEAR DAY YOU CAN SEE THE BROCKEN

Journal Writings
of a Time Spent in Europe, 1995

Introduction

In 1994 Jan Gasche, a park ranger from Hochharz National Park in Germany, took a bike trip with his girlfriend across the southwestern United States. On that trip they visited the Grand Canyon and, while there attended a ranger program I presented about wolves in which I told stories and anecdotes as well as presenting factual information. He liked the program enough that he went back to his park and recommended that they ask me to come and work there. They contacted me later that year. I decided that, since I didn't at that time have any major commitments, and since I had always wanted to improve my German language skills, I would take their offer and go to work in Hochharz National Park.

Hochharz* sits in the former East Germany, right on the border with the West in the state of Saxony Anhalt. Even though I went there

---

* The park was combined with Harz National Park in the neighboring state of Saxony some years after I worked there.

6 years after the wall came down, it was still a very different place than western Germany, which I had previously visited. The area had become a park partly because it was on that border and, since few people could go there during East German times, it remained in a relatively natural state. I say "relatively" because the forests, the landscape, had been changed, used, affected by humans for hundreds or even thousands of years. For instance, the forests had originally contained more high elevation spruce trees (which shed the snow better than lowland varieties), as well as many beech, oak, maple, and birch trees, however for the purposes of having a consistent source for lumber, they replaced them with faster growing lowland spruce trees. After becoming a national park they began to return some of the forests to their original composition. A few treasured spots had remained in their previous forest composition.

The name "Hochharz" means "High Harz Mountains" in German. The Brocken is the highest mountain in the park, and while only 1141m/3743 feet high, the top has a subalpine microclimate similar to much higher mountains and is the highest mountain in northern Germany. It is also famous for its history. J.W. v. Goethe hiked there in 1777, and they have a legend that on Wapurgisnacht (April 30) witches dance with the devil on the top of the mountain, which gave rise to a scene in his book *Faust*. The mountain was also a Soviet radio espionage site during cold war times, and much of that infrastructure remained at the time I worked there.[*] It's a fascinating place, really, and in spite of the some of the difficulties I faced in communication and such, I generally enjoyed my time there very much.

I went to work in Hochharz as a part of a program that Germany's national parks and natural areas had to "hire" interns to work in them. The program was sponsored and mostly funded by Commerzbank, one of Germany's major banks. Hochharz that year had three such interns: Christian, Silvia, and me. I don't know much about Silvia's background other than that she came from Dresden. Christian was my roommate, so I got to know him much better. He came from Halle, not too far from

---

[*] Most of the buildings are still there today, though the purpose of the buildings has changed.

the park where we worked. During one year of high school he lived on a farm in north central Oklahoma as a foreign exchange student. He went to an American high school & played football. He ate hamburgers. He drove a tractor (and got it stuck in the mud, like any teenager should). He let the cows out of the fence (again like any teenager should)...and helped to bring them back in. All German young people were supposed to do a year of community service. Many young men went into the military after high school, but Christian worked in a nature reserve, one I mention in the writing below. Our job as interns in the park was mostly to conduct environmental and experiential education activities for local school children who came to the park. As a visiting American, I also went to schools to do presentations and did some interviews with local media. During our time we also got to visit some of the other national parks and natural areas in Germany. We lived in the city of Wernigerode, where park head quarters was located.

This writing is a collection of journal excerpts from my time living in Germany and traveling in Europe in 1995. I filtered it a bit to remove some more personal items that either were not that interesting, or that I just don't want you to know. I will introduce you to Silvia and Christian, but I tried to keep away from revealing anything too personal for their sake. Most of the writing consists of accounts of my experiences and the philosophical wanderings of my own strange, sordid mind. I hope it all amuses you.

March 1995

30 March

So my journey begins. I'm on the train just pulling out of Gallup, NM. It was hard to leave Flagstaff, as I've made some good friends there and had some wonderful experiences. I'll miss them. But another new chapter in this continuing story of a life begins. My destination is Wernigerode, Germany, where I will spend 6 months as an intern in Hochharz National

Park.

31 March, Kansas City

Interesting Day yesterday. After Albuquerque I hung out in the lounge cars for a while and got into a wonderful conversation with this woman, Pat, who is the wife of a Methodist minister. She's a quilter and her daughter is an actress. Our conversation centered on social issues: on education, acceptance of other people and their lifestyles, how to change the world… you know…the usual stuff.

Later I was eating dinner in the lounge. In the next booth over were 2 women, one older, one younger. They started making conversation with me and eventually came over to sit with me. The older woman was a biker named Sunshine – very much a biker. Hard life based both on our conversation and the deep furrows of her face. She kicked her heroin addiction 10 years ago. Wants to go back and live in California, but she's in Chicago seeking protection of the bikers there because her ex-husband wants her dead.

The younger woman was Carly, an attractive 23 year old art student with interests in painting, dance, and art therapy. She used to have long hair, but now she sports a butch because she had been sick for a while and just laying in bed, so it had been difficult to take care of her long hair. She was born on the East Coast, but now her family lives in California. She lives in Chicago and is trying to get into the Art Institute. She worked in an amusement park for a while and had an interesting experience with a man who had seizures on one of the rides. I sat and mostly listened as Carly talked and Sunshine interjected now and then.

At one point we were interrupted by James. James is a young, burly Italian-American man with an odd short haircut, like a big pencil sharpener had gone wild with his head. His family has chosen a bride for him, but he doesn't want to marry her, so he's going to Chicago to see his family and he is not happy.

James has been drinking a lot and he likes Carly. At one point as I sat next to her with my arm on the seat behind her, he says "Move your arm!"

"Why," I responded.

"Cuz I don't want it there." His fist was clenched and he was staring straight at me. I looked back at him and tried to soften my eyes.

"Relax James, it's OK. I'm just conversing with my friends here."

He towered over me as I sat in the booth. He mumbled something in Italian and Sunshine tried to tell him to chill out.

"James, the ladies came over and sat with me and we are just having a conversation, OK?! Relax."

James sat next to Sunshine. He's very drunk and speaks in Italian.

"Speak English James," Sunshine says.

Eventually he apologized and went to the head and came out with his pants undone.

"James, zip up!" yells Sunshine.

"I can't."

James is not doing well.

Then there's Jeff. He drank very heavily as well, but he didn't pass out like James eventually did. Jeff just wanted to either 'fuck or fight.' He laughed a lot and slobbered on people. Sunshine loved him.

I just sat and listened.

Out the window in the morning there were deciduous trees, some tiny, but rolling hills in the distance, lots of farms, and little towns with white, wooden churches. Yep, it's the Midwest.

April 1995

6 April

It's amazing to me that last year on this day I hiked the Hermit Trail in Grand Canyon when I saw a hawk soaring up the walls of the canyon across the way. I put my awareness into the hawk, in essence "becoming one with the bird." I saw what he saw, felt the wind on my feathers, and soared above the treetops. In honor of that meditation I marked it down as 'Flying Day.'

Today I'm flying, by plane this time, to Europe. I didn't plan it that way. Just happened. But it gives me a sense of destiny, or better yet, synchronicity, that there is more to life and this world than meets the eye. Maybe there is a higher power overseeing what day I fly, the take offs and landings, the movements of stratus clouds beneath these wings. Maybe what I think is not wha*t* I think, but rather it is subject to laws, for lack of a better word, that govern what happens, laws which are beyond the scope of my, and perhaps everyone's consciousness. Could it really be just a coincidence? Maybe all this philosophizing is a crock of bull. Whatever the case, this is Flying Day, and I am flying, well, actually the plane is flying to Europe, and I'm just sitting here writing at 30,000 feet.

Since I last wrote much has happened to give pause for thought. The train came into Chicago an hour early, so I rushed to get on the 3:05 to Wisconsin. In the process I never said 'Goodbye' to Carly. I hopped off the Southwest Chief and waddled, heavily loaded by my worldly belongings (the chains I forge in life) into the station.

"Looking for a connecting train?"

"The 3:05 to Milwaukee."

"Down there (he points to my left). Take the first right to gate A3."

"Thanks."

As I trudged through the station I began wondering to myself. Why am I hurrying? I left a new friend behind without ever getting even her full name. What was I thinking?! I'll just end up getting to Racine early and sit with Dad and Margaret in the small TV room watching 'Wheel of Fortune' and listening to them comment on Vanna White's dress. All the while my legs were moving down the platform and into the train. I hoisted my bags up to the generous overhead compartment. 'Still time to get off' I thought to myself. Instead I sat down and waited for the train to leave. I was scheduled for the next train, and I could have at least said "Goodbye, have a nice life."

Justifying my actions I think how my address book is already filled to the brim with people I hardly ever, or never see. I only know them now by their handwriting and which words they choose to put on the page. I did know them better at one time. That was then, and this is now. I guess I figured this would be a good lesson in 'Letting Go.' It was easier for me to just leave the train, but easier doesn't always mean better, not by a long shot. Maybe it's time for me to learn the value of taking my time' and slowing down. It's time for me to learn to value friends made, whether fleeting or not. Next time I'll at least say 'Goodbye.'

Looks like Pennsylvania or western New York State down below: small valleys and ridges carved by dendritic drainage patterns and dotted with towns, most of them built on the floodplains. I can hear the owners asking "I just don't understand why the basement is always so wet!" (It's called a "floodplain" for a reason.)

When I arrived in Wisconsin it was typically cold and overcast. A few flakes fell as I headed for the station. I had to wait for a while at the Sturtevant train station; after all, I was earlier than expected. The station is being remodeled and is in an obvious state of disrepair. Inside sat a rather rotund gentleman, about 50 years old, wearing an open winter coat and one of those insulated winter ball caps with ear flaps. A hunting we will go! He just looked at me with an "I'm not quite certain of you" look. I wasn't quite certain of him either. Then his son came into the station. At least I think it was his son. Leather jacket, black, collar length hair, mustache, and "couldn't tawk too good." He had gone to the corner store. They pulled sodas, "Hostess Ho Ho's," and chips out of a bag, and chowed down.

From their conversation I gathered they were locals. They probably just hang out there for the excitement. I don't like to be condescending, but they did sound as if they had been hanging out at the nuclear power plant too long, or else they were poster children for inbreeding. An elderly lady came in to clean. I think she was a volunteer, because she looked like the woman that had been performing a 'labor of love' in helping with the renovation and care of the station, according to a news clipping posted on the wall. She looked around, did a little dusting and trash pickup, and left. The man in the hat made a remark about her not doing a good job cleaning. Then he made some remarks about women in general which involved sex and domestic violence. I just grunted in response. Dad arrived to pick me up shortly thereafter. I was happy to see him.

12 April

My first day of work: frustrating, but good. Now that's a bit of a paradox. A problem arose with the housing, but I'm sure it will be worked out one way or another. It seems they might have to move us to another place where there is no bathing facility. We'd have to bathe in the creek nearby. I'm frustrated with the language: everyone either wants to practice their English, no matter how little they know, or they don't know any. Either I'm listening to English or high speed German, the dialect of which I find nearly impossible to understand most of the time.

My current landlords are the Wiese family, husband, wife, and their 2 boys. The first thing one of the boys asked me was "Was isst Man in Amerika?" Only I couldn't tell at first the difference between "isst" and "ist" which makes a big difference in the meaning for "ist" means "is" and "isst" is a form of the verb "essen," which means "to eat". He was asking what people eat in America and I thought he asked what people *are* in America. Finally Herr Wiese caught onto my difficulty and explained, so I could answer the lad's question.

We went into the park on a hike to discuss plans for the children's programs. I saw numerous logged areas, but it's nonetheless beautiful. Lots of plants & birds & rocks & shit. You know, the usual park stuff. I love it.

My roommate and fellow intern is Christian, who's tall, thin, and eats like a horse. He's 20, plays in a punk rock band, and is from Halle. He's a good young man.

13 April

On television they are showing the movie "Trains, Planes, and Automobiles," dubbed in German of course. "Sie haben mein Taxi genommen!" (You took my taxi!) Well, it's one way of learning the language.

This morning Christian and I went to Sylvia's (a fellow intern) on his bike to get her bike so we could run errands. Christian "drove." I sat on his hard seat wearing his full pack, which was more than a little painful on my skinny butt, but I managed. At Sylvia's we picked up her bike for me to ride, which was of a more comfortable nature, but I went from a seat that was too high, creeping its way up my insides with each tiny bump ("It's OK, vee almost dare," Christian would call) and me grunting and groaning ("You sound like you're having a baby"), to a much smaller bike with my knees in my ears. (This was to set the tone for my entire time here in Germany.)

Then it was off to the public offices to:

1. register where I live,
2. acquire my visa,
3. arrange for insurance (wonderful thing, this national health care!),
4. and finally off to the bank to establish my account. We thought the offices opened at 8, but it was 9, so we went for a walk.

When the office opened we got through the preliminaries without too many teeth pulled, then went downstairs to the city information center for a map. "DM 7,50 bitte." I asked for a free one, which they managed to find, much to Christian's surprise. Then it was back to the visa office for some interrogation "Wie kann er mit kinder arbeiten wenn er nicht gut Deutsch spricht?" (How can he work with children when he doesn't speak good German? A good question, actually.) When that ordeal ended we were off to the insurance office. "No, we can't insure you." Christian was about to give up when I asked "What about Barbara Miranda?" She had been an intern a few years earlier. "Well, let me check....OK, we can insure you, but you have to come back next week. We have to figure out how to do this."

The bank was also not without its problems. "If I have an account, do you still charge fees to change traveler's checks? (DM 13,50 per check)" "Yes." "How about if I put it into my account?" "Well, OK, but just this once. You can cash all $1000 for just one fee." That little bit of dickering saved me DM 117,00. Christian was rather astounded that we were able to pull all this off, and I have to admit I was pleased myself. In East German times, which wasn't that long ago, you didn't ask twice. It just didn't happen.

Reflection:

The other day when I was on the bus to Wernigerode, I got on at Bad

Harzburg, paid my DM 5,00, and found a seat toward the back of the bus where I could fit my bags. This guy entered the back door. He wore a yellow raincoat, stood about 5'8" tall and of medium build, had short, dark hair and a short beard. He had a milk crate full of water bottles and 3 bags from the market. He couldn't carry it on the bus for it was too heavy, so I helped him.

He sat next to me and mumbled something unintelligible (not that I could understand much of what people said to me anyhow) due, in part, to an obvious speech impediment. During the entire ride, which lasted about 50 minutes, he would smile at me and rattle off something in garbled German. I'd just smile...or shrug my shoulders...and always looked confused. At least 3 or 4 times I said "Ich verstehe nicht. Ich bin Amerikaner. Ich spreche nur ein bisschen Deutsch." (I don't understand. I'm an American. I speak only a little German.) But he continued to smile and talk as if I understood. This game amused me at first, but as time passed it grew more and more tiresome. I looked out the window as much as possible and found myself fantasizing about ways to silence my mumbling seat mate. Finally, I jumped off of the bus, not knowing if it was my stop, but just glad to escape the monotonous game. It was, indeed, my stop. Funny how that works.

14 April

Beautiful, gorgeous day! Today I was off so I slept in...didn't arise until 10 a.m., and did lots of good Yoga, most of it outside in the cool sunshine. It's a relief given the constant rain we had endured since I arrived.

Yesterday I did some yoga in the house after work. There's a large picture window that looks from my room in the flat, out to the cherry tree where the two boys of Frau and Herr Wiese, my landlords, love to play after school. As the last part of my yoga I laid down in Savasana (lying on my back on the floor). At one point I became aware of voices close by, and opened my eyes to find Herr Wiese and the boys peering in at me. "Alles in ordnung?(everything OK?)" asked Herr Wiese. "Ja, kein problem (yes, no problem)," was my response. I arose, stepped outside, and did a little explanation in my broken German about yoga.

Later I ate brunch outside, then Herr Wiese took me to the Bahnhoff (train station) for a schedule of the trains to Grafenau, where all the interns will be heading in a few days. We had a nice conversation...my German is improving, slowly, but surely. Later I walked around, saw a local league soccer game, strolled to the hills, read, studied German, did more Yoga, and watched "Star Wars" over dinner. It was in German, of course, and it's always amusing to just hear the different qualities of the voices from their English counterparts. I figure I should spend more time with the boys. It might help me to understand kids better, as well as improve my German. Frau Wiese did my laundry today...Good people, the Wieses are.

16 April 12:30 a.m.

Just returned from seeing a German film called "Der Bewegte Man." Couldn't understand much of the lingo, but I think I got the gist of the film. Walked home through the mist, and as I moved along I saw lights in the windows occasionally. I wonder what sort of dramas are unfolding in those houses, and maybe more so in the ones with the lights off! But why were the people up at this hour? Who lives the life of an insomniac? They could be folks rising to go to late night jobs, although that would be odd given that not many places stay open 24 hours as they would in America.

Had a nice visit from Jan today. He's the reason I'm here, for he and his partner Stefanie saw my wolf program at the Grand Canyon. To tell the truth, I didn't recognize him at first. After all, it has been nearly a year since we met. I learned a few things about the park, and local flora and fauna. Later I biked into town and bought my train ticket to Grafenau. I found the nice tea shop in town, then wandered back here for lunch, wrote a few cards, watched "Dirty Dancing" in German, before going out for a wonderful evening walk. The dancing in the film was the same in English or Deutsch. I'm really pretty happy right now, an unusual feeling for me. It dawns on me more each day that I am actually here in Germany, and it is SO wild! I feel good about that fact.

17 April

Like always I seem to be nervous about getting away from here on time tomorrow. Truth is that if I wake up too late to walk to the Banhoff, there are several buses, buuuuut I'm still nervous.

Lazy day today: overcast, cold, rainy, tough to get out of bed. The alarm rang at 6, but I didn't arise until 8. Went to the wonderful Schloss that overlooks the town and had a good time just walking and looking in a lazy fashion. Later I became depressed, I think because I feel cooped up here, but some yoga and meditating on the feeling helped.

I recall the other night when Christian and I ate dinner, I had made spaghetti with lots of garlic. He asked me what was in the sauce, and when I told him he freaked. The next day we were to go to the government offices, and he worried that the people in the offices would consider us like Slavic people because we smelled like garlic. I told him not to worry about it. Although it was subtle, the next morning I could tell he truly worried about it. Sehr Komisch! (How funny!) Of course, everything worked out alright.

23 April

Lazy day. My body wants rest…lots of it. I took a walk into the city to buy Obst (fruit) and Gemüse (vegetables). I ran into Christian there and treated him to lunch. I ate meat, which is interesting, because I used to be a vegetarian, but I decided I'd have to eat meat in Germany.

Right now I'm sitting on the porch drinking a sort of wine cooler and catching up on my writing. I spent the last week in Bayerischer Wald (the Bavarian Forest). It was a good, but taxing and difficult experience. Here's a day by day run down of the events:

Day 1. Tuesday. A long day enroute to Bayern. I walked to the bus station early in the morning and arrived with 15 minutes to spare. I sweated on the way and the weather was cold, so waiting for the bus became uncomfortable. That same odd fellow from my bus trip when I first arrived in Wernigerode was here waiting for the bus also. He didn't recognize me as far as I can tell. I became frustrated at finding nothing to eat until I reached the train station in Göttingen. Traveling seems to make me hungry.

I met Christian at about Nürnberg and by that time we were on the train to Zwiesel, our destination. We realized that most people in the train were Praktikants (interns) in the same program as we. The Jugendherberge Waldhäuser (Forest House Youth Hostel) was very nice, but cold. I took the bunk below Christian. We had a party that night at the St. Oswald Museum with lots of good food and, of course, good beer. It was a difficult time conversationally for me, but good. A glass blower demonstrated his art for us. He was retired, but had been a real professional. Short, fat, and with an amazing smile. I had the chance to blow a glass ball. It's a lot more difficult than it looks. Great experience...and he gave me the beautiful blue ball that resulted. Funny, I had been thinking that it would be a ball (literally as well as figuratively) if I had the chance to try blowing. He had been making animals, but I just wanted a simple ball. I got one. Long day. Then I slept.

Day 2. Wednesday. Got up about 6:30 to do yoga. I didn't get much sleep, but the yoga felt good. Then we started training. I understood nothing. It felt incredibly frustrating, but I kept trying. The day was cold and some activities were canceled due to snow. We ate lunch at the Hans Eisenman Haus and I tried a Germknödel, which is a filled dumpling smothered in vanilla sauce. I don't remember much after that.

Day 3. Thursday. Not at all happy. Angry and frustrated at myself about communication problems. Started out the day with yoga and after breakfast we walked to the Czech border. I felt terrible, but it was nonetheless interesting. Afternoon sessions took place indoors and again it felt frustrating, but at least it was better than in the morning. I'm being much too hard on myself! That evening, one Praktikantin (female intern) took it upon herself to teach me German. Funny, but I don't remember her name. She was very nice. I do remember that she lives in Hamburg. That night we tried to go out to the pubs, but they were closed.

Day 4. Friday. Arose for the birdsong walk, but left about half of the way through and just walked on my own. Petted the dogs thereabout, which felt good. I could understand them. Even though communications frustrated me, I must say that everyone was patient and tried to help me. For instance, another Christian talked to me one night about how frustrated he had been when he went to England. I appreciated that very much, as I appreciated all of their assistance, but I realize now that I need to show that appreciation more. I get so caught up in my being hard on myself that I don't take time often enough to tell others how much I appreciate them.

Anyhow, we went to a Jugendwaldheim (environmental education center) and did some activities, which were lots of fun. I particularly liked one where we had a large sheet with a hole in it a couple of feet across. We laid it on the forest floor and tried to find all the living things that we could in the hole. There were more than you could imagine. After lunch we sat for a discussion of the national parks and the "Praktikant für die Umwelt" (Internship for the Environment) program, in which a Commerzbank representative was grilled about his company's environmental record. (Commerzbank is the German bank which sponsors the program). It was a glorious, beautiful day, finally. I caught a newt and a frog. That night we had another discussion session and a party – a good party. Lots of singing and drinking, drinking and singing, and more singing and drinking. Short night's sleep.

Day 5. Saturday. Started out with yoga and a shower, but there was no hot water to speak of, then had breakfast and said our scattered goodbyes before catching the train to Bad Harzburg. Good ride with my friends. I told a Grimm's tale called the Juniper Tree to four of them, which was pretty wild - an American telling a German story to Germans. Then I caught the bus back to Wernigerode and a long walk home.

I think I'm beginning to understand people better. This afternoon someone stopped me on the street to ask a question. I actually understood the question and found the words with which to answer. I don't think he guessed I was an "Auslander" (foreigner) and it felt good.

The Man on the Train

The day had dawned as a beautiful one, warm and mostly clear. In the air the sensation that Spring had finally arrived in force for the first time pervaded. Trees leafed out and cherry and apple blossoms bloomed in abundance. I boarded the train for Bad Harzburg along with my friends and coworkers, Christian and Silvia, and we sat down across the aisle from the man.

He gazed out the window with a sort of resigned impetuosity. The look on his face told me that he could see, outside his window, so many possibilities, so many potential experiences, but also that he had no intention to partake of them, and that it was alright. He had done his share. I guessed him to be at least 60 or 65 years in age, maybe much older. He wore a long, gray, somewhat tattered woolen overcoat, which he continued to wear in spite of the warm temperature of the train car. His hair thinned on top, but he wore it long on the sides and back, several inches past his collar. It seemed long for a German of his age. I recall his nose: the long straight line of it from his forehead down to a sharp point. He appeared short, of medium build, and sat slightly slumped in the seat.

He looked like he had led a long, eventful life, but I found it difficult to tell if the longing in his eyes as he gazed out the window at the greening German countryside was due to memories jarred loose from the archives of his mind, or from recalling dreams that never came to fruition. I began wondering about the history in the lines of his weathered face. He had lived through WWII. What role had he played in the war that dominated so much of 20th century history here? Had he marched as a soldier across this now peaceful scenery? Could he have guarded POWs, interred Jews at one of the now famous prison camps, or played the role of prisoner himself? Could he have been just a little too young for the uniform? Or had he been declared unfit for duty and watched the war happen just as he now watched out the train window, with his package of Butterkeks (butter cookies) awaiting his next hunger pang?

A woman and a child boarded the train and sat across from him. He glanced at them for a moment, then turned once again to stare out the window. I wondered…if something magic or catastrophic should happen, would his expression change, or would he just watch with keen eyes? Somewhere out there he had been born. Somewhere out there he had taken his first tentative steps. Somewhere out there he went to school. What kind of work had he undertaken? Had he wed the apple of his eye or remained single? Did he have any children? Were they around or was it just him? It all lay outside that window…somewhere.

As the train neared Bad Harzburg I pulled my backpack down from the overhead rack and had a few words with my companions. In my enthusiasm to leave the train I hadn't stopped to see where the man went. How did he walk? Had his impetuous expression changed? Did someone meet him at the station, or does he still sit there looking out the window eating another Butterkek? So many questions…so many possibilities.

When I am the age of this man what will I see out the window, and will some wandering soul with too much time on their hands write about me and wonder? And life goes on…

30 April

Walpurgisnacht tonight, a locally important holiday. It's the night when the devil is supposed to dance with witches on the mountain. This should be an interesting 24 hours. I'm working today to try and help keep the peace in Schierke where there's supposed to be a large gathering of skinheads who intend to cause trouble. If they go for me and my long hair, I'm running. We're supposed to report any problems and watch what goes on.

May 1995

1 May

Happy May Day Tom! I was right...it was a rather interesting 24-36 hours. The weather proved overcast and waxed cooler throughout the day. We all started the workday (I use the term loosely) feeling rather lazy. First we hiked down to the 'Parkdienst' (park employee) entrance station. There we ate lunch and hiked to near the top of the Brocken. It was misting and not much was going on except lots of people. On the way back we came across our first couple of skinheads, who gave us real bad looks, but nothing else. I'll admit to feeling a bit nervous.

Further down the trail we happened upon some newts swimming in the drainage ditches alongside the road. Wonderful to see my aquatic four-footed friends! Stopped at the train station for Pommes Frittes (French fries). We split up for a while and things seemed rather dismal until later, when our re-united group chanced upon a parade right through Schierke. It featured lots of people dressed up in witch or devil costumes and stuff like that. For a while I walked behind a guy with his wife and daughter. They were holding hands. The man was so drunk he banged into people, stumbling around. His little girl appeared confused and a bit scared. His wife was visibly disgusted, but she said nothing. It was a sad scene for them. Lots of that sort of thing among the unemployed former East Germans, unfortunately. Hard to be employed for all your adult life, then cast aside like a pair of old, worn socks. Those are the negative effects of the unification. Then again, maybe it's just hime getting drunk.

Later the parade led to a fairground. Most of us weren't into paying the 5,00 DM entrance fee, although Christian walked right in with the parade and nobody charged him. A few minutes later Christian had found a break in the fence and we all snuck inside. I didn't feel right about it, but I did it anyhow, and I'm glad I did experience the fair.

There we found a large circle of food and craft booths, all in medieval fashion, which included a fine herbalist shop, where I bought some good old American Echinacea, an herb for the immune system. There was also a stage with a great series of performances including music, dance, jugglers, fire breathers, etc. in an arcane style. A series of skits, mostly with "witchy" overtones, played upon the stage, then the main show featured a dancing re-enactment of the scene from Goethe's Faust, where witches danced with the Devil on the top of this selfsame mountain. It began with traditional dances, then transitioned into a more freeform style, until eventually some began stripping until several were completely naked. A good family show with lots of families present. And that's not just sarcasm. Not exactly something you see in the average American "Renaissance Faire!" Their dancing seemed so 'honest' that I wondered if they were indeed true Pagans. Beautiful women, though.

As the show waned, we rushed to catch the last train down the hill, which was packed to the hilt. I clung to the railing just outside of the back door of a train car, with bits of coal raining upon my countenance as we traveled. We rode down to Drei Annen Hohne where we stayed for the night in the ranger station. There were 5 of us and they asked me if I wanted to be in the same room with them. Right…I wanted to be the only single person in a room with 2 young couples in love…and with more than a few beers under their belts besides! I chose to be in the next room. Got to bed about 2:30 a.m.

Didn't sleep all that well, but I had lots of energy today. I arose before the others, not surprisingly, and washed my face in the morning dew…literally. Went for a morning walk along with numerous Schwarzenwegschneken (black trail snails). Stopped for tea at the Gaststube in Schierke and hiked back down the hill to Wernigerode. Danced around a larch tree along the way in my own Pagan May Day celebration. When I returned I showered, made a great dinner, & had a beer. It was a good day.

3 May

Early evening has arrived. I will get dinner ready soon, although I've already started the rice. Christian is hard at work raising my bike seat. He rode it and thinks it sits too low, but I hope he doesn't raise it as high as his. He has an old (well not that old) friend coming to visit. They went to Gymnasium together, what we Americans call high school. I did my first talk yesterday and it went rather well. Today we took the train to Drei Annen and studied the area where we'll conduct programs with the school groups.

After lunch they biked back and I had a great hike back home. I took my time and became familiar with the surroundings. The day was absolutely spectacular: warm, sunny, with a light breeze. I saw 2 mouflon, sort of like bighorn sheep, which, I gather, are rather uncommon. I startled them and they sped off into the spruce forest. There the two males stopped and gazed back at me. Beautiful! I spoke to them, then we all just stood still. Finally they moved. One snorted and stamped his hind leg, which I took to be a warning of sorts. I couldn't quite see, but I think they rammed heads. Then they snorted a few more times before moving slowly, cautiously away, stopping a few times to look back at me. One gave another snort and stomp and I began to saunter away. Finally they ran uphill until nearly out of sight and I left them to their own devices.

Later I saw 3 rothirsch (red deer), and an Eichelhäher, a bird in the Corvid family (jays, magpies, crows, and ravens). The rothirsch, apparently two adults and a yearling, retreated quickly once they spotted me. I also happened across an old sidewalk. Yes, an old sidewalk in the woods, which led to a shack with a "No Trespassing" sign on it. Two guys lay down sleeping by it. I didn't want to disturb them so I hastened back through the woods to the road.

As I neared the end of my hike I came to a place called "Der Silberner Man" (the Silver Man). (Note: Der Silberner Man is the name of a legend native to the Harz mountains.), and shortly after that I found an old ruined house. I searched its decomposing rooms and found it mostly devoid of interesting objects save for a fairly recent porn advertisement. I left it lay and walked home. I had a good hike, a good day.

4 May

I'm sitting on my porch drinking a beer on a beautiful warm evening. Christian's preparing himself for football practice, and I don't mean soccer; he plays on an American style football team. Apparently there are several leagues of amateur American football teams in Germany. I don't think they will ever supplant soccer from its lofty position in Germany, but interest in it grows at a snail's pace. The youngest of my landlord's two boys (what's his name…I'm terrible at remembering names) plays on the cherry tree outside my window.

Another hike today, this time with about 15 other people from the park in the area of Huy, a small town near Wernigerode. Beautiful place! A forest of beech trees dominated the area with larches, elms, chestnuts, maples, and oaks thrown in for good measure. Dr. Sacher led the hike, so we moved along at a rapid pace. I felt tired all day and just dragged along at the back of the pack, which didn't matter too much given the language barrier. Actually I did OK with the language today. I ate part of my lunch while we stopped to talk about plants or something, followed by a bite at the snail stop, and another where we looked at knoblauch kraut ("garlic herb"), an herbaceous plant with an odor resembling garlic. The hike mostly concluded at a Gaststätte (pub or café). I figured we had stopped just for a beer or something, but we had stopped for lunch. Had I known that I might not have eaten earlier. Actually I could have eaten more, but I chose not to do so. Just as well. On a tight budget.

As I sit here writing, my eyes also wander now and then to the neighbor woman walking back and forth watering her plants. She and her husband have a beautiful garden. As I watch them day after day they appear tireless, and yet they are nearly twice my age. The German people appear energetic to me in general. My yogis would tell me to eat a light diet and keep the intestines clear, but the German people eat a rather heavy diet, drink lots of alcohol, and yet seem to have tons of energy. Ah, paradox!

5 May

The following paragraphs are all broad generalizations, and while they are common, there are exceptions. People after all, are individuals, but our culture of birth, either through genetic or culturally learned means, does imprint the majority of us with certain characteristics. Even with what I have said, I still try to treat each person as an individual and not automatically place them in a box in which they must remain. It helps to keep an open mind.

Germans are interesting people. For the most part those I've seen are industrious 'busy-bodies' who also love to party. Even the more mild mannered Germans like their own kind of party. They drink a fair amount of alcohol, mostly beer of course, and eat an abundance of food, mostly meat, cheese, and breads of all sorts. In general they appear very energetic and have a gusto for life that is nearly overwhelming to me. They walk and, to a lesser extent, bike a lot. No matter which trail I walk I, more often than not, encounter many people. The men are usually dressed in the traditional hiking clothes of knee length trousers (sometimes even lederhosen), long socks pulled up to meet them, and boots or hiking shoes. It has impressed me that even the elderly folk will go hiking if at all possible.

I've remarked how much they eat or drink, but I've seen few people I would call obese; stocky yes, and men with ample bellies, but not REALLY huge like I see in the U.S. I think the key is their active nature. When they go "wandern" (hiking), they do so with the fervor with which they attack (for lack of a better word) most things. One can find Germans along the trail just sitting in peace enjoying the scenery, but mostly they keep walking at a fairly rapid pace. It appears to be a social and physical activity rather than a spiritual one, although tough to say on how many levels they appreciate it. Come to think of it, I seldom see Germans hiking alone. Of course, it's not really wilderness out there; the trails are nearly always well-marked with Gasthauses or Gaststättes along the way where one can get a beer and a meal.

Even though people generally work hard here, I often see people who look like they should be working, in the cafés and wandering around the market area. Then there are the government and office employees, who seem to work shorter hours than most other Germans. Most offices are closed Wednesday afternoons (including banks) and Fridays are short, light work days. Some places, such as Gasthauses, Gaststättes, and gift shops, are open on weekends, but most are closed or work short hours.

Germans are into shaking hands. For instance, Irmtraud, my boss, shakes everyone's hand when she enters a room. In spite of their official or businesslike manner when working or in public, they touch one another more than one would expect, mostly family and good friends. In other words they are not as "distant" with one another as they are often portrayed.

12 May

I haven't written for a few days, so to catch up:

Tuesday we worked with a group from the Fachschule (Junior College) at Drei Annen Hohne on the park boundary. The weather was awful, but it went well anyhow. I recall in particular a good time with the rope activity. It starts with the group wearing blindfolds and standing randomly in an area. We take a long rope tied in a circle and have each person hang onto it. The group then takes off the blindfolds (or leaves them on if you REALLY want to make it hard) and has to figure out how to make the rope, which is now in a rather complicated pretzel, back into a circle, with nobody letting go of the rope. It's quite a challenge actually and a good exercise in cooperation and trust.

After the group we returned to Wernigerode and had a birthday party for Christian. His parents joined us and I met them for the first time. Very nice people and we got on rather well. They seem a bit more affluent than I had expected given all the stories we heard in the U.S. about East Germany before "Der Wende" (The Change), which is what most folks around here call the unification. I must get into the habit of not letting Christian coerce me into eating more food; I ate way too much.

Wednesday we had a group on the Schlossberg (Castle Mountain), where the beautiful castle sits that overlooks Wernigerode. Cold and wet weather again. That night I went to my first class of "German for

Foreigners." I still have much to learn, but I feel more confident than previously.

Yesterday, after waiting in the cold for over an hour, I got a ride to near the top of the Brocken. There I hiked down to meet the group with Christian and Silvia, then back up to the top of the Brocken once again, which was totally socked in with fog. There we visited the Brocken Museum, ate lunch (they have wonderful pea soup), and rode the train to Drei Annen Hohne. We did a short nature walk and some activities with the group before catching the train down the mountain. I exited the train at Steinerne Renne (Stoney Run) and walked the rest of the way back to Wernigerode. It had been a strange day. Can't put my finger on it, but just strange.

16 May

The group at Drei Annen Hohne went well, although I am beginning to feel like a novelty ("The Token American"). This one little girl just hung on me and helped me with my German. It's wild to be 36 years old and taught to speak by a little child. It's pretty neat actually.

17 May

Big day! I saw my first live Fire Salamanders today. The first was on the way to Drei Annen on the train. I saw it at the Steinerne Renne Bahnhof (railroad station) as it tried to climb out from between the tracks. The second one I saw as I walked back from Drei Annen. I was walking on a dirt road and there it was on the roadside. It was Beautiful!! The colors are outstanding: bright, radiant yellow blotches on a glossy black background. Neat little bumps where the spine is located. He/she didn't like to be held and when I let it go it took off. It fell down the rocks on the steep hill, then landed on a branch where it sat still. Tonight Christian and I went to look for some in the cold, rainy darkness and found one near our house. Wunderschön!!

18 May

The morning was cold. We worked with a delightful group on the Schlossberg (Castle Hill), and my language skills seem to be improving. We found a fire salamander and I told them the story about how people used to believe that salamanders were born in fire because people heated with wood and salamanders often lived in the woodpiles. People brought the wood into the house and they placed it on the fire. The salamanders would then crawl out of the pile of wood. Hence the belief that they were born in fire. One member of the aristocracy in India had a coat made of salamander skin, which he believed would protect him from fire. It didn't.

Later in the day I walked through the town square. I had stopped to enjoy a Peruvian musical group performing near the Marktplatz, when I glanced back and noticed a rather attractive young blonde looking at me. She smiled. I smiled. After a few more times smiling at one another, I stepped over to say "Guten Tag." The conversation didn't go much beyond that, as I hardly understood a word she said. I did discover that she lived in Wernigerode, but not much else. For some reason I had a difficult time with her strong dialect. It was not to be.

19 May

Do flies have emotions? An interesting question. I'm sitting in the train on my way to see my friend Birgit in Leipzig. I have this car all to myself, which is an odd and rare situation in and of itself, and there's a fly on the window. A young one. Given the fact that flies only live 1-2 weeks, I'd say it is maybe only a day or two old. It's bouncing around against the glass the way flies are supposed to.

I tried catching it just to see if I could. I guess that's maybe an offshoot of the old "man vs. nature" contest. "Facing the wilderness alone" and all that crap. Or maybe it's merely me testing my physical prowess. "Prowess", now that's an interesting word for my physique, but that's another story. Could be that I'm just bored. In any case, I caught it on the second try. I didn't mean it any harm. It wasn't bothering me. So I opened my hand and let it go. The fly just wandered around the contours of my shirt until I blew on it to make it fly away so I could put my hand down without worrying that I would crush the poor little guy. The fly buzzed a few circles and ended up on the window again where it continued its ostensibly chaotic monotony.

It stood on the glass for a while not too far from my head, that is if one can call it 'standing' on a vertical surface. I blew on it. The fly blew around like a tornado inside a tea cup before flying back, bouncing off of the glass a few times, and then landing to scope out the filth situation, I presume. Then it occurred to me that the fly might be angry with me. If I were him I would be. But is it at all possible that this fly could have emotions such as anger. I'm sure that mammals, birds, and maybe even reptiles and amphibians experience some form of emotions. But insects?! This fly will live 2 weeks on the outside. Does it even have time to experience emotions? I mean, could you see two flies about to make love (to use a phrase which assumes they do have emotions).

"Not now, I'm just not feeling up to it."

"What do you mean you're not feeling up to it! You'll be dead in two days!"

"I know, but something just doesn't feel right about this whole situation. Can't we talk and get acquainted first?"

Could be a lesson for humans in there somewhere. I'm not sure what. Or where for that matter. But somewhere. And in the time it has taken me to write this the fly has disappeared. Another window perhaps. A pile of cigarette butts in the smoking car maybe. Or, hopefully it has found its way outside to a nice pile of shit…or German potato salad. By now it may even have gone through puberty, if it hasn't been smashed into oblivion by the conductor wandering by to check the tickets of non-existent passengers. Wherever it may be, I wish the fly well.

As the sun sets on another day in the Fatherland, my train passes farmers' fields where rabbits ('Feldhasen' auf Deutsch) chase each other among the clover. But that, as they say, is definitely another tail.

21 May

I need to start trusting what I hear. In the train station in Halle I thought I heard that the train to Ilsenburg and Wernigerode, my train, leaves from track one, but when I arrived I read the sign which said it left from track 8. So I went to track 8, got on the train, and after a while asked someone if this was the train to Wernigerode. No, it goes to Magdeburg. So I rushed to gate 1 and the train was gone. So here I am on the S-Zug (slow train) to Halberstadt, where I'll wait an hour for the train to Wernigerode, arriving there at a quarter to midnight. Then I'll walk home, about 1 ½ to 2 miles away. Long day.

On another note I had a great time in Leipzig. Ate lots of good food and went to a street music festival. Birgit plays in a group which does Celtic music and they are pretty good. We also saw a concert by the Thomanerchor (a world renowned choir) and Gewandhaus Orchestra in the Thomaskirche (St. Thomas Church), where Johann Sebastian Bach had been the Kantor (music leader) from 1723 until 1750. It proved a deeply moving experience with a sense of history that took my breath away.

The concert opened with an organ piece by Felix Mendelssohn followed by a choral arrangement of Samuel Barber's "Adagio for Strings," which was called "Agnus Dei." Magnificent! After that they performed two cantatas by J.S. Bach. It was a powerful experience to be in that church and to hear this beautiful music. It gave me a real sense of history. We also saw the Nikolaikirche (St. Nicholas Church) where the "Vereinigung" (Unification) got a major start. Birgit was involved in the demonstrations. They formed a circle holding hands around the old part of Leipzig, not to call for unification, but just to request certain reforms in the East German state. Tanks and soldiers waited just around the corner for the signal to crush the demonstration. That signal never came.

We stopped at a place made famous in Goethe's Faust (the name escapes me), then saw a movie called "Stargate." It started out good, but it was all downhill from there. Hollywood pales in comparison to history and real life. We returned late, slept in, and just walked around today seeing the sights, talking, and having a few shots of Schierke Feuerstein, before I caught the train. Had a wonderful time!

25 May

Today is Himmelfahrt (Ascension Day) also known in Germany as Father's Day or Men's Day or "Men Get Drunk Day." The tradition here is for men to drink beer while riding in a covered wagon pulled by horses. The wagon is decorated with birch branches, but nobody seems to know why. It's probably an old pagan tradition that became incorporated into Christianity and modern society, but whose meaning has been long since lost to most people, much like Christmas trees and Easter bunnies.

I went with Jan Gasche, Stefanie, Gunter, Gunter's son Matthias, and another woman I didn't know, up to a proposed cross-country ski area near the park. It actually goes into the park a short ways and they want to reroute it so that it is entirely out of the park. We did lots of walking in circles in the spruce forest and trying to read the map, but it was fun. Saw lots of men in their wagons riding around and getting thoroughly snockered (drunk). Then I came home, took a nap, and now as I write, Christian is flailing away at his guitar.

The other night Gunther and his family came to visit and they requested me to speak to Frau Karste's English class the next day. I told them the story of "The Wild Girl," a Moroccan story I received from my teacher Laura Simms, who had collected it in northern Morocco. Frau Karste requested I tell that story to her kids, which I did. They were a wonderful group – very attentive listeners, and I think they liked my presentation.

June 1995

I met Lisa and Marianne when I worked at a rock shop at the Grand Canyon in 1987. We went out for a hike together and kept in touch. I visited them on another trip to Europe, then again during my time working in Germany.

5 June

As I write this I'm sitting on the train returning from Switzerland to Wernigerode. Cool and rainy again, just like when I traveled to Switzerland. I had a great time there as always. I definitely noticed the prices more this trip, probably due to traveling on a more limited budget. Switzerland is an expensive country in which to travel. Where do I begin?

When I arrived my friends Lisa & Marianne met me with a warm welcome and we went out for coffee. We walked around Zürich's wet downtown a while, then went out to eat at a neat restaurant called Hitli. It has been a vegetarian restaurant since 1903. Good food – very good. Then we said "Goodnight" to Marianne who took the train home, and I went with Lisa to her house for a warm welcome from her family and a good night's sleep. Woke up and did some Yoga, including some with Lisa, who is eager to learn. I was not the most patient teacher today for some reason, however.

Marianne had to work, so Lisa and I set off for Luzern & Bern. In Luzern we saw the Gletschergarten (glacier garden), which was really fascinating. Nice museum about glaciation in the area and some neat rocks (mostly metamorphic) polished by glaciers. Good stuff for a geologist. After lunch we saw a photo collection on Picasso. The photographer was a friend of Picasso's during the last 17 years of Picasso's life and the photos showed him with his family. Very interesting! There were also a few of Picasso's artworks there as well, mostly drawings. I began noticing the role that sexual organs played in his work, which is not surprising given the connection between sexuality and creativity. In yoga, the chakra which is linked to sexuality is the same as the one which is linked to creativity. Then I began thinking "Maybe I'm the one obsessed with sexual organs." Probably it's a little of both.

From downtown Luzern we went to Tony's place where we found him outside scrogging in the mud digging up worms. He likes fishing. He's divorced now and looks very forlorn. He's a man with a deep emotional wound. I can relate. We had a beer, then met his sister Marta and her son. We went out to eat and then for a quick drink. Had a good conversation with Marta, who is a vegetarian. Her husband is English, but is away right now. We stayed at her house. Had pancakes as a late breakfast. She went with us to Bern by way of Beatushöhle, which is a fascinating cave in the Alps near Interlaken where an Irish monk, St. Beatus, stayed for a long time as a hermit. The cave has more human history than cave formations, but the most striking natural aspect is a stream that rushes through it, which emerges to a magnificent high waterfall outside.

We arrived in Bern too late to see Einstein's house, so we walked around and saw the sights of the beautiful inner city of Bern: tall stone buildings, archways, statues aplenty, a wonderful clock tower, a huge Münster (cathedral) with a wild portrayal of the so-called "Judgment Day." We left Marta at the train station after an introduction to Swiss government in front of the parliament building. Then Lisa and I went to see a movie at Kramgasse #72. It was called "IQ" and featured Walter Matthau playing Albert Einstein. Einstein put forth his theory of relativity while living in Bern at Kramgasse 49, right across the street from the theater. That felt pretty wild. Once again Hollywood pales in comparison to real life, as the film was an anticlimax after having seen the city, the cave, etc. We then, feeling very tired, drove back to Zürich.

Saturday began with breakfast at Lisa's, then went to pick up Marianne, and drove to Oberterzen. The weather was finally cooperating, and Oberterzen was, of course, gorgeous. Switzerland is truly an incredibly beautiful country. We met Tony at Oberterzen and dropped him off for fishing before heading off for a hike. We parked at Walenstadt, then hiked up the cliffs on the north side of the lake through a beautiful beech, oak, and maple forest. It never ceases to amaze me when we hike along through the woods, and then come to a Gastätte (café) in some place that seems so remote. We ate lunch, then after a short distance came to another one serving drinks and desserts. I ate an incredible slice of yogurt strawberry torte with a cup of peppermint tea. The peppermint was fresh from their garden and tasted fabulous.

After getting our stomachs well filled we hiked down to Quinten where we were supposed to catch a boat back to Walenstadt. However, the only day it doesn't run is Saturday. It was Saturday. Now what!! It was already 5:00 p.m., so a 3 hour hike back to the car didn't sound inviting. We had a drink and went with the boat back to Murg. There we ran to the train station and just barely made the train back to Walenstadt. Otherwise it would have been a 2 hour wait. Got back to Oberterzen where a wild-eyed musician named Heinz joined us. He talked and laughed a lot. Sometimes I understood him. Marianne made a wonderful risotto dinner, then I had a cup of Lemon Balm (Melissa) tea that put me to sleep in no time.

The next day we got a late start with another pancake breakfast (made by yours truly), then went to meet Marianne's family in Appenzel. Had a very nice time with them in the magnificent beauty of Appenzel, then off to Zürich. Wanted to see another movie, although now that I think of it I don't know why, since the movies are so pale in comparison to our other activities. Hmmmm.

9 June

As I write this I sit watching a futuristic film on TV (dubbed in German, of course), starring Sean Connery, and suddenly it dawns on me that in practically every film about the future that I've ever seen, life is not really any better than now, and in most cases it's a lot worse. Talk about a dismal view of humanity and the direction it is currently heading! Take this movie for instance. The people are aboard an orbiting space station and life is constantly like being in a 1930's factory. There's a drug ring mafia causing trouble. People drink lots of alcohol. There's a high level of violence. And nobody's emotionally, intellectually, and especially not spiritually more advanced than we are today. And that's not saying much! Technology has advanced, but we haven't. It's ever so common. Even the films in which the world is supposed to appear better off than it is today, they end up showing us that it really isn't, that it's all a charade. The "New and Improved Society" falls apart and we're back to the same old shit. The only possible exception I can recall might be Star Wars and the concept of the "Force." I guess the thing that truly bothers me about it is that if we can't even imagine a better life, how will we ever make it happen? How will we ever advance?

A Cowspiracy

Cows have the Swiss well-trained. Everywhere you go on every green piece of land in Switzerland you see cows. They have big bells hanging from their necks and everywhere you go it's not far between points of hearing the clang, clang, clang of them echoing among the verdant hills. They're mostly of the light brown variety with the same dumb looks on their faces as other cows you find around the world, but I get the impression that these Swiss cows are a little different.

Yes, it's true they are not often allowed to travel very far. They're not allowed on public transport. They can't drive the autobahn. And going to the movies is right out. But look at it this way, they constantly have some of the most beautiful scenery in the entire world: magnificent snow capped peaks surrounded by rolling hills of green velvet. They have lots of time for socializing with one another. And they always have the right of way on the streets. Humans usually have to schedule exercise time, but the Swiss cows get all they want, not that they appear to desire all THAT much aerobic exercise. Meanwhile Swiss people are racing around the office keeping track of time and doing tons of paperwork (at least in the cities).

Cows don't have to put up with Zürich traffic and don't worry about whether or not the train is on time. They never have to go shopping. They don't have to carry their passports or other personal papers with them. They don't pay bills. They don't have to worry whether or not they properly follow social norms or the rules of etiquette. I believe that Swiss cows have their people trained to think that they can't live without tons of dairy products. Everywhere you go you find cheese, milk, chocolate, quark, yogurt, etc., etc. For that reason the Swiss humans have cut acres and acres of beautiful forest land to make room for...cows, cows, and more cows.

I don't know, maybe I'm wrong, but the Swiss cow has a life that most of us say we're working our little butts off to achieve. If only we can have more money, more possessions, then we can have more leisure time and we can live like...cows. Meanwhile, Swiss cows keep chewing. And bells are ringing in the Alps. I call it ... a..."cowspiracy."

This is part of a letter I wrote in June to friends back in the US

Dear Friends,

I've wanted to write this letter for several weeks and now that I have time at home with nothing to do, for a change, I'm glad to finally write it. Of course, the reason I have time to write has to do with my learning a new German word: Lebensmittelvergiftung, known in English as 'food poisoning.' It's either that or stomach flu, but my doctor suspects the food poisoning. But, just as what little I've eaten in the last 3 days has rapidly done, this too will pass. Generally, however, I've been doing well.

It was rather humorous yesterday when a TV crew from Magdeburg came to interview one of the rangers and me. It took about 3 hours, most of it outside on a rather cold, wet day. First my roommate Christian drove me up to the meeting place on his old moped, about a 15 minute ride. Now, I don't know what it was like for him, but I smelled strong exhaust fumes the entire way. By the time we arrived at our destination, I felt as if my system had turned inside out and I had gone through my own digestive system with the apple from the previous day. Not a pretty sight. I'm learning German, but as of yet I don't speak the language that well on a good day. Needless to say, the initial interview proved interesting. No one in the room except me spoke English. After the interview it was time for pictures. Right! They wanted a picture of me with the other ranger (with whom I've never worked before), as we watch the steam train heading to the Brocken, the highest mountain in the park. So here we are, it's cold, I'm feeling like a grizzly bear had just played "Gut the Ranger" with me, and they're telling me to get really excited about seeing the train, which I ride nearly every day. I lived through the experience and can hardly wait to see the footage of me looking pale, weak, and incoherent broadcast to the entire region on the tube tomorrow night.

Christian and I live at the edge of the town of Wernigerode, and one of the most beautiful forested areas I've seen in this area thus far is only a 10 minute walk from here. Dominated by beech trees, it's also a mixture of oaks, maples, birches, larches, and spruces. Beautiful wildflowers abound. Even a short walk in the woods does wonders for my soul, especially after those difficult days when I just can't seem to speak or understand this odd language. Communication has been, by far, my biggest problem and frustration. I'm learning, but it goes slowly. Deep communication has been mostly non-existent. This is the former East Germany. People here learned Russian in school.

The most obvious thing one sees coming into town is the beautiful "storybook" castle overlooking the half-timbered houses of the old town. It really is an impressive sight. Then, however, you notice that the buildings, streets, and most infrastructure are in disrepair. But now, since the unification, the West German money has helped to bring in much needed renovation projects. The unification has also created some serious problems here, but that's a longer story. Generally Wernigerode is a rather nice looking town. The people are generally not very open until you get to know them better. The average person on the street doesn't smile much and won't usually go beyond business and weather talk. Interesting what a smile and a "Guten Tag" can do, however.

And as the sun sets on another day in Wernigerode, of course not that anyone can tell as it's cloudy, I'll go back to eating my toast, apple sauce, and bananas. Take care. Be well.

Yours in peace,
Tom

Photo from a newspaper article about my work in the national park in Germany. That day I was terribly sick from food poisoning. With me is a German ranger who was later arrested for having been a member of the East German secret police, called the "Stasi."

27 June

On the train to Waren to visit Müritz National Park.* It's warm and humid. I'm lazy and totally unmotivated for anything other than a bit of writing. We spent time in Berlin and saw the "Verdekte Reichstag," the parliament building covered by an immense silver metallic "curtain." An artist (Christo and his wife Jeanne Claude) did it as some sort of statement while parliament is out of session and being rebuilt. I found it interesting, but was not particularly impressed. What struck me more were the crosses and tokens on the north side of the building from those who had died trying to cross the wall. Silvia and Christian took me around town to show me the sights, but my low energy level precluded my being good company.

Saturday I arrived in Halle and had lunch with Christian's family who live just outside of town. We had a wonderful conversation, then Christian took me to town and showed me the sights. He's rightfully very proud of his family and hometown. Saturday night we ate dinner at Annette's family's weekend home. People in larger cities often live in apartments, but some, those who can afford it, have tiny cottages on the outskirts of town where they can have gardens. The places are packed together like RVs at a campground, although I've seen many campgrounds which have more space between RVs than these places do. That's the nature of a nation with such a high population density. It seems to be not only a place for people to forget about their workaday lives, but also to surround themselves with a little piece of nature. You can take people out of the wilderness, but you can't totally take the wilderness out of the people, at least not yet. Anyhow, I drank too much Greek schnapps. At one point I leaned over and told Christian that I suddenly could understand almost no German.

---

* Müritz is a lovely national park of forests, post-glacial landscapes, and over 100 lakes, with a wide variety of wildlife, including red deer, cranes, various water birds, white-tailed eagles, and osprey.

Müritz in June

Sunset afterglow
Painted across the lake
In brushstrokes
Pointed, circular, sweeping, dancing,
Carried on gentle waves
In the warm evening breeze.
At the far end of the pier
Children, 2 girls,
Play "Catch me if you can"
With the chill
Of cold lake water.
As they circle
Out, and in, and out,
Their ripples
Create a kaleidoscope
Of my lake landscape artwork.
Voices echo
Across a glassy surface
Otherwise still
But for fish popping up
To devour a mosquito or two
As birches, oaks, alders, and lindens
Stand watch in the cooling summer air.
Crows caw their requests
For a good seat on the branch
As they bed down for the night
In their favorite old, twisted oak.
I turn to see their playful competition
But my glance is captured
By the old fishing shed,
Boards weathered and gray
In hues glowing
Of sun's last gaze,

Thatched straw roof
Slowly discovering entropy.
I wonder
About the lives, the dramas
Played out upon its
Now sunken floor.
Who lived, who died,
Who got pregnant
While papa dozed,
His boat drifting
On waters that lap
Beneath this musing wanderer.
Swimmers continue splashing
In the fading light.
I stand on croaking boards,
The pier swaying ever so slightly
As I turn and walk
Across the field
Where earlier today
I heard cows
Voicing their concerns
As they bore their bulging udders
From one pasture to the next,
Farmers playing traffic cop
In their migration.
I see the stone tower on the hill
Windows still clinging
To the remains of the day.
Wandering back to the old farmhouse,
My brief and pleasant home,
I pass the ancient Linden tree
And wonder to myself
Why concerns weigh as they do
On these tired shoulders
Day in and day out

Wearing me down.
Because it's all there
And it all happens
In its own good time
In the right place
Pre-ordained or not is irrelevant,
Life still goes on
An endless horizon of possibilities
One following the next
Playing themselves out to the beat
Of the swift, sleek wings of swallows
Dashing overhead:
Always enough food
Always enough time
Always enough everything
Always enough
Until we ask for more
    Than we need,
And who could
On a night like this.
Written 30 June 1995 near Waren, Germany.

July 1995

11 July

The other night I stopped in an Imbiss/Café on Friederichstrasse. I asked the man "Haben Sie vielleicht Streichholzer?" (Do you perhaps have matches?) a line right out of one of the German tapes I listened to before I came here. The place was dark, but I could tell that the innkeeper had been drinking up some of his profits. I waited. He emerged with a handful of boxed matches. "Möchten Sie ein Feuer machen?" (Do you want to make a fire?) he asked. I wasn't quite certain how to respond. He had an intense look on his face and I thought he was implying that I was a pyromaniac. He repeated the question and I said "Ja," so he gave me the handful. "Ich brauche nur eine Schachtel." (I only need one box.) He insisted I take them all. Maybe he wanted me to start a fire for a little excitement. Hmmmm!

Also had a radio interview the other day which went rather well. I may learn this language yet.

16 July

Just returned from a trip to the Drömling area north of the Harz. Saw lots of storks and flat farm/wetland places and that type of stuff. Actually a beautiful area. The farms and wetlands seem to coexist quite well together as an intricate series of canals and streams carve the tilled earth, and the bird watching was wonderful. It's not a national park, but rather a "Naturschutzgebiet" (protected natural area), somewhat similar to some wildlife refuges in the U.S..

We arrived there tired and took a nap, then went out for a little 25-30 km (about 15-18 mi.) bike ride to the south part of the park. The biking is easy as it is so flat. I found myself wanting to say "Goddamnit Christian, let's stop and LOOK at the place," but of course I never actually expressed it. It was partly that I was tired, but also I just wanted to soak it up. Chatted with James, a volunteer from England who works there. He's had a difficult time with communicating and I can certainly commiserate.

The next day we took a much longer bike ride, about 70 km (42 miles). The day was warm and beautiful, and we went swimming in an old quarry. Late in the afternoon dark clouds began building and the wind increased with each passing gust. We picked up our pace as the storm grew. Branches swayed to and fro, some breaking under the strain as they blew across our paths. We arrived at Thomas and Doreen Scholz's house just as rain began to fly almost horizontally in the wind. We ditched our bikes in the garage of the old red brick farmhouse and were ushered into the kitchen for coffee, lemonade, kräuterlikor (like Jägermeister), kuchen (cake/torte), and pasta salad. (Pasta salad?). Christian had been a volunteer in the Drömling several years back and the Scholz family became good friends of his. Good people…and they treated us like royalty.

We ended up staying for a family reunion type party, during which we waxed rather "besoffen" (drunk). Had a wonderful time! I proved rather a novelty. Not many Americans travel these backroads. Here, as in several other places we've visited, I ended up in a deep conversation about life with the lady of the house. Seems to be a common theme with me. A common theme among the men was that of discussing/reminiscing about East German times. Most of them believed that life was better under the old regime. Rising prices accompany rising unemployment in many parts of the former East Germany, this one included. Also, this is farming country and with the European Union, German farmers find it difficult to compete in the changing market.

My perception of East Germans changes with each new group I meet. Yes, I liked them from the start, but I definitely find myself warming up to them even more so. I see very strong family values in most people, much stronger than in most of the U.S. in my opinion. Our ride back to our temporary home in the park headquarters after the party proved interesting. The storm had abated and all smelled fresh and clean, not that we could notice very well as drunk as we were.

23 July

I'm at Christian's parent's house in Halle. I find it interesting that his parents are so concerned about where I want to sit to write. It's been a major topic of conversation since breakfast. Christian, his dad, and I went to the neighbor's and helped him install a beam in the old barn he is renovating to become a house. Neat place with incredible woodwork. He's an unemployed carpenter and therefore he's been doing most of the construction himself with the assistance of his son.

The neighbor had just returned from vacation in Bayerische Wald (the Bavarian Forest). He made the astute observation that the "trails" in West German parks are so often asphalt and not "real" trails. A good point. It seems that in the interest of making everything "safe" and "pleasant" for visitors we so often separate ourselves from nature. We put in a handrail or pave a path or road. We make the crooked straight and the narrow wider. We put in trams and buses. OK, in some cases these are good things, but think about it. Is an asphalt path really any safer than a dirt one? Do handrails actually protect us from falling? Sometimes yes, but I've observed on many occasions people at the Grand Canyon who view railings as something over which to climb. They become playthings, obstacles to overcome, challenges of the physical world with which to test our limits. Is that really safer? Maybe if we put a wall like the Berlin Wall all around the Grand Canyon with peep holes through which people can peer, maybe then will we make it really safe, but when one learns of all the people who found ways to cross the Berlin Wall at great risk to themselves, merely to experience the possibility of more freedom, then one can only conclude that such a wall around the canyon would only produce a similar response. People in the interest of experiencing a "free" Grand Canyon, would find ways to try and cross the walls and some would still fall to their deaths. I have no doubt of that. And people would shake their heads and say "How stupid! Why can't they just look through the window like the rest of us?"

Why indeed! It's because life is really not safe. We all face the likelihood of dying one day whether we like it or not. As an old saying goes "A ship in a harbor is safe, but that's not what ships are for." So it is that the safer we try to make our lives the less meaning and fullness of experience they seem to contain. We need to venture out of the harbor. That, I believe, is a primary aspect of "living" as opposed to "surviving." Actually I believe it's likely that by trying to make life safer, we are really doing the opposite. The apparent safety of a wide, paved path through the forest has a tendency to make us feel less responsible for our own safety, in essence a false sense of security. By shortening the distance we must walk we often tend to get complacent about exercise and just moving our bodies in general which in turn has the impact of reducing the general health of the population. We ask for the rising cost of medicine. "Doctor make me well" instead of "Self, take responsibility for your own health." That's not to belittle the advances of modern medicine by any means, but I know that it's a constant struggle to keep myself fit. It's so easy to say "I'll drive there" when I really could walk or ride a bike. I find myself sometimes driving up to a beautiful overlook and looking from my car, but when I get out and walk is when I feel that I've really experienced a place. It doesn't have to be a megahike either. Just getting out and moving with the flow of it for a short while is enough to put me more in tune with the place, myself, and my own health. Oh, how simple it all sounds on paper!

23 July

Reflections on our Berlin Trip

Arrived Wednesday afternoon. It was warm in Berlin, warm the entire time, actually. I called Anja, who I had known from the Grand Canyon, and went outside to wait for her. There I was accosted by 2 teenage girls dressed better than me begging for money. Sorry, not giving right now. Saw a good Brazilian group at the Tempodrome that night. It's an outdoor music 'hall,' for lack of a better term, in the park not far from the Reichstag (parliament building). The next day I photographed the Reichstag and Brandenburger Tor before going to the Pergamon Museum where I saw an amazing display of ancient sculptures and sections of buildings from Greece, Rome, Syria, Babylonia, etc. It was wonderful and very impressive.

Found myself starting to think about life and what it means, as well as what future archeologists will find from our 'civilization.' What will they say about our lives, gods, etc.? In a nutshell, I got to thinking how these people spent their entire lives sometimes working on a temple. A king would say "We need this" and masses of people would toil to produce huge stone buildings so that they can end up in a museum somewhere with tourists going "Isn't that something, Harry?!" But it's what we do.

Anja and I met Grit on Thursday evening for a dinner at an Indian Restaurant and a walk along the East Side Gallery. That's a piece of 'The Wall' with fabulous artwork painted across it. It blew me away. Many of the pieces were beautiful and quite thought provoking. Lots of political satire, like the painting of Erik Honneger and Nikita Kruschev kissing. Some was just plain funny.

Friday I had a wonderful breakfast and conversation with Anja before going to Checkpoint Charlie. In the past it was the entry/exit point for traveling between East and West Berlin, but now it's a museum which has exhibits and artwork depicting human rights struggles around the world. Quite impressive and emotionally both draining and, in a way, uplifting. That night we went to Tacheles*, an East Berlin alternative bar/gathering place, mostly outdoors, that looked like it was something out one of the 'Mad Max' movies. Quite a scene! Saw an amazing fire breathing show there as people gathered around old buses and cars strewn across an open area between 2 nearly abandoned buildings. It had an apocalyptic feel to it.

Yesterday went to Potsdam and Sanssouci, the palace of Frederick the Great, King of Prussia, for a look at how the Kaisers lived in total contrast to the Tacheles scene. Later I hopped on the train and was off to Halle where Christian and I ate at the Tibetan kneipe (café). Neat place. Had some funny train mixups, but we eventually made it to his place outside of town. And here I am.

Here in Halle, Herr Stolberg is outside working in his garden attempting to make everything perfect. What's the difference! It's all so fleeting like the building of those stone structures that now sit in a museum. Maybe the meaning in life lay not so much in what we do as in how we do it and what we learn from it. Is our piece of the world... I was about to ask "Is it better for our having lived?" But that's really not such a major thing. Maybe the question is "Have we found ourselves and our connections to the continuity of life? Have we learned who, and what, we really are?" Ah, kvatsch!

---

* Kunsthaus Tacheles has its own page on Wikipedia. Interesting place.

26 July

Dresden. At Silvia's. Waiting around to leave for Oberlausitz. Arrived about 21:45 on Sunday and came here to Silvia and Torsten's place. Nice place. Very clean, which doesn't surprise me. In the Leipzig Bahnhoff, Christian dropped his saddlebags and broke his water bottle. There was water and glass all over his stuff. Nothing seriously ruined, but it was not a good night for him. Monday we toured Dresden. It's still a beautiful city in spite of the 'Zerstörung' in 1945 when the U.S. bombed the hell out of the city after the war was basically over. Of course it was war and it didn't matter that this part of Germany didn't support the German war effort. So far I like it better than any German city I've seen with the possible exception of Freiburg am Breisgau. Great sculptures! Took a few photos of them, including some representing the 'old time religion' such as Pan and Dionysus. Monday night ate some carrot 'pancakes' which were really good. I've got to try making those. Yesterday we did a hike with Jan, Stephanie, and Tobias (our guide) in Sächsische Schweiz (Saxon Switzerland) National Park, near the Czech border. Beautiful forest lands with impressive, steep sandstone cliffs and monoliths. I loved the hike which ended in typical German fashion: drinking beer at an Imbiss (food & drink stand) along the river Elbe.

27 July

Started the day out with biking to some of the Teichs (ponds) in the Oberlausitzer and did bird watching. Stopped at the office for the Biosphere Reserve and had a chat with one of the guys there. Here we were in this warm, stuffy room, listening to this guy ramble on (most of which I didn't understand) and after biking 15-20 km. I started falling asleep, which seems to happen a lot these days.

After lunch we hiked the 'Nature Trail' which was supposed to be 6.5 km and turned out to be 13 km. Silvia acted as guide with a brochure from the office. Poor job of a nature trail. The second info sign came after about 3 km, some of it beating through thickets of stinging nettles over

2m high. Good thing I don't usually react to stinging nettles. Swam a little that night in a beautiful pond.

28 July

We headed back to Dresden. Stopped in Bautzen to try and see a traditional 'Sorbish' community, which are a Slavic minority in Germany, the only official traditional ethnic minority in the country. The city itself was a Sorbish community, but today is almost entirely full of ethnic Germans. We eventually found one when we happened upon a community sign in a language that looked Slavic. Not too much to see, but at least we can say we were there Coming back into Bautzen we saw the town wall and towers, a very stately impressive sight! Quiet ride back to Dresden. We were all tired.

August 1995

2 August

Arrived at the isle of Ruegen yesterday then we rode our bikes to Jasmund National Park. Actually felt good to ride. After eating virtually no lunch, we hiked with Urta and Monika, two volunteers in the park, to Sassnitz, about 8.5 km or more. Beautiful beech tree forest atop white chalk cliffs dropping down to the Baltic Sea. Had a great time! We ate fresh fish right off the boats in Sassnitz. We were famished. Then we made it to the bus stop about 10 minutes after the last bus to Jasmund, so we had to walk all the way back. Went through a Tierpark (zoo) that had a very small pen with 4 wolves. I howled and they responded. That amazed my hiking companions. Didn't have the heart to tell them that wolves in captivity will howl to police sirens as well, although I do a pretty convincing wolf call. Had wonderful talks with Urta and Monika along the way, especially sitting atop the Koenigstuehl, a rock promontory of white chalky limestone overlooking the sea.

3 August

After a short sleep and breakfast, I went to the Herthasee (Lake Hertha). She was a Slavic goddess, I believe, and I had to take photos to show my Aunt Hertha. I did yoga in the woods, stretching and breathing deeply among the beech trees, which felt good. I needed it. We got a late start to Lauterbach to catch the ferry.

After lunch in Sassnitz we made a stop in Bergen. It was a long, hard ride for us, but we made it in time to catch the ferry with Matthias (another intern). It was a birthday ferry for his boss and we enjoyed free beer and kuchen (cake) as the boat slowly made its way around the island. We went to the Isle of Vijlm, a beautiful place where Matthias worked, with some of the most impressive old oak trees I've seen anywhere in the country. One of the reasons there are still some old growth trees on the island is that during East German times, this was a vacation spot for Erich Honecker and other leaders of the country. Few people were allowed here and the island was not to be found on any official maps. An interesting note is that there are wild pigs on the island of Ruegen about 2 km away. During the autumn when the oaks on Vijlm are dropping their acorns, the pigs swim across the strait from Ruegen to Vijlm, eat all the acorns they can, then swim back again. Happens every year. Matthias impressed me as he showed us around the island. He walked barefoot, bouncing and dancing about in a manner I've seen few Germans do.

Took the ferry to Lauterbach then the train to Altefaehr where I found a comfy site in a campground. I went to what supposedly is the largest Medieval Fair in Europe, which was wonderful. Interesting that here they call it a "Medieval Fair" and in America we call it a Renaissance Fair" even though much of it is very similar. I also noticed that only a handful of people did nearly all the entertainment: music, fire show, jousting, etc. I liked the Spilwut stage show on Walpurgisnacht in Schierke better, but this was quite good. I was spotted by Ina, a student at the Community College in Wernigerode who worked selling mead and other drinks there. I spent quite a bit of my time at the fair talking with her. She won't be back to Wernigerode until October anyhow, which is when I leave. I thought that I would like to work in a show like that, but I get the impression that it's not as glamorous or even as much fun as it sometimes seems.

17 August

Thursday of last week I had a good interview with a woman from a Leipzig radio station. My German was up to the cause and the interviewer was "gentle" with me: speaking slowly and distinctly and staying away from more difficult aspects of the language. After the interview I hiked up to the beautiful "Zeterklippe," then finished my hike at a party of many of the park personnel. It took place at a covered picnic area in the forest, a pretty spot called "Molkenhaus." I was expected to eat lots of meat and drink lots of beer and "Apfelkorn," a sort of apple liquor that tastes wonderful. I was up to that task as well.

An interesting group dynamic presided. I noticed that all the men drank beer and all but one of the women drank wine. Erich, the quiet ranger, expressed an interest in hiking with me and discussing the "old days" of the forest. He's been hiking these mountains his entire life and has much to tell, from what I can gather. Gunther and the Chief (the Superintendent) got into a raging argument regarding park policy. The Chief is more of a politician in his approach, and Gunther comes from a scientific background and is a man of very high ideals. The argument ended with Dr. Sacher starting a sing-a-long of traditional German songs.

One of the secretaries steamed during the party because she wanted to go home, but nobody would take her. I sort of made eyes with one of the other office women and we all got pretty drunk. Then, when night fell with a loud crash, we all piled into the cars and headed back to town. We made it safely, much to my surprise, and Friday became a wasted day for us all. I went to the office in the morning. Few people had shown up for work. Then I visited the market in the town square before heading home for a nap. And a good time was had by all.

27 August

Yesterday I visited the Middle Ages Market in Ilsenburg, part of the town's 1000th anniversary celebration. It had all the things I've come to associate with these affairs in Germany: various and sundry handicrafts, knights, fladenbrot (flatbread), met (mead), a fakir/fire show, musicians, jugglers, etc. Lots of fun, actually. It got me thinking about just why we are (and I am) so obsessed with the past.

The good old days are remembered with fondness by most people I've met. Golden oldies on the radio ('The Tears of a Clown' plays on the radio even as I write this), and museums, museums, museums galore. You name it, and somewhere, you can find a museum to it. Unbelievable just how many museums exist. Add to that all these sorts of celebrations of the past whether it's Middle Ages, Renaissance, WWII, Civil War, whatever. We are a people often so totally preoccupied with the way things used to be that we forget that we exist here today, in the present moment.

I really understand the attraction. As a kid I wanted to either be a Viking, an Indian, or a forest ranger when I grew up, depending on the year, month, day, or minute that you asked me. I've already been a ranger, although that was Park Ranger and not Forest Ranger. Close enough. But I think that Viking and Indian aren't too likely given the time and genetics of my birth, unless we have a rapid case of global socio-political change.

Certainly old songs bring back memories, nostalgia for what may have been happier days...or were they? Were the old days really happier, or are we the purveyors of very selective memories. For some, the old days may have indeed been happier, but if it was so much better back then, why did we change? If life was so good for us all, then why on Earth make the world into a place with which we seem to be so unhappy now? Hmmmmm! Maybe it's because there were enough people sufficiently unhappy that they used their opportunity and influence to make the rest of us miserable. If that's the case, then I'd like to personally thank whoever it was that decided we should be unhappy. I don't think I could live with the burden of a joyous life (this is called sarcasm). Really, I think that's part of it.

There have always been, and probably will always be, oppressed people in the world because one group of people believes they can't be happy without putting someone else down. Of course, those who are oppressed have to agree to play the game, at least to some degree. How else could you explain that a few Spaniards with swords and a couple of bullets could overthrow thousands of Aztec warriors?* Oddly enough, the so called poor, simple folk who are oppressed, often find ways to be happy, possibly based on personal relationships and contentment with what they have, not to mention that they have little to lose, and many oppressors are truly miserable, since they have a lot to lose. Hard to keep on top, you know. Got to keep watching your backside.

Am I saying that we need to oppress people to make them happy? Not in the least. Freedom is a wonderful thing, but it's not as easy as we often think. There's something called "personal responsibility" that needs to accompany freedom. That's another story, however. Back to the past for now.

I think that part of this hysterical historical obsession is that our memories tend to be rather selective. The good old days were probably not any better in many ways than life today, but we only remember the good stuff. Take the Middle Ages/Renaissance craze for instance. Do we really want to go to one of these festivals to be with people at close range who haven't bathed in a year? Or how about defecating out behind the house – and I don't mean in a chemical toilet? Do you want to go to a 15th century surgeon for a little blood letting with an unsanitized knife? I think not. So it's not a *real* old time experience. Then there's the fact that we go back home to the TV and central heating when it's finished. At least most folks do.

However, there are some things that make sense about our fascination with years gone by. It's fascinating to learn how our ancestors lived and experienced life. We descended from that bunch of folks who chiseled the statue, crafted the blade, and plowed the field. There's something in those museums that is a part of all of us. Could be some sort of biochemical/physical memory involved. A geneticist would have a field day with that one. Many people harbor deep longings for a simpler life, for the life as Grandpa knew it, maybe not the 'carrying water every day and riding

---

* I recommend *Guns, Germs, and Steel* by Jared Diamond for more perspective on that.

wooden wagons sans shock absorbers' type of life, although some have returned to such an existence. It seems that Joni Mitchell was right when she wrote "You don't know what you've got 'til it's gone."

Change happens; it's inevitable. We can't truly go back. It just ain't gonna happen, but with a little effort, soul searching, and creativity, maybe we can learn from the very good things that our ancestors had and find a simpler, more fulfilling life while avoiding some of the extreme pitfalls of days gone by. Like maybe it is better to bring a cloth shopping bag like Grandma had than to use all those endless paper or plastic ones that pile up in the kitchen cupboard until they reach critical mass and you either get rid of them or they smother you when you open the door. Besides saving on resources, cloth bags are much stronger. Simple toys, including homemade ones, are not only less expensive, but they may also develop a child's creativity more effectively than many of today's complex electronic games. I have watched children lose interest in the latest whizbang toys and go back to blocks, Lincoln logs, and simple dolls that can't pee when you push the right button.

The number of so-called 'time and work saving devices' has gotten to the point that we frequently have to spend more time working to pay for them, learning to use them, and finding storage space for them, than we did completing the work by hand before. Computers, for example, are great devices. (This is being transcribed on a computer from the original pen and ink writing). I love them, but I've seen people in offices spend more time trying to use the 'new, improved versions' than it would have taken them to do it on the old one. We've reached the point in our technological/sociological development that 'contentment' has suffered at the hands of 'progress,' and yet the two are not mutually exclusive. Where will it all end?! How much is enough?

Maybe it's time that instead of pushing ahead for technological progress, we learn to use what we have, combined with the lessons of the past, to make a more fulfilling & healthy existence. We've reached the point where technology is often decreasing rather than increasing our quality of life and health. Life is in many ways too easy – not enough exercise, not enough grit to hone the blade.

Finding the balance between the present and the past is not a challenge to take lightly. It means that we actually have to slow down and examine where we are, how we arrived, and what's really important in our lives. It means learning to stop, look around, and take a step backwards when necessary. It means accepting the idea that just because we can do something, doesn't necessarily mean that we should do it.

Of course it's easier to kick back and watch TV, so I think I'll do just that. Hmmmm! The TV doesn't seem to be working. I could get it fixed. Not likely on a rainy Sunday night. I could go out to a movie or a video arcade. Not in Wernigerode, Germany, at 11p.m. I guess I'll just have to pick up a pen and some paper…and start writing.

September 1995

During September I finished up my duties at the park and prepared to leave, although I returned for a gathering of the national park interns later. I provided a report to the park administration and did some storytelling at a public meeting for the park as well. I told stories of my experiences in American national parks, including some of my Alaska exploits. A reporter was there and her article ran the headline "Mosquitoes are worse than Grizzly bears, says American park ranger." Other than that, September seems to have passed by too quickly to write about.

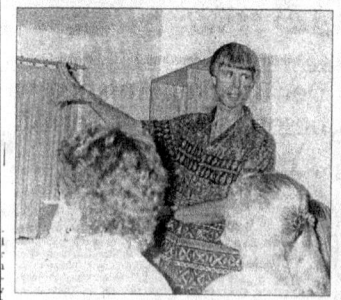

Article from a local newspaper about a presentation I gave on US national parks.

October 1995

1 October

Prague Sunday morning. I'm in a Tchibo (German chain) café by the Narodní Muzeum (national museum) looking out the window at a statue of King Vaclav on his horse. I've found most Czechs thus far to be very nice, but in the heavy tourist areas there's an air of shortness or resentment in their manner. Still getting used to it, I guess. It may be understandable given the number of Americans that live here, over 20,000 I'm told. I often find myself not knowing what language to speak. Some people know English. Some know German, although many don't want to speak it. I try Czech sometimes, but occasionally I open my mouth and a jumbled mass of consonants punctuated with a vowel or two proceeds forth, greeted either with laughter and smiles, or with that "Oh my god he's trying to speak our language" look. The city itself is truly beautiful and stately, a wealth of striking architecture and vibrant with arts and crafts, street musicians, theater (which I have yet to experience due to dwindling funds). The place is teeming with life, with vitality.

Prague is remarkably clean for a city of its size (about 1.2 million) and appears rather safe. I've had the chance to see quite a lot of the city, but have yet to see a "bad" part of town, although the southwestern corner with its Soviet Era apartments is not particularly beautiful. Still, for an apartment area it's not all that bad. I came upon it when I took the subway out to the last stops in all directions just to see what I would find there. The mass transport system is incredible. I've only used the subway thus far, but I see buses and trains everywhere. Haven't figured them out quite yet, but the underground is fast, frequent, and gets me to where I can walk just about anywhere. The central stations are a maze though, tough to find your way around at first. The escalators there are so high you could get serious vertigo from the top.

Later:
In the cathedral of the Prague Castle. Like many cathedrals and churches I've seen in Europe it's a real circus atmosphere, although this

one seems more so than most. This is a huge, impressive structure with very colorful stained glass windows. I can understand why people want tours and pictures etc., but I know that if this were my place of quiet religious contemplation I wouldn't want such a crazy scene in it. "Oh look Robert, it's a bishop!" That just doesn't sit well with me, nor does it foster a meditative atmosphere, but then, when you think about it, this is/was more a political than a religious structure in many ways.

At the time they built this cathedral, the church was the primary political entity or at least an important part of the political system. When you read through history you often find "Bishopships" and the like being set up in this place or that to establish the power of the church. That's political power we're talking about, and had nothing to do with saving souls. Still doesn't for that matter. So in spite of all the religious symbolism in this structure and in spite of its ability to "inspire," it remains a government structure tucked away in the midst of the castle with the royal palace next door. Still, I do hope that some people can gain spiritual worth between these "hallowed walls," all tape recorders, flashing cameras, and shouting tour guides aside, and in spite of the centuries of negative energy due to the church's oppression of the masses and attempts to keep us in the Dark Ages. It truly IS a beautiful building and just about the only way that it can be kept in such fine condition is through the money they receive from tours and the sales of books, film, trinkets, etc. And yes, I'd love to take some photos in here, but I will not out of respect for those who may come here for refuge.

Later still...

Sitting in the "Globe," an American/English coffee house in Prague. After that last writing I took a hike to the top of the hill across from the castle. I came to a park, Malo Strana I believe it's called, with a model of the Eiffel Tower in it. Nice place with lots of trees and a few old stone walls scattered here and there on the hillside. It felt good to get out and stretch my legs in the woods, although I'm not really getting tired of the narrow streets lined with tall, old buildings. It really is a beautiful city. I walked very quickly back to the castle to catch a concert. I thought it cost 150 koruna, but it turned out to cost 350, so I didn't attend. It's hard traveling on a very limited budget, as I always do. Instead I sit here checking out the scene, which seems pretty neat to me.

Most people in this café are Americans, but I'm sitting across from a nice young British lass who has lived here for 2 weeks. She's catching up on her letter writing. Teaches English and French at the London University here and likes it very much so far. On my way to the castle this a.m. I met a man, Bob, from Edmonton, Alberta. He was born here, and is back to visit for the 3rd time since the wall fell. He likes Prague and says that it seems to get better every year. He admitted, however, that it remains crazy to get anything official done. Old habits die hard. He said it's just like what Kafka wrote about. I've got to read Kafka. And more Kundera. And see the Kundera movie again ("The Unbearable Lightness of Being"). So here I sit with the dim lights, the smoke, and the sound of the espresso machine. I'm in Praha, the 'Paris' of the 1990s. The place to be.

4 October

On the train from Tábor to Bechyně in the Czech Republic. This was the first electric train in the Austro-Hungarian Empire, so I've been told. Across from me sit two old ladies chatting. They're happy to see one another. The train is clean, but old and not by any means spotless. In other words, just about right for me. A distinct scent of human bodies greets my nostrils, which I much prefer over the heavy perfumes that so permeate close quarters in many places. Outside I see rolling farmlands punctuated occasionally with towns, farmhouses, and groves of pines, birches, oaks, and horse chestnuts, the latter of which have taken on the multi-hued coats of early Autumn. I've been treated well here in Tábor. Today I figured out the train system enough to get on this one for a day trip to a small town, the sight of a mineral spring spa along the Lužnice River southwest of Tábor in central Bohemia. My friends have told me that Bechyně is a wonderful place, and I'm sure they are right. They haven't steered me wrong yet.

Later:

Sitting on the banks of the Lužnice River in Bechyně. I can hear the rush of the river rolling over a low dam just downstream from where I sit.

It forms a constant backdrop to the symphony of the town: a saw cutting firewood, hammers pounding, dogs barking, and cocks crowing. Someone tell the roosters that the day is getting on towards sunset. The music is that of a town renovating after years of neglect, one with an agricultural bent and appearing generally peaceful. The old, tattered buildings are receiving new support and a fresh appearance in this medieval place. Trees have begun changing as Autumn progresses, the vines that decorate their trunks already sporting a deep reddish purple. The air smells fresh and clear with a few whiffs of smoke from ever present charcoal home furnaces. Certainly it does not have the more serious pollution problems of the larger cities.

The temperature right now feels just about perfect for sitting on this park bench wearing a long sleeved shirt as shadows lengthen in late afternoon light. The sky above shines a radiant blue, a few high clouds sailing past in the distance. Up from the river on either side rise steep, rocky, forested cliffs. Not all that high, but enough relief to impress in a pleasant way. Not high enough to tire me out as I ascend. What can I say? The scene is idyllic to me now, and I feel glad and lucky to sit here. I deserve it.

I think to myself that I'd like to live here. Not an easy life I'm sure, but a good one. I know that not every day is like this, but several per year to refresh me would be all I require. Then I remember how it feels to stand at the rim of the Grand Canyon, my home if I even have one, as the sun sets on cold, clear winter evenings, painting the staggering cliffs with an infinite array of colors. I recall the powerful feeling of wildness and wilderness in Denali National Park, Alaska, as I stood next to a yearling moose freshly brought to its end by wolves just a short time before. Then there were the warm summer nights spent walking the calm, dark streets of my urban Wisconsin birthplace. And the majesty and awe I've felt as I stood next to Giant Sequoia trees in the Sierra Nevada Mountains of California. All of these experiences and many others are so dear and important, even vital to me. The makings of a full life…or several for that matter.

I think about all of these experiences and it occurs to me that I don't want much…I want it all. I want to live everywhere. Every place I've visited or lived has so much that is beautiful in spite of the harsh realities that they can also bring. I ponder where I want to live only to realize that I don't really know. It's all, the entire world, a place I want to call home. Then I realize that it IS all mine, the highs, the lows, the Springs, the Autumns, the rivers, the deserts, the mountains, the trees – those magnificent trees – all of this is mine. And none of it is mine. It's here. It is. As I am.

I will not get everywhere in this lifetime, at least I hope not. And if I never traveled again it would be OK. To know it exists is all I really need. Of course, experiencing it firsthand ain't bad either. But wherever I stand, there is beauty and the richness of life if I just open myself to it, to those infinite possibilities. Tucked inside the eye of the storm of our daily lives, there is always a place of peace. As I sit here watching the river, I know that I can be patient. For I will experience it all in its own good time. Just like the river. It is always here, and yet it moves on, becomes a lake, becomes a sea, becomes air, becomes rain and snow, becomes soil, becomes tree. It lives in that it gives life to all on this, the water planet. River is not just hydrogen and oxygen in a chemical pairing. River is also spirit. It moves ever onward, but is always here. Am I really any different?

And later still…

Laying in yet another temporary bed as is so often the case for me. Karel found me a room in a college dorm in Tábor, which suits me just fine. I have had a good time here so far in spite of a sore throat and the feeling that a cold is just around the corner. I will attempt to keep it there.

Karel Daňhel, my contact here, is a wonderful man, full of life and proud of his heritage. He has been a big help, but Alena, my "teacher," has been wonderful. She has spent much time with me helping me to learn Czech and showing me around. I truly appreciate it. Alas, but she's married and has a child. Probably a good thing for me anyhow. She likes to ski and jump from airplanes. She and her husband, who's a pilot, built a plane. Or maybe it was a glider – but still…!

Communications have been a challenge. Karel speaks some English, as does Marko, a friend of Alena's. Most of my time has been spent with Alena, who speaks no English or German, but I find it amazing how much we can communicate just by passing my Czech-English dictionary back and forth.

Tábor is a nice place. Generally quiet, as far as I can tell, and old.

Walking through the streets the other night I got the feeling that it is like the Hopi villages back in Arizona in many ways. The smell of charcoal burning in their stoves, narrow dirt or cobblestone streets lined with old, worn houses, the sounds of children playing, and the setting on a hill (or mesa) are things they share in common. Good feeling. Good place. Good people. Good night.

Several days later…I've lost track of the date:

Alena just left. Life is strange and wonderful as the last few days have shown. Take yesterday, for example. Alena picked me up in the morning and we went to her school where I did a program for the kids. I told a story of why the leaves change color, most of it in my broken German, which a teacher then translated into Czech for the children. I then used them to "build a tree," one child as heartwood, three as cambium, 5 as phloem, etc. I think the children felt a bit shy as this tall, skinny, long-haired American spoke to them in unfamiliar words, but I think they liked the experience. The school principle, who lives next door, showed me her collies, poodles, and golden retrievers. And a good time was had by all, bark, bark!

Then Alena and I prepared for a bike ride with her friends Marko and Zdeněk along the Lužnice River to a ruin called, I think, Přižnice. We had an enjoyable ride on the trail there, which proved a test of my fear factor and my concentration. Not that it was dangerous or anything, it's just that I'm not the most competent bicyclist and the trail was narrow and lined with slippery rocks. Beautiful place, good company.

We set up a picnic on the hilltop, roasted weenies wrapped in bacon over an open fire and drank some fine Czech beers. Far cry from the old "vegetarian park ranger" I used to be. At 5:50 p.m. I asked how long the ride back would take. "An hour or so," replied Marko. I then explained that I had to get to the theater by 7 to meet Dr. Bummerl. Apparently Alena thought that I was to meet him the next day, so after a little bantering back and forth, we packed our things and took off leaving behind a partly dowsed fire.

We rode in the darkening evening with only a dying flashlight for illumination. Had to stop for every car because a police car had been around and we didn't want to get into trouble with them for riding without lights while under the influence of alcohol. Apparently the police try to act as if they were still in a soviet state. When we could we traveled as fast as the bikes would go, while barely able to pick out the road in the darkness. Found a police road block and walked the bikes around it.

Finally we arrived at Tábor and my friends discussed the plan. We made it to the theater a bit late and looking a little the worse for wear. Watched Dr. Bummerl's program on Mt. Kilimanjaro and met the good Dr., one of the country's leading ecologists, after the talk. He invited me to his school the following day and we made plans to rendezvous early in the morning. Then we went out drinking with the gang.

At the bar I met a guy named Tony, who is into living history, but not Czech history: Cowboys and Indians. He showed me photos of his tepee and cabin (Fort Manitoba) at one of their gatherings, as we drank Budvar beer, the original Budweiser. The Czechs invented pilsner, which is named after the city of Plsen just west of Prague. Their beers are some of the finest I have ever tasted. They also make a fine liquor I've never seen before called Becherovka, which is made from the waters of the Karlovy Vary mineral spring spa. The stuff is fantastic, and of course great for your health. Packs a punch, however.

After a couple of pints, we roamed back outside and onto the town square where we blew Marko's trumpets until the police stopped by and told us to shut up. He had wanted to haul us in, but when he found out Marko was a respected artist and businessman in town, he let us go. Got to sleep at about 1:00 a.m. and had to awaken by 6:20 a.m. to meet Dr. Bummerl.

The following day I arose in time to meet Dr. Bummerl, and we then proceeded to his school, which is a thematic middle school specializing in ecology and environmental studies. He's about 70 years old, but still one of the few esteemed ecologists in the nation. I spoke with two classes by means of Marie, an excellent interpreter (as far as I could tell), after which we headed out into the field. We visited an old peat digging area, which has been reclaimed and is now a beautiful moor-type wetland, as well as a unique area of glacial dunes and a fish pond. What they call ecology is more reclamation of formerly impacted areas and more conservation than preservation in its focus, but the places are beautiful nonetheless. I felt exhausted from lack of sleep, but we pushed ever onward.

When the afternoon with Dr. Bummerl had come to a close, he dropped me off at my dorm. I showered and went to the theater where I spoke with Karel and Alena. She and I went for some leisurely boating on Lake Jordan with Marko and his son. Then we went out to dinner, after which Alena dropped me back at my temporary home. Quite a day! Tired. Time for bed.

9 October

Sitting in a hostel in Salzburg, Austria, watching "The Sound of Music." What a bizarre concept! They show the movie every day here. I arrived in town at about 3:00-3:30 and caught a bus to the hostel, promptly missed my stop, and the rather cross driver notified me after we had left the city limits. When I boarded the bus I asked him which stop lay closest to the hostel. He told me and I took a seat. He announced every other stop, but mine. So I exited the bus and caught one going the other direction and found the correct stop. Should have trusted my intuition as I had thought it was my stop when we passed it the first time, but I had trusted the driver.

Anyhow, I am here. It is a big place with numerous guests, mostly English speaking as far as I can tell. Took a walk around the city at sunset: Beautiful! Touristy of course, but justifiably so.

This morning I caught the train from Tábor with a certain sadness. I had a great time there, although had I stayed I would have worn myself out completely. Had to change trains in Česke Budějovicé, but there was some sort of problem with it so we were ushered to a bus and driven to another stop down the line where we caught the train. Aboard the train the conductor informed me that my ticket would only get me to the Czech/Austrian border, so I had to exit the train during our stopover in Hora Dvořiště*, the last station in the Czech Republic, and buy a ticket

---

* I could give you a pronunciation for this, but it would be to no avail. Just take my word for it.

through to Linz, Austria. After that my journey proceeded smoothly until the bus fiasco in Salzburg. These bags of mine are much too heavy, so I think I'll send off another box of books to the states.

I spent my last night in Tábor with my friends, Alena, Zdeňek, and Marko. Went out to eat. Tried to find a place to dance, but Sunday night in Tábor is not happening, so we wandered the streets back to my lodgings, arriving a little past midnight, and said our sad farewells. I had a great time with those people and look forward to the possibility of seeing them again.*

10 October

Augustiner Monastery/Brewery, Salzburg, Austria. It's 3:30 in the afternoon on an absolutely perfect Autumn day, except for a bit of ever-present air pollution. I had read about this brewery in my travel guide which listed it as the best of the beer halls in town. I expected a little place with old wood carvings in a quiet monastic setting. Wrong! After I passed through the door I followed the hallowed halls and descended the stairway to the beer hall. There I found a long string of small stands selling everything from salads to bread to the ever present meat to cigarettes to popular magazines (What YOU need to know about sex!) and everything in between. They led to the line of people waiting to have their beer poured from wooden barrels: Next…next…next…etc., at a price of 24 Schillings (about $2.50 American) per half liter. Purely an assembly line beer hall. There is a room with the carved wooden walls inside, but everyone's out here in the more than ample Biergarten sitting in the shade of horse chestnut trees.

In short, the "Brothers" have quite a money-making venture going here and they know it. It only serves to reinforce my attitude about the church. Probably one of the richest organizations in the world, and not getting any poorer. I guess the money made at the high-priced stands (even by Salzburg standards) and the act of rushing the customers through

---

* I have never seen them, though Marko has a sister in Oregon and came to visit. I wanted to see him, but it never came to pass.

whilst tapping one keg after another is good for spiritual development, a form of meditation leading to spiritual fulfillment, you might say. Of course, on a less sarcastic note, it is practical. Running a monastery costs money. These days people often will not donate money unless they receive something material in return. They are less convinced that tithing will get them to heaven. I suppose it is only logical that the monks try to cash in on it. They've had a long tradition of making wine and brewing beer in monasteries. Why, I'm not certain. Maybe making wine and beer takes a lot of time and patience, which few people besides monks have. Could be that they are trying to keep the general public "well-pickled" and therefore easier to control. Or maybe it's that they like to drink the end products themselves as a form of spiritual enlightenment and desire to share it with us. This last remark is only partly sarcastic. Maybe it is all of the above and more, or maybe there is another reason that eludes me now. I do find it ironic that these "spiritual" people, our religious leaders, make money by producing a product that is one of the most abused and abusive in our society. Hmmmm! Think I'll take another drink and ponder that one for a while.

Later:
Back at the hostel where the scene downstairs is raucous. The place is rampant with the hormones of youth. It's interesting, but maybe due to all the churches I've visited in Prague and Salzburg and the nearly overwhelming array of Catholic icons, today I actually considered the possibility of becoming a monk or a minister. The idea is not foreign to me, but this time I've been considering Christianity as a viable possibility. I've previously considered Buddhist or Pagan or Taoist paths, but not Christian. It doesn't seem like such a bad life, actually. There really is an attractive comfort of sorts in a monk's life, although I know that it's not as easy as it often appears. There's a great deal of personal control and deep self-reflection involved, which is often much more difficult to face than one suspects. No heavy drinking allowed, but that's not strictly observed I know. Just look at the brewery of earlier today. Not that I bear any resemblance to a lush, however. I wouldn't get to travel the way in which I've become accustomed most likely. I could probably live with that. The

vow of chastity could be a real problem for me. I like sex and I don't think there's anything wrong with that. Mind you, I'm not a sex fiend either. Of course, Catholic monks do have a long history of breaking their own rules, so it may not be such a big deal, but still I wouldn't want to enter a monastery with the intent of breaking the rules.

What attracts me to the monastic life is that I'd really love a chance to work on my own spiritual development with my main bodily needs taken care of. It's the trials and tribulations of everyday existence, paying the bills, etc. that bother me so much, and this idea of what to do for a living is still very troubling to me. As I've thought about religions other than Christianity, the problem that one faces is the tough battle for acceptance in this overpoweringly Christian society of Europe and the U.S.. It's not easy seeking involvement in those religions, let alone finding a place to study them in depth. So why not Christianity? Well, there is the issue of hypocrisy and lack of acceptance of other paths which is often so much a part of Christianity, although many Christian monks have also delved into Eastern meditation methods, especially Zen. Then there's the dilemma that while I can accept Christian symbolism, I just don't buy it hook, line and sinker. I don't see it so much as fact, but rather as metaphor, and I don't think they want a preacher who accepts Jesus Christ primarily as a symbol for our own personal journeys. Something tells me I would run into a real buzz saw on that one when it comes to dealing with my fellow Christians, but then there is much I don't know about the monastic world... I guess I'll keep looking, wondering how I fit into this religious scene, but now it's time for bed and the world of dreams. Maybe there I can find some solace...some answers. Good night.

20 October

I met a homeless man in the bahnhof in Offenburg. He had no shoes and his feet had swollen to the size of small watermelons. I tried to give him some food. He wouldn't take it.

> *I spent a few days in Hamburg, Germany, then up to Aarhus, Denmark,*

where I visited a large, mostly open air Viking museum. After that I took the ferry from Denmark to England and caught a train from the coast to Cambridge, after an intense discussion with an immigration officer who seemed to think I wanted to stay and soak up social welfare.

31 October

Happy Halloween!!

Cambridge...I'm in frigging Cambridge...Wild! Took a walk down to the old town and college area. Unbelievable! Fairly clear half moon night with groups of people, students most likely, walking the streets, some in costume & many decked out in suits and ties or fancy dresses. Must be their idea of a Halloween costume.

A light fog or smog sits in the city on its little cat feet while people wearing cloaks and scarves or capes wander through the alleyways in that air of mystery I've come to associate with England from movies and mystery books. You know, Sherlock Holmes and all that rot! I understand it much more so now. Then there's the architecture ...Incredible!! From small, cozy pubs, brick buildings and alleyways, to the massive stone structures of the churches and colleges. I felt awed at the intoxicating atmosphere of the city.

I wandered through the courtyard of Trinity College and wondered to myself "How can people study here?! This isn't a college, but rather a palace! Looks more like a place where people living in the lap of luxury make decisions about what to do with the poor, than an institution of higher learning." Ah well, may their studies bear good fruit.

November 1995

1 November

My conversation with Cherry, the young Australian woman sitting behind me on the bus, came to a subtle end as we crossed the Scottish border. My first time here. Hers too, as I learned. The sun had set just before Carlisle, but a fierce red and orange afterglow outlined a rolling horizon. A layer of pensive gray stratus clouds capped the intense colors, which then gave way to pale blue melting to darkness above, streaked by faint, wisps of light pink cirrus clouds. I could find no words to adequately capture the entire scene, so I just watched. I thought to myself "There is a god, and her name is Mother Nature." Good sign as the bus rode along into this ancient land, so new to me. Another 3 hours to Edinburgh, my rest stop for the next several nights. Wednesday night on the M 74 motorway heading north.

10 November

Not a good writing situation lately: hostels generally are not conducive to it, and while I've enjoyed the bus rides, they are often too bouncy to write. Such is life. Sitting in a café in Nottingham. My bus for Bath leaves in 3 hours. My friend in this old city will not return from Morocco for a few days, so I've decided to head to Bath and the Cotswolds.

I felt sad to leave Scotland. My journey there felt somehow 'unfinished.' Three days in Edinburgh, 3 on the isle of Skye at Kyleakin, and 2 more in Edinburgh. The weather on Skye appeared as expected: cold and wet, but even given the great weather I've had for most of my journey, it still felt hard to take. Enjoyed it nonetheless. The sunlight that did find its way through the clouds to play upon the hills and lochs was very special.

My first day at Kyleakin I did a few short walks near the town. That evening I saw a familiar name on a map in the hostel: Dun Ringil. It's the name of a Jethro Tull song which talks about the old gods playing there. I decided "Why not!" The next day was Sunday and no buses run on Sundays, so I hitchhiked. Enjoyed some nice chats as several drivers each took me part of the way there. I found the spot on the road where I needed to take off down a stream course to find the site.

Dun Ringil, a prehistoric village site, sits in a high level of disrepair, but I still found it impressive. On my way there I strode past numerous highland cattle, the long haired kind, and one in particular found me fascinating for some reason. Probably doesn't see many Americans dressed head to toe in rain gear, and he followed my procession with his gaze as I ventured there and back. The site sits atop low cliffs overlooking the bay near Kilmarie. Below in the cliffs stand a natural arch and a small sea cave (a grotto actually). Right on the edge stands a low, round stone-walled structure, mostly collapsed, but with an existing doorway. I crawled through and stepped over the fallen walls to get out. Farther from the cliff edge lay some oval building foundations and a series of walls, mostly grown over with heather and grasses, the latter in a striking shade of Autumn golden brown. Hawks circled over the hillside nearby as they've done since before these walls were built, and still farther upslope stood a spruce and larch forest, a timber cutting area. As I walked around the site I tried to imagine life here hundreds (or thousands) of years ago. What comprised the daily faire of these people? What thoughts accompanied their wanderings over these hills, their hopes and dreams, their trials and tribulations?

I left the site and strode back up the stream course forested with oaks, birches, alders, and other native trees. When I reached the road I hiked up the ridge beyond it for a spectacular view of the bay, a mountain loch, a waterfall, and the cloud-bedecked Cuillen Hills. I could see why people stay here their entire lives instead of wandering the globe like this lost soul. During the hike back I noticed a small stone circle in the distance, a mostly collapsed remnant of days gone by, but instead of checking it out more closely I chose to head for the road. Good decision as not many cars ventured my way in the pouring rain and my return trip proved much longer than the way out. Darkness comes early to this ancient land in November. I left the stones in peace.

11 November (I think)

Bath, England, Youth Hostel. Just told 2 stories to a couple of Canadian girls. I had forgotten just how good it feels to tell stories. I told then the story of "Why the Leaves Change Color" and "The King's Illness," the latter of the 2 just learned from a teller named George McPherson at the Edinburgh Storytelling Festival.

Took a bus tour today, a van tour actually, to Stonehenge, Avebury, Lacock, Castle Combs, and the Cherhill White Horse. Good day. Avebury favorably impressed me quite a lot. The village sits within a very large stone circle. The stones had not been honed as those at Stonehenge, but the size of the stone circle and the general setting just took my breath away. Magnificent! I could have spent a long time there.

12 November

Walked around the beautiful city of Bath today, with its streets lined by stately Georgian sandstone buildings. As I walked I often felt glad that I had forgotten my camera, although the habit of looking for the best shot dies hard.

So what do I do when traveling like this…how do I spend much of my time? Good question. Well, what I *really* spend much of my time doing when I travel besides the obvious activities of sleeping (or trying to) and riding in buses, trains, planes, ferries, etc., is attempting to organize everything in my backpack, looking through bookstores, and searching for a good and cheap place to eat. I'm constantly trying to get all my stuff organized and packed as neatly and bomb-proof as possible. And I try to do it quietly most of the time, because it seems there's always someone sleeping in my room at whatever hostel I happen to visit. What's the quietest way to open and close a zipper, or to handle those crinkly plastic bags so often in use by the shops? My pack is so loaded down with books, so what do I do? Well, I peruse the bookstores for more books I'll never really need nor probably ever read, and I spend a *lot* more time looking at menus in windows than actually eating. Hiking? Yeah, sometimes.

Walking around town? I do a fair amount of that too. Museums? Yes, that as well, but not as much as I do the searching bit. It's the story of my life… constantly searching.

23 November

Just watched a video by the late comedian Bill Hicks. Funny in parts, but more interesting to me philosophically, really. One concept of his I liked stated:

"Matter is just energy vibrating at a slow frequency."

Well, duh!! Yes, of course I knew this from my science classes, but it never really sunk in until now and it's fascinating how life changes when you view it this way.

He also talked of life "being a ride." I like that image. It feels much easier to accept than life as a game, even though I love James Carse's philosophy.* The game image goes against that part of me which takes life too seriously, but the ride idea fits better, especially given the "matter" statement above: bouncing along on this vibrating journey. I picture myself walking, running, driving a car, etc. on the globe, which is moving continually whether we know it or not – it just keeps going.

January 1996

The Circle Closes

After spending a few weeks in Wisconsin visiting my family, I made my way back to Arizona. Here are a few thoughts on my returning.

---

* *Finite and Infinite Games* by James P. Carse, a fascinating little book of philosophy.

22 January

The circle is about to come back to its point of origin…to come round full. I'm going "home," that is if there really *is* anyplace that I can call home. Back to the city in the pines: Flagstaff, AZ. I didn't sleep well last night, which, I guess, is to be expected. I felt a certain level of excitement as I realized that I would soon see old friends, including the mountains and the ponderosas. How have they fared these last 10 months? What's new? Who's still there and who's packed up and moved on?

I also feel a lot of fear and uncertainty. Jobs, living arrangements, decisions. I know that something will work out, but the questions of what, how, when, etc. all creep into my mind. Then there are the big questions relating to the future and what direction to take. Is it now time to settle down, at least for a while? There's definitely still wanderlust in me, but maybe it's time to stay still so I can face the wanderer inside of me. It's a lot less frightening to travel to Germany, or Nepal, or Africa, than it is to travel to the depths of my soul. I recall a quote I once heard:

"And the world cannot be discovered by a journey of miles, no matter how many, but by a spiritual journey of one inch; an arduous and difficult, but also a joyous journey in which we arrive at the ground beneath our feet, and learn to feel at home."

I think that I'm well along that journey, but I need to be patient. It's coming if I'll let it.

Looks like we're flying over the Great Plains somewhere. In just over 2 hours I'll land in Phoenix. The circle comes to a close…

When I arrived back in Phoenix, Arizona, I took a bus ride to Flagstaff, about 2 hours north. The following is a little piece of amusement that I wrote on the bus.

The Bus Ride

Written 22 January 1996

I had always wondered about those signs in the bus. You know, the ones that say "For passenger safety, federal law prohibits operation of this bus while anyone is standing forward of the white line." Sometimes it's a yellow line, but that's irrelevant. I wondered just what they meant by "prohibits operation." So what the hell, I thought, how about if I try it out.

The bus was practically empty: just me, two college girls, a Mexican couple, and a shifty looking old geezer in a long, black coat sitting behind the college girls. I wouldn't endanger that many people. And me? I didn't worry; I had made peace with myself and my god. I felt ready to die.

When Larry, the driver, wasn't looking I snuck up to the next seat ahead. His eyes glanced at the mirror. I sat still, as if nothing had happened. He didn't seem to notice. His eyes returned to the road. With stealth I moved up one seat at a time until I sat right behind Larry. Then...I did it. I stood up, put one foot across the white line, and brought the other forward. And Larry? What did he do? Well, just as I had suspected, as soon as I stood across the line and without even looking at me, he took his foot off the gas, his hands from the wheel, picked up a copy of Playboy magazine, and began reading an interview with Johnny Depp. So, somebody really *does* read those articles!

The bus began to slow, but then picked up speed as it left the roadway and started down the embankment, careening across the open desert, steering controlled only by the rocks we hit, dodging between saguaro cacti (good thing, I'd hate to flatten one of those venerable old succulents), and making a beeline for a deep arroyo. The ride got a little bumpy. Larry just kept reading. I stood there watching the rattlesnakes slither for cover as we headed their direction.

Of course, after the initial shock-induced silence, the folks in the back began screaming, the old man calling out "Down in front," and the others joining him in various octaves. Well, the noise began to get on my nerves and I had rather delighted in the experience thus far, so I turned and interjected "Quiet! Just chill out and enjoy the show!" As I turned to face the passengers, my feet went back across the white line. Larry put down the magazine, calmly grabbed the wheel, and turned hard left, thereby avoiding by only a few feet the edge of the arroyo and a 30 foot descent into its arid depths. The turn came so sharp and so sudden that I lost my feet and flew headlong into the windshield.

Next thing I knew, I opened my left eye, the only one that *would* open, and took a quick inventory of my body. My legs felt a bit numb. My right hand was totally unusable and throbbed with a deep, aching pain. My head? Well...I never hung one on quite *that* bad. I could feel blood dripping across my face and onto my right shoulder. I looked up. Larry sat, face stone cold sober, looking ahead at the road rushing under our wheels. He picked up a rag and said, "Here, wipe the blood off of the windshield, please. That's a safety hazard, having a dirty windshield. Just get what you can reach. I'll get the rest."

I took the rag with my left hand and started to wipe the glass from my crumpled position on the floor. "Sure," I said, "but hey, Larry...I'm in front of the white line. How come you're operating the bus?" "You're not standing," he replied. I guess some signs are supposed to be taken literally.

When we arrived in Flagstaff, everyone stepped over me as they exited the bus, several not bothering to lift their feet high enough to clear my aching body completely. Then Larry grabbed me by the shirt collar and dragged me down the steps, my head bouncing all the way. He left me lying by my luggage and climbed back into the driver's seat. "Thanks for the ride," I said. "No problem. Have a nice day," came the reply. The door closed, and the bus pulled away.

WORKING FOR THE MLC

After I returned from living in Germany in 1995, I eventually made my way back to Flagstaff, AZ, to look for work and find a place to live. Unfortunately, that winter proved to be quite a dry one, so the ski area north of town, which usually hired many college kids from Northern Arizona University, didn't have enough business to merit taking on winter workers and therefore every possible job in town was already filled by the time I arrived in early 1996. In spite of my fairly extensive experience I couldn't even get a job as a basic cashier, so I started looking into other options. I saw an ad for a job as the Sales Manager for the Mono Lake Committee (MLC) in Lee Vining, CA, and applied for it.

The MLC is a non-profit environmental group dedicated to making sure the very beautiful and unusual Mono Lake and surrounding area remain in good, natural condition. They operate a visitor center in Lee Vining, just east of Yosemite National Park and not too far from the Nevada border, where they sell mostly books and calendars with a few t-shirts and such thrown in for good measure, and publish some of their own materials which they also sell by mail order. They flew me out to CA for an interview and offered me the position. I borrowed some money from my friend Dale, who had done well with investments, bought an old Subaru station wagon, packed up my things, and headed to Lee Vining. I rented a small A-frame cabin in the town of June Lake, just south of Lee Vining and north of Mammoth Lakes, a ski resort area in the eastern Sierra Nevada Mountains, and started to work managing their visitor center and sales operation.

Mono Lake is a surrealistic landscape tucked between the eastern Sierra Nevada Mountains and the high desert at about 6500 feet elevation. The lake itself is very salty, but years ago Los Angeles, in its never ending search for water resources, began taking it from the streams that flow into the lake. There is no outlet from this lake to the sea so the water evaporates. With less water flowing into it, the lake began to dry up, revealing the amazing sculptures that had previously stood hidden underwater. Beautiful? Yes, but the lake was disappearing, taking with it a major habitat for many animals including dozens of migrating bird species. Biologist David Gaines discovered this fact when he was studying birds there and started the Mono Lake Committee to try to save the lake from drying up the way others to the south already had. Their approach was not to make things hard for those in LA, but rather to try and help them reduce their need for water. Gaines died tragically in a car accident, but the organization he and his wife had begun succeeded in what became a great success story for the environmental movement. I had nothing to do with that, sad to say. I just ran the visitor center.

How NOT to Do a Camping Trip

My friend Chris from England came to visit me during my time living and working near Mono Lake and we decided to go for an overnight backpacking trip in Yosemite. Chris and I had worked at the Grand Canyon together, he as a volunteer and I as park ranger, and hiking in the Canyon was the only backpacking he had ever done. We took a while getting up and ready, having gone out drinking the night before. I got my big backpack loaded with tent, sleeping bag, rain gear, food, a stove I borrowed from a friend, and other odds and ends. Chris came from his room with a small day pack and the pronouncement that he was ready to go.

"Chris, don't you think you'll need a little more than that?" I asked.

"What, do you really think so?"

Chris' idea of backpacking was the Grand Canyon, which, especially in the summer, is not your typical backpacking experience. The nighttime temperatures there seldom drop below 70 degrees F, and in July and August often stay above 80. One seldom needs a tent or heavy sleeping bag. A pad, a sheet, some food, and lots of water, that's all you usually need. We, however, were headed for Yosemite and an elevation of about 9000 feet.

"Chris, we're going into the high country. Temperatures tonight will likely get pretty cold, and we will probably encounter rain. We will also need to carry a Bear Resistant Food Container, so I suggest you take your big pack."

Chris agreed, we divided up our mutually needed gear, and set off for Tuolumne Meadows and the backcountry permits office. I had already arranged for our permit and we just needed to obtain the permit and get our Bear Resistant Food Container (BRFC) before setting off to our chosen destination: Young Lakes.

By the time we went through all of this and set off on the trail, the morning had pretty well flown away. We began hiking, and all our cares dropped off like Autumn leaves, to quote John Muir. The day proved a glorious one, with a few puffy clouds, lots of sunshine, and magnificent granite peaks all around us. Some larger clouds began building to the west a long way off. We had a great hike, reveling in the beauty of it all and the feeling of our bodies moving along in the wilderness. The trail is not a particularly difficult one, not much elevation change, easy to follow, with great views, and very popular. We enjoyed each other's company and took lots of photos.

Along the way we began encountering people coming from our destination and would ask them about their experience.

"Oh, it was beautiful, but someone not far from us had trouble with bears in their food. We didn't, however."

Some people with whom we spoke didn't get away so easily. Several had lost food, and some sleep to bears. Chris' eyes lit up when he heard about that.

"I'd really love to see a bear, Tom. Wouldn't that be great!"

I've had lots of experience with bears having worked in Denali and Shenandoah National Parks, which both have large bear populations, and I like them a lot, but I also know the potential problems.

"Chris, I'm not sure that's the way you want to see a bear."
"Still, wouldn't it be great to see one."

After numerous such encounters and a great hike, we arrived at Young Lakes and found a campsite near the first of the series of small lakes. It was a secluded spot, close enough to the lake for easy water access, but far enough to hopefully remain relatively mosquito free. We set up the tent and stashed our packs in it, then found a good spot about 75 feet away for the BRFC. Then we took a few things and hiked up to a gap in the ridge line above us for a view of the surrounding area.

Camping in the highland of Yosemite with Chris.

Along the way to the gap we passed a couple of snow fields (I told you it would get cold, Chris) and scrambled up some talus slopes, eventually arriving at a spectacular viewpoint on a promontory just past the gap. We stood enthralled with the 270° view of the Yosemite high country. I could really see why John Muir had spent so much time in this magnificent place. We hung out there just enjoying the view and taking a few photos for quite a while, long enough for that bank of clouds in the west to have caught up with us. It engulfed our promontory, the winds began blowing, the temperature dropped at least 15 degrees, and light rain began to fall, pelting us with little icy pin pricks. We reveled in the storm, the power, the beauty. We pulled out our rain gear. Chris and I both had raincoats, but I also had rain pants. I gave the pants to Chris, always wanting to be the magnanimous one. I, however, am the skinny one with the thyroid condition. Light hail began to fall.

We stayed as long as we could, but finally, when my hands started to resemble claws and my legs had goosebumps the size of chicken eggs, I decided that I needed to head back to camp. Chris agreed. We made our way back to the gap, then quickly, but carefully scampered down the talus slopes. About two-thirds of the way down I finally warmed up enough to open my hands a bit. When we arrived at camp, I told Chris to go to the lake and filter some water. I decided to start a fire with the stove I had borrowed from my colleague. I had never used it before…big mistake. With hands that felt like stone I took it out, found the matches, and began pumping to get the fuel pressure up. Then I tried lighting a match. Difficult thing to do when your fingers barely function. The matches kept falling out of my hands. Even when I did manage to hold onto one, I couldn't get enough force to start a flame. I grew increasingly frustrated and cold. Finally when Chris arrived back at camp, I got enough force on a match to light it and bring it to the stove. I turned the dial and bingo, fire. And more fire. And more fire! The entire stove suddenly became covered in flames that rose several feet in the air. I sat there dazed, wondering what to do. Chris saw the small bonfire and yelled "Run, it's going to blow!"

I stepped back and together we watched the flames dance upon our lost hopes for a hot dinner. After a few minutes, Chris looked down in his hands, saw the pot of water he had just filtered from the lake, and tossed it on the fire. Disaster averted.

"I guess I pumped it a bit too much," I said shivering. Chris went for more water, and I got out the food we could eat cold and began feeding my own internal fire. That and some warm clothing brought me up to a manageable condition. We finished dinner a little after sunset, then took a leisurely walk along the lakeshore as a silver dollar moon began rising over the eastern ridge line. I felt much better and so did Chris, as the soft light skipped across ripples on the water and frogs called to one another around the high mountain valley. We crawled into our sleeping bags at 9:00 and fell into a sound sleep.

Until...

I awoke at midnight to the sound of grunting and scratching. Chris and I had placed our packs twenty feet away from the tent. I had told him to take everything out, and anything remotely aromatic should go in the BRFC. When I heard the noise, I knew exactly what was happening. I leapt out of my bag and yelled "Go on, get outa here, go on!"

Chris startled from a sound sleep and tried to get his wits about him and I continued yelling at the beast somewhere outside.

"What is it, what is it, Tom?"

"It's a bear, Chris, and he's in our packs." Then to the bear, "Go on, get outa here!"

"Don't disturb him. Maybe he'll go away." Undaunted, I continued yelling. The bear just kept scratching and grunting. I opened up the tent and went out, much to Chris' displeasure.

"What if he charges you!"

"It's OK Chris, I know what I'm doing. Go on, get outa here!" I picked up some small stones and threw one at the bear. I could see the yearling bruin by the light of the silvery moon. Chris poked his head out of the tent. While I had seen bears many times before, Chris, however, had never encountered one in the wild. He had mostly lived a city dweller's life in England, with few wildlife encounters. When he stuck his head out of the tent, what he saw was a large, black shape, with bright silver eyes glaring at him at head level, not far from his nylon shelter. I knew he could be dangerous, but not likely. Chris didn't know the "not likely" part. I tossed a few more stones.

"Oh Tom, don't do that. What if he charges!? What if he charges!?"

"Chris, he's not going to charge. It's OK. I know what I'm doing." The bear walked off. After a few moments, he returned and resumed his digging into the pack. I continued shouting at him and tossed a few more stones.

"Tom, Don't. He's Going To Charge!"

"No, Chris, he's not going to charge." I kept up my shouting and throwing stones. A few more times the bear wandered off, then returned. Then he wandered off. We waited. He didn't return. I felt the way was clear. Just as I prepared to walk over to the pack, I heard Chris' voice, low and serious.

"Tom, there's another one."

I looked to my right. 50 feet away I saw mama, and she was really pissed off. In movies when they show bears as angry, they always show them standing on their hind feet and growling. That's not what they do when upset. Standing on their hind feet is how they see better. Bears don't have great eyesight. When truly upset a bear will pace back and forth, keeping her side towards you with her back arched. Then, instead of growling, they pop their jaws. That's exactly what mama was doing, just 50 feet away. At a speed of 40 miles per hour, a common run for a bear, she could cover that ground faster than I could get the urine down my leg and into my shoe. I picked up a much larger rock.

"Don't throw it Tom."

"Don't worry, I won't. It's just in case." I began then to talk to the bear in low soft tones. I told her how we meant no harm to her boy. I told her how we were sorry. I told her whatever came to mind, but in low, soft tones. Mama kept up her pacing. Back and forth. Back and forth. Then, finally, after what seemed like an eternity, she walked off in the direction where her young boy went, and we didn't see her again.

I realized then that it was cold outside and I was standing in my underwear. I returned to the tent to put on some clothes and Chris and I walked over to our packs. Mine was pretty much untouched. Chris' pack had been slimed by the bear and had a little tear near one of the zippered pockets. He opened the pocket. It contained one empty candy wrapper. That's all it took for this young bear to go after it with such vehemence.

We then walked over to check out our BRFC, which we had placed just beyond where mama had so recently paced. It remained untouched, with every stone in place on top of it. We returned to the tent and began chatting. Chris kept on saying "Well, I don't know about you, but I know I'll never get to sleep."

I responded "I think I might get back to sleep, but I doubt if I'll sleep well given the excitement. I'm not so worried about bears, but just have adrenaline moving through me."

Chris kept repeating how he would lie awake all night worrying about the bears returning. I looked up at the full moon above us. Then I looked at Chris.

"What about hiking out by the light of the moon?" When Chris and I had worked together at the Grand Canyon, I had told him of many times I had hiked in the Canyon by moonlight alone, using a headlamp only rarely.

"Tom, I know that you do that sort of thing, but not me! What, do you think I'm crazy?"

"Chris, think about it. We've just had a traumatic incident happen. You've already stated you won't get any sleep. I won't get good sleep, I know. It's a beautiful night. Look at that moonlight shining on the trail. It's a glorious time to be out and about!"

"But what about bears!?"

"Bears are not likely to be around the trail. They're here looking for food. Do you want to wait for them?" That got him. We gathered our stuff, packed up the tent and the BRFC, did a final check of the campsite, then headed into the moonlit night.

We had an uneventful, but positively beautiful hike back to the Tuolumne Meadows area and our car. The ghostly light of Luna* cast a mystical air over the landscape. We only had to use headlamps a few times. Stopping a few times to tank up on water and eat the last of our cold food, we made it back to the parking lot just as the moon set on the western horizon and the rising sun illuminated a clear morning sky. We returned our BRFC, grabbed a welcome pancake breakfast, headed down the hill to my cabin in the woods, and collapsed in our beds.

So that's NOT how to do a camping trip...that is...unless you want a story to tell.

---

* Spanish for the moon.

Pineapple Express

The winter of 1996-97 was a cold one and very snowy. In one storm lasting about 36 hours we had 6 feet of snow fall and by the end of the week we had more than 8 feet of snow on the ground. A tractor came to plow the road in front of my place, but I was left to shovel the snow from my parking area. Try as I might, I couldn't throw the snow high enough to keep it off of the parking space. With an A-frame house I didn't need to worry about the roof collapsing, but I had to shovel stairs from the top of the snow down to my doorway. In the higher elevations they had 15-20 feet of snow fall.

Then it all changed. My supervisor and her husband went away for the Christmas and New Year holidays and asked me to stay at their house and take care of their dog. After all that snow, a weather pattern called a "Pineapple Express" came through bringing unseasonably warm and wet weather. On New Year's Eve I settled in for a good dinner and to watch the epic film "Gandhi". Earlier in the day it had begun raining, the gentle falling drops turning to a downpour as the day progressed. The warm water falling from the heavens began melting all that snow. As I ate and watched the little Indian man in white shorts become a world hero on the TV screen, I listened as the small creek, maybe a meter across in normal conditions, became a torrent carrying huge rocks that tumbled down the mountains and gave tumultuous, bomb-sounding blasts as they slammed into one another. This went on all night.

While there was some damage in the Lee Vining area, other places got really hammered by the flooding. Just north of Lee Vining near Bridgeport, CA, runs the West Walker River that flows north into Nevada. Normally it's a relatively shallow river, maybe 6-8 meters wide and fairly easy to walk across, but the waters rose to more than 3 meters above the flood level, much higher in some spots, and this quiet little river washed away cars, trucks, and double-wide trailers in the biggest flood anyone could recall. All up and down the Sierra Nevada and southern Cascade Mountains and the lands they drain into they experienced floods and landslides of historic proportion. My supervisor's return was delayed more than a week due to the flooding and damage caused by the storm. Planes couldn't land at the airport in the normally dry and dusty Reno, Nevada, due to it having become a lake. Eventually they made it back and I returned to my cabin where the parking space had been cleared of all its snow. The little A-frame was still standing.

Leaving Mono Lake

After working with the MLC for a just about a year, they decided to change the position I was in to make it involve more marketing. I'm just not into marketing, even though in this case I did believe in the things I would have been promoting. I can come up with some pretty good slogans, but much of marketing and advertising just rubs me the wrong way. That's the Luddite part of me, I guess. Even though I was loving the natural beauty of the area, in spite of the cold, I decided I would have to part ways with the MLC. I talked it over with my dad and decided to return to Wisconsin to be closer to my family. My trip to Thailand the previous winter had shown me how close families could be and I thought I wanted that. I handed in my resignation. They had a small going away party for me and I set off the next day, but first shared with them this little essay:

Departing Thoughts

Tonight I said "Goodbye" to Mono Lake. True, I'm not leaving for two days yet, but I figured this would be my best time for a quiet time at the lake. After a walk around the rim of Panum Crater, something I've wanted to do since I arrived here and and finally got around to doing, I headed over to South Tufa. I drove unhurriedly, taking in the scene as I went along. The sun had just passed behind the Sierras between Mt. Gibbs and Mt. Dana and the world of shadows was beginning to overtake the Basin. The gravel road to the South Tufa parking area was in remarkably good condition given the kind of winter it's been. Just as I parked the car and began to head down the trail to the lake, stratus and lenticular clouds over the mountains began catching fire, the reds and pinks intensifying with each step. I quickened my pace. As I passed winterized rabbit brush, desert peach, and signs from previous lake levels (1959 – 6400 feet, 1963 – 6392, etc.), the western sky was coming alive in a torrent of color. I could see the array of shades reflected in the choppy, cold water of the lake, sharp contrast to the muted tones of post-sunset overcast skies in the Basin. I arrived at the lakeshore just after the blaze hovering above the mountains peaked, but the display of color was still nearly beyond belief. In awe I sat between tufa towers just absorbing the magnificent scene changing moment by moment. I stayed there until the reflection was nearly gone from the water, returning it to its algae-laden green hue, before I knelt closer to the water. I desired to taste it one last time. I dipped my finger tips into the cold brine, closed my eyes and brought my hand to my lips. I sucked every last drop from my fingers, caressing my own flesh with my tongue as I reveled in the bitter flavor of the salty water. It was like the taste of a lover's sweat and I was filled with a sensuous feeling of the lake as my partner. The lake became woman. And I realized then the extent not only of how she had been violated, but also how she, like many an abused lover, had begun to grow strong once again. For as long as she has the support of those who love her she will flourish with a renewed determination. I stood in the cool night air and said "Farewell". I turned toward my car, and began walking, the sand and stones crunching under my feet as the evening chill enveloped me. While I know that leaving is not only inevitable and soon for me, but also the best move at this point in my life, still I grew sad. I am leaving another friend, another very special place, another home, and venturing again to uncertainty. But that is the path I am on and I accept it. A breeze blew off the lake and kissed the back of my neck ever so gently. Then, like me, it was gone.

Written 25 February 1997

As it turns out I didn't stay long with my family. They didn't view the closeness thing I had seen in Asia in the same way I did. Thailand is a far away place in more than just distance. After staying in my hometown for a few weeks I found a job working at a nature center a few hours away near the Wisconsin Dells, a famous tourist area. The center had been started by and still served an organization called the 4-H, but we had people, children from many places come for either day trips or residential stays in the dormitories. When the season ended there in November, I decided to go stay with another part of my family, my sister Pat in North Carolina. So eventually I headed south and east for warmer weather and a different accent.

Thailand, December 1996

40 Hours in Thailand

In the distance come strains of modern-influenced, but nonetheless mostly traditional Thai music, as I lay myself down on the floor after a long day. I'm barefoot and wearing lightweight pants and a t-shirt ... and I'm comfortable. It's a far cry from the 10oF at June Lake,CA, when I left a few days ago. I'm at Doi Luang, near the northern tip of Thailand. It's paradise compared to Bangkok, but then it may be in some ways considered paradise when compared to most of the world.

My first impression of Bangkok was an interesting one. I had traveled there as an air courier, even though I ended up with nothing to transport. I guess they just wanted people to travel everyday and I got lucky, so I got a cheap flight with a layover in Tokyo, nearly all paid for, and didn't have to do anything for it. Once there I met with my German friend Birgit and a fellow American named Carol. We had all worked together at the Grand Canyon previously, Birgit and Carol as volunteers and me as a ranger.

Carol arranged for a taxi to take us to our guesthouse. She sat up front with the driver, who was moving along city streets at a rapid pace. They were talking. Carol began to get agitated. "Blah, blah, blah, service charge, ka. Blah, blah, blah, blah, ka," in fluent Thai. The driver, too, began to get agitated "Blah, blah, blah, blah, service charge, krap!", and the speed and recklessness of his driving increased in direct proportion to his increasing conversational fervor. Carol explained that he wanted to charge us 50 Baht extra for airport fees, but she knew that they were not supposed to do that and refused to pay it.

Before long he was taking us on a hell ride, passing cars by inches, rounding corners nearly on 2 wheels (I'm not exaggerating about that), alternately putting the pedal to the metal and slamming on the brakes, and several times scrunching us into closing spaces between 2 merging vehicles, missing them by less than a foot. I've seen some reckless drivers and I've been through police driving school, but he was definitely the worst I've experienced. When we arrived at our stop the driver slammed on the brakes, jumped out and threw our luggage on the sidewalk, Carol paid him, and he sped away. After a few minutes our sphincters began to relax, and our knees stopped shaking long enough to carry our things inside.

We got our backpacks, settled into our rooms, had our introduction to Thai toilets (if you can't squat, you're outa luck), and took a bus to go get some dinner. The bus driver had apparently been to the same school as our cab driver, but we nevertheless arrived in one piece. I was so looking forward to tasting some real Thai food, but Carol explained that she ate Thai food everyday and so would we, so therefore we ate at an Indian restaurant for my first night in Thailand. When we entered the foyer of the place, about 5 young Thai lads accosted us with cell phones exclaiming "You want call America, 50 Baht. You want call home, 50 Baht." We declined. I, for one, had no inclination to do so. The food was excellent, although I was still a bit hungry, so when we were back on the street I picked up a water buffalo satay from a street vendor. Tasty, but rather greasy. Back at the guesthouse, sleep came quickly. Jet lag.

In the morning we visited the Peace Corps office following a quick breakfast of Pad Thai. Then Carol had work to do at the office and Birgit and I set off for the famous Temple of the Emerald Buddha. If you've seen pictures of Thailand, and especially Bangkok, then You have probably seen the temple. It is a magnificent complex of buildings enclosed by a wall which has murals of the Buddhist version of a Hindu epic, "The Mahabarata," covering the inside of it. Throughout there are beautiful, although somewhat gaudy buildings and huge statues of temple guards with fearsome faces. Part of the the temple was closed to the public that day due to some official government activities. Thailand is 98% Buddhist, including the king, so temples and shrines are ubiquitous. Birgit and I were suitably impressed with the place, but after about an hour we grew tired from jet lag and the warm, humid 85° F temperatures, to which neither of us was acclimatized.

We headed for the gate and waited for Carol to show up. A crowd had gathered there and we discovered from an English speaking tourist that the king's representative was going to be coming through soon. The "honor guard" of about 6 Thai soldiers, 2 with bugles and 4 with rifles, was hanging out at the gate waiting for the dignitaries, leaning on their guns or mulling about chatting with street vendors. Then the announcement came that the representative's arrival was imminent. The soldiers stood at attention with the buglers blowing their fanfare, each in a different key, and a yellow Mercedes drove into the complex led by two motorcycle cops. In the car an old, thin man in an army uniform waved at us as he passed through the cheering crowd. As soon as he had passed, the fanfare stopped and the soldiers went back to their "at ease" positions. We continued waiting for Carol, and after about 15 minutes the king's representative drove back out to the same tooting fanfare and cheers from the crowd. Shortly thereafter, Carol arrived and we walked back to the guesthouse.

Our plan was to catch a night bus to the north country just south of Chiang Rai where Carol lived. We packed up our stuff and tried hailing a taxi (Oh, Boy! another taxi ride!). It was then that we realized it was rush hour in Bangkok (it's nearly always rush hour there) and we needed to get to the bus station quickly. We informed our driver of that and he was able to find a way out of the massive traffic jam and take an alternate route to the station. This driver, I'm glad to report, was very amiable and had no inclinations to driving like a bat outa hell. We arrived safely and no longer harried at the bus station 1/2 hour before our bus left, plenty of time to get our tickets and chill out a bit.

As we entered the bus, the TV was blasting, as was the air conditioning. We deposited our backpacks in the luggage hold and found our seats. The bus, in spite of what I've heard about buses in the third world, was as spacious and comfortable as any I have seen. In spite of the TV's raucous volume (which continued for the first hour of the ride) and the chattering of the passengers, I fell asleep soon after we left, exhausted by the changes and the day's activities. Didn't stay asleep long, partly because of the hostess (or maybe "ride attendant" would be the PC title) coming by to deliver our free snacks of sweet pastries and colas, and partly because, even though the outside temperature was dropping to a comfortable level as night fell, the AC in the bus was still blasting and we all woke up shivering. Birgit and I climbed down to the luggage area and retrieved our sleeping bags, mine rated down to 0° F, and eventually we were able to get comfortable enough to nod off.

My sleep again did not last long, since soon (about midnight or 1 am) we stopped for a break at the halfway point in our 11 hour ride. We pulled into the Thai version of a truck stop and were served rice soup (called congee), dried fish, and pickled cabbage. Carol and Birgit were unimpressed by the meal. I, in my usual unabashed fashion, devoured their leftovers. After another couple of hours of cold, restless sleep we were again served colas and several sweet treats in a Styrofoam box, and just before we arrived the hostess provided us with strong Thai coffee, highly sweetened. Carol mentioned that Thais are prone to lots of colds. If they ride the night buses much it does not surprise me, considering the frigid temperatures and the dietary disasters - sugar and caffeine.

We arrived at our stop around 5 am. The morning market was just getting underway in the dark, muggy, warm air. Carol went off to try and arrange a ride for us to Doi Luang, the national park where she worked, while Birgit and I perused the marketplace. The smells were wonderful: freshly made warm soy milk in big vats, deep fried bananas, chickens grilled over open flames. The tables were loaded with beautiful and varied fruits and vegetables, the heads of pigs, whole chickens, fish, and other wonderful items for sale. Carol announced that, rather than having to try to ride up to the park on the seats of three motorcycles as we had expected, she had found a friend of hers who had a car and could drive us to our destination, provided we stopped at her place for breakfast first.

Carol introduced us to Keminee, a part time English teacher who lived near the park. She was a delightful woman who was overjoyed to try out her language skills on us. At her home we were introduced to her husband, who was a successful artist, and their children. We had some congee and found out that she and her family were preparing food to give to the monks. Each day just before sunrise, the local monks wandered from house to house begging for food. Just like the Buddha had supposedly done, they begged once each morning, which supplied all their food for the day.

Birgit and I asked if we could present the food to the monks. Keminee agreed and explained the procedure.

The two monks, dressed in their saffron robes, were coming down the road as the first light of the sun was glowing through the haze of early morning. The food was ready on our plates. As they came close, we knelt down with our heads bowed and lifted the plates up to them. It was especially important that Birgit not touch the monks, since they are not allowed to have any physical contact with the opposite sex. They came to us and took the food from our plates, putting it into their begging bowls, all the while uttering a blessing over us. Then they walked on.

Keminee drove us up to the park, where, exhausted, we collapsed in bed for a few hours rest.

Forty hours in Thailand…our trip had only just begun.

Harvesting

One of the first things we did after hiking a bit in the park where Carol worked, was to go to a house out of the park to have dinner with some of her friends. We arrived in the afternoon on a pleasantly warm and sunny day, when they were involved in harvesting some of their rice crop. They asked if we wanted to help, and we wholeheartedly agreed. They had already cut the rice stalks, laid them out to dry for a few days, and then stacked them in sort of pillars. The next part of the harvest was threshing the rice, which, like all of this, was done by hand. First they put a plastic tarp on the ground and spread it out, then on it placed a wooden pallet. After that they used an odd-looking, but effective homemade tool to grasp the rice at the low end of the stalk. They had taken a stick, like an old broom stick about a meter long, then split it in half. They attached the halves on one end to a cleaned bicycle chain of the correct length. You wrapped the chain around a handful of rice, then as you brought the two halves of the stick into alignment, the rice would be held firmly together. At least that's how it's supposed to work.

They demonstrated for us, then let Birgit and I try to thresh their rice. I must admit, I did pretty well at it, not losing too many of the stalks after my first couple of tries, but Birgit, for some reason couldn't keep the rice stalks in the holder, and they soon started flying all over the place. Neither of us did it anywhere near as well as the farmers. We were both glad that Carol had told us to wear clothing that would cover as much skin as possible, in spite of the warm day, because the rice chaff flew everywhere and when it got on your skin felt itchy as hell. Even though this was the rice that would keep them eating for the next year, the farmers were good-natured about our lack of efficiency, and just laughed and laughed and laughed with us about the whole affair. This proved to be true of pretty much all of the Thai people we met on our journey: they were friendly, generous, and quick to laughter. Sharing and enjoying the experience was more important than making sure everything was "right" or "efficient."

After we threshed the rice, we pulled off any errant rice stalks from the tarp, picked up the pallet, shook it off, and then gathered the grains in the middle of the plastic tarp. Then we carefully picked up the tarp and used it to funnel the rice into bags for taking it to the mill to remove the chaff, which would happen after they had finished threshing the entire field. That we would not be around to see. Removing the chaff from our skin was the next order of business, also a joint activity, helping each other brush off the chaff we couldn't reach. When all was done, we retired to the house where we learned, with Carol's urging, how to eat modestly in the home of a poor subsistence farmer, in spite of having enormous hunger from doing physical labor. It's a good courtesy to become proficient at. Most of the world is a lot poorer than you or I. Only very few of the people we met in Thailand could even consider traveling the way we had to their country

Breathing

Keminee came to pick me up in her dusty, little car and drove me to a small, unspectacular temple somewhere in the woods not too far from the national park where we were staying. There were a few huts where the monks lived, and one large wooden platform raised off the ground a few feet with a grass roof above it where the monk with a few other participants waited to begin their meditation. Carol had told Keminee I was interested in Buddhism and meditation, so she took me to the monk with whom she occasionally meditated. This calm, peaceful man could speak a little English and asked me about my interest in meditation. What kind of meditation did I want, walking, breathing, or mantra? I told him I'd go with the breathing one. He and Keminee looked at each other and smiled. Then she sat down to do her own meditation while I sat with the monk on another part of the platform.

He instructed me to begin breathing deeply, repeatedly, to keep going and not stop. Try it sometime. After a few minutes you begin getting light headed and the urge to stop gets stronger and stronger. Whenever I slowed down or breathed more shallow he encouraged me to keep going and to focus on the breath going in and out, in and out. I continued breathing in, breathing out, deep breaths in consistent, continuous succession. After a while my body began to shake a bit and my skin tingled. Visions of my life popped into my head, then left quickly to be replaced by others, and still his voice kept encouraging me to keep going. I honestly lost all track of time, one of the few instances in my life where that really happened. While the meditation lasted less than an hour it seemed like it took forever because of the difficulty of continuing to breathe deeply in and out, and yet afterwards when I stopped and calmed down, it felt like it had taken no time at all, though I also felt like I had gone on a journey. There were no spectacular revelations or visions, other than the illustrations of my life, but I definitely had the impression I had been someplace else. When he got me slowed down and brought me back to a more normal state, I opened my eyes and looked around. Keminee and several other meditators just sat there smiling at me, along with the monk, and I had no idea how much time had passed. It took me several minutes before I could stand up.

We ate some fruit, I thanked him, and we drove off.

Years later I was to have a similar experience when I was living in North Carolina in 2000. I had gotten involved in a form of non-professional co-counseling and had planned an intensive session with 4 counselors in a row. I was going to "fix" myself for once and for all. It turned out the third counselor also did something called rebirthing as well as our co-counseling format, and she thought this would be a good experience for me. She did something very similar to that Thai monk, having me breathe deeply and quickly, though she did add some more interactive aspects, asking me what I was experiencing and giving me suggestions and encouragement. I had been curious about rebirthing breathing and had thought about trying it, and after this I realized that this is basically what that monk had done 4 years earlier.

In an Akha Village

Early on Sunday morning we arose, ate a quick breakfast of leftovers from the night before, and Birgit, Carol and I headed over to the nearby Akha Village. We got a ride part way from one of the park employees, then walked the rest of the way through the forest to the village. Along the way Carol, who had been working with this tribe for several months already, told us about some of their history. Originally they lived farther north in southern China. Some of them still live there in the province of Yunnan, and the Chinese call them the Hanizu, though they are also considered to be separate tribes by many of the Thai Akha. They practiced slash and burn agriculture, growing food crops for themselves, but some of them grew opium poppies as a cash crop. The Chinese were trying to wipe out the opium trade in their country, so they forced them into more food crop agriculture. Some of them still wanted the money from the opium, so they moved farther south into Myanmar (Burma) and then Thailand. The Thais also didn't want the opium grown there, so they pushed the Akha to grow food crops, particularly a type of sticky rice commonly used in north Thailand. By the time I visited in 1996, they had completely stopped the opium growing, but stuck to slash and burn agriculture, which can have its problems, so the Thai government weren't overly happy about the Akha people being there. Northern Thailand has many different ethnic groups, of which the Akha are just one. I don't know about the other groups, but there was a difficult relationship between the Thai and Akha, and there apparently were many cases of discrimination and attempts to make the Akha stop their traditional ways and blend into society.

Traditionally the Akha, like most such people, were animists, having a religion based on the belief in nature spirits. Many of the Akhas had adopted Christianity, however, and while I generally am a supporter of the animists, I have to admit that the story Carol told gave me a more open view of their conversion. It seems that traditionally they believed that when twins were born, it was an evil omen. They would often kill the children and the parents would be exiled from the village or forced into servitude. One time the village we were going to visit had a case of twins born, but the people took off in the night and traveled to a village nearby that had become Christian. There they were not killed, but accepted and treated well. When their village had heard about it, they were interested and ended up adopting Christianity as well. I guess such conversions aren't all bad.

On our way to the village that morning, we encountered our first traditionally dressed Akha women, which is something you won't forget. They typically wear basic black skirts with black jackets on top, the jackets embroidered with very colorful designs. On their lower legs they wear a sort of leg warmer that is of very colorful design like those on the jackets. They do all their own weaving of these. Their most famous items are their headdresses sporting numerous metal coin-like discs that jingle and jangle as they walk. Really beautiful, distinctive outfits. The women we met knew Carol and said a warm greeting, all the while looking Birgit and I over closely. They seemed to make some jokes to each other about us and we all headed for the village.

Upon arrival we went straight to the church for their morning service. The preacher was a woman. Women in traditional society did not have much status as far as village politics were concerned, but since their change in religion, this woman had become one of the top people in the village, in fact the "head person." The service had begun and we sat in the back. They were singing a song in Akha, a hymn which melody I knew. I sang along with my English words. After they sang a few songs and the preacher gave a short sermon, they decided to introduce us. We came to the front of the church and stood next to the preacher, both Birgit and I dwarfing her. We introduced ourselves and Carol translated our words. Then, as was to be the case nearly everywhere we went in Thailand, they asked us to sing a song. I don't recall Birgit's song, but I sang one of my favorites, Moonshadow, written by Cat Stevens. They asked us what the songs meant. I can't recall how I explained Moonshadow, but whatever it was, and however Carol translated it, the crowd ooed and ahhed. Must have been good. The song certainly has strong meaning for me.

We then looked around the village a bit, met some of the people she knew there, and visited some of their homes. They are built of mostly wood, with the floor several feet off the ground, most of them just one room, though I believe some had a small side room for storage and cooking. The roof is tightly thatched of some local grasses or reeds. They raised pigs and chickens, grew rice, corn, and vegetables, and gathered some items from the forest. We came eventually to a small open area near the wooden wall and gate at one side of the village, where a heated debate was in full swing. It seems they were discussing whether or not to share a Christmas celebration with the next village. As they talked, most of the men (it was almost all men) were squatting on the ground. A few were seated on the porch of the closest house, and the remainder, including the preacher, were standing at the edge of the group. The preacher lady, as the only member of her gender in the discussion, held a great deal of sway as to what happened, especially in regards to matters like this that involved not only the village politics, but also religion. After this we went to a hut where we bought a few items and where I learned a lot about buying in such a setting. These are poor people. Don't dicker over the price. Don't ask the price. Just buy the things you want and leave it at that. Today, these 20 years later, it might be a very different situation, but in those days when they were still very traditional, this was the case. We headed back to our housing area in the national park, but it was not our last experience with hill tribe people.

Doi May Salong

Several days later, the three of us took a road trip farther north, starting in the village of Doi Mae Salong (now known as Santkhiri), then up to the border with Myanmar at Mae Sai, then Birgit and I braved it on our own to a few other places before heading back to the national park near Chiang Rai where we again met up with Carol. By far the best part of this for me was Mae Along, a village tucked high up in the mountains near Myanmar, surrounded by hill tribe villages. Mae Salong itself was actually started by Chinese, and at the time of our visit, it was still more common to hear Chinese or hill tribe languages than Thai. As the Chinese revolution of 1949 began to wind down and members of the Kuomintang either gave up or got out of China, one group headed south into Thailand and founded this village. When we arrived in the late afternoon and after we checked into our guesthouse, we hiked up to the local Buddhist temple, then came back down and ate at a little Chinese restaurant.

I didn't sleep very well, and about 4 a.m. I was trying to find a way back to the world of dreams when I heard the morning market start up. I got dressed and ventured outside to walk the streets, looking at the pig heads and parts on tables, vegetables laid out on the street-side by hill tribe people waiting to be purchased, smell the fresh made soy milk and fried bananas, and watch the people in traditional dress, each colorful and unique, wander around buying or selling in the dim light before dawn. Eventually I went back and awoke Birgit to come out and experience the market before dawn ended and the heat of the day scattered people back to their homes.

That sultry afternoon the three of us went out for a long loop hike of about 10km or so, that took us around to a good many hill tribe villages. People were excited and curious to see these big, odd, white-skinned people wandering though their neighborhoods. We weren't the first foreigners they had seen by a long shot, but at that time it still wasn't all that common. We made a stop at a local school where we chanced upon an English lesson underway. We were asked in by the teacher and introduced ourselves, after which they requested that we sing a song. We obliged whole-heartedly. We went to the world map and showed them where we were from and they asked us questions, none of which I can recall 22 years later, but the children and their shy enthusiasm was absolutely wonderful. We said our goodbyes after a time, and continued our hike, starting back toward the village, which took us past the traditional Chinese cemetery and its vine-covered mausoleums. Then it was the steep way back up to the mountain village, where the afternoon market was in full swing. It didn't quite have the atmosphere of the morning market, but there were items we hadn't seen in the morning, such as the traditional Chinese medicine doctor and his various alcohols with snakes, scorpions, and ants well preserved in them. Most of the vendors at this one were Chinese. Then we retired to our room for some much needed rest before the evening meal. The next day, we disappeared.

Treehouse

I had always wanted to stay in a treehouse. As a child I loved watching Tarzan movies and thought it would be really cool to live in the trees the way he and Jane did. I dreamed about soaring through the air on a vine, so one day, when I was about 8 years old I took a rope and tried doing that on the metal pole our mom used for hanging laundry. That didn't turn out so well. But Wisconsin didn't have much in the way of treehouses back then, as far as I knew. Anyhow, after our adventures in the north of Thailand, we took a night bus down to the south along the coast where a friend of Carol's was the superintendent in a national park. The morning we arrived we were taken to our accommodations, which for Birgit and I happened to be in a lovely little treehouse that, while still in good condition, hadn't been occupied for a while. It had a porch with a gorgeous view of the park, an open air kitchen, like those all over Thailand, and a big, comfy bed. We put our bags in the treehouse, then set out to see the park. We stopped where one of the rangers presented a nature program for some school children and were promptly introduced as park rangers from America. They had questions for us, but first, of course, they wanted us to sing a song. We visited the little zoo of local animals and then late in the day went back to the housing area.

I somehow had mentioned curiosity about how they make coconut milk, and one of the cooks in the park let us participate. After cracking the coconuts in half, I sat on a little stool that had a round metal serrated plate that made it look like a star with many rays. Under the metal star they had placed a bucket and I sat on the stool scraping the inside of the coconut on the metal star, the shredded coconut falling into the bucket … or so it was supposed to go. I could do it, but my skill at this did not match my ability to beat the grains off of the rice, which we had done in the north of the country. Maybe I was just tired, but it was hard work. Birgit did alright with it, but we both tired quickly. The cook's abilities in this far exceeded ours, which on one hand makes sense, but on the other, it seems like a bit of labor that takes little skill. So much for that idea. After scraping a couple of coconuts, she put the flake into some boiling water and there it cooked for a while. Later, while we were back at our rooms taking showers, she had used some cheesecloth to separate the flake from the coconut milk, and that was it, fresh coconut milk. The taste of our curry that night was never so rich.

Later we headed to our respective rooms to sleep off a full day of activities. Earlier we had passed a tall observation tower that was open at the top for star gazing and good views of the surrounding forest. She decided to take her sleeping bag and go up there to let the night sky serenade her to sleep. I wanted the treehouse. As I got ready for bed I discovered that, like the kitchen in the park where we stayed up north, they had a resident Tokay Gecko. This is a lizard about 10 inches long with big googly eyes that hangs out and eats as many of the local insects as possible. A good thing in an open air kitchen. During the night they sometimes make a loud call that goes something like "d-d-d-d-d-d-d-d-d-d-d-d-d-tokay, tokay, tokay." Hence the name.

I washed up, brushed my teeth, and settled in for a good nights sleep in my first treehouse. With the lights on I read for a while then put my book down and turned the treehouse to darkness. When the lights went out, it came to life. First was a large beetle buzzing around above the bed. Then I could hear scurrying in the bathroom nearby. Soon bugs, lizards, and who knows what else were flying and scurrying around all over the bedroom, some banging into my face in the dark, others exploring the bed sheets, others racing across the floor. It became Grand Central Station for little critters. When the Tokay Gecko began calling, I knew there was no way I would get any sleep. I grabbed my sleeping bag, my pillow, and a pad and trudged under the starlight to the observation tower, where Birgit was nearly asleep. "What's wrong? I thought you wanted to experience the treehouse." "I did, and so did every little crawling critter in the park." I unrolled my sleeping bag, and lay down to get some rest.

I left Thailand soon after that and haven't been back since, though Thailand wasn't finished with me. On the flight home I came to realize that somehow I had picked up a bug that decided it would be good to clean me out. During the entire flight I had stuff coming out of both ends of my digestive tract, which, I'd come to discover, is not really much fun when you're in the air flying across the Pacific Ocean with limited restroom facilities. All things pass, and pass it did. By the time I was back in Reno, Nevada, I could handle eating rice, and when I got back to Lee Vining I was gathering my strength again.

Over the years I've thought back ever so fondly of my time in Thailand with Birgit and Carol and hope to return. Now I live in China where my wife and I have a little bit of Thailand. A few years ago we bought a second home, an apartment in southern Yunnan, a place called Xishuangbanna, where the majority ethnic group are called Daizu, basically Thai people with a slightly different dialect. It's also rich in hill tribe culture including the Hani, cousins of the Akha. So I guess in a way I did return.

Telling Tales

It's an odd bit of irony, telling stories about tellings stories, but here's the conundrum in which we find ourselves at this juncture.

So one day during my time at the Grand Canyon, I was looking around the research library, when I found a series of tapes called "American Storytelling". Intrigued, I looked through them and popped one that seemed interesting into the video player. A Native story of why the leaves change color, a Korean tale of a woodcutter, tales of life in Appalachia, an inner city black Cinderella, and on and on and on. Over the next couple of weeks I watched one after the other enthralled by the stories and the tellers. I talked with the unofficial resident storyteller of the Grand Canyon at the time, none other than Stew Fritts, the man with the face of a Grand Canyon mule, but a heart of gold. He had also seen the series and loved it, listing off all of his favorite tellers from it. I recalled how, in developing a nature talk about the forests of the South Rim of the Canyon, I had included a somewhat dramatized presentation of a story about the role wolves had played in forest health at the Grand Canyon (it has to do with deer) from Aldo Leopold's book, *A Sand County Almanac*. It was very well received and I saw how the story really touched people's hearts as well as their minds, just as the stories on the tapes had touched my heart. That storytelling experience later transformed into the program about wolves I mentioned in the section on Denali N.P. that, to this day, I'm very proud of. I hadn't known about professional storytellers at that point, hadn't seen a storyteller that I can recall, other than those in movies and TV, but I had done it based on my own intuition as to what would be effective. I started to really notice more and more the power of stories and began delving into it further. I looked online and found out more about these tellers, about national storytelling organizations, and the National Storytelling Festival in Jonesborough, TN. I had caught the bug ... I was hooked.

Between seasons working at the Grand Canyon, I went to visit a friend in Portland, OR, and happened to see an ad for a storytelling program at a local venue. The teller was Laura Simms, one of the tellers on the "American Storytelling" video series I mentioned earlier. It was an absolutely magical performance, and I went to talk with her afterwards, indicating I was interested in studying more about storytelling. At the time and for several years after, she did a week-long workshop every summer in the area of Jackson Hole, Wyoming, and she suggested I attend. Two summers in a row I arranged my schedule so I could travel from the Grand Canyon to Wyoming for her workshops, which were wonderful experiences in storytelling techniques and finding deeper meanings in the stories. Along the way they involved aspects of personal growth. She and I became friends as well as she my mentor. I brought what I had learned with me back to my job as an interpretive ranger and the storytelling bug passed from me on to several of my colleagues as well.

During one of those workshops with Laura, I was camped in the back of my pick-up truck one night and read through some stories from the German fairy tale collection of the Brothers Grimm. One of those was called "The Juniper Tree," and it's one that's always placed on the list of the "grimmest of the Grimms," because of its horrifying imagery and intensity. Read it if you dare. I talked to her the next day and said I had read an "awful" story called the Juniper Tree, but she responded, "That's a *wonderful* story." That took me aback. She said that when she was a young, eager storyteller she attended a workshop with teacher of mythology Joseph Campbell. They went around the room at the start introducing themselves, and Laura had said she wanted to be a storyteller. Later an established teller at the workshop told her, "Young lady, you'll never be a storyteller in my eyes unless you can tell the Juniper Tree and understand it." She told me I needed to go beyond the basic storyline and try to understand on a deeper level and in other contexts, so I set about to understand all I could about the story. Since then I don't know if I've gotten to what they called the "real meaning" of the story, but I certainly have found many meanings and contexts for it, including a more personal context, which I may discuss in another book. The first time I told it was at a birthday party where everyone was expected to perform in some way. I like that idea ... "I'll give you cake and ice cream and you give me a show." I once heard a saying from a Scottish storyteller along those lines when he used the phrase "Tell a story, sing a song, show your bum, or out you've gone." Anyhow, when I finished the story at first it was dead silence, people sitting there with their jaws agape. Then people started applauding, which nearly became a roar in the little art studio where the party took place. Over the years I have told the story many times to many different types of audiences, and it always elicits strong reactions, usually positive, though not always. It's not for everyone. And that's the thing about stories, there are many kinds, for many purposes, and many people, with different needs.

In 1997 I moved to Chapel Hill, North Carolina, where I wasn't far from the site of the National Storytelling Festival. Several times I attended the event, always inspired and enraptured by it. It's a simple art in a way, though I don't mean it's easy, and its simplicity is part of its beauty. I had the opportunity to meet many other tellers, both professional and amateur, over the years since then, especially while I stayed in NC where there is an abundance of them. I attended workshops and conferences, and eventually got my own gigs at times, starting down the road of my new avocation (I wouldn't exactly say I was professional, when you consider how little I usually got paid, if at all). Some of those were good gigs, many were tough audiences, not nasty necessarily, but hard to please. I focused mostly on a combination of fairy tales and stories from my own experiences, with a few poems and other stories sprinkled in.

One of the strangest gigs I ever did was for a group called La Leche League. "Leche" means "milk" in Spanish, and they are a group that promotes breast-feeding. They had planned a gathering at a local park and asked me to come and tell stories, as they thought the children would love it. Actually the children were mostly too young to understand what I was doing, but the adults liked it. What was strange, though, was that, since they promoted breast-feeding, I would be telling my stories, and about every minute another child would want a drink, so mom would pull out her breast and start feeding. I think breast-feeding is wonderful for the health of our children, but I have to say it was a bit hard to keep my focus in that situation. Delightful folks, though. Other gigs over time included, among others, small-scale storytelling festivals, bars, teahouses, schools, elder care homes, boy scout gatherings, parties, home concerts, and the following…

Before we leave North Carolina, let's talk about death. I was trained as a hospice volunteer back in Wisconsin, but hadn't had much chance to use my skills until I moved to NC, where they had an excellent inpatient facility and volunteer program in the area of Chapel Hill and Durham. I spent time on my days off both working in the inpatient hospice and doing home visits. One woman, who we shall call Alice, had been facing death bravely for some time before she came to the inpatient hospice. I had the chance to get to know her before she passed away. It turns out she had worked at the same place I was working at the time, Wellspring Grocery Store. She was one of those people with a strong personality, who often got what she wanted in life, except to live longer. You might say, though, that she packed a lot of life into her dying. One fall Sunday afternoon, I went to visit her in her room at the hospice, and we chatted for a while. She learned I liked telling stories, and asked me to tell her one. I chose a story about why the leaves change color. In the middle of the story, a family member called to talk to her. She said, "I can't talk now, I'm listening to a story." She said a cordial goodbye and hung up. She requested I continue, and I obliged. As the story concluded, she asked to go outside to breathe in the fall air and see the trees in their autumn foliage. We sat outside for a while until she got chilled and I had to go. Not too many weeks after that she passed away. I went to see her showing at the funeral home and meet her family. When I entered the room, I heard a clear, distinct voice say, "I'm not there, that's not me, I'm right here!" And yet nobody around me had spoken a word. Whether in the hearts of our family and friends, or in other ways, I guess we live on.

In 2001 I moved back out west, this time to Oregon, where I worked at Oregon Caves National Monument. As a geologist by academic training, working at a cave is logical for me, but I was also caught by the story of the cave's discovery and its discoverer, Elijah Davidson, as I mentioned in the section on Oregon Caves earlier in the book. This led me into more storytelling opportunities, both at the park and in other local venues. Now that I live in China I don't have much opportunity to tell stories. Most people's English language skills aren't high enough to really follow the stories and my Chinese is not up to the storytelling level. In my classrooms teaching geography and English, I did have a few successful storytelling sessions with the students, but now I mostly just type them out on my MacBook.

When living in North Carolina I had met a wonderful teller by the name of Milbre Burch. She was very helpful to me and based on my situation and my needs recommended people she thought would be good teachers for me, one of whom was Jim May, from northern Illinois, not far from my hometown. He lives in the town of Woodstock, IL, to be exact, which was where they filmed most of the movie "Groundhog Day", one of my favorites. You'll learn more about Jim and my studies with him in the following stories.

Oaxaca

Jim May and his wife Nan decided to get out of northern Illinois one bitter cold winter, so they traveled to southern Mexico, a state and city named Oaxaca (pronounced "wahaka") and fell in love with it so much that he decided to do storytelling workshops there based at a B & B called the Casa Colonial. Twice, in 2003 and 2005, I made my way from southern Oregon to Oaxaca to attend Jim's week-long workshops and to soak in the cultural and natural beauty of the place.

Oaxaca sits in far southern Mexico, only one state away from Guatemala. While Mexico City and more northern reaches in Mexico are famous for native Aztec people, Oaxaca has more Mixtecs and Zapotecs, and the population overwhelmingly consists of native peoples. Their artwork and beauty grace the place with an array of wonderful colors and patterns that can just take your breath away, if you let it. If you've seen pictures of Frida Kahlo, the famous artist, in her traditional flowered dress, well, that's one group of Zapotecs, those from Juchiteca, where her mom was born. Those flowered dresses are their blossoms of fire (also the name of a wonderful documentary about them). The climate of Oaxaca City (Oaxaca de Juarez) is fabulous, very comfortable most of the year with distinct wet and dry seasons, not unlike where I live as I write this in Xishuangbanna, southern China. There is a rich diversity of plants and animals, though I didn't spend enough time there to see much of that. It's also the home of chocolate. Well, one of the homes. Chocolate originated in parts of southern Mexico/northern Central America, though one variety seems to have originated in the Amazon area. Cacao, the plant chocolate comes from, is an important part of the local cuisine. Though fairly poor in terms of money, their culture is about as rich as you can find anywhere. The following stories will introduce you to some of my experiences in Oaxaca.

Sunrise over the city of Oaxaca, Mexico, one of my favorite places.

2003 - One Sunday Night in Oaxaca

The sun set on another beautiful night in Oaxaca. I left the confines of the state's cultural museum attached to the church of Santo Domingo, and strolled over to another church named Carmen Alto. Jim had told us of a fabulous event scheduled to take place that evening, the procession of El Señor de Esquipulas, the black Christ who first appeared in a town in Guatemala. There are various places where this figure is recognized and celebrated, with Oaxaca being one of the more famous spots.

Activities related to the festival had occurred throughout the day, but the most dramatic were to begin after sunset. When I arrived, the evening mass was about to begin. I felt hungry so I had a snack from a street vendor and took a seat in the back of the church. Just after the mass started, Trish and Diane, two members of my storytelling group arrived. The crowd was getting heavy, so I gave up my seat to an elderly woman and stood in the back just outside the door. At about 8 p.m., Trish, who's Catholic, told us that if the service follows the usual pattern of the mass, there was still quite a long while to wait until it ended. We couldn't understand most of the service anyhow, so we exited to the street to partake of some local culinary delights.

I had been eating food from the street vendors quite often, but others in my group had been heeding the advice of travel books and sticking to restaurants for our evening meals. They decided to 'brave' the food, and were not sorry for it. The empanadas with pollo amarillo (chicken in yellow molé) or pollo verde (in green molé), and squash blossoms were muy delicioso! All agreed and nobody got sick from it.

Just as we finished our meals, the procession began. A brass band led the way and a guitar/mandolin group brought up the rear, the two bands playing different songs. In between walked hundreds of people, most carrying candles in cups, and the bearers of the platform for El Senior de Esquipulas, a crucifix with a black Christ. In the crowd, we were reunited with the other members of our group. The brass and strings played on as we joined the throng, chatting with joyous and friendly people along the way and trading flames as the breeze snuffed out our candles. A full moon rose above the hills and rooftops, while on Earth a glowing procession moved on through the streets in the neighborhood near Carmen Alto. When the entourage returned to the church the crucifix was placed on the altar, where faithful parishioners, some in tears, stepped to the front and kissed the feet of El Senior de Esquipulas.

The Black Christ, Sr. Esquipulas, in the church of Oaxaca.

The time for fireworks was drawing nigh. Church members carried a series of wicker frames from the courtyard out to the street. All but one of the frames were small, about 4 feet high and mounted on figures of bulls or horses. One frame stood out from all the rest: the grand finale rose about 20 feet above the cobblestone street. As we watched in anticipation, a participant would put one of the frames over their head and shoulders, the fuse was lit, and they danced around the street to the music of the brass band. The fuse ran continuously through the bamboo frame, and as it reached different parts of the structure, it would ignite a series of spinning wheels, firecrackers, and bottle rockets. We dodged as bottle rockets occasionally shot along the street and ricocheted off of stone and adobe walls. When one participant was tired, another would take over. The frames were ignited one at a time and the crowd grew in anticipation of the grand finale. Many of the frames ended with a flaming wheel that launched itself 50 or more feet into the air, landing where, I cannot say, and neither could anyone else. Several fire department representatives behind us kept a watchful eye, well away from the flaming figures.

After the smaller frames, they prepared for the grand finale. Couldn't have a break in the action, however, so little bamboo cars were ignited and shot to and fro around the street and sidewalk, people hopping to avoid being run over. As they finished, the big frame ignited. It was constructed just as the smaller ones were, but when each section ignited, the fireworks lit up the night sky like a host of comets at close range or the front row of a welding conference. Not 20 feet away from me the bamboo erupted with reckless abandon. I kept thinking 'This would NEVER happen in the U.S.' and pondered. The brass band played on as we laughed and dodged sparks, until the crown of the structure shot high into the night sky, signaling the end of the night's excitement. It was magnificent!

The time was after 11p.m. and we headed to the zocalo to wind down with hot 'chocolate de agua,' and rave about the night's activity. Then it was back to our rooms at the Casa, and the world of dreams. With any luck, or proper planning, I hope to be at many more celebrations of El Senior de Esquipulas, preferably in Oaxaca.

When I returned to the U.S., I drove to Chimayo', New Mexico, the northernmost place where El Senior de Esquipulas is honored. The Sanctuario there is impressive in a much more subtle way than I had seen in Oaxaca. The church is an old Spanish structure from the early1800's. The rustic designs of the interior brought me back to Mexico. On the altar stood a crucifix, not as black as the one in Oaxaca, but more resembling complexions of those living in this Indian/Latino village. I stood in the back, struck by a certain presence, which had not been dimmed by the more touristy signs outside. I noticed people going to the front and into a side door by the altar. I ventured there myself, and entered the place of the 'healing earth.' The first room was adorned with the letters and crutches of those who have been healed by the soil of this place. A little chamber off to the side had a hole in the floor where people reached in and grasped handfuls of the blessed ground. I did the same, taking only a small amount. I figured that if it did have healing powers, the amount did not matter, rather the belief. I held it in my hand and wished. Then I left a donation, walked to my car, placed it in an empty container, and drove off across the high plateau of northern New Mexico. The soil sat on a special shelf in my humble Oregon home, reminding me of Oaxaca, Chimayo', and the ground beneath my feet.

18 Enero … Oaxaca

Sitting in Juarez Park, northeastern Oaxaca. It's not the park with the big Juarez statue on the hill, which we go to most mornings to see the sunrise. This one is much lower key, which is why I like it here at this time late in the day. The Zocalo, town square, is wonderful, but very busy. Here, the traffic around the park may be fast, but the pace of the park is slow and easy. Benito Juarez was the first Indian president of the United States of Mexico and ruled from 1858 to 1872. His time in office occurred during a very difficult and tumultuous time in Mexico's history and he is widely admired in Mexico, especially among the native peoples, who are often neglected and downtrodden, not only in Mexico, but throughout the world.

The storytelling workshop I attended over the last week has come to a close and the people with whom I've shared this brief, but intense relationship have flown to lands far, far away. As water pours from the fountain behind me, a man walks past with his little girl. She's in her school uniform of white shirt, red vest, blue skirt, white socks pulled up to her knees, and dark tennis shoes. Her beautiful, long, black hair she wears tied back with red and white ribbons, and she carries a pink shoulder bag with a white strap. Her father, a short, stocky man wearing simple clothes, laborer's clothes, carries his daughter's pink backpack covered with pink and pastel little girl patches, like Barbie and stuff.

(should next par. be past or present?)

They walk hand in hand, then sit down on one of the green, Victorian style wrought iron park benches close to the street. Or at least HE sat down. His little girl set to playing, dancing around a large tree trunk. She picked up a switch from the ground and began swinging it here and there, the thoughts, visions in her mind known only to her. I wonder to what worlds she travels in those fleeting minutes before her mother, wearing dark slacks and a bright yellow pullover, nears them from across the street. They share hugs and kisses, the three of them. Then they walk off hand in hand to wherever they go every afternoon at about this time. Or at least I guess that's what they do.

A moment later as I sit writing this whilst seated on the stone rim of the fountain, I catch a movement out of the corner of my right eye and turn to see a young man with his daughter walking towards me. The girl, my guess a first grader, walks on the rim of the fountain on which I sit. She, too, wears a school uniform nearly identical to the other girl's, but for a plaid pattern on her skirt, which comes down to nearly cover her knee socks. I rise to move and the man motions for me to remain seated, that they could go around me, but as he prepares to pick up his daughter, I stand fully, bow, and let them pass. He smiles, says "Gracias," and continues following her around the circular rim of the fountain.

Children need to know that they can walk on the edge, and that, more important than us pulling them away from it, we will hold their hand.

A minute or so later I turn around and see that they have reached the 180º point around the circle. The man sees my glance and greets it once again with a smile. His daughter's gaze remains fixed on the stone beneath her feet. Again I turn to look just a moment later and see them walking away hand in hand. Just then a small, familiar flash of black, white, gray, and bright yellow catches my eye. I turn to see a yellow-rumped warbler (common also in parts of the U.S.) land near me on the volcanic stone of the fountain walkway not far from my feet. It picks up a few morsels and flutters off to the grassy area about a stone's toss away. I arise and walk in that same general direction toward the Benito Juarez statue at the center of the park, past lovers in warm embrace on park benches, and other wanderers like me in quiet contemplation. When I reach the statue I stand looking at it for a moment. Then I turn to a middle aged woman seated nearby and say in Spanish "I think Mexico, and the world, need a leader like Benito right now." She nods and says, "Si, verdad." It's true. I turn and continue my walk across the city of Oaxaca.

As I walked out of the park, I saw a little boy, very early grade school age, getting his shoes shined by an old man. The elder had a beautiful face carved with age and experience, and eyes that sparkled like stars. The lad sported an uncertain look on his face and eyes like big brown saucers that sought reassurance from his young mother seated next to him. You know, the kind of look little boys and girls get when they have the chance to do what big kids and even adults do.

When the elder tried to polish the back of the boy's left shoe, his foot kept slipping off of the stand. The elder and the boy's mother, with patient smiles, placed his little foot back on the stand and explained to him that he had to push his foot down and resist the polishing cloth. They did this 5 or 6 times, always with the patient smiles, until the boy got it correct. His right foot didn't need the same coaxing. When they had finished, momma helped her son off of the chair and paid the elder, whose calm, knowing smile shone brighter than the little boy's shoes, sort of like an old, content sun shining in the early evening sky.

He shined the boy's shoes
And the sparkle in his eyes
Outshone the polish.

Oaxaca 2005

When I first visited Oaxaca, Mexico, 2 years ago, what brought me there were both a storytelling workshop and my sense of adventure. What brought me back was, once again, a storytelling workshop, but also the love I've come to feel for this special place, even though I've known it ever so briefly.

I landed in the dark of night and was greeted by cool, comfortable air, as well as the scent of the air pollution that plagues even this wonderful city. I noticed it much more this time than last, either due to an increase in the amount of pollution, or to my increased sensitivity having lived two more years in a place with some of the cleanest air and water in the U.S.A.. It was probably some of both. Oaxaca has maybe 500,000 residents, so it's not a particularly large city, and the pollution comes almost exclusively from the metal monsters that so often clog its veins and arteries. Were it not for the traffic, this place would welcome visitors with the less noxious scent of natural gas used for much of the people's cooking & heating needs, a bit of trash here and there, as well as the sweet smell of the bougainvilleas, jacarandas, and all the other flowers that bless this place.

From the airport I headed for the zocalo, the town square, where I first went to get a bed at the Magic Hostel, 60 pesos ($6.00) per night, then set off to find dinner. I love the street food of Oaxaca and that first night I ate tlayudas, a large crispy tortilla covered with your choice of toppings. I decided on frijoles, guacamole, col, y pollo con salsa picante: beans, avocado sauce, chopped cabbage, and chicken, with hot salsa. I had returned. Life was good.

The next day, Tuesday, I visited the mercados (markets) and eventually went to Casa Colonial, the Bed & Breakfast which again served as the site for our storytelling workshop. I planted some temporary roots in my room and did a bit of writing and sight-seeing. As others in the class arrived I shared hugs with old friends and made some new ones. That evening our workshop began with lengthy introductions. People often ask me what we do in storytelling workshops. The content is nearly as varied as the stories we tell, but this workshop's focus was personal narrative, basically working with the story of our lives. To do that, one needs to spend time looking in the mirror and facing demons (and maybe a few angels), old and new, so workshops in this vein often end up being as much group therapy as storytelling. This one proved no exception.

That evening as we made our way around the room for the introductions of each of our members, we shared not only our names and where we are from (both originally and currently), but also what's new and good in our lives, why we were there, what we wanted to leave behind for the workshop, what we wanted to invite into our circle, and any resolutions we chose to make. Some themes which emerged from this discussion were those of members feeling uncertain about their place in our group, wondering why they were there, grief in its many facets, and the balance of Fire vs. Water, mythologically speaking. Jim, our teacher, and I were the only men in the group with 8 women, appropriate for a city where the patron saint is the Soledad, our Lady of Solitude, and her image or that of the Virgin of Guadalupe can be seen everywhere, even affixed firmly to the grills of some cars and trucks. During the next 5 days we would meet in the morning for 4-5 hours for the class, then explore the area during the afternoons, and maybe meet again in the evening, depending on our whims. Our first assignment was that of writing at least one poem every day. On that first night we also decided to form a grief group that would meet every evening to share our feelings, our losses, our hearts.

Because I so like to wander the marketplaces, I became the group's reference person for the hot scoops on shopping. I enjoyed sharing the arts (weavings, carvings, pottery, etc) and especially the delicacies of Oaxaca with them, alegrias (amaranth cakes), chapulinas (fried grasshoppers), moles (the special sauces of Oaxaca), and, of course, chocolate. The place has such a rich culture that it nearly overwhelms you, in striking contrast to the abject poverty of many people here.

During our time together we shared much and developed a special type of bond, one born out of baring our souls and trusting that our other group members would be there for support. We explored our culture of birth, our culture of choice (how we live today), and looked at both to begin to define the "myth we are living", as psychologist Carl Jung would say. We then looked at a traditional tale using a technique originated by famed teacher of mythology Joseph Campbell, himself a student of Carl Jung. We then applied that method to our own lives, with results sometimes funny, sometimes sad, sometimes enlightening, but always in some way profound.

The evening grief group met in a quiet little corner of the Casa, where we set up an altar and created a sacred space, which proved an invaluable place for us. In the group we shared our losses: of friends, of family, of relationships, of opportunities, of our own childhood innocence. I had once experienced a ritual foot washing as part of an Episcopal Service on Maundy Thursday during Holy Week that made a deep impression on me. I suggested to the group that we do such an activity, that it would aid the process in which we had engrossed ourselves. They all agreed.

On Friday night we gathered in the alcove in front of our altar. We had a pail of water, which could have been a bit warmer, towels, incense, and a bowl with a mermaid design, appropriate for our foot washing.

We decided to do the ritual in silence, and to have each person wash someone's feet, then have theirs washed, dried, and anointed with oil, after which they could sit in the silence and digest, or metabolize, the experience. Jim and I started the cycle with me washing his feet. It is humbling, intimate, joyous in a quiet sort of way, awkward, tender, and at times even humorous to perform such a ritual. When it came time to have my feet washed, Kathleen's eyes pierced to my very soul as she gazed up at me. I found it difficult to face the honesty of her eyes, but that's part of the process of washing away our defenses. As we made our way around the circle, it became more that a foot washing…it also became a bit of a contest to see who could give the best foot massage with the oil. As we drew to a close, put our shoes back on, and prepared for the evening meal, I still am amazed that nobody slid out of their shoes and landed flat on their backsides, given the amount of oil used on their feet. Humor and reverence should go hand in hand more often.

On Saturday our goal was to give each person 30 minutes to do whatever they chose. The group would then give feedback based on what the focus person wanted. Some people shared formal writings. Some presented prospective performance pieces. Some shared journal excerpts and chatted. In my past workshop experiences I had not often felt pleased with my presentations, so I decided to tell a story that I thought I could tell well, and also one that has always been very powerful for me, a Grimm Brothers tale called "The Juniper Tree." Due to time limitations, my presentation happened that evening after a long day of activities. I wore the shirt that 3 classmates (mis tres hermanas – my 3 sisters) helped me buy that afternoon. We gathered in a back room away from the other guests at the Casa. I sat down, composed myself, and let the story emerge. It felt good. I needed that. After my presentation…Party Time. Even I danced a little!

Our last day focused mostly on appreciations, for our distinguished leader Jim, for the class, for the Casa, for Oaxaca, and for each other. That afternoon the Casa had scheduled a jazz concert and during the break several of our members told stories. We then headed off to the procession of El Señor Esquipulas, the Black Christ, which is a beautiful event, carrying the huge platform with the crucifix through the streets on the shoulders of 20 men, lighting off fireworks, singing, carrying candles, and enjoying the good company of all in the procession, just as described above.

The ending of the class was rather anticlimactic, saying quick farewells in the dark, late night hours of the Casa. Everyone except me left the next day, although mis tres hermanas and I had the chance to walk the streets of the city together before they had to leave for the airport. My good friend Angela, also in the workshop, had told me about an angel in the Basilica of Soledad that she said looked just like me, so the four of us went to see for ourselves. She was right. It felt rather eerie to look into a face fashioned in plaster and painted that so unintentionally resembled me, in a place where the people tend to look short, stocky, and brown-skinned. He even had my long eyelashes!

I took an early morning flight back to the States, and a reunion with my own four-footed best friend. Ten short days for me…a lifetime for Pedro. His eyes told me that. And the shudder of his body as I held him told me he had missed me even more than I had missed him, if such a thing is possible.

I've traveled a great many places in my life and each of them has a special place in my heart, even if it's just because I was glad to wash the dust from my feet when I left, but Oaxaca remains one of my favorites without a doubt. Walking through the markets, smelling the rich odor of cacao, corn, and chiles, looking at the delicate, colorful artworks, the hills, the sunrises and sunsets, the sense of history, the colonial architecture and the ancient stone temples, and the realities of modern life, are all part of the fabric of this place, part of the fabric of me, now. I long to go back there and spend more time, though don't know if I'll make it. Someday, maybe. Someday.

On the next page is one of the poems I wrote while in Oaxaca.

Chocolate scent rises from
Hovels along the side streets of
Oaxaca as my feet
Carry my nose and every pore along in
Orificial ecstasy. I soak in the aroma,
Linger on each nuance of the sensation
And dance at the idea of
Tastebud heaven, as grinning, I
Enter one gate of paradise to partake in the ritual of
Sensual
Sensory
Spiritual Celebration.

It's hard to justify going back to places like Oaxaca when I have not yet seen even a small percentage of China, my home since 2010, and there is certainly a lot of history here to soak up as well. I've only just begun, but that's another story.

WEDDINGS

Weddings are rites of passage that punctuate the lives of so many of us, as well as great symbols of love, compassion, and commitment and I've had the opportunity to attend some rather interesting, wonderful, odd ones over these past 60 years. They reflect differences in culture, personality and time of life of the participants. There have been traditional Western style weddings, each with their own quirks, such as my sister's first wedding where my dad and I, both participants in the affair, had temperatures of about 102F/39C as we battled the flu, or my dad's second wedding in which I had the strange honor of being his best man. There have been German weddings, Chinese weddings, Native American weddings, Pagan weddings, Atheist weddings, Theatrical weddings, Old weddings, Young Weddings, Outdoor weddings, Indoor Weddings, and many others, including those just at the government offices in charge of such things. I even attended the wedding of a rock musician friend that when the pastor asked if there was any reason they should not be joined together, a heavy pregnant silence settled over the room for what seemed like an eternity as the other woman he'd been sleeping with recently sat in the back of the room with a mischievous grin on her face. She didn't say a word, and neither did anyone else. Don't know if they're still together. I'd rather doubt it.

The sweetest and most low-key wedding I attended (well, maybe besides my own wedding) took place on the North Rim of the Grand Canyon and involved my friends Tom and Marcia tying the knot. They were coworkers, both, I believe, in their 50s at the time of their wedding, both had been in the Peace Corps, and both had been married before.

They met while working on the North Rim. They chose to get married after the summer busy period had quieted a bit and when the fall colors, the lovely golden aspen trees, were at their peak. Dale, our supervisor, and Ernie, another ranger, sang songs, Dale's wife Katie conducted the ceremony, and I told a story. The loving couple wore floral rings on their heads and dressed beautifully, but casually. Many years later they are still happily married, living near the North Rim in a wonderful house at the base of a red rock cliff, and it all began in our close-knit family of park rangers one summer in the early 1990s.

My friends Kai and Claudia got married in Claudia's hometown of Aachen, Germany, which sits on the border between Germany and the Netherlands. I had met Claudia and her sister when I was working at the Grand Canyon years before, then visited them during my first trip to Germany in 1992, when I also met Kai. I don't recall the church wedding service as being much different than weddings back in my hometown, other than speaking in German and all. My German at the time was quite limited. Still is. But anyhow, after the service the newlyweds were carried off to the mini-reception by means of a shiny, black horse-pulled carriage. Never saw that in Racine, Wisconsin. The mini-reception was a cake and coffee gathering held on the first floor of an old windmill that had been preserved as somewhat of a museum, complete with all the operating parts. It wasn't operating that day, however. The big reception later was held in a gastaette, a German café/beerhall, that, if memory serves me right, was run by her family. The food was amazing and the beer and schnapps plentiful, accompanied by many games, sometimes involving embarrassing moments in Claudia and Kai's respective pasts. Some of these I could not quite understand, given the language barrier, but I distinctly recall a milder part of the festivities involved people pairing up and drawing pictures of their partners, so as to have a record for the loving couple of all those who attended the event. Unfortunately, they will never guess who I drew as my talents in this art form are basically not much past making a good stick man. The last thing I recall about the event was driving Claudia's parents home, as I had had significantly less to drink than her father. Before heading to bed in their guest room I sat down for a chat and a nightcap with her dear ole dad, discussing the issues of modern

Germany, comparing them to those in the USA. What I mostly recall about that was his level of acceptance and the beautiful, dark woodwork in his sitting room. The next day I left to take a position in Hochharz National Park, but that's another story.

One of the more unusual weddings I attended took place in Flagstaff, Arizona, many years ago. I have lost touch with the couple, can't even remember their names, so let's just call them Bob and Carol. They were an older than usual couple at the time they decided to tie the knot, as I recall maybe in their 40s, possibly married before. Carol owned a vintage clothing store and a costume shop. Everyone attending the wedding was instructed to go to the costume shop and check out a costume of their choice to wear to the event. There were witches and warlocks, princes and princesses, knights and devils and angels and all sorts of other characters, some of them identifiable only to themselves. I wore a wizard costume (I was one of the last to go to check one out and didn't have many creative options). For the ceremony they rented the old theater just a block off of Route 66 in downtown near the railway station/visitor center where I worked at the time. It was a jovial affair with music provided by the local reggae/rock group, with one of the best names for dance band I ever heard: Limbs Akimbo. As of this writing it's been nearly 30 years since it took place, so I don't recall particulars of the ceremony, and the reception must have been good as I don't remember it either. I just recall everyone's delight at seeing each other in costume and how the party atmosphere of the revelers flooded into the street on a sunny afternoon, bringing joy to all who passed by.

While I'm on theatrical weddings, I can't escape talking about the wedding between my friends Deb and Steve, proprietors of the Frog Farm in southern Oregon where I lived at the time. They wrote their own ceremony, a musical play about how they got together based on the traditional song from the British Isles entitled "Froggy Went a Courtin'". The play included frog costumes, fairy costumes, a giant sun puppet, dancing mushrooms, and me as narrator and was held in the corral by an old barn along the Illinois River in the small, but potent town of Takilma. Other songs included "Don't You Fall" (Be Good Tanyas), "Buckets of Rain" (Bob Dylan), "I'm in Love with a Big Blue Frog" (Peter, Paul and

Mary), "The Bramble and the Rose" (Barbara Keith), and "Galaxy Song" (Eric Idle/Monty Python, John Seed/Dana Lyons version), all performed live by participants. The story was a partially metaphorical version of how they met and eventually got together after Steve's persistent efforts and Deb's reluctance, so Steve was Froggy and Deb was an "Oak Fairy" and we sang and talked through the whole experience for an appreciative and rather amused audience. More than 200 people attended, and the whole event, complete with feast and lots of homemade wine, came off as a great success. Southern Oregon in August can be quite swelteringly hot, and the day ended up being warm, but manageable. One personal note on the event was that the area of the ceremony had lots of poison oak. For some of it, they just put up a sign to keep people away. We couldn't do that with all of it, though, as there was just too much. The farm's goats helped a bit, but since I had never had a reaction to poison oak, I was the farm's designated poison oak puller. If you're not familiar with poison oak, be glad. People who touch it normally end up with a nasty rash that itches like mad and often ends up spreading the more you scratch at it. I spent hours in the heat trying to make the place safe for the large group of people and succeeded pretty well. Unfortunately I think I reached my limit for poison oak contact in spite of taking precautions to not have it contact my skin directly. I didn't get a very serious rash like many people get, but it was enough to make me think twice about continuing my status as the "designated puller." It was worth it, however. I was more than glad to have done that for such wonderful people and happy to do my part to make the wedding come off so beautifully.

I can't write this next one any better than I did after it happened many years ago...

8 April 2004

Last Wednesday I left work at noon, drove to my house to change, load the car and pick Pedro up, and hit the road. Given that my 5 ½ day trip would consist of 3 ½ days of driving and 2 days of wedding activities in which my dog Pedro could not really involve himself, I chose to leave my four footed friend at a very fine kennel in Grants Pass, about 30 miles from our home and right along my travel route. My destination: Second Mesa, AZ, on the Hopi Indian Reservation and home to my friends Gerald and Yvette, who are in the process of getting married. Why in the 'process of getting married?' You'll see.

A veteran of long drives, I traveled the 1300 miles to Second Mesa in a day and a half, arriving at 11 p.m. Thursday night after a stop for dinner and grocery shopping in Flagstaff. The Hopi mesas lie in northeastern Arizona, 3 high flat "tables" of rock ("mesa" is Spanish for "table") in the high desert country of the Colorado Plateau. The tops of the mesas are about 6000 ft. (1800-1900 m.) in elevation, and dotted with small pinyon pine and juniper trees in a sea of sagebrush and other desert shrubs. Several villages sit atop each mesa, with steep sandstone cliffs at the edges of each village dropping off to the lower plain below. A few roads wind up to the mesa tops, each an umbilicus connecting the villages to the rest of the world. I had checked the weather forecast, which called for breezy, cool, skies and scattered showers. Normally a wedding would not welcome that sort of weather, but not in the high desert of Arizona. I knew we all would welcome the rain as an honored guest at the feast, and in fact it did bless us a few times during my stay there.

At first glance, many people might believe the Hopis to suffer intense poverty, but while they do have their share of economic, social, physical, and political woes, some do quite well for themselves and most are rich in ways other than monetary. Life in the villages is not easy, especially for those who follow the traditional Hopi path. In a world that constantly changes at an ever increasing pace and cries for technology, wealth, and feeding the social beast, maintaining those traditions is difficult to say the least, even for a people who by many standards live in a remote corner of the world. Many of the homes do not have running water, including my friends' double wide trailer. Outhouses dot the edges of the villages and most also use an in-house 'chamber pot.' They obtain water by driving to one of the standpipes that tap local springs or other water sources and filling whatever containers they have. Most houses do have electricity and that flashing eye on the world, TV, graces most homes I've visited. Cell phones work on a limited basis, but some homes do have regular land lines connecting them to the rest of humanity. The traditional life involves an extensive cycle of ceremonies and social events throughout the year. Weddings typically take place in March and April as opposed to the June celebrations which punctuated my childhood. June is needed for tending crops: corn, beans, squash, melons, fruit trees, and others. Some Hopis also raise cattle or sheep.

I arrived on Thursday evening, and on Friday morning I drove to the standpipe at the Hopi Civic Center to fill some of my friends' water containers, and then proceeded to Shungopavi, Gerald's family village and the location of most of the wedding activities. The wedding had actually begun at least several months previous, for when I visited them in February they had already begun baking pastries, preparing corn meal, stockpiling flour, and giving gifts to one another's families. Much of the wedding centers around the bride and groom and their families courting one another to convince them their family member is a worthy match. The in-laws also test their future family member to determine their mettle. Yvette lived at her in-laws' house for a couple of weeks, cooking, grinding corn using traditional stone manos and metates, and making piki bread, a ceremonial rolled filo dough type of bread made from blue corn meal.

At Shungopavi, I found Gerald busy with some other men cutting sheep which had been killed for the traditional dish of mutton and hominy stew. Five sheep had already been slain and more awaited their fate in two livestock trailers near the house. I pitched in and helped where I could, but like many such activities only a few men at a time would usually do the work while others stood around, drank coffee, chatted, and oversaw the operation. Meanwhile, women stood outside by the fires, above which huge pots of water heated for the stew. Also in this house, called a 'piki house' and constructed special for ceremonies like the wedding, we set up and cleaned a series of shelves for the pastries which would flavor the ceremony. Inside another house, some of Gerald's aunts began grilling Yvette as to how she thought she could be good enough to take their boy away from them. As was traditional, the process erupted into a mud fight. The women first splattered Yvette, then broke out of the house and began slinging mud at everyone and everything. I saw my little green Honda get smeared with the gooey gray slime. Then when I went out to get a better look, I stood by the house as one woman snuck up from behind me and splashed a bucket of muddy water down my neck and back. I retreated to the piki house. A bit later I again ventured out of the piki house and one of the women grabbed me by my jacket sleeve, hung on for dear life as I tried to spin free, and she shouted "Why are you helping them?!!" Finally she got her muddy hands on my face and hair. I retreated once more to the house, but this time the women overpowered a man who desperately tried to close and lock the door, and they smeared the lot of us, including yours truly. Late in the day when I knew they had finished, it took me a good 15 minutes to wash the mud out of my hair under a spigot of cold running water, and much longer to comb out the knots.

After the mudding, lunch was served, a feast of several different stews and breads, along with fresh green onions we dipped in salt. The afternoon we spent unloading more sheep, wood for the fires, cleaning, and in general preparing for the evening's activities. A short time after sunset the families prepared their houses for the arrival of the gifts, cleaning the mud from floors and shelves. Then they set dinner on the tables as we all awaited the caravan from Mishongnovi, Yvette's village. Numerous gifts, mostly of food, had already arrived at the houses: canned goods, fruits, vegetables, meats, soda, breads, etc. for the various meals during the ceremony. In the chill of the evening, we stood waiting and chatting. Eventually, as we gazed across the mesa, we saw a row of car lights proceeding out of Mishongnovi. I began counting, but stopped at 25. I would estimate that the caravan consisted of at least 50 vehicles, possibly many more, traveling slowly across the mesa top as our anticipation and excitement mounted.

Gerald asked me to film some of the phalanx of arriving gifts, so when they drove around the corner of the kivas and came up the alley, I grabbed the video camera and began recording. Most of the vehicles which arrived were pickups loaded with flour: first, hand-ground corn meal, then 25 pound bags of wheat flour, as well as boxes and laundry baskets loaded with breads. A line of men and boys facing one another passed the gifts into the first house as the camera caught their efforts and calls of "Askwali" and "Kwa Kwai" (respectively the women's and men's ways of saying "Thank You") rose from the lips of participants. When we had filled the first house, the line continued out the back door to another house. The camera battery eventually died and I joined the line, passing bags of flour and shouting "Kwa Kwai." A few times I called "Askwali" in a high pitched voice, which met with chuckles all around. When that house had received its fill, we moved down the alley to another. After the flour had been unloaded, then came the pastries as pies and cakes in abundance passed through the hands of the women and into homes and the shelves we had set up in the piki house. I would estimate that I handled at least 300-400 twenty five pound (11 kg) bags of flour, and I filmed most of the procession, so the total number of bags must have been 800-1000. The number of pastries also reached enormous proportions. The total number of livestock donated included at least 24 sheep and 2 cows. Of course, Gerald and Yvette and their family will never eat all that food; what's important is the show of support for them, their families, and their traditional way of life, and I must admit it felt both joyous and overwhelming. After the ceremony, they distributed all the unused food, flour, sheep, etc. to various friends and relatives around the reservation. Once it all had been unloaded, a process which took at least an hour, we all sat down to dinner. Four houses, maybe more, had prepared meals and we shared numerous soups, stews, breads, meats (mutton, beef, chicken, turkey), salads of fruits and vegetables, sodas, juices, and desserts aplenty. Thoroughly satiated with food and tired from the day's activities, I drove back to my cozy sleeping bag and tucked in for the night.

Morning came early as they set the stage for the ceremonial hair washing. Women from both families would wash the hair of my friends as they knelt on all fours, their heads bent over wash basins on the floor of the house in Shungopavi. Preparations began at about 4 a.m., as the women heated water and cut the root of the yucca plant, putting it in the water and swirling it until it formed a heavy lather. Then we waited until all had assembled, the women making occasional remarks, most apparently humorous and mostly in Hopi. I again filmed the event as women took their turns washing Gerald's and Yvette's hair, first separately then together. I take it as a washing away of the old life and joining the new as the two became one. After their hair had been washed, the women washed the hair of Gerald and Yvette's 3 beautiful daughters. Given the nature of Hopi weddings, all the preparation and expense, most people married after they had already lived together for some time. My friends were no exception.

Breakfast came after the hair washing, and then the time arrived for butchering meat for the feasts of the following days. We took a couple of sheep at a time from the livestock trailers and led them to the butchering site outside of the piki house. The men sat on the sheep's back, pulled up the head, brushed the wool away at a spot on the neck, and slit the throats of the twitching animals. Once the throat had been slit, they pulled their heads back to allow blood to shoot out into a basin held by one of the women, who collected, cleaned, and prepared the blood for blood pudding & sausage. They then turned the sheep on its back and began cutting away the skin, which they laid out to dry for later use. Several of the men helped cutting out the internal organs and intestines, which the women collected in basins and joined one another in cleaning and preparing them for various foods. We cut the animals into halves which we then hung out to drain and dry. I helped with some of the butchering, but also worked making and tending fires for the pots of beans and hominy. (For the benefit of those not familiar with it, hominy is a type of dried corn). Later we all helped kill and butcher a cow, most of us once again standing by and chatting while others took turns getting their hands bloody. Others chopped and stacked wood to keep the fires going.

While women continued cleaning the entrails of the animals, we took the fresh meat down into one of the kivas, underground ceremonial chambers, and began cutting it into smaller pieces. In the dim light of the kiva, about 30 of us sliced away at the meat, while others ran the electric meat saw for cutting the bones, especially backbones, and a small contingent of women sat in a circle wrapping a sweet blue corn meal mixture into corn husks and leaves to be boiled for the evenings' feast. I cut in silence as others tossed jokes around the circle, most of them in Hopi. What little English they bantered consisted of jokes, including many with sexual overtones. I also became aware that some jokes concerned me, and later learned that a fair number of Hopi jokes regarding this lone "Bahana" (white guy) had passed the circle. I took it all with a grin and an air of amusement. I just felt glad they included me.

After lunch, we set to work cutting more wood, tending the fires, and cleaning the area. About mid afternoon I began feeling a bit off: weak and very tired, so I retreated to the house and rested. The evening's feast was huge. I returned for a part of it, but retired early to rest for my long ride the following day.

In the morning I packed my car and prepared to leave, then stopped at the village to say farewells and numerous thanks. I was directed to Gerald's kiva, where I sat in the back of the room while a core of men sat in the middle smoking their pipes, others joining from their seats by the walls. We waited in meditation, a few words spoken here and there including greetings to all new arrivals. Eventually a call came from outside and shouts arose from the men in the kiva as they arose and set up another line for passing food down through the entrance in the roof to the back of the room, while calling out "Kwa Kwai" as each item passed their hands. When all these gifts of food, had found their way inside the kiva, we ate breakfast including blood pudding, various cornmeal items, beans, pastries, and others. I wanted to try the blood pudding, but just didn't feel up to it, so I settled for corn meal cakes, coffee, and jello. I then thanked everybody, said farewell, especially to those with whom I had conversed the most, and arose to leave. They stopped me, thanked me for my hard work and contributions to the ceremony, and gave me a box of piki bread and a pie to take with me. I felt honored. I then said farewell to Yvette and the women who ate breakfast as they sat surrounded by piles of flour, corn meal, piki bread, and other gifts in the houses. Just as I approached the door to leave, Yvette arose and told the women that I had traveled far to attend the wedding, had worked hard, and had to go. They all thanked me for my contributions of work and food, then gave me a bag of flour and a bucket of the special blue corn meal, which I accepted with deep gratitude. Under the mosaic skies of a Sunday morning in April, I drove out of the village and headed for home.

Hard act to follow, but let me finish off with some more recent weddings.

Now I live in China. These days on the mainland, Chinese weddings mostly tend to be a big party, sometimes with an actual wedding exchanging of vows in the dining hall, but often not, as the official wedding usually takes place at a government office. Typically the bride wears 3 different dresses during the evening, although the groom just usually stays in the same clothes. As usual, men have it so much easier. There will be a big feast and some entertainment, which may involve games or karaoke, called KTV here. Occasionally they have some type of ceremony, especially a tea ceremony involving the parents, which is more traditional. In many places, especially outside of the big cities, weddings will follow more of the traditional ceremony, including the bride being carried to the event in an enclosed cart carried by several young men. I saw that once as I was walking the streets of my mother-in-law's hometown of Bishan in Chongqing. Wedding guests sometimes dress up for the event, but others just come in whatever street clothes are comfortable for the time of year, even shorts and a t-shirt. Typical wedding gifts are, like for almost any formal gift-giving situation in China today, red pockets, little red envelopes full of cash, the amount dependent upon how well you know the people and how closely you are related.

Our daughter's wedding included some traditional elements from both China and the USA, but with another twist: the ceremony took place on a small, remote island in the Maldives, off the southwestern coast of India. The trip there involved a five hour plane ride to the capital city, then after a few hours wait, another hour plane ride to a smaller southern island, then a 20 minute high speed boat ride over rough seas to the island where we stayed. Rain on the day of the wedding didn't dampen our spirits. The wedding began with the Chinese portion, the couple offering tea to both sets of parents and the giving of gifts from the parents to the bride and groom, the common red envelopes full of money. For that Yini wore a traditional red dress with magnificent brocade, absolutely stunning.

For the western-style wedding ceremony she changed into a white lace and satin dress. To get to the ceremony the resort ferried us to a small sand spit a short boat ride away where they had set up a canopy and chairs. Even though Yini is not my biological daughter, she asked that I give her away, so we were the last to go to the site. The time spent with her as we awaited the return of the boat, chatting, taking pictures, and sitting in contemplation was one of the highlights for me.

At the sand spit we had some picture time, with the ladies' high heels digging into the sand as they tried to manoeuvre around. Then a small band in a tent at the back played music as I walked her to the altar and passed her hand to Yang Yu, her husband. The Maldives is a Muslim country, and it was the local Imam (Muslim preacher) who conducted a typical American style ceremony. In the not so distance, a storm slowly approached with dark, foreboding clouds and flashes of lightning. I went back and forth between listening, crying, and watching the storm on pins and needles. After the Imam finished, there was more picture time as the storm continued to approach and the winds grew in strength. We drank from coconuts and chatted and watched the clouds.

Pei and I with our daughter and her new husband at their wedding in the Maldives. Note the storm in the background.

Returning to the resort proved more of a challenge that expected. The tide had started going out and the boat struggled to get off of the sand with each load of people. We arrived back in the resort just in time before the storm hit, and waited while Yini, in Chinese tradition, changed into a third dress, a gray evening gown. The magnificent dinner involved local curries, lots of seafood and plenty of champagne (not a local item).

My own wedding was not quite so spectacular, but had an interesting prelude. In Autumn of 2009 I was working at Oregon Caves National Monument as a seasonal park ranger and living at the Frog Farm in Takilma, which I've previously written about. One evening after work and dinner I went to my little wooden cabin and began checking my email. On the side of the page I saw an ad for a website called "ChinaLoveMatch" and thought "What the hell, why don't I check it out." I had been interested in Chinese culture for quite some time having studied taiji, qigong, and Taoism, and even though I had no intention of moving to China I thought it might be fun to look.

I was somewhat surprised at the wonderful, diverse group of women that I encountered on the website and decided, just to see what would happen, to post my profile on the site. Much to my surprise, I started getting 10-20 requests per day, in spite of the fact that I specifically stated that I was not the "rich American" they might be looking for, and in fact had very little money at all. Some of the women obviously didn't buy that I was poor, but many didn't seem to care and, more surprisingly to a typical American, few expressed any interest in moving out of China. There were a few that really struck me, and one in particular because she wrote in poetic form. I had stated an interest I writing poetry on my profile, and I did my best to answer her back in my free-form poetic style. Before too long she was the only one of the group that I continued communicating with.

Wang Pei and I eventually began chatting everyday, which was made possible by my job being seasonal, and the season had ended. I was basically unemployed, but with promise of a job in the springtime. I was just doing my farm work and chatting with a lass thousands of miles away. We did some video chats and got to know each other quite well, and I eventually decided that I needed to find out if this could be the real thing. I arranged for a Chinese visa from their consulate in San Francisco and planned for a visit of about 4 weeks in January and February, so it included the Chinese New Year. I purposefully told only a few people about the trip so that I wouldn't have to answer all those "How did it go?" questions if it didn't work out. I said "Farewell" to my friends at the Frog Farm and my beloved dog Pedro, and made haste for San Francisco en route to Shanghai.

Wang Pei met me at the airport and we kissed for the first time. I recall everything about it, her brown fur hat and black coat, her long, black leather boots, the broad smile on her soft face, the feel of her warm lips against mine, her firm, but tender hug, and her consternation at being a few minutes later than intended. We went to her car, a black Subaru Forrester, and headed for her apartment. She had always told me that she was great with directions, yet she got lost trying to get from the airport to the Hongkou district where she lived. As a geologist and map enthusiast, I asked her to hand me the map, even though it was in Chinese, and by using pattern recognition of some street names and my navigation skills, I was able to get us back on the road to her place. At least on some level, I guess I earned my keep in my first hour in China.

The next day she took me to the police station to register and we began to explore Shanghai ... and each other. Three days after I arrived we began talking about a possible future together and the subject of possible marriage came up. We really got along great right from the start, so, casting caution to the wind, I pulled out the ring I had brought, one made from a diamond on my deceased mother's earrings, got down on my knees, and asked her to marry me. She immediately agreed.

Several days later we went to spend a night at an antique water town called Xitang, where part of one of the Mission: Impossible movies was filmed. After we returned we began planning for a trip to her hometown of Chengdu, Sichuan, where I was to meet her family for the first time. As my hair was down to the middle of my back and in China I hadn't seen any men with hair longer than their collars, I went with her to the barber to get it cut. Didn't want to scare them all. Two days before we left for Sichuan, we began discussing this marriage thing. If we were going to do this and I was going to be going back to the USA in 3 weeks, when could we get married? I said I thought it took a while to get approval for a foreign marriage in China, and she began looking on Chinese websites about it. She said that much of what Western websites wrote was not required, but recommended and that all we needed to do was to go to the office on Caobao Road with the proper ID and we could get married. I looked at her and said, "So, do you want to get married?" She said "Sure."

I said "Let's get some lunch first." We went to a noodle shop (Lanzhou Lamian) and set off for Caobao Road. We took care of some paperwork, said our vows, and were married, simple as that.

After we returned to the apartment, her daughter Yini had come home from school and we got ready to go out to eat at the Pudong Shangri-La across the river. The dinner with the 3 of us was a bit strange, but oh so very wonderful. Yini was gracious and tolerant with our googoo eyes to a point. The only food I can recall was the roast pigeon … hadn't had that before. I remember that we sat there for a long time. Yini left early to be with her friends, and Pei and I tried to get a cab back home, but none wanted to cross the river. It was getting late and the subway was not running anymore. It looked like we'd have to walk back, a long, long walk. Finally we found a cab that was willing to take us across the river to the apartment and arrived around midnight. We've been together 9 years as of this writing, and going as strong as ever, at least with the relationship. We are getting older, after all.

BIGFOOT SERENADE

Journal Scribblings from a Hike in the Siskiyou Wilderness

Introduction

In July of 2007 I went for a walk in the woods. I had intended to hike for 3 weeks, but it ended up lasting only 13 days due to a sudden loss of food. My intent was to be alone in the wilderness for the entire time, if possible, and to connect more deeply with Nature and with myself, not necessarily to undertake a great feat of hiking, pun intended. I took with me no reading material, other than a few maps, and my journal. I had no watch, no cell phone, no camera, no toilet paper (Nature provides), but plenty of food. I carried a food cache in to Young's Valley before the hike, a location about 40 miles into the hike, then had arranged for friends to check in with me at a place called Poker Flat on the 13th day of the hike. The food was in a Bear Resistant Food Container (BRFC), which is like a big piece of PVC pipe that is sealed but for a screw-down lid on one end.

    I left on the morning of July 1st from the trailhead of the Clear Creek Trail (called the No Man Trailhead), about 10 miles south of the blessed little town of Happy Camp, CA. My good friend Laurel dropped me off and took care of my canine companion, Pedro, while I spent time away. From there I hiked up the trail to Young's Valley (YV), and finally to Poker Flat where I met Pedro, Laurel, her dog Osha, and other good friends John and Annette. Along the way I also hiked up the West Fork Clear Creek Trail, to Devil's Punchbowl, Rattlesnake Meadow, Kelly Lake, and made several other shorter side trips. From Poker Flat I had intended to hike to the Red Buttes Wilderness on the California/ Oregon border, then on the Boundary Trail to Mt. Elijah, and finish off at the Oregon Caves. That part of the hike, alas, never happened, although I've hiked most of it before.

The landscape of the Siskiyou Wilderness consists of beautiful clean rivers and lakes, steep-walled valleys and moderately high mountains (up to over 7000 feet), covered with shrubland and forests, often dense, which consist mostly of Douglas-firs, Pacific madrones, several varieties of oaks, true firs, 2 species of cedars, with an understory of buckbrush, ceanothus, huckleberry, bay laurel, and other various and sundry small trees and shrubs. The geology is complex, but the rocks are mostly igneous and metamorphic, especially granite, diorite, a little marble, some gabbro, and serpentinite. Winter tends to be cool to cold, and fairly wet and overcast, with summers being hot and dry. The record high temperature in Happy Camp, CA, for instance, is 115F. Temperatures on this hike mostly reached over 90F, but went as high as over 100F. The area seldom gets hiked compared to many other places in the region, but it is nonetheless magnificent. I dearly loved it.

The Pacific Northwest from northern California to British Columbia is Bigfoot country. Most of the sightings of this supposed wild man took place in the forests of this area and if you travel much in the region you're likely to see various statues, paintings, business names, or other media that relate to Bigfoot, not the least of which is the huge metal statue in downtown Happy Camp, CA, population 1,190 as of 2010. I mention this only because I was living near Happy Camp at the time and the hike takes place in this area, hence the name of the writing. If you're thinking I'm going to tell you about sighting Bigfoot along my hike, you'll be disappointed. I know people, some reputable, who have claimed to have seen Bigfoot, but alas, the closest thing I saw to Bigfoot on this hike was one normal human and a few bears.

I did see a Bigfoot trap, which obviously didn't work, when out on another hike. Believers often say they are intelligent creatures, but most bears I've know could have outsmarted the trap. Yet another time I was hiking from the Oregon Caves to the Red Buttes and came across a mango and an apple sitting on a log. They looked delicious and I was tempted to grab them for my hike, but thought they might belong to a nearby hiker, though I saw no other sign of people. When I returned late the next day the two fruits were still there. The apple had been partly eaten by a Stellar's jay, but they were otherwise untouched. I sat down and ate them before finishing my hike. Later I realized that they were possibly left for Bigfoot to eat, as most people who believe in them seem to think Bigfoot is a fruit eater. A curious thing. Apples are native to central Asia, though have been grown in Oregon for over a hundred years, so a Bigfoot might recognize one as food. But a mango? Mangoes are tropical, likely native to South Asia, so how would a Bigfoot recognize one as food when the nearest mango vine likely is 1000 miles or more away? If Bigfoot does exist, I think he's likely more intelligent than many of his admirers. But back to the subject at hand.

My walk covered about 65 miles in total, not all that much for 13 days, but I did have a heavy pack, rough terrain, and intent to meditate more than exercise. Also, while I have backpacked before, the longest trip I had done previously was 4 days, and that took place more than 15 years prior to this hike when I was 34. My longest solo trip lasted 3 days. I would consider myself a veteran day hiker, but not a seasoned backpacker. So this was a test for me emotionally, spiritually, and physically, to some degree. As you read the following pages, you may get the impression I don't like people, but that's not at all true. It's just that I wanted to be alone and see what would happen.

This writing consists of excerpts from my journal during that hike, altered a bit to remove anything incriminating or too boring even for me. My purpose in presenting this is mostly to share my experiences, but also to show one perspective on what goes through someone's mind when their only communication takes place with Nature other than humans. Some wanderers and hermits have gone out for much longer times, but most people have, I believe, no clue as to what such an experience means. I've included a few of the poems I had written along the way, such that they are. I was going through a very dark period when I started this hike. There are references to Sufism (mystical sect of Islam) and Nature spirituality, which helped me deal with that darkness. There's also much written about the flora and fauna of this special place. I hope you find it at least partly as fascinating as I did.

1 July 2007

And so this journey begins. Just had a moment with a dragonfly: white and black with narrow abdomen bulging at the tip, and a back humped like a camel – well, almost like a camel. S/he just flew in to land on a rock in the creek, sit for a couple of minutes, then move on. I've stopped alongside a very small, but delicious creek that cascades o'er the rocks on its way to meet Clear Creek below. Not sure of the name of it, but who cares. Beside me stand Azaleas, just past bloom with their wilting flowers arching from their perches atop the tips of branches. Some sort of legume grows around me. To my left are maidenhair ferns and Port Orford cedars, among others.

Later

It's my first of the ten or so campsites I will set up somewhere along Clear Creek, I think about 2-3 miles from the confluence with West Clear Creek. It's a nice campsite at a big bend in the river. I'll try to write as I sit outside, but the stupid mosquitoes here don't seem to know they're supposed to hate citronella oil, which I've rubbed on my exposed flesh. Rough day's hiking in rather hot weather, much of it exposed to the sun, first on red rocks, which always seem hot whether or not they are. Then for a while on black rocks, which do soak up a lot of heat, then on white rocks, which reflect lots of solar radiation that toasts you in a different way. However you put it, I felt well-baked, like an overdone loaf of bread.

The bats have come out. Hooray for the bats!! Die demon mosquitoes!

2 July

It's interesting the stuff that goes through my head as this trip progresses. Lots of songs, most of which I don't want there, i.e. Delta Dawn, the Green Berets, etc. I did hear the call of ravens, probably my favorite birds, for the first time on my trip. Glad to hear from them.

Anyhow, I've been able to get the songs out of my head with a little effort and time, mostly by focusing on my hiking, the environment, or by substituting something else, such as the Rumi poem which I've rewritten as:

> Today, like every other day, we wake up empty and scared.
> Don't open the door to the study and begin reading.
> *Take a walk in the woods.*
> Let the beauty we love be what we do.
> There are hundreds of ways to kneel and kiss the ground.

A poem written today:

Sunlight Flows

> Through a window
> In the canopy
> Cascading o'er the trunks
> And leaves and branches
> As streams shine down
> Upon the landscape
> Rays piercing through
> Bilious cumulus of rock
> And a solitary wanderer
> Sits at the base
> Of a strong, stately Douglas fir
> Wondering why it took so long
> To come to this place
> To find the Beloved

In the green foliage
Of a spreading laurel
Kissed with sunlight
The bark at his back
The mosaic of leaves overhead
And the firm, but gentle ground
That nestles his buttocks,
The rush of Clear Creek
His soothing serenade.
The longer the journey
The sweeter the kiss
At the end.

3 July

Today I hiked most of the way up the West Fork Clear Creek Trail as a day hike with a small pack. I started out with the idea of making it a light day, and if I could just get at least as far as I did yesterday evening that it would be enough. Once I shook off the sluggishness of a night without much sleep, I got to feeling really good, unburdened as I was without my heavy pack to weigh me down. I started to tire as I got close to the point where the trail ends, and began pushing myself to try and get there, but my intuition told me to stop and turn around before I wore myself out completely. I had many creek crossings and downed trees to negotiate before I could rest back at camp and I didn't want to wipe myself out on a hot day so early in my 3 week hike. I'm glad I did that, although I'd at least like to know how close I got to the end. Kelsey Ridge seemed a little ways off and I think I could have done it, but... My goal is more spiritual than physical, although 3 weeks of hiking is enough of a physical goal in and of itself, especially for someone like me who hasn't done that much backpacking.

The Elder

My walk was interrupted. Headed back to camp, I heard a voice call out in a very subtle sort of way. It called to me from the shadows. Quiet, but firm. Not pleading. Just a simple request. "Please, come sit with me," he asked. I stopped, turned, and pondered for a moment. I wasn't in a hurry. Just needed to get back by dark, a few hours distant. Nobody awaited me, nor any appointments to keep. So I walked back to him and sat down. We remained in silence for a time, just sitting and being together. Then he told me of his life, how during his many, many years he had seen changes on the land. Homes built and destroyed or fallen into disrepair due to lack of use. Stream channels changing location. Flash floods, lightning, fires, earthquakes, and a great many friends come and gone. Old trees fallen and new ones born. Dramas lived out before his gaze. And he talked of his own offspring, some living good lives, healthy, strong, with young of their own, and others fallen before their time. The pain of watching your own children pass grieved him, but he spoke also of the acceptance of life in its heights and its depths.

He told me also of his own physical pain, the illnesses that have weakened him in some ways, maybe made him stronger in others. The wounds, the broken limbs, the essence he had shed, how the winds of life had taken their toll and nearly toppled him. He said he felt weary, that while he did not wish to hasten death, he nonetheless would welcome the rest that only death could bring. But he also admitted that having the chance to sit and chat with a friend assuaged his weariness and made the long days more worthwhile. How it gratified him also to have his family ever so close, to watch his children and grandchildren grow.

Then he said he knew I'd have to go soon and expressed his gratitude for the time I'd spent with him. I too, thanked him for the chance to get to know him if only for a short time. He asked if I would return to visit. I said I didn't know, that it was my first time in his neighborhood and I hoped it would not be my last. I told him it might take a while before I could visit again. He told me I was a good man and that wherever I wandered in this big, wide world of ours, if I took the time to sit with an elder, to listen to their story and tell them mine, that he would be there with me. That felt good. So I stood, turned toward him, and gave him a big hug. He sighed. I thanked him, wished him well, put my lips to his bark, and then, with a tear in my eye, I turned and walked away. Long may the old trees stand. And long may we listen.

Water Dance

>Snippet of Old Man's Beard*
>Cast into the current
>Of a cascading mountain stream
>Riding the surface for a time
>He saunters upstream
>Protected in the eddy
>Then spins around
>Dives under and dances
>Swirling in and out
>Twisting, turning
>Spinning in summersaults
>So elegant, so graceful
>Turns back around
>Do-si-dos it all again
>Then, when this part
>Of the dance has ended
>He bobs into the mainstream
>Bows to an audience of one
>And then falls in the falls
>Heading to new adventures
>New performances
>Somewhere beyond
>He ever thought he'd travel
>Then, this audience
>This initiator of the journey

---

* Old Man's Beard is a type of lichen that grows on many trees in this area.

Continues his own dance
Somewhere up the trail
Hoping for as much grace
As he saw in a simple twig.

4 July

So there I was debating in my mind, or actually trying to justify, the merits of using soap to wash my hands in such a pristine place (is it bad for the creek water or even worse for my health not to use it?), when the creek took the soap away from me. I laughed at the irony. I have more for when I need it.

Arrived at Wilderness Falls sometime before the sun stood straight overhead, and it is a truly wondrous place. The main falls funnels the creek down to a narrow spillway about 2 feet wide that drops a total of about 12-15 feet to a large emerald pool. On the east side of the pool rises a sheer wall, 20-40 feet high depending on where you measure, and the west side rises more gently to an open rock terrace before the ground cover, then the trees, envelope it. The rocks are mostly, maybe entirely, granitic in type, gray to salt and pepper. Around this island of open space rises a mixed forest, mostly conifers, primarily tall, stately Douglas firs and Port Orford cedars.

Above the main falls on the west side, sits a small pool. When I approached it I noticed a baby garter snake sunning herself on the rocks alongside the pool. I watched her for a moment and then went over to check out some potholes in the rocks that contained lots of mosquito larvae. I returned to the other pool and saw that the snake had moved, and on further inspection found her under the water swimming around on the bottom. I watched her as she came to the shore, then very slowly crept up the rocks. I continued watching as she sat there, still but for her tongue darting out of her mouth. Flies danced across my naked body, but I didn't flinch, not wanting to startle her. When I began thinking I'd leave her to lay still, she opened her mouth in a sort of yawn. I wasn't sure if that's what I saw, but then she did it again with a much wider opened mouth. Hmmmm, so snakes yawn?! I can't say for certain that's what she did, but it sure looked like it to me. She moved a bit, and as she did, she wiped the side of her head on the rocks, first the right side, then the left, almost like wiping something from her nose. Then she headed back to the water where she proceeded to move rapidly along the contours of the subaqueous rocks, and appeared to follow a definite pattern, almost as if she were running a well-worn circuit. She finished her underwater adventure by rising slowly out of the water, watching for signs of food or danger, I imagine. After another couple of moments I arose and left her in peace. Time for my lunch.

At nightfall:

Just heard something BIG fall up the creek somewhere. Think I'll see if anyone is around. No response to my call, my first loud words in days, and my food's OK. Spent some time thinking about my priorities in life and what I should do after I finish this hike.

Time for bed.

5 July

Afternoon:

This morning as I began breaking camp, I set my pack against a log by my tent. Unfortunately I set it over a yellowjacket nest. I went to pick it up and saw it swarmed with what I thought were flies. It was all backlit by the sun and I couldn't quite tell what they were. As I grabbed the pack, one clamped onto a finger on my left hand and really bit me. I swiped the offender away, but it's been hurting all day. Sometimes cold water helps, but later in the day it actually increased the pain. A cream I bought for this sort of thing has also had mixed results. Anyhow, I snuck in during a lull in the swarm and pulled the pack away. One of them was trying to bite my pack and I killed him. I kinda feel bad about that. I apologized to the yellowjackets, stayed away from the log, and they left me alone. My finger's OK now.

So here I am at a popular fisherman's camp called Trout Camp, a place I've dreaded, given what I heard about bears stealing people's food here, but I think I'll be alright. I believe my stuff is hung high enough in the trees and I suspect that the incidents are related to bad food management, based on the way these camps look. But then, ya never know and we'll see how the night goes. Arrived here late morning, set up camp, then got ready for a day hike up to Devil's Punchbowl, which turned out to be a very steep trail in parts. However it's a great view from there, my first place on this trip for a big overview of the area.

After hiking up I came to a lake and was rather disappointed from what I'd heard about the place. A faint trail continued up the valley, but there was a washout, so I thought that this was the main lake. The scenery around it looked great, but except for the newts and jumping fish, the lake itself appeared as nothing that special: just a shallow, muddy bottomed, small lake, not as nice as others I'd visited in the area. Then I thought, "Well, I'll just see what's beyond that rise over there." So I went back to the trail and easily maneuvered the washout. The trail just kept on following rock cairns over granite until I came to this amazing natural amphitheater in the mountain with a huge emerald lake at the base... Spectacular!!!! There really are not words adequate to describe the place. It was one of the few spots along the trip where I really, really wanted to have a camera with me. Just sat there for a while in the high elevation sun and then felt the need to head back to camp. After not having slept well, the steep hike, the sun beating down on me on a very hot day, I felt I needed to be extra careful on the way down, so I took my time and tried to be careful, and all went well.

If I were to title this walk, two possibilities are "Bigfoot Serenade" and "Dances with Insects." The first relates to every evening at about dinner time I hear music; well, I hear it a lot, but mostly at dinner time. I suspect a combination of the sound of the running water, animals, and hallucinations/ mind games, but it seems so vivid that tonight I made a special trip to the creek to see if anyone was camped on the other side. I found nothing, nada, nobody. I could have sworn that someone was there... I suspect Bigfoot of playing mind games with me.

The second, of course, relates to the fact that when you're out in a place like this, people often imagine the wild animals like bears, mountain lions, coyotes, or other charismatic megafauna. In reality it's always the insects that play the biggest role in the day to day dance of life, flies, mosquitoes, ants, yellowjackets, dragonflies, etc. In reality, the most dangerous creatures on Earth besides humans are likely mosquitoes.

Up until today I hadn't really missed personal contact with friends all that much, but during my morning hike that longing really hit me. Yes, I miss people, but mostly I miss my dog, Pedro. Funny how that works. I still have 16 days to go in total, 8 before I see friends. For the most part, though, I'm doing well thus far.

Devil's Punchbowl

>Glistening in the summer sun
>Diamonds on an emerald mirror
>You sit tucked among
>Sheer, rocky granite cliffs
>Circled by ancient trees
>Some, remnants of a distant age,
>Just like you
>Fish jumping 5000 feet
>Every day you simply sit
>And express your beauty
>For all the world to appreciate
>Providing daily sustenance
>For bears and their friends
>And all we can do is admire you,
>Come feel your cool water,
>Let your spirit fill us,
>Then walk away.
>How trivial and unnecessary
>The workings of congress,
>Car troubles, arguments with lovers,
>Wearing the right clothes,
>Fretting over oil supplies,
>And so much more,

When held up to
Your presence and simple beauty.

6 July

Today I learned a good lesson from Preston Peak. I started out this morning from Trout Camp, and hiked up to the intersection with the Rattlesnake Meadow Trail. There I made the decision to hike my full pack to Rattlesnake Meadow, rather than find a campsite along the creek and do a day hike up to the Meadow. My plan was to camp at Rattlesnake Meadow, hike to the top of Preston Peak, then camp again in the Meadow, before moving on to Young's Valley to get my food cache. The hike up to Rattlesnake Meadow was not all that long, only 2-2 ½ miles, but very steep, climbing over 1300 feet, most of it in the first mile. It was hot, but not as sweltering as it had been. I stopped about half way up for lunch and a good, long rest. The hike would have been hard anytime, but with a full pack on a hot day it was grueling. Then I pressed on to the Meadow. Don't know why it's called Rattlesnake Meadow, as at that elevation (5200 feet) there aren't likely many rattlesnakes, although I could be wrong on that. I just saw one garter snake on the trail. Maybe someone found one there and was surprised, so that's how it got the name. Maybe it was for the rattlesnake orchid that grows in the forests here. Anyhow, what I saw most was lots and lots of evidence of bears, including more scat than a person should see in a lifetime, and numerous plants pulled up for their roots (Angelica sp.). I finally found the campsite that people had established, complete with piles of bear scat, and evidence that people haven't always kept food away from the bears. I could see the remains of the ropes people had used to tie up their food in trees around me, most looking like they had been broken by someone big and furry.

I walked around a bit to see the sights – great view of the valley below and the surrounding mountains. And a spectacular view of the top of Preston Peak 2100 feet above me. I looked at the route to the peak and it didn't look all that bad. I felt I'd be up for it the next day, even if my legs and shoulders were a bit sore from the hiking lately, especially up to the Meadow. Then I sat down and thought about things. The amount of bear sign troubled me. I love bears and highly respect them, but prefer to admire them from a safe distance. On the other hand, if I stored my food properly, I'd not likely have a problem. Then I checked in with my heart and it said that I should not climb this peak, even if I'm capable of it. Preston has an astounding presence, a dignity, even though it's not all that high (7309 feet). I'm sure it would be a great view from there, but I believe that just because we can do something doesn't mean we should do it. I came to the conclusion that I would not climb Preston. There will be other peaks, I'm sure, that I will hike to the tops of, but not this one. There are places we maybe should just leave alone, even as hikers.

I felt disappointed, but believed I was right not to do it. Well, what about just staying the night and going down tomorrow? I got up to look around. About 200 feet away I saw a bear foraging for food. She looked beautiful, her silky black fur shining in the summer sun, rippling with her movements like waves across a mountain lake. I watched her for a moment, then to see what would happen, I clapped my hands. She looked up at me. I called out to her, wanting her to know I was human. Bears don't have great eyesight. She walked over and sat down in the shade of a couple of trees. I talked to her, the first deliberate regular volume sentence I've uttered in over 5 days. She just lay down. I loved seeing her, but her actions troubled me a bit. Most of the bears I've seen are pretty shy with humans, especially those in the Siskiyou Mountains. They've always made a swift exit when they discovered I was human. This one didn't. I felt pretty tired after my day's hike, but I decided to leave this place to the bears. They say that discretion is the better part of valor. I think people should visit a beautiful place like this on its own terms, including allowing the bears free rein. Yet another good reason to not hike the peak.

Since I already felt exhausted, I dreaded the idea of going down that steep, rocky trail, but I said goodbye to the bear and wished her well, then turned, hoisted my pack on my back, took a big slug of water, and headed back downhill. I walked carefully in the steep sections and made it down in time to set up camp and eat dinner before dark.

Trout Dancing

Silver ships glowing in the night
Passing through a sea of stars
Far below, in the dark depths of the ocean,
A solitary figure
Stands among the towering
Bastions of the forest
Bathed in the light
Of a waning half moon
He begins to dance
Feet caressing the ocean floor
Arms, legs, hair, swirling
In the waters of night
Moving to a rhythm
Of a creek nearby
Dancing on the rocks
Chaotic, entrancing
He spins and bounces
With no other fish
There to watch and judge
Just moving in whatever way
The beat and the spirit call
The spirit?
Did I mention the spirit?
Ah! The spirit conducts
The orchestra playing
In the ocean of forest
Under the sea of stars
And the silver clouds
Passing beneath the moon
While the mountains sing the song
If only we could hear it
In the concrete jungle where tempers can flair
Over many a meaningless matter

And an overwhelming glut
Of useless information
Turns us away
From the calling
For what is joy
But a soul
Dancing with circumstance
In the moonlight
Just before the dawn.

7 July

Morning:
    I have noticed that I tend to always have a musical theme in my mind, but it's different from the songs that often catch my mind and linger there for minutes, hours, days. These are not songs per se, but just short musical phrases & rhythms, which are very simple and while they may sound similar to things I know, I can't attribute them to any song or musical piece in particular. I can say that today they tend to sound a bit like contemporary Celtic music, maybe even Celtic new age. Oh, no, not new age!! Yes, but these are just simple themes above which one could do any number of things if one chose, add a melody, dance, calculate higher math. Anyhow, what often seems to happen is that as I walk along pondering a Rumi poem or focusing on being present in my hiking, the words that constantly run through my mind fall into the rhythms in my head. While this is not entirely new to me, it does tell me that rhythms and musical themes are more important to me than I often give credit and maybe I need to incorporate them into my life more. Also it feels good to have my own rhythms and melodies rather than the "store bought" variety.
    A thought popped into my head while looking at a cedar tree: "In a way we (the trees) are all just as old…we're all timeless." How positively cosmic! ☺

Evening:

Today I wanted a leisurely day, and though it has not exactly been a hard day, I did end up hiking to Young's Valley (YV) to check out my food cache and see how things were up there. Didn't' see anyone camping in the area. Found a GeoCache and the last entry was dated July 3 of this year. There was another entry from May 18 in which the people had left on May 13 from No Man's Trailhead, the same one as me. "No Man's Trailhead". Sounds ominous, like no one could survive. Or maybe they only want women using it. Anyhow, the really exciting news was that my food cache didn't appear to have been touched at all. Very good news!

Just went down to the creek to rinse off my hands, as well as other parts of my anatomy, and I noticed in some water that's so very gently flowing, but almost like a mirror as it's so smooth, the presence of these neat little whirlpools, small and delicate whirlpools that I only noticed in the late evening light. They danced around the rocks in the flow of the current. They came off the side of one rock, then the next rock had a little divot in it that caused the whirlpools to divide around the rocks. It was *So Cool!!*

Sitting by the creek, when my head is just right, I can hear bees buzzing, but I think it's just an odd sound from the water of the creek, though it could also be from the cedar tree I'm leaning against.

After what I wrote this morning, the musical theme in my head is driving me crazy today. I hear it in the creek along with voices singing various melodies to it, but no words. I began thinking that I might want to end this odyssey early. After I pondered it, I decided to keep going.

8 July

Sitting atop a small peak just to the south of Cyclone Gap. The elevation here is about 5800 feet. It was a relatively easy hike up, very little climbing involved. From here I have an incredible view. To the north sits El Capitan, the southeastern bastion of Young's Valley. To the west I see too much to describe other than that it's everything from just south of Bear Mountain (Devil's Punchbowl) north to Young's Peak at the northwestern corner of

YV, and beyond towards Broken Rib Mountain (what a great name!). I'm sure I can see into the Kalmiopsis Wilderness and down to Kelsey Ridge. The east shows me the Marble Mountains, Mount Shasta, and everything in between and around. The south is dominated by the most impressive view of Preston Peak I've had, with Copper Mountain in the foreground. The area where I sit writing is covered with Manzanitas, Ceanothus, and other shrubs I don't know. There are twisted and stunted Douglas firs, incense-cedars, Brewer spruces, white pines, and others. Sulphur flowers, penstemons, and other flowers are in bloom, including the most vibrant Indian paintbrush I've ever seen, almost neon in its reds and oranges.

It's been a good day for seeing birds. Earlier I saw a grouse and her 2 chicks, then a couple of hairy woodpeckers. I saw a brown creeper, the first in quite a while. Then there was this brown bird with what appeared to be a reddish brown tail, and he sang a gorgeous, fluting and trilling song. It's a glorious day, still quite warm, but cooler than it has been. It also helps to be a lot higher. It's breezy with hardly a cloud in the sky, just a bit of haze to the west and some cumulus clouds in the very distant southeast. Saw a garter snake on the hike as well.

I saw a person today from my perch high above them and heard other voices. I felt a bit shocked. So my solitude has ended. Their group is camped at YV and I've now heard the first human voices outside of mine (and the singing in the creek) in 7 days. Haven't spoken to them yet, but my guess is it's inevitable. I will spend time at Raspberry Lake tomorrow, hike the East Fork & Black Butte Trails (or whatever I find out that end of the valley), and maybe hang out at Cracker Meadow, although that may be a problem depending on how long this group will be here, since my goal is to be alone. Maybe I'll go to Twin Valley early and spend an extra night there. The truth is that this whole experience has thus far been special and spectacular and mystical, but in a more subtle way than I had anticipated. Maybe, though, it would have been better to have undertaken this trip not during the peak tourist season, if I didn't want to meet people, but that's what worked out. Maybe I'll do another 10-14 day camping trip with Pedro in the desert this winter and I can have more solitude. But this trip ain't over yet and I intend to make the most of it.

Tonight as I watched sunset hues change on El Capitan, I saw some dragonflies out buzzing around way above my head. They are SO AMAZING! I need to learn more about them. Also I want to know more about hummingbirds and woodpeckers.

9 July

The music I hear in the flowing of the creek has turned to a more jazzy type of thing with guitar chords like two minor 7th chords a full step apart, then a crooning male voice singing over it in a rather soulful mood. It's really quite nice.

I've hiked up to Raspberry Lake and it truly is a special place, a beautiful emerald green lake, although not as bright as the Devil's Punchbowl, but more intimate in its presence. It sits tucked along the side of the ridge of Preston and Copper Peaks, of which one can see only a little bit from the lake. I loved the hike up to the lake. Found an abandoned mine along the way with some neat rocks, looked like possible copper ores. Great views along the trail, though the hike is not as easy as the map seems to indicate. I wondered about the quality of the water when I first arrived and saw some dead fish near the shore, but then saw lots of live fish and newts, so I suspect it wasn't the water quality. Rather it was possibly the fishermen who are very much in evidence here, their campsites still rather trashed with some chalk graffiti on the rocks in places. Probably some teenage fishermen (fisherboys?) likely based on the "Beau loves Martinelli" and other such scribblings. Only saw one bear scat so far. I think they all hang out at Rattlesnake Meadow. I can see logs in the bottom of the lake, but a lot of them on shore as well, one on the right quite popular with the local blue damselflies. I'm sitting where the ridge to my left breaks to the flatter area to the right, which is where this little cirque opens to the world. A butterfly flew past me that was as loud as any I've ever heard. Also heard a sound from the Stellar's jays I've never noticed them making before. It's sort of like a donkey "heehaw" with the tone of a hawk and a whistle combined. Hmmm.

Giving Birth to Herself

At Raspberry Lake as I prepared to check out the west side of the lake, the flat side, and after having taken a dip in the lake. I went to put on my waist pack when I noticed that attached to it was the exoskeleton of a dragonfly larva. And trying to get out of it was the new dragonfly, her abdomen still partly in the old skeleton. In other words, she was in the process of shedding, of changing from a larva to an adult. In a very sort of 'exhausted, low energy' way, she periodically writhed trying to get all the way out. I pulled the skeleton off of my pack and placed it on a nearby small plant with spatula-like leaves 2-3 inches long, and low to the ground. The plant stood maybe 4-5 inches tall. I've read that when they emerge they like to crawl to the tops of plants to dry themselves off. I've also seen their exoskeletons on plants before. Then, even though I knew I should not, I cheated a bit and helped her out of her exoskeleton, her old dress. She grasped the leaves as best she could, but I could tell it was agonizing for her, so I placed a stick in the plant to try to help her get a better grip to climb up it. At this point she had a green body, the color of pea soup, with black eyes and the wings? Where were the wings? All I could see was a white and lime green mass on the back of her thorax. I decided to watch her as long as I could, hopefully until she flew away, but I had no idea how long that might take.

Eventually I had to return to camp some 2-2 ½ miles distant and almost 1000 feet below me. The time passed with long periods of her just sitting there drying out, separated by moments of intense effort to 'come of age,' and we all know how difficult that is. Much of her work of going from larva to adult looked agonizing to me, and I certainly empathized with her. Slowly her wings went from a lump to wing-looking things that still flopped in the breeze, sort of like a hot air balloon as it fills, but at paint drying speed. As they did, she struggled to climb higher and I did what I could to help, but I knew it was mostly up to her. Her little legs gripped at the leaves, but they seemed a bit too slippery for her. At one point fairly early in the proceedings, an ant came and tried to have a go at her. I took a stick and drove him away. I know all that stuff about letting nature take its course and all, but I figured we have enough food around for ants, and I wanted to give my dragonfly a fighting chance. As time passed she looked like she was gaining her strength, so when ants came up to challenge her, she brushed them off herself…Hooray! During all this her wings began to get more clear except for one little lime green patch, and they were still stuck together instead of laying flat like they do on adult dragonflies. She also changed eventually into a bronze color on her body and an iridescent metallic blue gray on her eyes. Each time she struggled I'd urge her on with words of encouragement. Finally after all that struggle to climb the plant and fill out her body, I was looking right at her when her wings went 'Pop!' and opened up flat. I cheered with a sudden Hooray!

It was a while yet before she gave her first little flutter of attempted flight. Her wings still flopped in the breeze and one, her left rear, still looked crinkled and milky white, while the others had become completely clear and full. That worried me a bit. Was it common for them to have wings like that, or did she have a problem? And how long would it normally take until she could fly? I had no watch so I don't know low much time passed, but I'd guess it was often 5-10 minutes or more between each flurry of activity. Finally she gave her first flutter of trying to fly. It started with just a vibration. Then they started to flap and I again cheered. It took several more of these false starts before she got off the ground and fluttered a few inches, then crashed. Undaunted she kept trying every so often, but with the same results. However, she seemed to have reached a wall in all of this and didn't seem to get any stronger.

I put my finger into the lake and, thinking that since these are aquatic insects she needed water, I held my finger to her. She climbed up it and did put her little mouth to my skin. Was she drinking? Hell, I don't know, but it seemed to help her, so since dragonflies do usually fly over the water and emerge from the water, I took her closer to the lake and placed her on a rock by the shore in the sunlight. She again tried to fly and fell into the lake, where her wings seemed to get waterlogged. She, with great struggle, climbed the rock to dry out. Maybe that wasn't such a great idea on my part. What do I know about what dragonflies need?! By this point the sun was reaching toward the western horizon and I realized I needed to get moving soon. I watched, my thrill turning to sadness every time she fluttered and faltered.

Finally I needed to go. Her one wing still didn't look right, but there's nothing I could do to help. Maybe the help I'd already given was a detriment to her, but maybe not. I think her relatives, the damselflies, knew I was trying to help one of their own, since for the first time in a long day by the water, some flew over to me and hung out with me just before I left. As I arose to head to the trail, I wished her well and blew her a kiss, feeling honored that she chose my pack on which to give birth to herself. She just sat there, clinging to her rock as I walked away. And I clung to the hope that she eventually spread those wings to fly, diving in acrobatics over the water like her brothers and sisters. Maybe she got eaten by a bird, maybe she just was one that didn't make it, or maybe I just didn't wait long enough to see her take off. That night, as I sat down to eat dinner, I looked to the sky. In the breaks of the forest canopy I saw dragonflies darting about after mosquitoes and other tasty morsels. In my heart I cheered them on and thought about my friend, wondering if she was doing the same.

Evening:

Well, now what to do? I'm camped at the southern end of Young's Valley and went to check on my food cache. A bear has gotten my cache and I have some beans and a few grains (very few), and one tin of fish left, so it's time to make for the road. All I found of the well-placed Bear Resistant Food Container (BRFC) was the lid, heavily scratched, and some remnant shreds of plastic bags. Oh, and some twist ties. The bear moved, but did not take my extra fuel canister, so I can cook for quite a while. If only I had enough to put in the pan. The creek sounds like a rock and roll song, 5-4-1 progression. But time for bed now. Long, good day at Raspberry Lake.

I've faced some fears about backpacking on this trip. I wasn't entirely sure I could do this, but thus far I have and it's gone well. Many avid hikers have never been out solo for as long as I have already and it's not yet finished. I've felt surprised at how well I have managed with only my own company, I know I can do well with Nature, and what I really need to work on is my relationships with people. I'm not sure this hike is going to help me in that regard. Glad I didn't find any people in Young's Valley when I hiked through there, though.

10 July

Sitting in Twin Valley swatting flies, eating lunch, and looking out at Lookout Mountain. Two main thoughts come to mind:
1. How do I feel in regards to this change of events, my loss of food?
2. What to do now? What to do now? What to do now?

When I discovered that the BRFC had been violated, of course I felt surprised, then amused and somewhat relieved. Disappointed also, but not that much. If this journey ends sooner I believe it still will have been worth the effort. I will have proven to myself that I can do this and have accomplished most of my goals. Feeling rather worn out, but that's also due partly to poor sleep last night and not having much food. The next few days without food may be the toughest. Now for questions 2.

Do I continue hiking today or camp here for the night? Food and bears are concerns here. Looks like good bear habitat, but haven't seen much scat. I have little food left and it may be best to hike while I still have it, but it feels best to stay here for tonight and tomorrow go to Poker Flat to await my friends a few days hence.

So I'm sitting under this magnificent Douglas fir and this little black jumping spider crawled up on my pants leg. My trousers as I sit here have these ridges in them, sort of like the ridges of these mountains in which I've been hiking around. She was climbing slowly up one ridge and up the other side came a tiny insect of some sort, about the size of a gnat. Anyhow, the spider and 'gnat' reached the top at the same time and in an instant the spider sucked up the gnat and it was gone. Such carnage on my very appendage! Right now the spider's on my boot keeping watch for something else to happen her way. I just heard a very loud crash some distance up the valley. Hmmm, I wonder what is going on?

11 July

Not great sleep again last night, partly due to the storm that struck with a beautiful vengeance. First I noticed the clouds building to the east. Then as nightfall neared, the winds picked up and I got that excited anticipatory feeling I always get before a really good storm. I headed into my tent as darkness loomed and the clouds overcame waning sunlight. My tent was well anchored, a good thing for the winds began tugging fiercely on my little nylon world. I glanced outside a few times to see the lightning pierce the darkness and bring instantaneous daylight to this valley. Then, the rain began pounding my humble abode, but I stayed dry as I faded off to the dreamworld. Getting some rest this morning, but want to get on the trail before a squirrel appears and starts scolding me for my sloth.

Later

And now it's time for the hilarious situation comedy "Tom Hangs His Food Bag." Stay tuned for uproarious laughter as Tom tangles the rope on every branch in a 20 foot radius, and even on his own feet, arms, nose, and other body parts. See him throw the carabiner everywhere but the place he wants it, catching it on wrong branches, bouncing it off of tree trunks, careening back at him nearly bonking him on the head or putting his eye out. Chuckle as he wiggles the rope in every possible fashion, trying to get it to drop far enough below the branch so he can reach it with one of the various sticks laying around, some of which will make you roar as he struggles to pick them up while standing on them, getting it caught on every other branch in sight and stumbling as he tries to maneuver them from the ground to the rope above. And you'll find it dreadfully amusing when he finally gets it put together, only to find it's still too low to keep it from the bears.

Ah, such nightly fun! Well, that won't be necessary again for a while. Ironic that I write this while hanging virtually nothing, as I'm out of food except for a few bay nuts. Very tired. Today was ideal for hiking: mostly overcast and cooler, much cooler than it has been, but still warm enough for just a t-shirt. The hike was actually quite delightful today with some great views of the mountains, including Preston Peak and some "bear's ears" looking peaks in the distance. I'm at Poker Flat, my destination on this leg of my journey and possibly for the entire trip. The food is gone but for some dried onions and deer jerky, oh yes, and some coconut oil. The jerky is good and I'll eat some if I absolutely need to, but it gave me such awful farts it was almost suicide to stay in the tent. I finally scraped some charcoal off of the bark of a tree and ate it to deal with the gas, which helped immensely. I decided not to eat any more, though. With friends coming soon I think maybe it's time to fast for a few days and wait. Maybe it will do me some good.

I still haven't communicated with people for over 11 days, just that distant glimpse of one man and I heard voices from his camp. It's funny, but when I saw that guy in Young's Valley it reminded me of that famous film of the Bigfoot walking through a forest, a sort of lumbering walk, but it's just that this man had clothes on. Looking forward to seeing my friends, though don't know how it will be to actually talk to someone. This is even longer than the meditation retreat I did where I wasn't supposed to speak for 9 days.

I was outside just now when a deer walked up to the campsite. I stood completely still and she came closer. Then a bug flew in my eye and I flinched. The deer turned and decided "Well it IS human after all." She made a slow retreat. Then I walked the road along the meadow's edge. This really is a gorgeous place, a beautiful rolling meadow in bloom with some pretty wonderful trees surrounding it, mostly true firs with incense cedar and Douglas-fir mixed in. As I walked from where I had lunch over to this campsite, I noticed a bear at the far corner of the meadow. I think she made a retreat when she saw me, although I didn't see her go. During my saunter around the meadow, grouse startled me twice and a few hummingbirds were out sampling the penstemons and paintbrushes. On a more personal note, I know I'm well-hydrated during this fast, as I peed 3 times during my short walk.

I'll see what the weather brings tomorrow. If it's raining as it was this evening I may end up in the tent quite a lot, otherwise I'll head over to Kelly Lake to see what I can find. Saturday morning I'll prepare for my departure and make the decision on what to do next. Now that I'm closer to 'civilization' the original musical themes I'd experienced have given way to a bad rock song whose name I can't even recall. I kept it at bay by reciting some Rumi poems. The days sure are long, now. Sky seems to be clearing a bit.

12 July

Morning:

    I awoke this morning to the meadow shrouded in a mist. A dozen different bird songs serenaded me as deer grazed outside my tent under clear skies. There is still a chill in the air, but then it is a morning after a rain at 5000 feet elevation. The sun has melted the mist into thin air. A jay squawks from a nearby fir, other birds sing their sunshine songs, and the flies have set about on their daily, very rapid rounds. I guess you have to move fast when you only live a few days. It's now been 11 days with no direct human contact. Yes, I miss my friends, but in general I'm really OK with that. I'll see them soon enough. Also, it's my first full day of fasting. One bay nut, a bit of ginger, some garlic powder, and now some herb tea with coconut oil in it. Feeling pretty weak right now, actually. It will be interesting to see how this progresses.

    Just noticed that on the butane cartridge (fuel for my stove) it reads "Contents may catch fire." Well, I certainly hope so!! Amazing the grasp we have of the obvious in this society. I keep hearing a loud noise like a big helicopter and wonder if maybe a fire started from the lightning the other night.

    Change, meaningful change, seems to usually happen both slowly and subtly. I've become more confident in the backcountry on this trip, which only makes sense. Before this hike I wasn't very afraid of bears, but I'll admit that as I started out I was concerned about them, being alone for such a time on my own. My relationship to them and to cougars I think has improved being out here. I think that any fears I had came to a head at Cedar Creek (Day 3) and then dissipated. Maybe more than anything this journey has helped me be more accepting of myself, which is always a good thing, unless you're Hitler, I guess. I think noting my physical & psychological limitations will in the long run serve to make me a happier, healthier person, although I've also shown that I can push those limitations, but maybe only so far.

Afternoon:

I just did a very languorous, but wonderful hike over to Kelly Lake, or should I say near Kelly Lake, because I saw people there so I turned around just before the shore. I didn't want to have them try to make contact with me, even if they were all on the far shoreline. It's not that I hate people. It's just that I wanted a certain type of experience, one that entails solitude. Anyhow, it's a beautiful hike and there are some great trees along the trail.

On the way there, just a short time before I caught sight of the lake, I encountered my first rattlesnake on this trip. I had let down my guard because I didn't think they lived this high in elevation around here. None have been seen at Oregon Caves, which is lower in elevation. As I walked the trail coming up to a pile of rocks, to my left I heard the telltale sound and jumped back about 10 feet. OK, so I didn't jump back that far, but I did jump back and it got my heart rate up more than the trail did. I looked into an opening in the pile of rocks and sure enough, there lay the little guy coiled up and reeling back in a defensive position. Beautiful black pattern on a white background on his back. I scoped out my options and the best one seemed to be making a hasty jaunt around the back of the rock pile and the snake. Hopefully he wouldn't have a back door to his little house through which he could strike me if he chose! It worked fine and I continued my hike as planned. On the way back I decided to carefully move past that spot as quickly as I could. The way the rocks sat, he wouldn't have a good view of that side, so I thought I could slip past without getting him riled up. It worked. I looked back and saw the snake coiled in his little hovel. I left him in peace.

I also encountered an odd looking frog when I stopped at a creek to rinse my face with cool water. She looked so white I thought she might be dead, as she lay on the bottom of the creek bed, but she moved after a minute, curling up in the mud. I couldn't tell if she had brown spots or if that was just the mud of the creek bed on her. Her head looked a bit more like a lizard's head than that of a frog. Hmmmm.

I finished my hike and got back to camp to find my food bag on the ground. The rope had broken (it is a pretty windy day), or possibly the cord has been chewed by squirrels. They seemed to have taken an interest in this entire food set up. This morning I heard my pans rattling and looked out of the tent expecting to see a bear, but only squirrels ran around near it, so I assumed they had played with it or at least had used the rope for high level transport. Not much in it anyhow, mostly my pans and utensils. I'll either put it in the tent or use the parachute cord to hang it in an alternate spot later in the day.

Man I'm hungry and tired!

Just had as odd insect walk past. At least I think it was an insect as he had 5 legs and I think it more likely he lost one rather than 3. He was about ½ cm long (about ¼ inch), basically round, and had a pattern of minuscule squares on his back, mostly black, but a few light gray. Insects are SO amazing! Wish I knew more about them.

Yesterday as I tied one end of my food line to a fir tree with lots of dead branches, a nuthatch, likely a pigmy nuthatch, flew over to the tree and hopped, branch to branch, down to the point where she perched within about 2 feet of my face. We shared a moment gazing into each others' eyes, then she flew off. Wonderful!

I keep expecting John, Laurel and Pedro to show up early for some reason. I wonder about the fires, how close they are. More smoke over near Kelly Lake now. Part of me wants to get out of here as soon as possible and get something to eat, but part of me wants to stick it out, continue fasting, and be out for the 13 days that will have passed at our designated meeting time. The hike to Kelly Lake made me REALLY hungry, and the breeze chills me even though I sit in the sunshine on a pleasant summer day. Looks like now only 2-3 hours before the sun dips below the ridge. At the creek getting water earlier I had a black and white dragonfly land near me. Symmetry: I started this hike with one, and now at the end of the Siskiyou Wilderness portion of the hike I find another come to visit. Maybe it's an indication to end the hike here. Not likely I'll continue on as weak as I am.

I see faces and odd shapes in many trees, and sometimes in rocks and other places one generally doesn't expect to find them. Still having the same aural hallucinations as well, the music I've mentioned. The creek sounded like a woman singing beautifully and I could have sworn I heard Laurel and John talking, and Pedro's tags jingling.

Black and White Dragonfly

You've come to visit
At the journey's end
Just as you did
At its beginning
Many miles and many
Moments in between
All things come full circle
Your life, my life
This walk in the wilderness
Spiraling through time
May we meet again
In another turn of the wheel
Shadows stretch themselves
across the meadow
as hermit thrush presents
his sweet invocation
sounding the end
of another unique
and special day
as a lone wanderer
saunters to a gentle rhythm
saying 'goodnight'
to old friends
he's come to know
for the first time
friends of feather and fur
of wood and herb
of black and white
with transparent wings
who offer their tidings
for a quiet sleep
under a forest canopy
with stars, and with

dragonflies
to watch over him
as this day
and this journey
reach their ends.

13 July

Busy morning! Lots of nuthatches, chickadees, jays, hairy woodpeckers, juncos, and a host of other birds I don't know, all busying themselves with obtaining nourishment, flitting about, and in general keeping themselves plenty busy. Some seem to be looking for nest repair material. Who knows what the mischievous jays are up to! Nuthatches sure are gregarious and curious birds. Several have been busying themselves on a tree about 8 feet away, and they often cast glances at me and fly close to me before returning to their tree. And a couple of hummingbirds came by to say "Hello," one only 1-2 feet from my face. Amazing what happens when you sit still!

Feeling pretty weak today – hard to catch my breath and my heart beat is very prominent. I feel chilled as well. These things usually happen when I fast. I've been sauntering along the road 1/2 mile or so, sitting among the trees and just letting thoughts run through my mind and heart.

I'm looking at a bizarre insect crawling around on the cut face of a log laying on the forest floor. It seems to extend something out of its abdomen even as it walks, sometimes sending it into cracks in the wood. Maybe laying eggs. Got to look that one up when I get back. Also had a bear sighting, again on the other side of the meadow like the last one. I had just gotten up from sitting at my campsite when I turned and saw a good-sized brown colored black bear across the meadow. She made her way from left to right and I just observed her quietly. I watched her for maybe 15 minutes (what is time without a watch?), then I moved around to do something, turned, and she had apparently gone. As opposed to the one I saw at Rattlesnake Meadow, both the bears I've seen here seem pretty shy with humans. I guess there's more human use here and this is also a place they might be hunted, so the bears know whom to stay away from. Both of these bears disappeared when they saw me moving around, or at least that's what I assume. Who knows? Maybe they are still out there watching me.

I just said a fond farewell to my walking stick. I found her at Cedar Creek on day 3. Somebody had done a bit of work on her, but she still had a small remnant of branch that I had to knock off. Don't know for certain what kind of wood she is, but I suspect maybe cedar. She isn't very heavy and has a reddish cast to her, and while it didn't look all that much like cedar outer bark, I can see where it might be the inner bark. Doesn't smell like cedar, but then cedar doesn't always have a strong smell. She served me well, especially on those occasions when I had on my full pack and had to negotiate steep, rocky trails. I thought about hanging onto her, maybe using her on future hikes, such as the possible jaunt to the Red Buttes that may succeed this one after I get some more food and get a little strength back. But my heart said she ought to stay here. She belongs to the Siskiyou Wilderness and here she shall stay. I walked over to the creek to refill my water bottle and took my stick with me. On the return I propped her up against a fir tree and bid her adieu. A sad moment indeed. A symbol of the end of this part of my journey. I hope another hiker sees her and decides to make good use of her, rather than using her just for firewood. I'll never know. But I felt she should have a chance for more adventures in this beautiful place. I doubt that as a tree, she ever thought she'd travel so far, see so many inspiringly beautiful places, and make many new friends along the way, especially me. So fare thee well and happy trails old pal!

Lots of helicopter activity tonight, but I neither smell nor see much in the way of smoke. Hopefully things will be OK.

14 July

In a few minutes I shall finish the last little bit of preparing my pack, and begin hiking towards the road, towards humans. Where yesterday it was clear, today brings some light clouds and quite a bit of smoke. It's possible the road has been closed, but it seems strange nobody would have swept it, so I think it's probably not, but I'm going to start walking just in case it is closed. Don't want to worry my friends too much. I've considered that they may already have begun worrying, but nothing I can do about it now, so I'll just do what I can, which is to start making for the road. In the coming weeks I'll have more to write in reflection of this part of my journey, but for now I've written enough. So I bid thee farewell Poker Flat and my campsite, and I offer my hopes and best wishes for surviving this fire, and for a long and healthy life to you and all your inhabitants. May you bear good fruit, have many children and grow healthy and strong.

A short time later:

Just as I began hiking out of Poker Flat, a pickup truck pulling a trailer carrying 3 ATVs (all terrain vehicles) pulled into the camping area. Good time to leave. About a mile down the road Annette and John, two of the three people who were to meet me, drove up. They wanted to see Poker Flat, so we drove together to the meadow where Laurel and, of course, Pedro met us shortly thereafter. We had a nice picnic…it was slow eating after my 2 ½ days without food, but once I got started I began stuffing my face. It felt good. And it also felt good to see my friends, the first people I had talked with in 13 days. I found talking difficult due to my fasting and not having used my voice much at all for that time.

Reflection:

So, what did I learn from this experience? First I learned that I can do it, and from a physical or logistics standpoint, even under adversity, such as heavy storms, difficult trail conditions, bear issues, loss of food, extreme heat, I can handle it. Yes, I moved slower than others might have, but I did alright for someone approaching 50 alone in the wilderness. I learned that music must be very important for me. Otherwise why else would I keep hearing it for nearly two weeks almost constantly! I need to consider ways to make better use of it in my life. I learned that the world is an amazingly beautiful place. This is not really new to me, but it certainly was reinforced ever so strongly. I learned that being in raw nature is very good for me, but that being with people is where I need to improve, where I need to focus. I know I can be a very good friend, but I need to work on my relationship skills. It's even more important than I had realized before.

I learned that sitting and meditating is good, but walking is a meditation in and of itself. If I should ever do this again, I think I would just keep going and see what happens, spend more time on the trail and less just sitting in camp. That doesn't mean I shouldn't stop and notice things, not by any means. What good is it to be out there if I don't take stock of what's around me? Some of the best parts of this journal are my observations of Nature, whether in descriptive prose or poetry. I've learned that "mystical experience" is usually subtle and comes when you least expect it, so don't go looking for it. It will find you if you need it. I also question its value. Maybe it can change a life, maybe it will just enhance what's already there, or maybe it just passes with little or no effect. Life is what it is here and now. What more do we need? Too much of our beautiful world, including humanity, has been destroyed by people looking for something more than what we have right before us.

Travels With Pedro

I had the world's best dog. I know a lot of people will tell you their dog is the best, and in some ways they may all be right, but nearly all my friends agree that Pedro was the best dog they had ever seen, and certainly he was the best dog for me. I grew up with dogs. When I was little we had a medium-sized black dog that kept us company. I have some memories of her, but not a lot. Later, when she passed on, we got a beagle/spaniel mix that stayed with us for over 10 years. After she left us, my parents didn't want another dog, but my older sister got one, a big Siberian husky, who loved to run whenever he could. Both my sisters have had numerous dogs over the years. I worked with dogs in Denali National Park. I've been around plenty of dogs, and believe me, Pedro was the best.

The following are a series of letters and journal entries I wrote during my time with Pedro, mostly us together, but a few not. I've added a few other stories as well. He was my best friend and companion, from our first encounter in 2003 until I got married and moved to China in 2010. How could I pack up and move to China, leaving him behind? It was one of the hardest things I've ever done, but I'll tell you about it at the end of this chapter. For now just let me say that if you don't know how someone could get so attached to a dog, then you never met Pedro.

You will learn much about him from the following stories, but let me give you some basic info and fill in gaps not in the narratives. Brown, with touches of white and black, not the least of which were his four white paws, he weighed about 70 pounds and for much of his life was a strong boy who loved to chase after things, especially animals like deer. I saw him run like a bat outa hell through blackberry thickets, with their sharp, woody thorns, yelping from the pain yet not slowing down at all as he chased after a deer. I never saw him catch a deer, but I often didn't see where he went in the forest. Only he knew. That was the nice thing about living in southern Oregon as we did… lots of forest and room to run. Anyhow, he had a strong heart and will. My friend Annette trained dogs for many years, as well as having many of her own, and when she saw him and the way he stood she said, "There's a dog who would pull you out of a burning building." That's the kind of spirit he had. The fact that he chose me is downright humbling. I think he would have made a good working dog, and one of my biggest regrets with him is not trying to get him trained for search or other duties. I became his work.

Pedro and I by our cabin in Cave Junction.
(*Photo by Alan Laurie*)

Pedro had a bit of a wild streak in him in his first few years with me. I recall once having to work overtime at Oregon Caves, coming home at 9 p.m. I was too tired to take him for a walk and he had been outside all day, so I figured it would be OK. When I took him off of his chain, he started going for a walk and I told him to come back. He just looked at me with that "I need a walk!" glare, and took himself for a walk, returning in about 15 minutes. That was early on in our relationship, and before long he settled down quite a bit.

Annette gave me some pointers for training him, which worked quite well. We often walked without a leash, but if I said "Heel," he would come next to me, at least most of the time. Usually if I just called his name, he would look at me and stop what he was doing. I gave him a lot of leeway, but also expected good behavior, which he was happy with. He loved nothing more than to please me. I didn't make him that way; it was all his decision. Pedro had probably been abandoned, and his biggest fear was that it would happen again. At first he didn't want to get into the car for that fear, but once I got him in, he didn't want to get out either. After a while, he got used to it and our travels, as you will see, were good times for both of us.

When Pedro first came to me he was aggressive with other dogs, which is common for street dogs as well as Akita's, which he likely was, at least part. His desire to please me led to him becoming tolerant and even friendly with other dogs, after I corrected him several times. It didn't take him long to learn. He was also a very serious dog at first, but once he met our friend Alan's dog River, who was a very playful adult dog, Pedro lightened up and the two became great friends and playmates. This gentler side of him served him well most of the time, but on two occasions he was attacked by other dogs and ended up the worst for it, and I think it was because he had just become too trusting. His human is often like that as well.

Pedro did not seek for attention at all really, and was just content to be part of the group. Mind you, he liked to be in the middle of things, but he didn't need to be the center of attention. At my storytelling gigs he would go to the side of the stage or somewhere near me and just lay down to rest and watch. Same at a party. If his human was there, he was satisfied. If anything, you had to watch not to step on him. As a brown dog he blended in with wood floors and many carpets. He had amazing patience as well, and would wait for me until the world ended, if he had to. Watching the movie "Hachi" made me cry like a baby, because that was so much like my boy.

Pretty much all dogs like to eat whenever the opportunity arises, but if Pedro had a fault, I guess it would be gluttony. Again, that's common among dogs who had been abandoned and known real hunger. If he had unlimited access to food, he would eat until he got sick, then go back again as soon as possible. It caused him problems at times in his life and he didn't outgrow it until he became an elder in the dog world. But we all have faults. His were minimal.

I guess those are the basics about Pedro. Most other things you will learn about him through these stories. May you all be blessed with such love and loyalty.

22 August 2003

I have been adopted. That's really the only way I can say it. About 4 weeks ago, a dog showed up near my house. He had apparently been abandoned by his previous family. He wore neither a collar nor other means of identification. One day he was just there. I tried a few times to get close to him, and after a several attempts I coaxed him near me with a bit of food. After a week of this sort of thing I began buying food for him, setting it out morning and evening, and of course he began spending more time by my house. I considered the possibility of adopting him, but thought that it would not be fair to him given how much time I spend away from home either working or traveling, not to mention the fact that my lease on this little house says 'No Pets.' Most of my neighbors have dogs or cats in spite of the 'rule' but I thought I would not press the issue. That's just how I am.

I bought some film, took his picture, and made a poster which I distributed to numerous local businesses, in an attempt to find the dog a good home. I planned to have him 'neutered' because I realized that few people would want a nearly adult male dog who had not had 'the operation,' especially given his size. Also, it just makes sense to prevent the situation which causes dogs like him to be abandoned. Only 2 people called, the second of which had just lost her dog, one that looked a bit like the photo on the poster. She sounded like the best possibility.

I made an appointment for his operation and took him to the woman's place to see if they would be compatible with her chickens and cats. Getting him into the car was quite a challenge, as he had probably been dropped from a car when he was abandoned, so entering an auto required picking him up, sliding him on the seat, and closing the door quickly behind him. The first attempt resulted in him sneaking out when I opened the driver's side door.

The next day I tried again, this time with a collar and rope attached to him, and it worked. During the entire drive he lay shaking like an Aspen leaf on the passenger seat with his head in my lap, mouth drooling on my thigh. The visit was an apparent success. He walked around, looking with curiosity at the cats, chickens and goats, but not showing any interest in chasing or attacking them. He scent marked the area and appeared to feel somewhat at home.

The woman, Sheri, asked me his name and I didn't know what to say. I always figured that his new owners would name him, so I had just been calling him 'Puppy Dog,' which is what I call dogs if I don't know their names. I tried to think of a name that sounded a little like that and the only thing that came to mind was 'Poppy,' which is one of my favorite flowers. He didn't look like a poppy, however, so then 'Perro' came to mind, which is Spanish for 'dog.' For the time being I thought that would work fine.

The next day I took him for a walk and again had to pick up his shaking body to get him into the veterinarian's office. The price for the operation depended upon how much he weighed. I had told them that the dog was about 40 pounds (16kg), but when placed on the scale he weighed out at a whopping 66 pounds (25kg). Lots of muscle. He shook the entire time I was with him and it was hard for me to put him in the cage and leave him there for those 24 hours. The operation was a success and the next day as I took him from his cage and walked him back home he was scared and disoriented. The following day I took him to be with his new family, and this time the ride in the car was easier for him. Again it pained me to let him go, but I told myself (and Perro) that it was best for both of us.

The next morning I was awakened out of a deep sleep by my phone ringing at 6:00 a.m.. It was Sheri. She said that Perro had tried to run away, and she had been able to corral him back home, but then he hid under her son's trailer and would not come out. When she tried to get him out, she said he growled at her. I had never heard him growl. She requested that I take him back. A few hours later I drove to her property and found Perro under the trailer behind the house. He lay there shivering with fear. He appeared to want to come to me, but conflicting emotions confused him. Finally he crawled like a snail, out from under the trailer. Just as he emerged, I heard Abe, Sheri's son, call out 'What are you doing?' I said that Sheri had called for me to take Perro back home, but Abe insisted that Perro would be fine (he actually called the dog 'Earnest') and that he wanted to take the dog to Berkeley, CA, with him. I asked if there was enough room for 'Earnest' in Berkeley and if he would be well cared for. Abe insisted that all would be fine. 'Thanks for the dog,' he called as I walked to my car. My intuition had its doubts, but it also said to give this a try, so once again my heart bled as I drove away. Sheri called me at work that afternoon and said that the situation was better and she believed all would go well.

Three days later as I fixed dinner I saw a familiar tail pass by my kitchen window. I went to the door and, sure as the sky is blue, there stood Perro, happy to see me. A short piece of chewed rope remained on his collar. My heart filled with honey to see him and as I scratched him behind the ears his tail wagged like a pine branch in the wind. He looked around as if nothing had ever happened, for he was home. I later talked with Sheri who told me of her attempts to catch him as he ran away from her place. Perro knew where he was going. He traveled nearly 5 miles as the Raven flies just to come back to me. I couldn't argue with that any more.

So now I have a dog. The name 'Perro' didn't seem quite right, so I tried 'Pedro' which feels much better for both of us. The landlords like him, so it should be no problem with them. What it means for me is a change of lifestyle. It means I find ways of not working so much overtime, which will be good for me as well. It means my food bill will be a bit higher. It means less traveling, unless I can take him along. It means that

I have someone to greet me when I come home from work, someone who loves me unconditionally, which feels really good after so many years of being alone. It means all my letters will be signed from both of us. All is not easy and I still have my doubts, but for now the relationship is working.

And that's the latest news from Cave Junction.

Peace,

Tom and Pedro

December 2003

Pedro has kept me so occupied that I have not had much time to keep up with my correspondences. After talking to a very good vet and a few people who know dogs well, I think he is probably an Akita mixed with possibly pit bull or boxer. He definitely has an edge about him, which makes him somewhat independent, even though he's very bonded to me, and also very special. I have much to learn from him, just as he has much to learn from me.

Now, though he shows no symptoms of it, he has tested positive for heartworm, which can be fatal if left untreated. The most common treatment is not only expensive, but also potentially fatal. I gave him an aspirin every day to thin his blood for the treatment, and on Dec. 4 he went to the veterinarian to spend the night and receive the medicine. Now he must remain inactive for about 6 weeks. Normally we walk 3-4 miles (5-7 km) each day, so we are finding 6 weeks without exercise very difficult. He just sits by the door, eats and drinks nearly nothing, and looks at me with big brown eyes not comprehending why he can't go out for his usual long walks. I don't know if this feels harder for him or me, not that it matters.

Before this heartworm stuff came up I took Pedro to Ashland, OR, where I attended a workshop with Martin Prechtel. The first thing to know is that Pedro almost never barks. During the Friday night pre-workshop talk I sat in the back of the hall with my boy Pedro, and at one point Martin said something about the need to speak up and raise our voices regarding serious issues facing humanity. In the moment of silence after Martin's remark, Pedro let out 2 barks, the only time he barked during the entire evening. It couldn't have been more appropriate if it had been planned and we all had a good laugh.

The skies, which shown of beautiful blue throughout the summer and autumn, have turned gray and foreboding. Snow paints the mountain tops a dappled white, and a damp chill creeps into this humble abode. Here I sit, typing away as Pedro sleeps on the floor nearby.

March 2004

Our unseasonably warm and sunny weather has departed in favor of more normal cool & wet Springtime conditions. Pedro lies asleep in the next room, and here I sit wondering just how I can write about my recent trip to the Southwest. Do I merely recount what, where, who, and when? Do I formulate a poem of scattered images that evoke the moods of my experiences? Do I try to wrap it into a package with bows and pretty wrapping paper and present it as a gift? Or do I combine all of the above?

My travels took me across familiar landscapes seen for the first time, took me to highs and lows and in-betweens. I met old friends with new faces and new friends with familiar airs as I wound my way through a mosaic decorated with stately eucalyptus and twisted junipers, rolling verdant hills and red sandstone cliffs, stark desert simplicity and complex urban loneliness under broadly orchestrated skies.

Pedro, my constant companion through all this, proved up to the journey. Cleansed of his heartworm parasites, he apparently cast aside his anxiety over cars and abandonment as a puppy, and accepted the roadway, new surroundings, and long hours of driving with mostly good natured gusto. There were a few instances of note in that regard. One occurred while we visited friends in Aztec, New Mexico. Pedro and I rode with my friend Marti in her car to the library in Farmington. We left my four-legged companion in the car while we used the computers in the library. Marti decided to return to the car to go pick up her boyfriend while I still perused the internet, but when she returned to the vehicle, Pedro greeted her with a firm, deep growl. "We will go NOWHERE without MY HUMAN." Marti shut off the car, slowly exited, and returned to the library.

During most of our drives he lay on the passenger seat with his head on my lap, which I much appreciated except when he drooled while sleeping. Based on the looks I received from truckers standing nearby, it must have appeared strange as I emerged from the car with a wet spot in a conspicuous part of my trousers, followed by a dog.

A particularly memorable moment with Pedro occurred while Marti, Gary, Pedro, and I hiked in the Bisti Wilderness, a magnificent, barren landscape of rainbow rocks just south of Farmington, New Mexico. As we made our way back to the car battling a stiff headwind, Pedro bounded just ahead of us, turned, and stopped. In his mouth he carried a frisbee-shaped piece of dried cow dung while his face bore a look of playful intent. And me without my camera!

Our journey had begun with a quick jaunt visiting friends in the San Francisco Bay Area, then hiking in Las Trampas Regional Park. Pedro and I then headed to Victorville, CA, for a couple of fine days with other friends: great company, beautiful desert sunrises, and delicious Mexican food. Our whirlwind tour continued with a stop in Flagstaff, AZ, then up to Second Mesa on the Hopi Reservation to enjoy the generous company of Gerald, Yvette, and their beautiful family, who graciously welcomed us in the midst of preparations for their wedding and the demands of the Hopi Bean Dance Ceremony (See the "Weddings" section for more on that).

This year I experienced the village of Mishongnovi's Bean Dance during the day and that night the Kachinas danced in Kykotsmovi, which I attended, our prayers rising to ask for much needed rain and abundant crops. In my cave tours at work I often shine my flashlight on the cave walls and ceiling, drawing attention to drops of water that shine like diamonds. I tell people that these drops have more value than diamonds, a remark which often meets with chuckles. I don't discourage laughter, but my statement is not meant as humor. People who have never lived in the desert or experienced extreme drought cannot appreciate the true value of water, for gold, silver, and diamonds are folly in comparison, beautiful though they are.

From the Hopi mesas Pedro & I ventured to Aztec, NM. After Aztec Pedro & I traveled to the Taos, NM, area by way of Jemez Canyon, a drive of exquisite beauty, for a good visit with friends and a dip in their local hot spring. Along the way, while driving through snow covered forests in the New Mexico highlands, I noticed steam rising from a spot along the road. I stopped and checked my map, and yes, it was a hot spring. I grabbed a towel and we made our way down the incline to the creek below, then up the steep hillside to the spring that bubbled out of the rocks into a small set of pools. I bathed while Pedro explored the forest and returned periodically to give me that look like "What the hell are you doing? Honestly, who would sit in water for fun?"

The last week of my 3 week vacation found me in Ojo Caliente, New Mexico. The town's name means literally "hot eye," but is also interpreted as "hot spring" in Spanish, and the place is known for its wonderful healing hot springs. I bathed in the pools a few glorious times, but I traveled there for a writer's workshop with my teacher Martín Prechtel, and much of my time I spent either writing, or thinking about writing as Pedro and I explored the local mesas and canyons. He dodged amongst the sagebrush with agile aplomb chasing hares and squirrels as I watched his tail, like the dorsal fin of an Orca, cutting through crisp desert air. Periodically my silent predator surfaced to breathe, breaching from this pale green sea as he leapt over chollas and prickly pear cacti.

The workshop lasted 7 days and proved a valuable experience for me. In the past I have attended storytelling workshops and taken one writing class when I lived in Chapel Hill, NC, but nothing that quite immersed me in writing to the extent of this workshop. Pedro was not allowed in the building at the request of the resort management, so I tied him up outside while we were in our sessions. From the window I could see him watching the door, waiting for me to return. One day the snow began falling, gently at first, then increasing to near white out. I could still see his nose and eyes through the falling snow, pointed right at me. He has incredible patience, and doesn't mind the cold and snow the way "his human" does.

It certainly was not all fun and games. After one of our morning sessions, I had become rather despondent feeling that my writing did not prove up to par, a perception I alone expressed. There exists a part of me that would love to become a professional writer, but it is a part that I have not adequately fed, and therefore it becomes especially unhappy if I think that this dream is no longer on my horizon. I stopped in the makeshift bookstore at the workshop and a book called Art & Fear caught my eye. I bought it and took it back to my hotel room. The first quote I saw when I opened the book gave me a new perspective on the situation: "Writing is easy; all you do is sit staring at a blank sheet of paper until the drops of blood form on your forehead" (Gene Fowler). I began writing and what emerged received some much needed positive comments from Martín and the group during the evening session. I felt much better.

After the workshop we returned to Oregon, back to the land of tall trees, to our day to day lives. For what is a vacation if we don't have a regular life to return to?

July 2004

In July Pedro learned a new word… skunk. One night I returned home from work just as night had fallen. I decided to take Pedro out for a short walk as it was late and still pretty hot. We had walked only a short ways when Pedro saw something in the shadows on the road ahead. It looked like a cat and he loves chasing cats, among other things, and took off in a flash. It wasn't a cat. After a moment, Pedro returned, moaning his displeasure, rolling on the ground, and trying to rub up against my leg in a futile attempt to get the awful smell off of him. Needless to say, I wanted no part of his new perfume and walked him quickly to a grassy area where he could roll around and try to get rid of it. I felt surprised that I didn't find the skunk cologne all that offensive, though not a smell I care to encounter on a regular basis. Pedro certainly would rather not have discovered this new olfactory experience.

We then hurried home where, as he waited impatiently outside, I prepared to give him a shower. The traditional remedy for such a thing is to bathe in tomato juice. I had none at the time and certainly didn't want to go to the store, so I tried apple cider vinegar instead. I took Pedro through the house and into the shower as quickly as possible, not wanting him to rub up against anything. Usually he hates showers, but this time he accepted its inevitability. I washed him off as well as I could, then dried him with his towel as I attempted to discern if we had succeeded in eliminating the worst of the odor. It helped a bit and I just accepted it as the household potpourri for the next several weeks. As I said earlier, it didn't smell as bad as I thought it would and we lived with what was left of the skunk smell just fine. Pedro has not chased a skunk since that time, and whenever, during the course of our walks, we encounter the now familiar smell, he gets a pained look on his face and doesn't bother to follow his nose to its origin as he does with other curious odors.

Note:
Pedro had two more encounters with skunks while we were together. The first occurred while we were still living in that same little house along the river in Cave Junction, and not far from where the first incident happened. Pedro saw something moving and ran to investigate. He saw the tail and recognized it just about the same time I did, and he turned 90 degrees to avoid it, but the skunk caught him just a little. The smell wasn't too bad and it was obvious he had learned his lesson the first time. Curiosity just had gotten the best of him.

The second time happened during our travels. It was a winter night in the Arizona desert not far from Tucson, and we had driven up a mountainside to camp for the night just sleeping in the little Honda. I had opened the door to let Pedro stretch his legs and sniff around while I got the car ready, and just a couple of minutes later he came back stinking and rubbing his face on the ground over and over again. In his defense, it was pitch black that night with no moon and even some clouds to cover the stars, so he couldn't have seen the skunk at all, and of course, by the time you smell them, it's too late. We drove down the hill to a drug store that was open and got what I needed to wash him, including hydrogen peroxide, baking soda, and a few other things including several gallons of water (it was the desert after all). Then we headed out to the open desert south of town and I washed him as best I could in the dark and the dusty desert. He handled it stoically, including some shivering, and we ended up with a decent, quiet night without too much odor.

February 2005

This morning, Pedro and I arose later than usual, prepared to greet the Sun, and went out for our first walk of the day. Low clouds perched atop the ring of mountains that border the Illinois Valley, the peaks of some dressed in mosaics of white, green and gray. Winter in southwestern Oregon. The air that kissed my face did not feel as cold as that on previous days. After saying our morning blessings, we headed over to Forks State Park, which lay across the bridge on the far shore of the Illinois River from our humble little home. Mist clung like ghosts to the tall Pine, Cedar, and Fir trees around us, their branches draped with pale green lichens that paint a mottled palette across which a pair of Mallard ducks flew, honking their concerns all the while.

We are back in Oregon after our 6 week hiatus. From the time we left this valley in mid-December until the night we returned, we drove nearly 7000 miles (11,200km), saw numerous friends and family, made a few new ones, and spent 10 days apart from one another while I warmed my bones in Mexico.

We left on 16 December after an evening of stories and poetry at Cave Junction's one, and to my knowledge only, monthly public literary event. We had gotten most of the way to Grants Pass, about 30 miles (48 km) away, when I realized that I had the wrong shoes on my feet. We returned home where fog and 32° F (0° C) air still held the town relatively still. Ah, the fickle quirks of memory! With hiking boots on my feet I again started the car and headed down the road while Pedro just looked at me with that air of bewilderment that he so often wears whilst quietly observing me.

Our first destination was the San Francisco Bay area, where we spent a few days thawing out and enjoying the company of a couple of good friends, but these visits, like all of them on this trip, were much too short. Pedro and I did, however, find time to hike up to some of the old gun bunkers that dot the Marin Headlands, remnants of the cold war. Now newts swim in the ponds formed where mighty canons once sat and grass creeps up through cracks in the concrete, claiming ground where polished leather had once stood guard. Where have all the soldiers gone? Well, that's another story. Huge waves pounded the north bay shoreline as we bid fond farewells and left the West Coast en route for lands far to the East.

Spent a night in Reno, NV, with good friends who had recently relocated there, and after wishing them well we made haste for family in frosty Wisconsin, pausing just long enough in Utah to taste the bitter salt of a lake now mostly dry. For much of the drive, Pedro occupied his usual spot in the passenger seat, his head on my lap. Just before arriving in the state of my birth, Pedro and I went out for a walk along the Rock River. It was cold…very cold. My nose dripped on my jacket and before I could dab it off with my mitten, it had frozen solid literally in the blink of an eye…in the sunshine. We tried finding postcards in the little town of Oregon, Illinois, to send one to my coworkers in the Illinois Valley of Oregon, but they must not get many tourists. I think I found them in the fifth place we looked.

Finally we arrived in Wisconsin and spent our first couple of nights in the abode of my niece and her 2 beautiful children, who I'm sorry to say I hardly know. It's been 2 years since I've seen them, and it had been 2 years before that since the previous time. The hazards of being a wanderer. While outside the red line in the thermometer strained to reach 0° F/-18° C, my four footed companion and I stayed comfortable, warmed by the hearts of family, whether niece, sister, aunt and uncle, cousin, or father. I had the pleasure of accompanying my dad to a lunch meeting of one of the charitable organizations to which he belongs. Under white hair, his cheeks, rosy from the cold air, brimmed with a proud smile as he introduced the members to his son, a park ranger in Oregon. That was Christmas for me. I think it was the first time he was ever noticeably proud of me.

But our feet could not stay still for long as we soon headed to North Carolina, where we once again could thaw out and visit Pat, my other sister and Lacey, her special little fluff of flowing, white, canine hair. Lacey's an aristocratic blue-blood, and wasn't quite certain what to make of the 70 pound/~30 kg street-wise mestizo with a curly tail that she encountered when Pedro entered her domain, but eventually Lady and the Tramp found their common ground and peace settled in for most of the brief weekend we spent in Chapel Hill, my old stomping ground.

After another good family visit we brushed off the moss and headed south and then west. After Wisconsin's cold, the warmth of the Deep South felt great. We traversed across South Carolina, Georgia, Alabama, Mississippi, Louisiana, and finally Texas, before settling in for a couple of days with friends in Carlsbad, New Mexico. I like that area and wouldn't mind spending more time there, but Phoenix, AZ, called to us. (Note: I debated on going into New Orleans, but decided against it. Bad choice. Hurricane Katrina hit there before my next travels.) My friend Ellis, who had just retired from the National Park Service, was due to run a half marathon in Phoenix and I had a date with a flight to Mexico. Pedro, unfortunately, had a date at a kennel, but more on that later.

Ellis rode with us to Phoenix, and Pedro hardly let him forget for a moment that HE usually rode in the passenger seat. Two very sad canine windows of the soul kept a vigil on Ellis from the back of my Honda. It was a chance to catch up with my good friend and mentor, and we shared some delightful conversation on the ride westward. In Phoenix I left Ellis at his sister-in-law's. I stopped inside to call my friends Lynette and Mark, at whose house I was due to stay. We left Pedro outside, off leash and unattended. Ellis' brother-in-law went out a moment later to check on him and returned to say that Pedro seemed to have run off. I knew better, but said nothing. On nearing my car I could see Pedro already curled up on the front seat of the car. He had jumped in through the open back window. He likes his car seat.

I found my friends' house shortly thereafter, and as I reunited with them, Pedro and Carly, their dog, introduced themselves. Carly wasn't happy about being invaded by this brute. Pedro just curled up on the floor and made himself comfortable. Eventually Carly grew to mostly accept the situation. She's a good dog…just a bit territorial. And who can blame her? It's a nice place. After a few days, we found a good kennel and took Pedro there, and then they took me to the airport. My destination was Oaxaca, Mexico, to attend a storytelling workshop, which you can read about in the section called Telling Tales.

Upon my return to the states, Pedro and I both nearly peed on the floor, so happy to see one another. Then we set off for the high elevation of Flagstaff. I stayed there with more good friends for a few days, then headed up to Second Mesa on the Hopi Reservation. Gerald was away hunting, but Yvette and the children welcomed us in. We had the opportunity of experiencing both the Buffalo Dances and the good hospitality of friends in Mishongnovi, Yvette's village. I had seen the Buffalo Dances before, but this time it struck me more than ever how much of a rare privilege it is to experience such a venerable tradition, when so many people have lost both their tradition, and the roots that grow from it. We spent time with them making traditional Piki bread, a sort of rolled phyllo dough usually made of blue cornmeal. Again, it was a much too short visit, but the weariness of the road pulled at Pedro and I both.

We headed west to Victorville, CA, for a few delightful nights at my friend Angela's place on the edge of the desert. After that we made the mistake of driving through Los Angeles as we got into "rush hour." I put that in quotes, because I found that it's more like "rush hours…and hours…and hours…" We found a place to exit and went for a walk on a side street for a while, but when we tried to get back on the road, it was still the same 'stop and to a little bit' traffic as when we had left in an hour earlier. Eventually we got out of the the ever-so-slow moving river of cars and about 24 hours later, we found ourselves back in Oregon, where we will remain, until we get the urge and opportunity once again to hit the road.

December 2005

Here in the Illinois Valley as I gaze out my window, the sky bears its customary gray, foggy appearance and the temperature hovers barely above freezing. My last day of work this season was December 2, and soon I will fly to Wisconsin to visit some of my family for the holidays, before taking Pedro to mostly warmer surroundings in California and the southwestern deserts. My idea of winter sports is hiking in the warm sunshine of the arid lands both north and south of the Mexican border.

Pedro is well and has a new friend with which to play. In July, Alan moved into a neighboring cabin and his dog River, a black & brown terrier a bit smaller than Pedro, have spent many wonderful hours together playing and exploring the local woods. River is a wonderful dog with a real gusto for life. As soon as he hears Pedro and I leaving our humble home for our morning walks, he insists that Alan let him out to join us, and comes bounding out the door, jumping to greet us, hanging in mid-air like Michael Jordan dunking a basketball, or like a dark cloud wearing a big smile, wafted on a sea breeze. It's a real pleasure to see the fun they have together.

Pedro had always been a dog of rather serious demeanor, but both his friendship with River, and his growing confidence in having a stable home have lightened his step and lifted his spirits. Pedro loves to dig for ground squirrels, and often during our journeys I see two tails, one black and one brown & white, thrust into the air as their noses and front paws try to excavate the hole some squirrel has long since abandoned for another of its maze of passageways. Alan, a truly fine artist, has become a good friend and positive influence on both Pedro and I as well. I have often thought that I would like to move on to another park or another type of work, but the longer I stay here, the more reasons I find for lingering… good friends for Pedro and I, good food from the local farms, and the magnificent forests. Still, I look forward to my travels: seeing family and other good friends, and enjoying warmer climates which suit this thin body and cold hands and feet. The cave in which I so often find myself, while beautiful and intriguing, stays 43°F/6°C, and the climate above ground remains rather cold to me most of the time, except for the hottest summer months, rather uncomfortable for the likes of me.

One night, Pedro and I were just finishing our evening walk along the East Fork of the Illinois River. Our friend River had already reunited with Alan back at their house, when Pedro spotted a furry head with long whiskers jutting out of the water near the opposite shoreline. Shortly after we first saw it, the head dove back into the drink, leaving Pedro and I standing perfectly still, our eyes fixed, watching for the head to re-emerge. After several minutes, we then continued our path towards home, but kept glancing back to the other side of the river. At one point, I heard something scramble in the brush, then saw 5 sleek, dark shapes bounce towards the water and dive under. Otters: five fully grown otters.

Pedro ran across the river and jumped onto some logs watching for the shapes while trying, only partly successful, to maintain his balance on the wet logs beneath his feet. He may be a good hunter, but a water dog he's not. Good thing for him, as otters have very sharp teeth. I didn't worry for either of them however, and watched as the 5 shapes popped out of the water a short ways behind my fearless hunter, over another log, and back under, as Pedro kept his gaze fixed in the opposite direction while dancing on smooth, slippery wood. I watched a moment longer before realizing they had gone into open water. I called Pedro, who returned with great reluctance, and haven't seen the otters since then. To this day however, Pedro looks back to the place he last saw the otters every time we walked near there. So do I. If there is such a thing as reincarnation, I think I'd like to come back as an otter; they always seem to have so much fun, sliding down the banks and swimming in spirals, and eat all the salmon they want. What a life!

Pedro the Stoner

Sometimes when I was at work, my neighbor Alan would take our dogs for a walk, often late in the day. On one such day, I returned home to find Pedro chained up outside our house looking dizzy after their walk. He got up and tried to greet me, but stumbled and couldn't walk straight. I let him off of the chain and he just couldn't stay upright, only lay on the ground, his head wavering, and appearing confused. Numerous times he attempted to get to his feet, but didn't stay there for long. I called Alan to come over and asked him what had happened on their walk, but he said nothing unusual had occurred. Pedro and River had played and did their normal activities. He had no idea what might have happened. I first suspected a neurological problem, like a head injury, so I asked if Pedro had hit his head, but he said he hadn't seen anything of that sort and that Pedro was alright when he left him a short time ago. The only thing he said might be unusual was that they had been digging into an old compost pile in the woods near the cabins. I also questioned him about the possibility of Pedro getting into some marijuana, as there are lots of pot smokers and growers in that area. Alan insisted he didn't think that had happened. I was frantic with worry about my boy and needed to figure out what was wrong. It seemed like it could be serious.

It was getting on to twilight and the veterinarians in town had already closed. I called one of them and they told me there was a place in Medford that had a 24 hour animal hospital. I called them and they told me to bring him in ASAP. The drive took over an hour, even with my excited state and pushing the speed limits. Pedro just lay in the front seat next to me, his head wavering, continuing to look dazed and confused. I brought him into their facility and turned him over to the vet who had an assistant get him into their emergency room while she questioned me more about his condition. Then she went to examine him. After a half hour or so she came out and said that she didn't think he had a head injury or other neurological problem. She thought he might have ingested something that made him sick, so she gave him activated charcoal. I told her I wish I'd done that earlier as I had some at home, but of course, I didn't know if it could be something else at the time. She recommended keeping him there for the night and I could come back in the morning to see how he was doing, but she thought he would probably be fine. She told me to go home and get some rest. I finally got to bed at nearly midnight, and planned to go as early as possible to get him. With my worry and not having him around, I didn't sleep well.

In the morning I returned and it seems he had made a nearly full recovery. The doctor suspected he had eaten some pot and asked if I knew where he could have gotten it, giving me that look like "I know you have it." I said, "I don't smoke the stuff myself and there's none in my house. My neighbor told me he knows Pedro didn't eat his either." "Really," she asked, implying I was not telling her the whole truth. "Really," I responded, "I work for the U.S. Government and am subject to random drug testing. For me to smoke pot would be just stupid. I've used it before, but didn't even like it, so no, I don't have pot in my house." I could see she still didn't believe me, but she didn't pursue it after that. It's true, though, I have done it, I didn't like it, and I didn't have any, but attitudes die hard and people from Cave Junction are often assumed to be using drugs of one sort or another, usually pot. I told her I suspected maybe he had eaten some mushrooms when he dug into the compost pile the day before, and she said that was possible. Either way, Pedro didn't have a head injury and he would be OK. I felt ever so relieved. The truth, though, is pretty wild. One way or another, Pedro had gotten stoned, had taken a journey of a different kind. One look at him told me he didn't want to go down that road again. We went home and he never did it again.

22 April 2006

Our lives often take interesting and unexpected turns. I had always traveled alone, well, at least as the only human, with Pedro during my winter vacation, but this year I traveled with another actual human, my friend Laurel. My job at the Caves is called a "subject to furlough" position, and requires me to take between 2 and 8 weeks of unpaid leave time each winter when the cave is closed for bat hibernation. I generally plead for the full 8 weeks, but it depends on the situation at work. With the government and its budget these days, I didn't have to do much begging to get the longer furlough.

I took part of my furlough to visit some of my family in Wisconsin for Christmas. When I returned I went back to work for 2 weeks, journeying to Arcata, CA, to take a course in Wilderness First Responder (emergency medicine). They thought they needed another certified emergency medical person in the park, and since I used to be one I was the logical choice for the training. Then, after a brief stop home in Cave Junction, I headed to meet with Laurel at her family's home just north of San Francisco. We spent a few days there, feasting and enjoying the company of her family, then headed south, Laurel, Pedro and I, in her pick-up truck to camp in the Anza-Borrego Desert of southern California. Here is our journal of that trip:

Winter 2006 Travels with Tom, Laurel, and Pedro

1/19/06. And so begins this journey and this journal. We're finally on our way from the Bay Area en route to the American Southwest and northern Mexico. Pedro sits tucked in behind the front seats, the little side window cracked for his comfort. Laurel is driving, which is good, cuz otherwise it would be hard to write this. The truck's loaded with essentials including, of course, chocolate, as well as other food stuffs, warm clothing, sleeping bags, tools, emergency stuff, bug spray, Laurel's travel guitar, books, maps, etc., etc., etc. For a change, the sky is mostly blue with scattered cumulus and cirrus clouds. I gaze across the rolling hills of central California dotted with eucalyptus, palms, barns, silos, power towers, phone poles, and a few windmills turning slowly.

We stopped near Los Angeles for some dinner at the lone decent diner we could find amongst the swarms of fast food restaurants, then ended up at our first of many campsites, this one a short ways into Anza-Borrego Desert State Park. The night temperature dropped to chilly, but comfortable. We felt tired, and we soon drifted off to sleep. In the morning we quickly fell into what became our usual pattern of Pedro and me heading out for our morning walk whilst Laurel kept vigil over the warmth in the bed in the back of her truck and explored the world of dreams. We camped 4 nights in Anza-Borrego. The desert sunrises and sunsets were stunning, and we especially enjoyed our stay in the Wind Caves, sandstone hovels overlooking the Fish Creek drainage from their high perch. I think it's actually illegal to camp there, or it was illegal to have Pedro there, but either way, I recommend it as a great campsite, just don't tell them we sent you. We enjoyed long walks in the desert, mild days, cold nights, and good meals cooked on a camp stove. Pedro didn't think much of the place. Yes, he loved chasing jackrabbits, that is until he had his fill of cholla cactus spines firmly lodged in his paws. He got to the point of looking the other way when he saw one of the large bunnies, just to resist the temptation of running at full speed through the desert after them. Our last campsite there overlooked our next destination: Baja California, Mexico.

Monday. Much has passed in these last days – camping 2 nights at

Indian Hill (cold, but fantastic!), wonderful hikes in the desert, good simple meals cooked on the camp stove, a feast in El Centro, an easy border crossing. We were concerned about getting Pedro across the border, but nobody even looked at his papers, and barely glanced at our newly acquired tourist cards. Here we sit in Mexico at Campo Las Cabanias – we the only campers. One guy's hanging out waiting to talk with the campground owner about buying a house near here. He's from L.A. and wears a Green Bay Packers sweatshirt, but the owner's away. Does that mean our camping tonight is free? It's a balmy night…well, maybe a tiny bit chilly. And all of this I share with my constant companion Pedro, and my dear friend Laurel.

I think it's Wednesday.

After driving for hours most of that time on rough roads, we reached Puertecitos and decided to continue further south a ways. We pulled off on a side dirt road toward the shoreline and found an ideal spot to camp on a flat perched above the water maybe 6-7 meters. The flat continued to our north, to the west rise beautiful anticlinal mountains, to the south volcanic hills, some prominent islands, and more distantly, another mountain range. To the east, of course, is the Sea of Cortez, blue and glistening in the sunlight. The tide is out, as it was yesterday upon our arrival, and the path to the water is mostly rocky with a prominent high tide mark. The landscape is dotted with desert scrub, mostly creosote with some ocotillo, deceased (or dormant) brittle bush, and a few other shrubs. We explored the tidal pools for a while, finding a starfish with 20 arms, numerous hermit crabs, limpets, mini sea urchins, snails, and some tentacled thing (probably brittle stars), among other life forms and wonders and rocks and stuff.

For dinner Laurel made tacos with leftover chicken from our El Centro feast, canned mackerel, jalapeños and garlic sautéed in olive oil, with cabbage, avocado, and lime on corn tortillas. Tasted absolutely delicious! Dessert consisted of chocolate and camote (sweet potato candy). I cleaned up and we prepared to tuck in for the night. I read to her from Disobedience of the Daughter of the Sun by the light of the camper shell as Orion began his trek across the sky. Then we shut off the light. I cast a few glances towards the stars and the sea, and began to catch glimpses of greenish glows in the waves, which I took to be reflections of the stars or moon. I brought them to Laurel's attention. As we both watched them, we realized that they weren't reflections at all, but luminescence in the water. There was no moon and it only happened where the water moved, such as the tops of waves. We decided to go to the shoreline and explore at closer range. We put on our shoes and a few more articles of clothing (it was a wee bit chilly after all) and scrambled down the slope to the water. When we arrived, we saw tiny pale greenish dots in the water which lit up in the turbulence of water on rock. I squatted down and moved my hand through the water, causing a rush of light to emerge from the waves I made. I splashed and the landing of the water on water lit like flashes of the aurora borealis. I cast a stone across the top of the water and it sent the light in arcs across the palette of wet. When my hand emerged from the water, some of the glow emerged with it. Laurel waded in. Stirred light followed wherever she broke water in a neon phantasy we'd previously never imagined. Eventually we returned to the truck bed, buzzing with delight, with wonder. Pedro wondered what all the excitement was about. He just lay down and led us into the world beyond consciousness. As we tucked ourselves in, the winds began, which blew like banshees until morning. Now, here I sit in the sunshine finding it all difficult to believe.

Thursday, I think. Just north of El Huerfacito. Camped once again on the beach, this one at the end of an arroyo with steep volcanic walls on either side of us. Walked up the wash this afternoon. Saw some plants which looked very interesting including a wild tomatillo. The volcanic rocks somewhat baffle me in their variety as I'm just not up on their interpretation - not my geological area of expertise. There are also some wonderful sea caves, small ones, and some lava grottos as well. The rocks here along the shore are crawling with little crustaceans that give Laurel the creeps.

We spent the night in the company of coyotes. We saw one in the waning daylight, then heard a large pack howl just after a dramatic sunset. It sounded like sweet music to my ears, and piqued Pedro's instincts as well. Laurel and I decided it would be best to keep him close by. He had other ideas. At one point in our dinner conversation, he bolted from his blanket and took off into the darkness, in spite of my calls to return...

instinct is stronger than friendship sometimes. I prepared to set off after him, when he trotted back into camp, his hackles standing at attention. I chained him to the truck, then at bedtime put him in a comfy spot in the cab of the pickup. I was not about to have my friend become coyote bait. The coyotes likely are attracted to the dead seal which lies not too far from our camp. It might have been better to camp further away.

The next day as the sun rose over the islands in the gulf, we prepared to turn back north and make our way to the border. As we finished packing the truck, we spotted a whale, probably a gray whale, swimming in the distant waters. As we watched the mighty cetacean, we also spotted two prominent fins moving parallel to shore, just a bit closer to us, but still too far to see well. My guess is that they were Orcas...killer whales...the first I had ever seen in the wild. Whales, coyotes, magnificent frigate birds, pelicans, gulls, starfish with 20 arms, 'sea cockroaches,' glowing algae, leathery, dried triggerfish, shells of various types, and many others, were our neighbors for several wonderful days. After a few hours drive north we returned to San Felipe where we gorged ourselves on tasty fish tacos, then found another campground between there and Mexicali. As Chinese New Year was rapidly approaching, we stopped just before the border and ate in Chinatown, Mexicali. Then back to the States.

We spent several days in Tucson preparing for our next foray into Mexico. Here we sadly parted with Pedro, who had to stay in a kennel, and caught a night bus to Los Mochis, in the state of Sinaloa, Mexico.

2/2/06. Thursday – I know because I checked my watch.

The busy streets of Los Mochis have fallen behind us replaced by rolling hills of varying shades of brown and green, farmer's fields guarded by wood, grass & adobe huts, cactus, mesquite, other species unknown to me, a few cottonwoods along the arroyo, and men, women and burros weathered by time and a desert climate. Laurel watches out the window as I write/glance/write/glance. The bus, a comfy one, resounds with the voices of school children who clambered aboard in San Blas. Ahead lay El Fuerte, the Fort, and the gateway to La Barranca del Cobre, Copper Canyon. Anxious, excited about our adventure. Our own metal burro sways with the casual rhythm of this two-lane secondary road in the desert, leading to another world, another story, another day, one breath, one step at a time.

3 Feb. On the Ferrocarril de El Fuerte a Creel, after a lovely night in town at the Casa Pascola. A school class of boys just ran past en route to the dining car and Laurel and I sit writing and watching as the swaying rhythm of the train caresses us along the way. Outside the distant hills, farmer's fields, and desert scrub forest ride past. We, the center of the universe today, the stationary travelers as the rest of the world and the day move along. The general elevation rises while here and there the land beneath us drops off as we continue. Memories of last night and the previous day linger. We arrived in El Fuerte and asked directions to the Casa Pascola, although I was doing most of the talking and in my usual fashion confused the name: "Casa or Hotel?" "Pascola or Pascula or Posada," the latter the name of a posh hotel on the square, which ended up with wrong directions, although our place, a new and pleasant hostel, lay not far from the Posada. A few minutes ago the conductor and porters were singing in the back of our car. Just discovered we're on the wrong train – we'll get off at Loreto and change, but the conductor who came by to collect the fare, I asked him what I should pay for the ride to Loreto and he said "Is no problem." Also saw a beautiful bird this morning on our way to the station. Our cab driver (I have to get better on remembering names) told us the name, but like his name, I've forgotten it. It had the size and general shape of a large jay with a crest and loooong blue and black tail with white underneath and some black lines along the border and face.

So back to yesterday, we found our place, right next to a Pacifico beer stand along Calle Morrelos about a 4-5 minute walk from the beautiful palm-bedecked town square. After resting a few minutes we walked into town to buy bug spray, water purification, and, of course, limes and avocados. Then we walked up to the fort, but along the way our attention diverted to the square where a brass & percussion band struck up a wonderful concert, playing with not only talent, of which they had plenty, but with such an air of joy in the music and life that was infectious, almost prompting these 2 weary, sleep-deprived wanderers to get up and dance. We didn't, but rather sat and rested, letting the sensation dance within us, admiring the band, the onlookers, the palms, the gargoyle light posts, and the tall stump near us which had been carved with numerous animal shapes in the year 2000, or so it read. After a while we headed up to the fort to check out the museum and admire the 360° view of the landscape, the attractive Pueblo of El Fuerte, the Rio Fuerte, and hills & fields fading off into the distance. The museum had some interesting photos and articles from the Mexican Revolution and from the native Mayos (not to be confused with Mayas, who are very different) of this area, but mostly of Spanish conquest and settlement. Expeditions that began near here later founded Los Angeles, San Francisco, and San Luis Obispo, among other missions in California as far north as Sonoma. Of course it played down the fact that they slaughtered numerous (to put it mildly) indigenous people along the way, including here in Sinaloa. Felipe Bochomo led a revolt of the natives in the early 1900's, but eventually it was laid to rest as was he.

Then we walked back to the Casa, during which, for the second time a pit bull surprised me by barking, jumping, and growling at my ear through a fence. After showering and resting we set out for dinner at a great little taco stand southeast of the square a few blocks. Ate splendid beef and tripe tacos and bean with ham soup, guacamole, salsas, and Jamaica juice. Had a great muy picante hot sauce! Wonderful family business – beautiful people. Chatted for a while, then set off. Returned after buying a banana to show their daughter the 'talking banana' routine, where I carve a face with movable mouth into the fruit. (He speaks Spanish too!) At first the little girl was terrified and hid in the car as I started to carve up the silent fruit, and didn't want to peek out to see the banana talk, even though it began to sing the first verse of "De Colores." Mom & Dad tried to get her to come out, but she hid farther down and cried. I made the talking banana anyhow and figured I'd give it to her parents for later. They loved the gig and we all had a good laugh. When she heard us laughing, the girl looked up from the depths of the floor on the passenger side of the car. Her mama took the banana from me and showed it to her, which brought a twinkle to her eye, and slowly her smile grew until it spread wide enough that the car could barely contain it.

Just boarded the second class train, but had to wait for another to pass, a train full of Americans in RVs – yes, their own RVs loaded onto the

Copper Canyon train – bizarre!! To each their own, I guess.

Anyhow, we left the taco stand and walked back to the Casa. Along the way we were stopped by a man and his 2 daughters, who talked with us about the U.S. He works in Las Vegas several times per year – a wonderful man with a bright smile. His teenage girls were shy, as most children seem to act with strangers, a good thing to a point. Didn't get scared by the dog on our way back to the Casa, where we finished most of Laurel's ballena (big bottle) of Pacifico beer and hit the hay, tired after a long day. Actually Laurel finished off the beer. I'm a cheap drunk...a few sips and I'm gone. This morning I got up early, went for a walk and said my blessings for the day, then bought fresh corn tortillas and went to the Casa for breakfast.

The next day we got a ride from the guesthouse to the train station and hopped aboard what we thought was the second class train. As we chugged up the tracks along with lots of tourists and some school groups, the conductor told us we owed him 1000 pesos for the two of us. We were expecting more like 500-600 pesos. We wanted second class...cheaper with fewer tourists and more local people. The conductor said it was no problem and he told us to exit at Loreto, the next stop, and wait for the second class train. Loreto has a train station, or had a train station. It's now in serious disrepair, with no viable windows, lots of mouse dung, and some intriguing graffiti. We were joined there by a family waiting for a ride home to the area of Urique, inside the mighty canyon we had come to see. While Laurel played "knock the bottle off the rail" with the youngest boy, I attempted to help Angel, the older brother and an eager student, with his English lessons.

Finally, the train pulled into the station, such that it is. Angel and I sometimes continued our lessons on the train, but Laurel and I had come to see Copper Canyon, so there were frequent breaks for scenery. Copper Canyon is actually a series of canyons all linked together, which in total are larger than the Grand Canyon. I, however, believe that such comparisons are odd at best, as they are very different places, both beautiful, both huge, both unique. The train ride is literally awe-inspiring...there is no other way to describe it, winding up through constantly changing vegetation from desert scrub to pine & fir forests, beneath impressive cliff faces, along rivers sunken deep into Mother Earth, through tunnels, and spiraling up trellises, which in at least one place reaches a point where the front of the train can look down on the tail end of the train. Dotted along the route are a few towns, where the local Tarahumara Indians come to sell their wares to train passengers.

The Tarahumara, who call themselves the 'Raramuri' in their own tongue, still live in many parts of the canyon, most trying to follow their traditional way of life, with the addition of making wares for tourists, especially baskets of pine needles, sotol, palm, or other materials, beautifully woven and sturdy, as their resistance to the wear of our journey back to Oregon can attest. The word 'Raramuri' means something to the effect of 'fast foot', referring to the running for which their men, and some of the women, are known. A Raramuri man won the Leadville 100, a 100 mile foot race in the high country of Colorado, in his first attempt. Like so many other indigenous people, the Raramuri too often fall prey to the press of 'civilization', which often places them into the demeaning role of tourist oddities, when all they really wanted was to be left alone to live their traditions. May they never completely succumb!

Just a bit before Divisadero we stopped at San Rafael where two Tarahumara women walked to the train loaded down with baskets. Rather than hawk, they just stood there waiting. Finally I asked the conductor "Cuanto tiempo pase el tren aqui?" "Solo unos minutos" came the reply. ("How long will the train stay here?" "Only a few minutes.") I returned to my seat. We sat there a while and I finally arose, went to the door, and bought my first Tarahumara basket for 20 pesos, a beautiful, tightly woven, hand painted basket of fresh pine needles. It smells incredible!

Divisadero is literally the high point of the train ride where several of the canyons join at one of the highest points along the rim, about 10,000 feet/3000 meters above sea level. Here the desert scrub is replaced by pines, junipers, and madrones. It's the only real 'photo stop' along the ride, and it truly is an incredible view, but I ran out of film!! I bought 3 baskets from a lovely lady named Isadora. She shook my hand shyly, her eyes diverted to the ground. Then we hopped back on the train and continued on to our temporary destination.

Rolled into Creel and exited our iron horse, entering the throng of young men, kids most of them, accosting us with requests to stay in their hotel. We negotiated the maze of pubescence and met Samuel, who showed us his card. We took it and told him we'd stop by, but wanted to look around ourselves. He said 'OK'. We went to one, a very nice place, but settled for Samuel's based on a combination of price and setting – a rustic room with log beams, good wood doors, and tin wood stove. Everyone calls it "Luli's Place, but it's also known as the Hotel Huespedez-Perez. Luli, Samuel's mom, is a bundle of energy, so eager to please that she almost kills you with hospitality. Our room was rather cold, but she threw some wood into the stove, dowsed it with kerosene, and torched it. After a few tries, it got the room comfortable. When hunger set in we walked through town and ended up at a taco stand near the tracks, the only one in town as far as we could tell, and had burritos de barbacoa – very tasty. Later got apple empanadas for desert. And here we are in Creel.

We had intended to stay in Creel for 2 nights before going into the canyons, but realized the next day that no bus went into the canyon on our planned day. We found a couple who had rented a pickup truck and were able to get a ride with them into the canyon a day earlier than planned. The road proved dusty and pretty rough in places, but it is a spectacular drive, one not recommended for the faint of heart. Our route took us to the bottom of one canyon, back up to the rim, then down to the bottom of another canyon to the town of Batopilas, an old silver mining town from days long since gone. It's a wonderful place, stretched out along the banks of the Batopilas River at the base of the steep canyon walls. We stayed at Seniora Monse's guesthouse on the town plaza for one night, then, the next morning, set off on foot for the village of Satevo', the site of a large, old, and somewhat anomalous church, much beloved by the small local population. Along the way we began finding these things that were about the size of a small tennis ball, but with thick spikes protruding from them. Most of them had been cracked in half and were empty. We eventually found a small tree that had some hanging from its branches. As we marveled at these biological curiosities, a Raramuri man happened along riding a bicycle and he stopped to talk with us. Ramòn said the spiky things were called 'papuche' in his language, and that people cracked them open, removed the seeds, which were held together by a gooey brown liquid, and sucked the juice off of them. We chatted a bit more with Ramòn and then he rode off towards Satevò. We found an uncracked papuche and tried it...remarkbly like chocolate...who could argue with that?!

Shortly thereafter we came around a curve in the road and got our first view of the beautiful village of Satevò, a wide, flat spot along the Batopilas river, dotted with farm fields, groves of trees, some houses, and the church, surrounded by the steeply rising walls of the magnificent canyon in which we stood, held in the bosom of Mother Earth. We made our way to the church and sat down in its shade to eat some lunch. While we ate, 2 young girls let their curiosity get the best of them and they ventured over to us, their shy smiles glowing on their faces in the shade of the iglesia. We began talking with them and offered them some of the greens (purslane) we spread on our tortillas along with the avocado and other tasty items. Like many children of their age, they weren't too interested in the greens, but when I again made the last banana I had with me talk, their amusement grew. Tanya and Jasmine became two more friends of many in this long journey.

After lunch we asked the girls where we could get the key to open the church so we could take a look inside. They pointed to the house immediately behind the large edifice. I walked through the yard, causing their turkeys to scatter, and knocked on the door. An elder woman with a face wrinkled with life experience and desert air, answered and pointed to the key ring hanging from a nail on the wall. Laurel and I both tried the key numerous times with no success. Other visitors arrived and also had no luck. Then our young friends brought Alejandro, a middle-aged, thin man with a gentle face, who had another key which opened the door. The building was striking in its simple beauty, the interior painted blue and white, with several vivid statues of Mary and Jesus Christ. After we had spent some time in thought in the church, we asked Alejandro about camping alongside the river, and he promptly showed us a route across river and pointed to some viable sites. We thanked him and gave him a few pesos for his trouble, and set off to find a suitable spot. We eventually settled on a place overlooking the river just downstream from the iglesia, quiet but for a couple of visits by small herds of goats. We camped in the open air under a star-spangled night sky, hardly able to sleep for the beauty of the magnificent setting in which we found ourselves. In the morning we headed back for another night at Señora Monse's, before leaving the next morning at 5 a.m. for an inspiring sunrise drive back to Creel. We returned to Luli's place for a night, then took a bus to the city of Chihuahua.

Chihuahua is not a hot spot on the tourist circuit, but we found it much to our liking, with interesting history, good, simple food, and friendly people. We found a decent, cheap hotel not far from the cathedral and market area. We enjoyed a couple of days there checking out street vendors, the Pancho Villa Museum, a paleontology museum with skeletons of wooly mammoths, chambered nautali, and a gray whale, and spent a lot of time hanging out in the various halls and alleys of the market, buying medicinal herbs, sweet treats, avocados, tamales, and some maguey honey...maguey is the plant from which they make mescal & tequila. Then, after a hellish rush hour bus ride to the intercity bus station, we prepared for a night bus back to Tucson.

In the Chihuahua bus station:

Lots of nervous energy lingering in my muscles, bopping about like Pac Man on a binge or bees in the hive trying to settle in on a windy night, always re-energized with each swell of unsettled air. A man just walked past: short man, maybe 5'2", relatively long arms, wearing red pants, not a bright, but more of a dirty red, and a sports-type jacket of blue with orange sleeves. Wears a dingy cowboy hat with a high crown which sits high on his head. Gives the appearance of a head much too long for his body. In his 50's or 60's maybe. Carries 2 things in his left hand, a bag of chips and a candy bar. He sauntered by, looking from side to side. Walked past me, somewhere around behind me, came up from behind way over by the ticket counters, then to the other end of this echoing hall of a bus station, much too large and of hard building materials, which give the intercom a resounding echo that makes the words pretty much unintelligible to me – would be in English let alone Spanish. Lots of people sitting around, trying to pass the time, looking about, most of them with much less baggage than Laurel and I, who are loaded down with sweets and Raramuri handcrafts.

Another man just walked past, one who works here. Not particularly tall either, maybe average for Mexicans. He's maybe in his late 50's, but more likely in his 60's. Chewing gum with his mouth closed. Dressed in blue from his plain blue ball cap to his faded blue long-sleeved sweatshirt, blue slacks, and blue well-worn tennis shoes. A man of sturdy build, but with a limp born of old age and a hard-working life. He's pushing a dust mop, a very wide dust mop with a shaft near as tall as he and a handle like a lawn mower's. He shuffles back and forth in the long, football field sized hall, back and forth, back and forth, how many years back and forth. Followed by the pungent odor of the oil-based compound they spray on these mops to keep the dust together. How many miles, or should I say kilometers, has he walked pushing that broom? What stories do the wrinkles of his face and hands tell? How many pairs of tennis shoes has he worn through? Who waits for him to come home, or sits on his lap to hear stories on Sundays, holidays? The floor looks clean and shiny.

Two little Raramuri children run around the hall playing. It's all a game. The boy, younger of the two, wears fairly typical clothes for most kids his age. The girl floats about the hall on quiet, bare feet, her billowing, colorful, flowered kerchief flapping the back of her head like a flag in the breeze or a cottonwood leaf on a summer afternoon. They play some version of hide and seek, occasionally stopping to ask people for pesos. A smaller girl sometimes joins them, bundled in a mid-weight jacket and mostly black dress, trying hard to keep up with her siblings. Life in the bus station wanders along on a Friday night in February.

North of the Border

On our return to Tucson we headed ASAP to Pedro's temporary accommodation to get him checked out of his "room". When I had left him there I asked if they walked the dogs daily. The lady said they did not, but because the pens in which they stayed were large, the dogs always exercised themselves. I told her that Pedro likely would not do that, but would curl up and wait for me to return. When we came back she was amazed to tell me that's exactly what he had done during our week-long journey, hardly touching his food. "He's not like any other dog I've seen." I'll agree with that.

So it's Wednesday or something and we're in Bisbee, AZ, sitting in on a class at the herb school with Michael Moore (Michael Moore the herbalist; not the film director)...very knowledgeable man and very opinionated, which doesn't surprise me. It seems that most people who make something of themselves in this world, who go to the forefront of their professions or become famous teachers, seem to be intellectual end products in their fields. They are opinionated and tend toward the curmudgeonly side, while those of us on the other extreme who try to keep open minds and lean towards affability tend to meander through life looking for a niche that can prove elusive to find. I know it's not always the case, but that's how the latter seems to have happened for me.

Laurel had studied with Michael in 2001, becoming one of his prize students and a good friend. We spent a couple of nights staying with some of his current students before moving north again, making our way slowly home. Our next destination was Second Mesa, AZ, on the Hopi Reservation where we enjoyed the good company of Gerald, Yvette, & their family. On this occasion, we had the chance to see the Kachinas come out for the Bean Dances at one of the villages, including the "Dirty Girls", who tried to catch people and have mock sex with them, using candy and other goodies as bait. And a good time was had by all. Like all of our visits with friends along the way, our stay at the Hopi Mesas ended too quickly as we left the cold, wind blown mesa tops for California.

Road weary and filled with experiences aplenty, we headed to Laurel's family home north of San Francisco, where we rested for a couple of nights in relative luxury. Then, Pedro and I left Laurel and returned to our humble home in southwestern Oregon. Hard to go back to regular life after such a journey, but soon I found myself at work in the February cold of Oregon Caves getting ready for the next season of tourists to arrive, and Pedro reacquainted himself with familiar smells.

November 2006

What was a stream, is now a roaring river. What was tranquil flow, has become a torrent. Sunny skies have given way to overcast, mist, and frequent showers. I live along the East Fork of the Illinois River, and can tell that the soil in the upstream land has become saturated with rain and snowmelt as the river suddenly swelled to its wet season base level overnight. While I love warmth and sunshine, I also welcome this time of year, for it indeed has its own beauty, its own foggy mystery. The rains are the reason for these magnificent forests with trees that reach into the clouds 100, 200, 300 feet (30-90 m), dwarfing me and my simple problems, reminding me that life is so much larger than we may ever truly know.

Right now as I gaze out of the Visitor Center at Oregon Caves 4000 feet (1250m) above sea level, the world lies covered in snow and flakes continue to fall, making the trees and these old, rustic buildings look like a million typical Christmas cards. Tomorrow at 4:00 p.m., this visitor center will close for the season, will close for the last time during my tenure here. This pending change in my life comes with a certain amount of fear of the unknown. Is it the right decision? I believe so or I would not leave this job. But to paraphrase a thought from Milan Kundera's The Unbearable Lightness of Being, if I had two lives to live I could live them both and see which one is better, however I only have this one. You pay your price and you take your chances. Change is the only constant in Nature. I leave this job and go into the future with both eyes wide open.

My new home is on a beautiful piece of land 8 miles from Happy Camp, CA, which we call simply "The Land." Awfully creative, isn't it? Supposedly the town got its name due to a series of murders many years ago. People wanted to change the mood of the town after that, so it became Happy Camp. There is no land phone and cell phones are of limited use. We have no internet service on the land, so I will have to go into town once or twice a week to use the computers there. Water is from China Creek that runs along the property, and is very good, clean water. Electricity is currently by a generator that charges batteries. We try not to use it too much, although I intend to do lots of writing, so this laptop computer will have to make use of it. In the future we will have a solar system. Heat is by wood stove. The nice thing about wood heat is that it warms you twice. First it warms you when you cut, transport, and stack it outside your home, then it warms you when you burn it. The house has a nice kitchen, and the land has lots of beautiful trees for my inspiration (as well as firewood), so I will have much good food for both soul and body.

Pedro loves it there. He's most at home in the forest and loves exploring the land. Still, it will be hard for him to get used to not living in the place we have shared for over 3 years. He flows with the changes well, however.

In October I traveled to Port Angeles, WA, for the Forest Storytelling Festival, which was wonderful. I heard lots of great stories, and hiked in the woods with truly fine company. Pedro enjoyed those parts of the journey that he could attend. We had a trying encounter with three raccoons at an ocean front campsite in Olympic National Park on our way back home. They insisted on checking out our spot, whether we liked it or not, and whether we were there watching or not. Pedro wisely kept his distance from them. I recently read a book called Kinship With All Life, which discussed communication with animals and how we can reach agreements and understandings with them. I tried to talk with the raccoons, but I don't think they had read the same book. No matter what I tried they continued to get as close as they could before I chased them off. Not even peanuts laden with cayenne chili pepper dissuaded them. Eventually I broke out my slingshot and kept them away for short periods, but they persisted. Finally after I had eaten, I took the dishes to the restroom area to clean them and make a phone call. When I returned the campsite was untouched and the masked bandits had gone. I guess they just wanted to inspect our site, then did so when Pedro and I walked away (not leaving any food for them), and wandered onto the other occupied sites, where I heard them being chased off sometime later. The rest of the journey passed without incident.

January 2007

Greetings from along China Creek and Happy Camp. The wood stove has been well-fed and so have we. Pedro lies on his blanket near the fire looking for sticks from the woodpile on which to chew. Laurel sits in the comfy papasan chair also near the fire reading Harper's magazine and eating the last of the banana bread I made the other day. I find myself sitting by the fire at the dining table digesting the homemade tortillas and split pea soup we had for dinner and writing this little slice of life on my computer. Most of what we do, if it's inside, which most things are in the cold of winter, we do next to the wood stove. No place else here has heat, so we spend a lot of time in the kitchen/dining area tending the fire and preparing meals.

Of course, every day starts at the crack of 8 or 8:30 (it's pretty dark until then) when Pedro and I go out for our morning walk, usually along one of the dirt roads that wind through the woods. Actually it's through the woods here everywhere we go: Douglas firs, madrones, tan oaks, canyon oaks, sugar and ponderosa pines, etc. We get a pretty good workout given the steepness and Pedro spends little of his time on pathways, preferring to chase whatever he desires through the bush, disappearing for long periods while I contemplate the day and my part in it. Depending on the weather, our walks last from 30 to 90 minutes. Then it's back home for breakfast and stretching/yoga, although recently we have had to add fetching water from the creek to our morning routine since the water lines that take the water from the creek to the holding tank and to the house have all frozen. The house sits on a north-facing slope, so it doesn't get much sun or warmth this time of year. After breakfast is ready (Pedro always eats first) we settle in by the fire to warm my icicle feet, eat, and write poetry or read until it's time for hauling more wood from the pile, splitting wood, or doing other chores. Then it's time for light lunch. If the afternoon is nice we head down to the open flat area below the house, which does get some good sun, to warm our bones and just hang out with this beautiful place and all its residents. Pedro and I go for another afternoon walk regardless of the weather. Once or twice a week we go into town to do laundry, use the computers, check mail, etc. Happy Camp is a town of about 700-800 people with one grocery store and a few other amenities, but pretty simple and quiet. It's a nice place. I arranged to tell stories for the after-school program in town.

Nine to ten in the evening means bedtime. After dark we fix and eat dinner and read, write, or work on making or repairing things. I've taken up weaving and have thus far produced three belts, thanks to my terrific weaving teacher back in Cave Junction who got me started. I've never been good at working with my hands, other than cooking which I can do relatively well, and it feels great to finally, after all these years, be able to make something more permanent with my own two hands. The sleeping area we do not heat and while I often have problems feeling warm enough I find that with enough covers I stay warm and sleep rather well, better than I have in many years. Don't know if it's the cold, quiet, general lack of stress, or those 3 combined that helps me sleep, but all that matters is that I sleep well sometimes.

So that's what life is like here in this little piece of northern California. Sounds boring maybe, but it's a good, simple life. We do have our share of adventures and soon it will be traveling time, so more tales will unfold.

June 2007

June 7. I decided to head for the hills. At the time I was still living in Happy Camp, CA, and since June 8 is my birthday I thought I would do something special and spend it alone with Pedro in the area of the Red Buttes Wilderness near the Oregon/California border. We packed enough stuff for a couple of days, grabbed my map of the area, and drove up the dirt road to a high pass near the boundary with the wilderness area. We weren't going to backpack, I wasn't in the mood for that, just some car camping and day hikes, which are often more my preference. It was cool and partly cloudy in the area near the pass where we chose to camp, with glorious views of the surrounding countryside and a spectacular scene looking up the steep, rising spires of the Red Buttes above us. After arriving we explored a bit, then cooked up some dinner and prepared for a night under the stars.

In the morning we set off to walk a rugged dirt road and contoured along the ridge we were on. In my little Honda, it wasn't a road I would choose to drive unless I had to, and I do like walking on old, seldom used dirt roads in the woods. I figured we would later hike the trail into the wilderness, maybe after lunch. After several miles of very enjoyable walking, with some side trips off of the road to ponds, rock cliffs, and the like, we reached a point where I thought it would be good to make our way back for lunch. Pedro was doing what Pedro did, running off into the brush to chase rabbits, deer, or just for the fun of it. I had to caution him a few times about steep cliffs below us, but he's smart enough not to chase squirrels over the edge. Just as we began to turn around, I called Pedro, who was on the steep slope above me exploring the scrub brush, and when he heard my voice he popped out on top of the straight drop of about 20 feet. I called for him to come down and head back to camp. He tried to turn around and get back to where he had ascended, but the shrubs were pointing out in such a way that when he turned around, they pushed him right off the perch that he had found and he began to fall butt first. His back end slammed into some rocks jutting out from the cliff, which caused him to spin around and fall face down until he landed behind shrubs on the roadside. I watched in horror, thinking I had lost my beloved friend, that this was our last hike together, then ran over to find him. Just then he darted out from the brush and shook himself off, before heading down the road. My jaw dropped, then I gathered myself enough to tell him to stop, which he did. I ran to him and hugged him… gently, because I knew he'd be hurting, then began to check him over. He had some cuts on his paws and his back end, but I couldn't see that any bones were obviously broken. I think his adrenaline had kicked in and he wasn't feeling the pain because of it, but I knew he would soon. I tried to pick him up, to carry him back to the car. He was OK with that, but after a few hundred yards I knew I couldn't keep it up all the way back to the car. We still had at least 3 miles to go. Also, he seemed to be doing alright. I set him down and watched him walk, limping some, down the road toward the car. After about 15 minutes he began to slow down and limp more. I knew the adrenaline was wearing off and he was starting to feel the real impact of what had happened to him. We continued to walk, as quickly as he could, back towards the car. The beauty around me, the clouds opening and closing, birds and lizards darting around, became just background noise as my focus became Pedro, Pedro, and only Pedro. I could tell he was in pain, but his stoicism led him on. There's another lesson I have to learn from him.

 We made it back to the car and I let him lay down for a bit to lick his wounds. I gave him some water and treats, though he wasn't much interested in eating at that point. I found my tea tree oil antiseptic and put some on his cuts, and after a more thorough exam and some loving attention, I helped him into the car and we headed down the road, both quickly, but also carefully, not wanting to exacerbate his pain any more. I was relieved to get back to the paved road where we could make a swifter pace toward home.

Back at the Land I helped him to his bed and Laurel also checked him over. The nearest veterinarian was at least 30 miles away on winding roads, much farther for one who would likely be open by the time we could get there. We decided to care for his wounds and hope nothing was seriously broken, which we didn't think was the case. The next day Pedro was too sore to go out for our usual morning walk. We called a vet and at the doctor's advice, watched him closely, giving some approved medication for his pain and mending his cuts. We made sure he had plenty of water, but he didn't have much interest in eating. He limped outside to pee, but lifting his leg the way he usually did was obviously too much for him, so he squatted instead. That proved challenging enough. The following day he improved to the point where he could go for a short walk and take care of his business, but it was nearly a week before he was really well enough to go for our usual walks. I was amazed at his recovery. I would likely have been in the hospital for weeks after such a fall. But he was Pedro, my rock. Nothing kept him down for long, not for many years.

December 2007

> In frozen white dawn
> First sunlight, crimson mountain
> Fire within, I dance.

As the year comes to a close I find myself care-taking the Frog Farm, the home of my friends Deb and Steve, while they spend a few weeks in Arizona. On this frosty morn, I have thus far done my hour of writing, walked the dogs and myself, danced, stretched, fed the chickens, ducks and geese, checked for fresh eggs (none today, but 4 last night), fed the dogs and cats (no eggs from them either), written 3 haiku poems including the one above, started a fire in the wood stove, and had breakfast. It's 10:00

a.m.. I'll stay here for another week, then return to my regular 'home for now' in Phoenix; that's Phoenix, Oregon, not Phoenix, Arizona. I stay in a castle-like house that a friend and now landlady, Didar, inherited from her mother some years ago. It's an odd place and I'm glad and grateful to her for the accommodations. Pedro and I had left our previous home in Happy Camp, CA, and moved to Phoenix, OR, in July, which I think is about the 45th time I've moved in my life.

In this last year, much has happened, too much in fact to allow me to cover it all, so I'll just try to give a synopsis of the main events. I did not work a steady job at all this year, but I definitely did work, picking up jobs here and there, mostly yard work and light construction. I did the same to pay for my rent in the places I lived and as work trade for workshops I attended. I also worked a few days as a guide at Oregon Caves, did some babysitting, and even got some paid storytelling gigs. Most recently I helped Didar with her holiday mistletoe business.

For those of you who don't know about mistletoe, it's a plant used for Christmas/Solstice decoration in the U.S. and northern Europe that has an interesting tradition around it. People hang it from ceilings or doorways and if you see someone standing under it, you are supposed to kiss them. Usually it's a male/female thing, but times change. Mistletoe is a parasitic plant that grows on other plants, the Christmas one mostly on oak trees. Didar harvests mistletoe from the oaks around the Medford/Ashland area in Oregon, prepares them, packages them and sells them to stores to sell for Christmas. This year Pedro and I were her assistants in harvesting the plants. We had a crew of people to help prepare it for sale, mostly local people from Mexico and Guatemala, but also, of course, Didar and I. Pedro just couldn't get the hang of tying the mistletoe, largely due to a lack of opposable thumbs, but also a distinct lack of interest. He gave moral support.

When I lived on the North Rim of the Grand Canyon back in the summers of 1992 & 1993, I made some good friends that I've more or less kept in contact with since. Two of those, Tom and Marsha, live in Kanab, UT. Tom caught the storytelling bug, partly from me, and decided to put together a storytelling festival in Kanab. He asked me to come and tell stories for it, which I did in October. It was a wonderful 2-day event held in an old barn and I felt glad to be a part of it, as well as to see my good friends again. Kanab, Utah, was the filming site for many Hollywood cowboy movies, and one of the tellers told tales of working as an extra in some, meeting the likes of Frank Sinatra and John Wayne. After the festival Pedro and I headed to New Mexico, where we visited other friends from the North Rim and spent a week helping with the construction of a new building to house the school and workshops of teacher Martín Prechtel. Then Pedro & I headed west toward Joshua Tree, CA, where I visited a friend and did a fun storytelling gig for a nice crowd at a private house.

On the way to Joshua Tree, I decided to camp out in the mountains west of Kingman, AZ, for a night. Just before arriving at the place we camped, the alternator light on my car came on. I parked so that I could easily start the car without needing the battery, just in case it wouldn't start by itself in the morning. Thank goodness for manual transmissions! Pedro and I bedded down under the stars and moonlight in the open desert and went to sleep. In the middle of the night, I awakened to him barking at some beastie lurking in the shadows. I looked around, but could see nothing. I did hear what sounded like a large creature in the brush nearby, and pulled out my flashlight to see. It had big ears...very big ears. And it was dark. As it moved around the clearing in which we lay, it came into the moonlight, and I could get a better view. Pedro continued to give low barks and growls every few seconds. When I caught his profile, I confirmed my suspicions as to the identity of the creature...a feral burro. Burros were used by the old time miners in this area, and when the miners died or went away, the burros remained. They have since become somewhat wild, although still often have a tendency to look at people as sources for food.

The burro approached, inching closer and closer. I wasn't really frightened of the animal, but since I didn't have experience with feral burros, I remained cautious. Pedro didn't like the burro at all and couldn't quite figure out what to do about it. Burro appeared not too crazy about Pedro's barking either. I talked with this beast of the dark, and made a few shouts to try and send him packing, which didn't work at all. I made some sudden movements toward him and he retreated a few feet, then turned and watched us. Moments later he approached again. I wanted to go back to sleep and so did my brave companion, who huddled behind me as I chatted with the burro. I felt no ill will towards the burro, just wanted to be left alone. I ran at him and tried to get him to remove himself. He began to bray, loud and long, echoing from the cliffs around as Orion chased the seven sisters through the night sky above us. He most likely wanted food.

I then did what I knew was the wrong thing to do. I've worked as a park ranger. I know you're not supposed to feed wildlife. I know the problems it causes, such as them not leaving you alone. But, I also had tried various things get rid of this overgrown jackrabbit, and nothing worked. I wanted to show him some compassion. This was his home and not mine after all. So I did it, I pulled out a stale wheat tortilla from my car, and I threw it to the burro. He sniffed it, then looked back at me. Maybe he preferred fruit. I threw some apples out into the desert, then one at him, to try to get him away from us. He ate a few and then returned. I decided we needed sleep, and chasing the burro off was not happening, so I picked up my sleeping bag, pillow, and Pedro's blanket, and we got in the car to settle down for whatever sleep we could get after our experience. True, it's a rather small Honda, but I've slept in it before and likely will again. We did get back to sleep, and awoke in the morning, free of the night visitor, somewhat rested, and me a little sore. We went out for a walk, then headed into Kingman, where I found a mechanic and had the car checked out. New alternator needed. So much for the money I made at the storytelling festival! Ah, such is life!

Lest you think Pedro lacks bravery because of his staying behind me in the burro encounter, I'll share another incident that occurred in August during a hike to Pilot Rock on the Oregon/California border. Just as we returned to the car, I saw a flash of black out of the corner of my eye, and turned to see a fairly large bear running through the woods…and Pedro chasing him. He was only about 10 feet behind the bruin, who ran as fast as possible to get away from my intrepid canine. Pedro barked as he ran, which likely made it hard for him to hear my calls. When he finally did stop and return to me, I wasn't certain whether to yell at him or give him a medal. I guess he chooses his battles carefully and the burro down in

Arizona had just looked too alien in the moonlight, but the bear appeared more normal. He's likely smarter than me on that account.

March 2008

The wheel of the year has turned to Spring, and snow queen, daffodils, snowdrops, and others peek their heads above ground to brighten the days. Large flocks of robins have returned to their roosts in the hills around here, and vultures once again soar overhead before perching in their favorite dead oaks. Morel mushrooms will soon thrust themselves from the moist dirt and hopefully some will grace my plate, as a tasty green plant called miner's lettuce already has.

As the seasons change, so do I. The winter, and frankly the last year or so, has been a time of intense looking inward and self-examination. I believe that it has borne good fruit, but only time will tell. Outwardly, the change that comes is for the wheel to come back to a place it was not so long ago. In 2006 I left Oregon Caves feeling burnt out on the job. I worked a few days there last year just to help out and keep some income heading my way. Now I have decided to go back to the caves as a full-time seasonal guide, working just until early September. While I have some misgivings about it, I believe that it will be a good thing for me, and while I will not be making as much money as I did when I was the Head Guide there, I will likely have fewer headaches.

It should be an interesting season at the Caves. First there are the gas prices and economy which will keep many people home. Then there's the fact that the Caves have no communications due to someone having stolen 8-10 miles of their high-tech phone/computer line. Yes, that's correct, 8-10 miles of phone line stolen. Lots of poverty in this county, so it's not entirely a surprise. More of a surprise that the NPS didn't do anything about it for quite some time...they've had no phones for 4 months. I have moved into a cabin at a place called the Frog Farm with my friends Deb and Steve in Takilma, OR, just south of Cave Junction.

In January, when I was still living in Phoenix, OR, I decided I needed to go back to work and applied with a temp agency. They offered me a job doing light production (factory-type) work at the Dagoba Chocolate plant in Ashland, OR. Even though it only paid just above minimum wage, it was more than I was making before, which was nothing, and besides, I love their product. So I took the job and worked nearly 2 months there. It was a good experience and I worked with some fine people, not the least of which was my supervisor Ruby, who worked hard to treat her employees well, and was as generous as she could be with chocolate and cacao. I very much appreciate that, and will have chocolate to share with friends for months to come. I spent much of my time sifting and packaging cacao nibs, which for the uninitiated in the world of cacao, are the broken beans of cacao (cocoa), the material out of which chocolate is made. Oddly enough, while people like me do like eating them, many of these cacao nibs were being sent to beauty shops where they would be crushed and used to give women very expensive facial cleanses. The main drawback to the work was all the bleach we use in cleanup and washing my hands what seemed like 110 times per day. For the most part, it beats raiding their dumpster like I used to do. Actually they now have a trash compactor, so you can't do that anymore anyhow.

Pedro is doing well and likes the change to living on the edge of the woods where he can run more freely. I hope to do more storytelling here, and have an upcoming gig in Yreka, CA, on April Fool's Day. I still have regular gigs at some assisted living centers, including one in the Special Care Center (dementia unit), which is always interesting. I don't know if they understand my stories much, but they like Pedro. So the days are packed with work at the Caves, working off some of my rent at the farm, writing poetry, working on stories, and, of course, walks with Pedro. Life just keeps on rolling.

Walking in Takilma

One day Alan and I were walking our dogs on the road behind the Frog Farm and we came upon some people who had recently moved into a cabin on the Kauffman's land along the dirt road that ran from the river to the main road. Alan's dog River went into their driveway to greet their dogs, and one of the dogs didn't much care for that, so there was some tension between them. When the couple complained and said, "Git yer dogs off our land," Alan said something like, "Just relax, they'll be alright." I told Alan that we should get our dogs and move on, which we did. I didn't much like the looks on the faces of these newcomers to the area. A couple of minutes later as we neared the main road, we heard gunshots from the direction of that cabin, and bullets screamed past our heads, landing who knows where. It wasn't long after that I moved away, but in the interim I didn't take that road any more. For some it's still the Old West.

My little cabin at the Frog Farm in southern Oregon. I lived in the right side where the new wood is.

December 2009

It has been a big year in many ways. Once again I returned to working in the land down under, no, not Australia, although I'd love to visit there sometime. I went back to the world of dark and damp, the Oregon Caves. I started on a part time basis in Spring, then just after the 4th of July went to full time. This year proved busier than the previous couple of years, I'm sure due in part to the perception of a better economy, but mostly I think due to the fact that it was a big year for the Caves and Oregon. This place I've come to call home celebrated her 150 year anniversary as a state. Then in May, the Chateau at the Oregon Caves, our stately hotel, celebrated the 75th anniversary of her opening in 1934. And to top it all off, Oregon Caves National Monument passed the 100 year mark, having become a monument on July 12, 1909, named by President William Howard Taft, who likely never visited the Caves since he was our most circumferentially challenged president...he would not have fit through the narrow passageways. We marked the event with cake and ice cream (none of which I could eat), some served by Oregon's governor. We also had a reading of the original proclamation, special tours, and a visit by the Caves' discoverer, Elijah Davidson, represented by yours truly, since the original Elijah passed away in 1927. It was the first time I have portrayed Elijah in the presence of the man's descendants, and it went well. I felt it a great honor to do so, and they appreciated my performance

One day in late Spring Pedro and I went out for our evening walk with our friends Alan and his dog River. The dogs were out of site of Alan and I when they encountered two others. When I saw River run back towards us and heard the sound of a dogfight, I ran ahead and found the two nasty beasts with their jaws locked onto Pedro's back. I scared them off and we headed quickly back home. Pedro ended up needing some surgery to drain the wounds. While under the anesthetic, the vet's assistant needed to help with his breathing, which had stopped, but when I stepped up and laid my hand on him, he began breathing on his own again. He was on pain killers and antibiotics for a while, but within two days he had bounced back and again felt ready to resume our twice or more daily walks. We saw those other dogs only twice briefly after that, and now I think they have moved away. Pedro and I don't miss them.

In October, Pedro and I again traveled to the wonderful little town of Kanab, tucked among the red rock cliffs of southern Utah, to perform in their third annual storytelling festival. It's a beautiful place with a fascinating history. Besides the fact that it was a site for filming western movies, it was also the home of the first woman mayor and all woman town council in the U.S., dating back to the early 1900s. The town now has another woman mayor-elect, so we had the new mayor and a costumed portrayal of their first woman mayor, both in attendance at the festival. My storytelling went well and it was overall a quite successful event. I also did a delightful gig in Seattle for their storytelling guild, and continue to do monthly gigs at an assisted living center in Medford, OR.

Now on the horizon I have a number of options. I've applied for some jobs in various beautiful and fascinating places and am waiting to see what happens with those. Also on the horizon I see a distant dragon, not the fearsome one of European folklore, but the more robust, joyous Asian variety. In my future I see wild horses that race like the wind, and a Thornbird singing sweetly in her flowering tree. I also see that I will be mostly out of contact from late January through most of February on retreat. I suspect that my greatest adventure lies just ahead of me. We shall see, we shall see.

Conclusion

The ending to this last letter foreshadowed my move to China and a new chapter in this varied and chaotic life, the next story in a long line of them, both real and imagined. One thing I have only touched on about Pedro is how he helped me. What I've said so far has only scratched the surface. You see, Pedro saved my life.

Ever since I was in my teens I have had problems with depression and anxiety. Over the years I had taken a number of medications, some of which helped and some which didn't, and been to see many counselors. At times I considered suicide, a few of those times were serious. One of those, maybe the worst, was when I was living at my little cabin in Cave Junction with Pedro. We had already established a close relationship and lived through some of those experiences in the stories above. One night I got into a very dark place personally and was just sitting in our place with a bottle of pills by my side crying and contemplating taking the pills... all of them. I didn't know if they would kill me, but I wanted to try. Pedro lay on his blanket watching me ever so closely not quite knowing what to do, but he knew something was very wrong with his human. I sat there, looked at the pills, looked at Pedro, looked at the pills, looked at Pedro. Then I thought about him. He had been abandoned, left to die. He had found someone he loved and trusted, someone who cared for him. What would happen to Pedro if I died? Who would care for him? Would he find another person who really loved him? He certainly deserved it, and didn't deserve to be cast aside once again. My sense of responsibility kicked in and I realized that, if for no other reason, I needed to be there for him. I picked up the phone and called the suicide hotline. The next day I was on medication again.

You could say that Pedro didn't really do anything. He just lay there watching me. But it was his love, his undying trust in me that made me decide to seek help, and brought me back from the brink of oblivion, and for that I will be forever grateful to him. I was to have lots of dark times after that still, but I never gave suicide such a serious thought as I did that night. He helped me through those subsequent dark times as well. I had other friends who helped me, but none was as loyal, attentive, and attached to me as Pedro had been, caring though they were. So yes, Pedro saved my life, as sure as I had probably saved his those years before.

In the fall of 2009, Pedro and I were still living at the Frog Farm and I was working at Oregon Caves National Monument when I met my future wife, Wang Pei. See the section in this book about Weddings to get more of the story regarding that series of events. At that time we had been living at the farm for nearly 2 years. When we first moved there, they had a wonderful, gentle dog named Sage, who loved digging up stinking things she had buried months ago and bringing them to you to share with you, and had some of the worst farts that ever graced a nose. She was also a good watchdog for the farm and a real sweetheart to all of her friends. Our first year at the farm, Pedro and Sage spent a lot of time together and became good friends. But Sage was old. She could go for walks with us, but not very far. The winter after we moved to the farm, Sage passed away and they buried her on the property. Deb's affections turned to Pedro and the two of them became very good friends. While I headed off to work up the mountain during the day, Pedro just lay on the cool floor of Deb's office or like a pancake on the drive in front of it. When I wasn't there, he followed her around wherever she went and during those 2 years became very attached to her. It's not hard to do. Deb and Steve are good people and Deb in particular is very kind. I was still his number one person, his "rock star," as Steve often said, but Deb was becoming a close second, with Steve, Laurel, and Alan (River's human) rounding out his human family.

When I decided to head to China to meet Pei in January 2010, I planned to be away for a month. Pedro saw me getting packed and figured I was getting ready for another of our winter travels. When I got into Steve's truck to go to the bus station for my ride to the airport in San Francisco, Pedro followed the truck to the gate incredulous that he was not joining us. I saw the pain in his eyes as we drove away, and a knife pierced my heart. It was something I had to do, but there are many things we have to do that are hard. Of course he was that much more overjoyed when I returned a month later. We spent a lot of time together those next couple of months before I moved to China, and I considered the possibility of bringing him with me, looked at the options and the costs. I was not, after all, a person of means. I could have him come over, but then he would have to stay for a month in quarantine with Chinese authorities. I later learned there were agencies that would expedite the process for you, but the cost would be nearly all the money I had left in the world, so it's a good thing I didn't know about them at the time. Once in China he would have to stay in a small apartment on the 29th floor of a high rise apartment building, going for walks on the crowded streets of one of the world's most populous cities. Then also, would he take to Pei the way he had taken to Deb? Much as I loved him and wanted him with me, I didn't think it would be a good situation for him. The decision was a very hard one, but in the end I had to weigh what would be best for him in the long run. He had people that he loved and who loved him in Oregon, he had canine friends, he had room to run and forests to explore, and he had already grown attached to the farm, become part of the structure of the place. I felt it was best to leave him behind. When I moved away in April, it was one of the hardest, most painful things I have ever done, like cutting off my own arm.

Could I have found someone to marry in the US? Yes, probably, but that's not what happened, though not for lack of trying. Things just didn't work that way. So I moved to China and Pedro stayed at the Frog Farm for the rest of his days. A year later I came to visit, bringing my new wife with me. When he saw me he began to shake all over, like a child in freezing water. While we stayed there he followed me wherever I went, and I was glad for it. I could see that his attachment to Deb had grown even deeper, however, and that felt bittersweet. When Pei and I moved to a larger place outside of the city, I considered having him shipped over, but felt it wouldn't be fair to Deb or to him. They became closer and closer over time. The next visit I made to the farm, he still often followed me, but it was plain to see that Deb had become his main human, his security blanket.

Pedro grew old at the Frog Farm. His eyesight began to go first, and the next time I saw him, he had to smell me before he began shaking all over. Eventually his legs that had run so many, many miles both with me, and since, grew weak, and later he stopped being able to control his bowel movements. You could tell he felt bad about that, but there was nothing he could do. He was in pain. He knew me, but it was Deb he went to for comfort. One day in 2016 as I drove to work in Shanghai traffic, Deb called me on my cell phone. Pedro had passed away quietly in his sleep. I pulled over to the side of the road, and just wept for a while. Three years later, I still grieve for him. He was buried where he belonged: on the Frog Farm underneath a beautiful walnut tree. But a piece of him will always live in my heart, just as a part of me rests there with him. Do I regret not having him with me in China? Sometimes. But I still believe that overall I did the right thing. Deb and Steve don't regret it. When you've found such a great love, it's important to share it.

Pedro at sunset over the Pacific Ocean on the Washington state coast.

A Few Odds and Ends

At the Oriental Drug Store

The Oriental Theater, an old, magnificent building dating back to 1927 decorated with South Asian design, complete with minarets, elephants, Buddhas, and the like, stands on North Farwell St. on the Lower East Side of Milwaukee. When I attended the Wisconsin Conservatory of Music back in the late 1970s, I lived on South Farwell, not too far from the theater, and I used to occasionally go there to see cheap movies. More frequently I would head to the Oriental Drug Store beside the theater to have dinner at their sandwich counter, which served as a focal point for more local color than a writer, or a psychologist for that matter, could handle in a lifetime. I was new to living on my own and still a bit cautious and reticent of life in the big city, but I also began growing a profound fascination with watching people in this rather eclectic neighborhood. The Oriental Drug Store, while not as scenic as the theater next door, was a great place to do just that.

One particular evening as I sat waiting for one of my staple fried egg sandwiches, a woman, a bag lady to be more precise, came in from the sidewalk and sat at the counter directly across from me. A plate from a previous customer still sat on the counter decorated with a tomato slice, some lettuce, and a few pickle slices. Two quarters sat alongside the plate: the tip. The woman sat for a few minutes, then she stood up, holding the tomato high in the air with her left hand, brandishing it like a nervous bank robber with a pistol, and loudly announced to everyone there "All I want is the tomato. I don't want their damn money. I just want the tomato. OK?!" After a brief moment of pregnant silence, she devoured the tomato and proclaimed "That's all I want. I don't want the damn money. They can have it for all I care. Just want the tomato." She stepped away from the counter and slowly, deliberately headed for the door. After exiting the store, she stood on the corner looking around for a minute or two, turned left, and walked down the sidewalk and out of my view.

A guy working behind the counter leaned across and said to me from under a bushy mustache, "She's been coming in here for years. It's a shame. I guess her husband died quite a while ago. She began by bringing in his old clothes and stuff in paper bags and leaving it in the corner for homeless people. Now she's homeless. She gets worse every year. It's a damn shame." He shook his head, turned around, and went back to work.

I finished my sandwich. It had gotten cold.

Spider and Caterpillar

Sometimes we encounter the wild in the smallest and simplest of places.

Twenty years ago I lived in Chapel Hill, North Carolina, and worked as cashier in the café of a Whole Foods Market grocery store. The room where I stayed occupied part of the loft in the third floor of a house in the woods north of town and my kitchen sat on the second floor. A stairway from the kitchen led to the first floor, but I mostly used an outside stairway that descended from a door in the kitchen to the ground level. Just outside that door was a little porch where I sometimes sat to eat my meals on warm, sunny days.

One such sunny day I had the late shift in the café and decided to make a big brunch before heading to work. I whipped up a simple meal of hot spiced eggplant with pork (I was learning to cook Chinese food at the time) and settled down in the chair on the porch to eat. My view consisted mostly of the canopies of oaks and hickories which encircled the house, with sunlight shimmering on their leaves as gentle breezes kissed them now and then.

As I sat eating my meal, I noticed a caterpillar making his way atop the 2 x 4 that acted as a railing one foot away from my head. He stretched himself for about an inch and a half to two inches and wore a woolly coat with a series of long, hairy spikes running down his back, like a punker's spiked coif. Hair covered his face and tail end such that had he not been moving in a certain direction, you couldn't tell one end from the other. I began eating, glancing up often at the wonderful trees and that delightful caterpillar.

Caterpillar neared the upright that would pose as a dead end for his current route, and in the corner where the upright met the railing a spider web connected the two. I could see two spiders in the center of the web, one larger than the other. I wondered if the larger one had trapped the smaller, as spiders will sometimes do. I continued eating...and watching. Caterpillar kept cruising along, and as he did, his hair began to brush against the spider web. Big spider came down to see what the disturbance was all about. Upon seeing the caterpillar sauntering past her web, she began dancing around above the intruder, back and forth, sort of in a circle. She would dance for a bit, then come back up higher in the web and rest, her breath coming in great puffs (I could discern all this perfectly with my keen powers of observation, and some imagination). I thought to myself "There's no way this small (maybe ¼ inch body length) spider can do anything to this much larger caterpillar."

My interest in the unfolding drama piqued and brunch became only a secondary operation. Caterpillar reached the upright, turned, and went back towards me, once again alongside the web. Big spider continued to dance around caterpillar, rest, then dance some more. I noticed then that the hair on the caterpillar began getting pulled back away from his face and tail, and it all pulled together into a single spike, sort of like Alfalfa's hair in the Little Rascals. My meal sat neglected in my lap as Big Spider sped over to Caterpillar's face and bit him right on the snout. A small drop of clear liquid fell from the bite onto the railing as Caterpillar writhed in agony, twisting and turning around. Painful to watch, my initial reaction was to try and save Caterpillar, to stop the carnage. Then I looked around at the trees. If we have too many caterpillars, they defoliate the trees, those one-legged people I love so much. That would seriously impact my shade on sunny days like this. So I just observed the action and chose not to participate in it. Best to let Nature take her course, and besides, she had already bit the caterpillar.

Caterpillar continued to squirm in pain, and as he did so, he curled himself into the web. Big Spider retreated to the center of the web as Caterpillar wrapped himself in the delicate threads and, when secure in Big Spider's tapestry, lay still. I then realized that Little Spider was not dead at all, (??) in fact was the male. The two of them came down to where their quarry lay dying and did a little dance of joy about their sudden abundance. "Oh, we're going to eat well now!" I could hear them say to one another. Then they returned to the center of the web and rested.

I sat for a moment, stunned at the drama that had just taken place before my eyes. Then I realized that I would need to hustle to get to work on time, so I finished my cold Chinese food and retreated to my room to get dressed. As I passed by that railing on my way to my car, I looked at the spider web, the two inhabitants, and the dead caterpillar, and decided to check it every day to see how long it would take these two to finish off their prey.

The day at work passed unremarkably until just before sunset, when a raging storm blew into town. Winds whipped the trees around as rain flew horizontally and the store windows rattled and hummed. I love a good storm and when I had nobody at my register I stood transfixed watching the power of Nature manifest before my eyes. I finished my shift and headed outside where the air had that clean, but warm, humid, and sultry atmosphere you often get after a North Carolina gully washer.

When I arrived home, I climbed the stairs to my kitchen. On the porch I paused to see how the spider web and its inhabitants fared in the torrent. Gone. The web, spiders, and deceased caterpillar had all disappeared. Had they perished when thrown against the house? Had they climbed to safety beneath the porch? Would the arachnid couple return to build another web? They never did, at least not on this railing, and I can only speculate as to what became of them. I imagined that maybe the spiders had climbed aboard the body in their web and ridden him like a surfboard on waves of wind, making a skid landing on the dirt path below. What truly happened, I know not and never will.

Faye

I remember Faye, a thin, wisp of a woman whose heart, much too big for her little frame, reached out and touched everyone around her with a warm, gentle kiss. I lived in Chapel Hill at the time, having moved there from Wisconsin in late 1997. Four years I stayed in the lovely Southern town, working as a cashier, and on the side telling stories, delivering groceries, and doing hospice volunteer work. It was in this latter capacity that I met Faye.

I'd had some other patients and worked at the inpatient facility in Durham, and then they assigned me to Faye, who was dying of breast cancer. She wasn't bedridden, but was very weak and needed someone to help prepare food, run errands, and help around the house. She had tried mostly alternative therapies, though had also done conventional ones, but to be on hospice you have to accept death and not be actively trying to fight the disease, so when I met her she had come to that point. There is much I don't recall, these many years hence, but I believe she had two children who mostly stayed with her other family members. I saw them only a few times. She had other helpers besides me, in fact nearly an army of people who truly cared about her and did what they could for her. It was hard not to love Faye, not to want to help her. People had spent time with her, but as her disease continued, they dropped off and others took their place. Most still came to see her from time to time.

Faye, like most people in her situation, had good days and bad days. Sometimes she could barely get up, and others she seemed as though it were only a mild case of the flu. Soups are not my forte in cooking, but I did what I could to make her soups, salads, and whatever else she could tolerate. She liked my sautéed vegetables, once I got them to being bland enough that they didn't upset her stomach. Sometimes we would just sit and talk. She loved listening to me tell stories, whether fairy tales or some of the stories in this book. On one of her better days I recall taking her to pick blueberries just outside of town. I did most of the picking, and we ate a lot before they made it to the bucket. We laughed a lot, enjoyed the flowers, and chatted about things that mattered.

What was it about her that was so special? It was the quality of her relationship with you, whoever you were. When you talked, she listened as though there was nobody else in the world. She was present and gentle, and had a way of just making you feel better when she was with you, and yet, she was the patient. I don't know what she was like before she got sick. Maybe it was coming to terms with the illness that brought her to that kind of quality of personality, which wouldn't surprise me at all. I had several patients that I worked with for the years I volunteered in hospice, and they usually were at peace with death, though not always as calm about it as she. It was usually their family members that had the biggest problem with the situation. So yes, she may have changed a lot as a result of her imminent passing.

Eventually Faye decided to seek a treatment that took her off of hospice, I guess because she wanted to spend more time with her family. Hospice gave me the option of continuing to work with her, but it would be on my own, not part of their program, and I did that for a few months. Then I got busy and another of Faye's friends took my place. Faye knew I loved stories and poetry, especially the poems of Rumi, so before I passed the torch on to someone else to help her, she gave me a beautiful book of Rumi poems and stories, richly illustrated. I tried to stay in touch and did for a while, but you know how life goes. Just like so many others of her friends.

Several months later Faye passed away. I came to her house for the wake and was overwhelmed by the number of former caretakers who showed up, some of whom I knew, much to my surprise. No fancy casket for her, she lay in a simple pine box, her requested last home. I said my farewells and kissed her lightly on the cheek. Faye looked very much at peace, just like the last time I had seen her. She was buried at the edge of a small forest, a quiet spot away from the madding crowd. The book she gave me still sits in a prominent place on my shelf.

My Friend Jack

I first met Jack in the summer of 2001 when he visited Oregon Caves with some of his relatives. I had a strong interest in the history of the area in which I lived, and Jack was introduced to me as a piece of that history. At the time he was, I believe, 89 years old, and for many years he had worked in the county assessor's office in Josephine County, Oregon. His job took him throughout the county and he learned much of the history firsthand. Later in his life he traveled to various parts of the world, and when I first met him he spoke of other trips he would like to take.

Jack lived in Merlin, OR, at the time. He told me that he loved to write letters and asked for my address to add to his long list of correspondences. I gladly gave it to him, and asked if I might visit him should I get to Merlin. He said that would be wonderful. His eyes sparkled and his quick wit was obvious to me in that first short conversation we shared.

A month or two later I had the pleasure of visiting Jack at his home in Merlin. It was early in autumn. He had a wonderful place overlooking the land to the north of Merlin, rolling hills of beautiful verdant forest. His hearing wasn't so great, but after a few knocks I got his attention. He welcomed me in and told me that the place was heated by means of a wood stove, which he had stoked up making it comfy. He said he liked it that way because getting his own wood and seeing to the stove kept him in good physical shape, while writing letters and keeping up with the news of the day honed his mental abilities.

Did I already say that Jack loved to write letters? I was amazed by the extent of his writing. He kept a tall filing cabinet filled with copies of his letters as well as the originals that people sent to him in response. He wrote to people in foreign countries as well as the U.S., including several prison inmates. He wrote to people from all walks of life and all ages. Basically, anybody who wrote to him received a response, along with a little bit of his philosophy on life.

Jack always kept the television on with the sound turned down, always tuned to news channels. Due to his hearing difficulties, he had gotten used to watching the news subtitles and turning up the volume when he desired to hear details of the stories. Jack always liked to discuss politics, for he watched it all with an air of amusement. The back and forth, up and down, in and out aspects of the political spectrum appeared often as folly in his eyes, given his many years of historical perspective.

I, too, am fond of writing letters to my many friends scattered about the globe, so I corresponded with Jack on many occasions. Jack's letters generally were short and to the point, but written in an almost whimsical style. They were always typed. Sometimes I received little things along with the letters, items collected in his many years of travel and enjoyment of life. For example, given my profession as a park ranger, he sent me a brochure about lodging in Yellowstone National Park...from 1936. One treasured item that I received from him I had posted for years on the wall next to my front door. It's business card sized, with a picture of a little girl in an attic who is trying on old clothes she has found there. The caption reads "Let the child in you out to play." How apropos given the way I often take life way too seriously.

Jack moved into an assisted living apartment in 2002. He had loved taking care of things in his house in Merlin, but when I visited him in his new abode, he spoke of how wonderful it was that they took care of him so well, the food was good, and he could focus on his writing. He had begun using a computer and could write to so many more people via email. I gave him my email address and continued to correspond with him.

One Saturday I visited the grower's market in downtown Grants Pass, when who should appear, but Jack. He walked with a cane and told me he had taken a fall, nonetheless he said that life was good, except that some of the people in his building acted like old fogies sometimes, spoken with a gleam of amusement in his eye.

Jack lived in a couple of different places in Grants Pass during the next year and a half. One of his letters told of the brain surgery which he had undergone, informing me that his writing might be a bit irregular for a while. When I visited him he continued to be upbeat, even if the conversation was a bit scattered, and the letters I received were not quite as coherent as those of earlier days. At one point I received a letter informing me that he was again living in Merlin. After the typed portion was a handwritten note from his daughter Jackie saying that he had entered a nursing home.

I recalled the nursing homes I had visited where my grandmother and grandfather had lived years ago. It was with a bit of trepidation that I visited Jack there. The man I found was so different than the man I had known for the past 2 years that I found it difficult to comprehend. Jack could barely utter words. He sat facing the TV with headphones firmly affixed to his ears. I brought a copy of my latest "friends" letter and tried to read it to him, but when I removed one ear of the headphones he became a bit agitated, so I placed it back on his ear. My dog Pedro had come with me, but Jack was mostly unresponsive and just focused on the only bit of security he had left, the TV.

I again visited Jack twice in the waning weeks of 2003. The TV was no longer on, but sat silent on the table next to his bed. Jack lay on his side. When I entered he appeared to sleep, but after a few minutes his eyes opened and the small curve of a smile creased his face. His hands remained clenched on the railings of his bed. After his moment of recognition, he ostensibly faded to sleep once again, and continued to go through cycles from sleep to various levels of consciousness every 5 minutes or so. I put my hands on his and just sat with him. I had little to say, but sat in silence watching his face, his breathing, and holding his hands. At one point his hand left the railing and held on to mine. His fingers were pale and cool. In such a short time Jack had gone from a spry, sharp-witted elder, to a bed-ridden, mostly incoherent old man. It felt hard to stay, but also hard to go. I kissed him and stroked his head before I walked out the door.

Early in January of 2004 I again stopped to visit Jack. I walked to his room and noticed that his name no longer appeared on the door. I stood looking at the room when a nurse asked who I sought. "Jack Hawkins." "I'm sorry, but he passed away about a week ago." I had expected him to pass away sometime soon, but it still hurt to hear those words. I certainly would not have wanted him to linger in the debilitated state in which I had last seen him, but still I mourn the passing of a friend, and of an era. I walked out the door. A light rain began to fall.

Local Man Creates Stir in Takilma

And now for something light:

This just in from our newsroom, Frog Farm resident and local busybody Tom Siewert has today washed the large picture windows on the dining room of the main house at the Frog Farm. In what has been regarded as a "monumental achievement," farm owners Deb Lukas and Steve Orr stared in amazement as years of filth cascaded down the glass and into the planter, where, until recently, passion flower and lemon grass grew in abundance. "The plants grew so well there for a while, but they've died off due to a lack of light in recent years," said Lukas. Orr added, "I don't know that this has ever been done before. I knew it was possible, I just thought it would never happen."

Siewert used a mixture of vinegar and warm water applied with a long handled sponge/squeegee combination tool to wash the windows. "The water in my bucket turned black when I rinsed the sponge after my first swipe. I've never seen anything like it!" remarked Siewert. When asked what prompted him to do this he responded, "Well, I don't know. I guess I just realized that what we saw from the window didn't look anything like what I saw outside. I wondered why the sun never shone in the house through south facing windows."

His actions were not without controversy, however. Many neighbors expressed outrage upon seeing the clean windows. "Well, you can see glass whereas before it looked so much more natural, what with the dirt and microbes and all," stated one. Another who described himself as a professional ecologist exclaimed, "They've destroyed an entire ecosystem. Possibly new species of algae and mites have just been wiped off the face of the Earth, and they don't seem to care. Where was the public comment period? Where was scientific input? This is reprehensible, way beyond anything I could have imagined!" Others were apparently unfazed by Siewert's actions, "They did what? Who the hell cares!" said one community member as he emerged from his rusted bus on blocks to see what all the commotion was about. "Hey, you want a hit? Some pretty good shit, man" he continued as our cameraman stepped away.

Local officials could not be reached for comment. In fact, our top news people couldn't even find out who the local officials were and where we could contact them. Pedro, the Frog Farm dog seemed apparently unaware of the significance of the event. When asked for his opinion, he just licked his genitals.

Note: The above item was based on a real event... I really did clean a window at the farm that, if it had ever been washed, it was a long, long time before. Many particulars, such as the interviews, are fictional, though Steve was truly amazed and Pedro did lick his genitals.

China

For almost any American, any European, moving to China would be a huge undertaking, a real adventure, and encounter with the exotic, and yes, for me it has been one as well, but mostly for very different reasons than what many would expect. What sets my life apart from many people is the fact that it didn't follow the usual pattern after college of get a good, steady job, get married, have children, buy a house (along with the mortgage), etc. That would have been a good, full life in and of itself, as it is for many, one with much of its own type of variety, but variety within a narrower spectrum than my chaotic existence has brought me. Less exotic, if you will, more of the small, daily kind of variety and adventure.

In truth I had always wanted to get married, but for one reason or another things never worked out. Most of that was due to my own choices, often not very good ones, though I also got dumped by a great many attempted girlfriends. My constant struggles with depression and anxiety didn't help matters. So this "normal" life was one major thing that eluded me. In many ways, China is the most exotic place I've ever been, and yet I went there to do the "normal" thing, to get married, get a steady job, commute to work, buy a house, have children (actually my wife already had those last two items), have grandchildren, have a couple of dogs, do weekend projects, take care of parents, watch TV, retire, and all kinds of other stuff like that. It took me until after the age of 50 to do what many people do in their 20s or 30s. I've always been a late bloomer. The reason for my coming to China, how that all happened, is recounted in the "Weddings" section of this book, so I won't repeat it here, rather

I'll fill in the blanks and add some later points of interest. In reality, most of my life in China has been a pretty normal life, just with a much harder language ... and chopsticks. So this is a difficult chapter to write for that simple reason, it's mostly just regular stuff. It's also hard because it isn't over yet. As I write this I'm still in China and going about my daily activities, and it's hard to know what are the most significant aspects of it. For now, let's start here:

In truth I had been interested in China for a long time before I ever ventured across the Pacific to the Great Dragon. I studied taiji (tai chi) at the encouragement of my guitar teacher at the Wisconsin Conservatory of Music, who believed it would help with efficiency of movement and quality of performance on classical guitar. Since then I dabbled in it over the years whenever I could find a teacher, and along the way I tried out some other Chinese martial arts, including Bagua, Choy li fut, and some simple Shaolin forms. I still practice taiiji to this day, having studied with a teacher in Shanghai to finish the Yang Long Form that I had started learning 30 years earlier. Hard to finish things when you move as much as I have. This study of taiji also sparked my interest in the philosophy behind the forms. Taoism, which is native to China and provides the theory behind many Chinese martial arts, became one of my favorite philosophies and I read several books on the subject starting in my 20s, including, of course, the *Tao Te Ching*, as well as crossover books like *The Tao of Physics* and *The Dancing Wuli Masters*.

I didn't have health insurance for most of my adult life, so when I got sick I often couldn't afford to see normal Western style doctors, though occasionally I splurged when the need was dire. Usually I ended up seeking the services of alternative medicine providers, and that often included doctors of Chinese traditional medicine, including acupuncture. I found some relief from my aches, pains, and maladies in this way and grew interested, as is my tendency, in the philosophy behind it. I read a number of texts on the subject, most notably *The Web that has No Weaver*, one of the most complete books in English on the subject at that time. My realization I could no longer eat dairy (1995) led me to seeking out Chinese restaurants frequently, and whenever I went to a big city like San Francisco, Los Angeles, New York, etc. I would hone in on their

Chinatown where I always found good food and neat, inexpensive things to buy. When living in North Carolina (1997-2001) I got interested in cooking Chinese food, so I picked up cookbooks from the library and even went to Chinese restaurants to try to learn some things from the chefs.

I worked out a deal with my friend Kim, who was an acupuncturist, to cook her Chinese meals in exchange for treatments. She was a practicing Tibetan Buddhist whose teacher was a famous lama from Bhutan, known as the Gangteng Tulku Rinpoche. She often described him as the "Bhutanese Dalai Lama." When her teacher came to North Carolina to do some presentations, she had me cook dinner for him, his assistant and his local students, a total of about 8 or 10 people. Most Buddhists I knew at the time were vegetarians, but of course, he was a Tibetan-style Buddhist from the Himalayas, where they don't grow many vegetables. I asked her what Rinpoche liked to eat and she replied, "Beef, lots of it, and very spicy. And rice. He will probably push vegetables around on his plate, but not eat much." She also said that the American students of his were vegetarians, so I should have something available for them also. I made a rather successful spiced beef dish with a couple of good vegetable dishes. I hadn't cooked rice for more than 2 or 3 people before, and it turns out that was the part of the meal that was rather sub-standard. Rinpoche was gracious, though, and I think overall they were pleased with it.

Also in North Carolina I had volunteered to help a visiting Chinese scientist with his English. I got to know him and his good family, and tried to learn a little Chinese along the way. After he left town I took a few lessons in Chinese, but gave up quickly due to the difficulty and my own level of frustration.

The last thing pointing me to the Far East had to do with my good friend Lyneah, who was a spiritual healer as well as a massage therapist. As a friend I helped her deal with issues related to her divorce. I also gave her occasional massages and taught her qigong (like Chinese yoga) in exchange for some of her healing sessions. She did a "reading" of me one evening and said she saw a spirit guide of mine who looked like an old Chinese man with a scraggly beard. Oddly enough, with all of this pointing to

China, I still had no inclination to visit the country, due to what I had heard about the pollution, crowding, and oppressive government. Then came the fateful night when I had checked my email, seen an ad for chinalovematch.com, and checked it out. The rest, as they say, is history. For now I'll move to what happened after my marriage and subsequent move to the "City on the Sea," the Pearl of the Orient, Shanghai.

"Hi dad, I'm in China."

"Oh, that's interesting."

"And dad, I'm married."

"(Chuckles) Well congratulations!"

I remember one conversation with my dad a couple of years before I met my wife in which he had been telling me about a biography he was reading regarding a man who had spent much of his life wandering and seeking adventure. The tone of admiration in his voice and his demeanor were obvious to me. I told him that my life, while maybe not quite so glamorous as the one he described, was also one of travel and adventure, not all that dissimilar to what he described. He just scowled and shook his head. Apparently the wandering life was fit for others, but not his one and only son. So before I left for China I didn't want to hear his criticism, nor that of others, and I told only a few people where I was going, only one of them a blood relative. To most I just said I would be out of contact for a month or so. I must admit that when I called my dad from the house of my wife's parents in Chengdu, Sichuan, his reaction was much more positive than I had imagined, and I was overjoyed to not have to explain myself and my actions yet again. He just accepted it. I guess he was getting soft on me in his old age.

Soon after we got married, Pei, Yini, and I left for her hometown, driving as quickly as we could nearly half of the way across China. I felt justifiably nervous about meeting her family, but the fact that I couldn't understand much of the language helped. It was harder on her than me, really. Her aunties grilled her about me at first, looking for flies in the ointment, wanting to know if I was scamming her or if I was just going to take her away to the United States. They seemed to be satisfied with her answers and accepted me into the family. I think what helped as much was how I behaved at the hospital. Pei's dad was not doing well and was in long-term hospital care, too weak to get out of bed due to complications of diabetes. He didn't know much of what was going on around him, though he had moments of clarity. I helped bathe him and care for him while we were there, and comforted my darling as she came to terms with the failing health of her father, with whom she'd been very close. Maybe as much as anything, that helped to convince her relatives that I was serious about this, though of course, that's not why I had cared for him.

After visiting her mother and other relatives we had to get back to Shanghai so she could return to work and I could catch my plane. I didn't want to leave, but Pedro awaited me and I had much to do before I could get back to China. On the return trip we stopped briefly in Xi'an, her father's hometown, to see the tomb of emperor Qin Shihuang and the terra cotta warriors. It's really amazing to see just how many figurines were constructed with such fine detail, only to be buried with a dead man. Odd how humans sometimes pay more attention and give more thought to death than to life. Fear is a powerful motivator. On the road back I also had my first taste of Chinese holiday traffic, stuck for hours and hours in jams along the way. It's gotten significantly worse since then, which is why we avoid traveling during major holidays if at all possible. Soon I returned to America to work for a few months, then tied up my loose ends, put some things in storage, and moved to China, where I have lived ever since.

We lived on the 29th floor of an apartment building in the heart of Shanghai when I arrived. When Yini was trying to go to college the following winter we needed money, so we sold the 29th floor apartment for quite a profit, and rented a fifth floor place for a few months while our house was getting finished. Pei had already started buying a house outside of town, a three floor townhouse with a basement, but it was just basically a concrete shell. As is typical, the people doing the work in our new house moved into the place and lived there while they were doing the work, one man bringing his wife with him to help and do the cooking. We lived there for nearly 8 years. We visited Xishuangbanna in southern Yunnan province one year and loved the place. Pei used to work in real estate, so when she saw that apartments there cost about one tenth per square meter compared to Shanghai, we decided to buy one, if only as an investment. It sits along the Mekong River (Lancangjiang) with mountains close by, not far from the borders with Laos and Myanmar in the city of Jinghong. It, too, was a concrete shell, so we eventually had it finished. When we moved out of our house after retirement, we got a small apartment in Shanghai, but for much of the year decided to live in our southern place, and that's where we find ourselves as I write this. Those are the basics about how I, we, ended up where we are today. Now let's take a look at some details.

Need to Know Basis

China has been referred to as the "Most frustrating place you'll ever love." I think it is an amazingly accurate insight, and when trying to adapt to this place it's something I've always tried to keep in mind. Remain flexible at all times, had become my mantra quite some time ago, and it's especially appropriate in China.
- "Classes start this Thursday. Be ready." Thursday arrives and there's nobody in my classroom. "Where are my students?" "Oh, the seventh graders have aptitude tests today." Ok, back to the office to rework my curriculum.
- "There's a practice for the New Year's Program today and a few students in your 8th grade class will leave ten minutes early." "Ok, I can work with that." Class begins and five minutes later half the students leave. "I thought you were leaving at the end of class." "Teacher wanted us to rehearse an extra time because it didn't go so well yesterday." And off they go. What do you teach to half the class?
- "Darling, what are our plans for tomorrow?" "I don't know, it's my day off and I don't have any plans." Tomorrow arrives and I'm relaxing with a basketball game on TV at 9 a.m. "Darling get ready, we have to go to Carrefour to buy things for our dinner tonight with Sabine." It seems that whether it's school, or home, or wherever, you're on a need to know at the last minute basis.
- At the police station: "I need a temporary residence permit. Here are my documents." "You don't need this one." "You said I needed it last time." "And you don't have a letter from your housing unit. We need

that or we can't give you the permit." "But the last guy didn't tell us that." "Well, you do need it."

- "At the bank: "My dad sent me this check for my birthday and I want to deposit it." "Let me see your passport. Hmmm. The check says your name is Tom, but your passport says it is Thomas." "Yes, Tom is short for Thomas." I'm sorry, the names have to be the same." I sent it to my American account.
- "You have 96 traffic tickets on your car." "But if I was driving the wrong road with my license plate every day, why didn't anybody ever tell me?" "Is this your address?" "Yes." "Well, they should have." So you go and pay a guy under the counter to find people he pays to take your points for you, otherwise you lose your driver's license.

And the list goes on, and on, and on, and on… every one with a story behind it.

The richness of culture, the incredible natural beauty, when you can get out of the city to see it, the verve for life and family that the people exhibit, sense of history and the shoulders that people here stand upon, and even the frustrating language, which is so rich and varied and beautiful, these are the things that draw people into China, and I love them as well. So while yes, it is frustrating, it's wonderful as well.

Teaching

The children screamed and cheered when he entered the room, the walls shaking with their excitement, the sound nearly deafening. He walked to the microphone and they went silent. You could hear a pin drop. He said a simple, "Nihao!" (hello), and they again erupted in applause and cheers. The children listened intently to his presentation. After he had finished they descended in droves to get his autograph, and eventually he was just writing his initials as quickly as possible on any piece of paper that came his way as hands were thrust one upon another in an attempt to get his scribblings. Was he a famous actor? An Olympic champion? A rock star? No, he was a foreign teacher… me.

Once I had arrived in Shanghai in April to take up a new life with my new wife, I set about looking for work and found a job with New Oriental Language School, where I worked for 4 months. It was a good job, but most of my clients were high school kids or young working people and the times they had available were evenings and weekends, which were also the times I had to spend with my dear wife, Pei. I hadn't waited so long to get married only to not be able to spend time with her, so I kept looking for other work. I responded to an ad for teaching geography and English at Shanghai World Foreign Language Middle School (SWFLMS, now SWFLA, the 'A' for Academy) and was promptly given an interview, then in the middle of August 2010 I started working there. I was lucky on both accounts. There are many shady language schools and shady hiring agencies, even for good primary or middle schools, but my experience with these two went pretty well, as far as hiring logistics and the basics of the jobs were concerned.

SWFLMS is one of the highest rated middle schools in Shanghai, which, according to the annual PISA tests is one of the highest rated cities in the world scholastically. The school is private, but mostly follows the local administrative guidelines. There are two campuses in the main school, one teaching the local curriculum, but with more added English, and the other an IB school, which is a European-based international educational system. The vast majority of the teachers and students are Chinese. The simple version of my work there is that I taught mostly geography with some English, starting at the local campus, then moving to the IB campus my second year there. In my last two years I did more English, this time at two other campuses that had been added. My first year I had over 400 students at the local campus, and at my peak level of activity I was teaching 26 classes per week, with 4 levels of English at the IB campus, and two levels of geography in the local campus to a total of over 300 students. Even now I can't imagine how I did that or if my teaching was any good, but neither the school administration nor students and their parents complained, and many students said they really liked my classes.

The IB campus did some community outreach and for several years in a row the 8th graders would travel for a week in April to a poor school in a rural town called Taihe in northwestern Anhui province, one of the poorest provinces in eastern China. Taihe is a farming community, and our well-to-do students had mostly never been to such a place before, so it was an eye-opening experience for many of them. Of course, it was also quite an experience for many of the poor students as well, though it's harder for me to evaluate that aspect of it. I went along on one of those trips, and it was amazing for me in a different way. I went to do some talks at a larger school in town and for many of these kids, I was the first real foreigner they had ever met. My appearance at that school was the account you read in the first paragraph. Aska, my Chinese co-teacher, and I were brought up to the room where hundreds of 8th graders were packed in like sardines. We did a short geography lesson with a question section at the end and it went smoothly, the kids stayed very well-behaved, only going crazy at the beginning and the end. After that the administrators took us out for lunch, and in typical Chinese fashion we were served more food than we could have eaten if we were three times as many people.

A common conception of Chinese students, is that they are obedient and well-behaved. That's often true in the public schools where discipline is strict, though even there they can be pretty noisy at times, such as my experience in Taihe. Since our students were from mostly wealthy families who paid a lot of money for their children's education, they had many of the foibles of children in schools in America or other wealthier countries, though they generally had more respect for teachers (and didn't carry guns). That was certainly not always the case, however, as we had our share of spoiled brats. Overall I loved the children, even most of the badly behaved ones, in spite of how much I had to raise my voice at them. Middle school ages are tough no matter where you happen to live, what with hormones kicking in and all, and I'd have to admit that class discipline is not my strong suit. Class sizes at SWFLMS were much smaller than in the state schools, usually between 20 and 30 per class, though I had several larger and a few smaller classes.

I ended up working for for SWFLMS for 8 school years, before retiring in 2018. There was much I loved about the job and I would still be doing it, were it not for family factors that convinced me to stop working, although I also have to admit that I felt exhausted by that point. In my last 3 years I had became a liaison between the school administrators and the foreign teachers, helping to facilitate management from both sides, so I got in the middle of problems that arose. Gladly, there weren't too many.

Language

One day when I was working for New Oriental, I headed out to a school summer camp at a place I hadn't visited on my own before. I had in the past taken the company van to get there, but they had none at the time of day I was due for work. I took the subway, then a city bus to the far edge of town, then got off near the school and hired a "sanmenche," a big three wheeled bicycle, to get the rest of the way there. The woman said it wasn't far and she gave me a good price. It was raining and I sat in the covered part while she wore rain gear. She tried talking to me on the way there and the general pattern of the conversation went: "Blah blah blah blah blah blah blah," to which I would respond, "ting bu dong," meaning "I don't understand." She would throw up her head and laugh a great cackling bellow. Then she'd try again, and the same thing ensued. I felt glad to amuse her so much, but also glad that it was a short trip. When I got off of her bike, I noticed a sign for the bus I had exited earlier, so the rest of the time I took the bus right to the school door. While at that time I knew very few Chinese characters, numbers are no problem.

If you drive down the main streets of Shanghai they can look like New York or Los Angeles, with some signs even written in English or pinyin, the official way of writing Chinese using an English alphabet. In most cases, though, the language would be the main way to tell them apart. Turn down the side streets and the differences begin to emerge. The architecture begins to take on a Far Eastern look, street vendors selling baozi or stinky tofu, three old men with scraggly whiskers wearing blue, Mao styled coats in conversation, a woman holding her tiny daughter in a squatting position so she can pee in the gutter, people sweeping the streets with brooms made of fresh bamboo fronds, and bikes and scooters outnumbering cars. China is, at heart, very much a nation of farmers, and when I was still taking the subway to work you could see corn, beans, eggplant, or leafy greens growing along the tracks in any open piece of soil. Even our upper middle class neighborhood had many people raising chickens and planting vegetables in place of grass. Having come from living on a farm in Oregon, I like that aspect of life here very much, but it's still odd to see it all within the limits of one of the largest cities in the world. It is one aspect of things that made my transition from country to city, from West Coast America to East Coast China, easier than it might have been.

But then there's the language. I've tried learning languages before. I travelled in Mexico independently on my limited Spanish, though I never spent the time immersed in it to get fluent enough to have a really decent conversation. I lived in Germany for six months and took a basic "German for Foreigners" class, so my German got to a higher level than Spanish, but I was still nowhere near fluent. I seem to get really good at the basics quickly and my pronunciation was always good, but I never made it over "the Wall," that internal barrier that keeps you from going much farther. When it comes to learning languages, my experience has led me to the conclusion that the earlier you learn, the better you will get, and once you've learned a second language well, it's easier to learn new ones after that. Had I moved to Germany for longer or moved to Mexico, or taken an immersion class in one, I might have gotten fluent at one of those languages, but Chinese is so completely different that for someone with my challenges (read "language incompetence"), getting serious about learning after the age of 50, it's nigh unto impossible. Still, I've tried.

My wife made it clear to me that she would help with the language a bit, but she said she had no patience to be my teacher, so I tried other methods. I used books and CDs, I attended a few weeks of a language course (limited by time and funds), I listened to podcasts, I watch Chinese TV and movies, listened to Chinese radio, I talked with teachers at school, I talked with people at the market and on the street, I read children's books, and I still keep on trying. The truth for me is, it's just so fucking hard. The research I've read on learning seems to indicate that you learn a lot while you're sleeping; that's when the things you've learned during the day get shuffled into their correct places to settle in and start working. I guess I have a legitimate excuse, namely I don't sleep much, and haven't for most of my adult life. That's what I'll tell people, anyhow.

The buzz saw I've run into with some languages, especially Chinese, but also to an extent German, is the dialects. What you learn is usually Mandarin Chinese, the official dialect, but my colleagues at school often spoke Shanghai dialect, my wife's family speak Chongqing dialect, the cleaning ladies for our house mostly spoke Anhui dialect, etc., etc., etc. We are not just talking about accents here, these are legitimate dialects. My wife was born in Sichuan, then lived in Tianjin and Shenzhen before moving to Shanghai, and it took her several months before she could really understand the Shanghai dialect. When we moved to the Qingpu district of Shanghai, they have another dialect, and the older people there she still had trouble understanding. What chance did I have?! One of my biggest frustrations is when people tell me they think I speak Chinese really well. It never fails that the next thing that comes out of their mouth becomes totally unintelligible to me. It's nice to hear compliments, but they seem to totally derail the language train running around in my brain. Overall, not having gotten better at the language is the biggest disappointment of my time in this vast, absolutely fascinating country.

Even when I do speak Chinese, people often don't understand me, either due to pronunciation or because they don't expect me to be able to speak the language. I got into a cab near school one day and asked to go to the South Railway Station, only one kilometer away, called in Chinese "Shanghai Nan Zhan." He looked at me quizzically, "Nali?" (Where?). I repeated the phrase in Chinese. He was baffled. I said, "Dao huoche zhan, jiu zai nar." (To the railway station, right over there - pointing.) I repeated this several time and he finally realized, responding, "Ah, Tsanghai nan dzan," in some local dialect. He took me there directly. It would have been easier to walk, but easy isn't always where it's at.

Hiking

I've loved hiking for many years. Of course, what's not to like? Working in national parks, traveling to natural areas wherever I've gone whenever possible, putting one foot in front of the other and watching the trees, the birds, the little critters, the big critters, breathing clean, crisp air, these are the things that have helped me through life and given me a large part of what joy I could eek out of this existence, often in spite of my own physical and mental limitations. I lived in southern Oregon before coming to China and there I could walk out my door, Pedro by my side, and head through the woods up a mountain, hardly seeing a soul as I went, and from there, if I wished, I could walk for a hundred miles to the south and likely see only a few people, if any at all. China isn't quite like that, at least not where I've lived. Parts of the west are as wild as you want and so remote you could easily walk a year and see only a handful of people, but most of those areas are strictly limited in accessibility, though some are still available to 外国人, waiguoren, foreigners. Thus far, the closest I've gotten to there is just west of Chengdu, Sichuan, so there's still a lot more to explore someday.

Tom and Wang Pei visiting the thriving metropolis of Takilma in 2011
(*Photo by Alan Laurie*)

The nation of China is covered with mountains, up to 70% of the total land area, but you couldn't tell that living in Shanghai. The highest point in Shanghai is a place called "Sheshan," which is all of 100 meters high, if that. Shanghai sits on the coastal plain where it meets the Yangtze River plain, and while it has some nice parks and green areas, it isn't exactly a hiker's paradise. The wildest place would be Chongming Island in the midst of the Yangtze, which has a nature reserve part and a lot of natural or organic farms. It's a nice place to hang out if you have the time, which I did during a school trip. Kairen, our foreign high school biology teacher my first year at WFLMS, decided to lead a trip out to the island with his students and asked me to go along, since I had some knowledge of ecology and had begun learning the birds of the area. The students had projects to work on while out there and took off by themselves, most of them more interested in each other and their phones, but being good students they did get their assignments done. I ended up not doing much bird or plant ID with the kids, most of it was with Kairen. We had a nice chat, though, and it was a lovely day, chilly, but pleasant. Typical class field trip. That was my hiking in Shanghai, that and Sheshan, which is a nice walk with some oak trees and a verdant bamboo grove, but only for an hour or two if you walk really, really slowly and stop for lunch.

For real hiking you need to get out of Shanghai at least an hour and a half to two hour drive. That can get you to several places, the most famous of which is Hangzhou, a small city of nearly 10 million people south of Shanghai. The city sits on the edge of the coastal plain where it greets the mountains of Zhejiang province. I also went there with a school field trip and we did just a little walking in slight elevation to some old historic Buddhist sites for a couple of hours. Most of our time we spent at West Lake, the most culturally famous lake in China - it's even on the money. Not a particularly eventful trip, but good in its own way for the kids and for me. Good to be there on a weekday, as weekends and holidays are packed with visitors. Mogan Shan was more of a real mountain. I went there with a fellow teacher in rain and fog, which was nice as it again avoided tourists, for the most part. Anji is another area with lovely forest and mountains not too far away, and a little farther can get you to Da Ming Shan, a really beautiful mountain in western Zhejiang.

The thing to remember, though, about hiking in China, is that people have been doing it for a seriously long time, and I have yet to visit a mountain without fairly extensive infrastructure. The mountains usually hiked in China are steep and over the years they've constructed stone steps up and down most of them, so instead of the dirt and rock switchbacks you usually find on American mountains, you have cut stone stairs that go straight up and down, as well as rest houses and hotels at the tops, which are often not served by any roads, requiring them to hire wiry little guys who carry supplies up and down them all day long. You'll be hiking along, thinking what a wonderful hiker you are with your little pack, then see an old man carrying 40+ kilos of drinks, vegetables, meats, and anything else needed for the comfort of visitors, divided between the two ends of a bamboo burden stick carried across his shoulders. At least the men look old. Maybe they're 35 year olds who have been doing it for 20 years and that's the toll it takes. They do this all day, everyday, and that's how you get your water bottle at the rest stop or beer at the hotel. It gives new meaning to the word "strength." Hard way to make a living, but then again, they have the beauty around them every day.

Hiking on these mountains, as I've alluded to, you are seldom alone. With a country that has so many people who mostly have the same times off you do, it's not likely you're going to experience mountain solitude. During Spring Festival (Chinese New Year), one year we went to Chengdu to see my wife's family, and spent a night at the base of Qingchengshan, one of the most famous Taoist mountains in the country. Famous mountains in China are often classed as either Buddhist or Taoist, depending on which religion has monasteries there, though some have both. Mountains play a big role in Chinese culture, especially religion, art and poetry, as well they should. Anyhow, I set off fairly early up Qingchengshan, but was packed in a huge line, several people wide and hundreds or even thousands long heading up the mountain. I just used it as a meditative practice and figured the crowd would thin the further I went up, which it did, though not as quickly as I might have thought. I stopped to see the temples and other historic buildings on the way up, but from the top I found another way down where I encountered almost nobody. There are often alternate routes that are much quieter than the main ones, but you'll miss the historic or religious points of interest. I often try more than one route, since I like both nature and culture.

In August 2015, shortly before school started back in session again, Pei and I made it to the most famous mountain in eastern China, and one of the 5 most famous mountains in all of China, Huangshan (Yellow Mountain). Though it was crowded by my standards, it was wonderful and I can certainly understand why it's so famous. I've seen and hiked many mountains in my 60+ years, and Huangshan is among the most awe inspiring for its sheer beauty: the granite rock formations, pine trees clinging for life on the cliffs, trails of nerve-shakingly steep stairways, and the clouds that block the view often, then open dramatically creating mosaics of amazing views, giving the feeling that it is much higher than the 1864 meters (6115 feet) height. We spent two nights in a hotel at the top, then one near hot springs by the foot of the mountain. I needed the hot springs, as I got drenched by a summer thunderstorm on the way down. Pei had taken the cable car. Unfortunately I had most of our clothes in my pack and they got pretty wet. Oops!

Even at my age and physical condition, I don't intend to stop hiking completely, but I won't likely do any more Huangshans. You never know, though. Generally I set my sights on simpler fare. Sitting at our apartment in Xishuangbanna looking out the window as I write this, it's just good to see the mountains there patiently waiting for me, for someone, for anyone.

Lookin' for Chicks

May 2012. I drove along on a sunny Saturday afternoon feeling the warm breeze on my face through my open car window, as well as the warmth of family, my wife beside me and daughter Yini in the back seat. We had just picked Yini up from the East Xujing Subway Station and were making our way home. Suddenly I became aware of the sound of birds chirping. It didn't seem to come through the car window, but rather from the back seat. I looked around figuring that a sparrow had flown in the window and noticed a smile come across my wife's face. "It's in the back seat," she announced. "Yini has bought some chicks." Sure enough, when we came to a stop at the next traffic light, I looked back and saw two soft, yellow chicks in a tiny cage on the seat behind me. "Well, you said we couldn't have a dog right now, and rabbits smell too bad, so I bought some chicks." This, of course, was before the dogs had arrived.

We stopped to pick up some things for them, including a plastic storage box that would serve as their temporary home until I could build an outside coop for them when they got big enough. We kept them inside for the first week, but the following weekend I went to a local lumber store and bought materials for a coop. After the first weekend, one of our little ones passed away. I told Pei and Yini that chickens don't do very well by themselves, so we should either give this chick to someone with chickens who can give her a good home, or we should get more. I figured the novelty of the little fuzzy peepers would have worn off after that, but I was wrong. My good, loving wife came home with two more. Back in Oregon I lived on a farm with chickens, so it is, of course, my duty to care for them and build their enclosures. That became my weekend work: constantly making changes and improvements on our original little chicken home.

Things went well at first, though we did have quite a scare one day. I came home from work and only found two birds in the coop. Where was our Xiao Huang, Little Yellow? I looked all over the place, but it was futile, she was nowhere to be found. When Pei came home we looked again, but as before were unsuccessful. I figured a cat had gotten her. Even more of a mystery was how she might have gotten out. I couldn't find any possible escape except for one tiny hole on the side of the coop caused by the fact that our yard has a slope and I had to prop it up to keep it level. Just as I was pondering this, I heard Yini call out "We found her." I hopped over the wall from our backyard and into the front. It seems our neighbors had our little chick. Their little girl had been crawling around outside and noticed the chick underneath their car. So our little 2 week old bird somehow squeezed through that minuscule hole and got out of our backyard by crossing over a fence more than a meter high. Never underestimate the potential and the fortitude of small things. I blocked up the little hole and we had no more such incidents.

The coop became part of an enclosure big enough for the 3 birds even once they were fully grown. Another passed away before long, and we were left with two. They grew, and it became obvious we were never going to get any eggs: both of them were roosters. Eventually a dilemma presented itself. They were about 3 months old when it became time for us to head to the United States to see my family and friends. What would we do with the chickens. They were nearly full size, though without much meat on them. I decided that finding someone to care for them for those weeks (Yini had already left for school), we should take them to the nearby market and have them killed and plucked, ready for soup. I suppose we could have given them away, but the story would have ended the same. People here wouldn't think too much of chickens as pets. They already look at me weird. There was, indeed, not much meat on them, but it was good, if tough, meat, and we know they had eaten good food and were well-cared for while alive. May they rest in peace.

Dogs

It's not uncommon to find racks of preserved meats hanging outside of homes or restaurants, usually chicken, duck, pork, etc. When living in Zhaoxiang on the outskirts of Shanghai I passed by one such rack outside of a restaurant, and couldn't quite figure out a particular half of a small animal that I saw. Then one day, I noticed the foot and it dawned on me: it was a dog. One of the reasons I had chosen not to take Pedro with me to China, though not a major reason, was because of what I'd heard in regards to people eating dogs and my concern for his well-being. Pei had assured me it was something I shouldn't worry about, but old ideas die hard. The truth is that in China, there are people who do eat dogs. As I understand that's mostly popular in southern China, in Guangdong, Guangxi, Guizhou, and mostly in the poorer areas, though as my Zhaoxiang experience told me, it's not exclusive to there. To be honest, most of our ancestors were dog eaters at some point in time. When people are hungry, and I mean REALLY hungry, they eat what they can get, and with dogs so near, they were sometimes the fare. China still has a lot of really poor people, and all of the country was poor not long ago, so the situation is understandable. And yet while walking to work from the subway, or later my parking place, I would see people out walking their dogs, some of them quite old, and many in designer clothing, so dogs here are often treated quite well, sometimes too well, judging by how fat some of them are.

One day I was on my way home when my cell phone indicated a message. Normally I don't take messages while driving, but it was an ok situation and our daughter Yini was writing to me, which is rare, so I looked at the message. She indicated I should come home quickly and it was important. Considering how little she usually reveals to me, I figured it was some sort of emergency, so I made haste. When I arrived she was sitting on our porch steps, and sitting next to her, was a little, scruffy, white Bichon Frise. I asked what the emergency was, and she said it was that this dog had been following her all day and seemed to be lost. "Can we keep it?" "We'll talk with your mother," which is always the best answer, especially in our situation. In the meantime, we took the dog inside and gave him a bath, which he sorely needed. Pei didn't appear overly pleased by the situation when she got home, but she conceded to it, so we had a dog, Baobao, by name. It's one way of saying "baby."

The deal was that Yini needed to take care of the dog, which, if you have kids and at least one dog, you know pretty much never works too well. Before long she went overseas again to study, so I became the dog man. I love dogs, though prefer bigger ones like Pedro, but I love him nonetheless. One otherwise relaxing Saturday, Pei and I went into town to wander through the video store and check out a pet store to spend ever more money on Baobao, this time for flea repellent. We decided to take him with us. Pei had purchased a doggie carrying bag and we wanted to try it out. Getting him into it was a bit of a comedy, him fighting with all four feet to not be caged in, something that he utterly loathes. Once in the car he set about crying, whining, moaning and eventually barking for us to let him out of the bag. Then, about half of the way to town, he began to scratch and chew at the webbing. About 5 minutes later, with our car firmly embraced in a herd of auto, his nose poked out of the screen over the door of his little prison. A few minutes after that his whole head emerged. Since we were stopped in traffic, I pulled the bag to the front, put it on Pei's lap, and had her pull him out before he choked himself to death. The compulsive little beastie trashed the bag in less than 30 minutes.

We got Baobao the "operation" so he wouldn't make other dogs, and got him all of his shots. Being as obsessive as he is, he wouldn't leave the wound alone, even while wearing one of those odd collars that makes him look like a dog flower. It got infected a bit and he drove us as crazy as it probably drove him. Not too long after that it became apparent he had some sort of skin problem, itching…constantly…obnoxiously. We took him to the vet, who said he had a fungus problem. We used the special shampoo as directed, gave him the medicine as they requested, but to no avail. After several weeks he was itching just as bad. Then we took him to another vet, who said the same thing. We did his treatment for a month, after which he did some more expensive tests and said, "Good news, the fungus is nearly gone." Well, his itching wasn't, instead it was just as bad as ever. We tried pills bought on the internet, which worked well, so we used them for a long time. Then he developed bad diarrhea, so we tried another doctor. She smelled his skin and said that he didn't have a fungus problem, as dogs have a distinctive smell when fungus is an issue. She thought it was an allergy, which is what I had suspected. Three to four thousand dollars in allergy testing later, we never found the source of the problem, so to keep him from chewing his toes off, the doctor put him on low dose prednisone, which he has taken ever since. We've tried other medications, but it's the only one that works with few side effects. Oh, and he also takes thyroid hormones everyday, just like his human. We're quite a pair.

Yini went away to the US for school and came back after a year. Then she went to England for half a year to school, and came back. Soon after she returned home I heard her arguing with Pei, "Please Mom, she's so cute and I will take care of her I promise." Yini pleaded with her to bring her dog from England to live with us. Her mother steadfastly refused. The dog arrived in a crate 2 days later. How life and children drag us into things, often kicking and screaming! Our newest addition was a bizarre, nervous little schnauzer who hated the word "No" for an answer…just like Yini in that regard. For the longest time, the little bearded beastie decided that it wasn't a good idea to pee outside. Yini would take her out and sit with her for 10, 20 30 minutes and she wouldn't pee. Then they would come inside and within a couple of minutes there would be a yellow pool somewhere on our floor. She actually started pooping outside before she finally figured out it was ok to pee there also. We still occasionally had gifts on the floor of the house for a while, but then they tapered off to nil. She had also called her Baobao, so she said we had Baobao white and Baobao black. I told her that doesn't work and will be much too confusing for the dogs. Baobao, beibei, and baobei all mean "baby" in Chinese, so I said that one was Baobao, and the other would be Beibei. She agreed, and it's still that way today. Yini, of course, no longer lives with us, so I'm still the dog person. Pei helps when I'm not available and she loves them more than she will admit. Yini loves them, but has a new baby to care for in Beijing. I get plenty of walking time, and so do the dogs, the noisy, obsessive, loving little dogs. There's an old saying, "If you're too fat, your dog is not getting enough exercise." I'm far from fat.

Everywhere we go, there are a lot of dogs, mostly pets or farm dogs. I know of cases of people eating them. My wife ate dog satay once when younger. But mostly people just have them around. Some are tied up all the time and seem to be guard dogs. Quite a few just run around freely wherever they pretty much want unless their human yells at them. Some, more than I care for, are poorly behaved. Not a lot of dog training here. When they run in the street, people do their best to avoid hitting them. In Shanghai, quite a few have fancy little coats. In our southern place, in Xishuangbanna, coats would be much too warm. We've taken them into many restaurants and some less expensive hotels, mostly small guest house-type places. Here in Jinghong, Xishuangbanna, nearly all of the grooming places, pet stores, and pet hospitals are all on one small alleyway. That sort of things is common. Nearly all the bike stores are on the adjoining street. People still have often bipolar ideas of dogs: either dogs are dirty, dangerous and best kept at a distance, or they are best friends that can do no wrong. There are currently no rules protecting animals, just rules protecting personal property, but I think they will come in time. It will just take some people in government having dogs for that to happen. Dogs are here to stay. Baobao and Beibei certainly are.

Driving

On my way home from work one evening during my first year here, approaching Siping Rd. I was cruising along a very narrow one way side street. A car had stopped right near the intersection with Siping Rd, sitting in his car reading his phone. I say "stopped" rather than "parked" because there is no parking allowed there, and he was, in fact, in the only driving lane. A bus tried to turn on its route from Siping Rd onto the side street, but couldn't make the turn because of the stopped car and was beeping furiously at the man, who just continued sitting there reading his phone, waiting for whomever. Over the 5 minutes I watched, the traffic completely blocked the intersection and backed up along Siping Rd, a major street in that area. The guy just sat in his car reading, but did glance back once or twice in an irritated fashion. People shouted at him from cars, though nobody got out to tell him to move. One passerby said something and he just shrugged. I crossed the street and it was still all honking when I headed down my path toward home.

Like Americans, Chinese people have fallen in love with cars, especially big cars, and driving. Last year they bought more cars than Americans, and with a population four times as big as the U.S., a place where it wasn't long ago that hardly anyone had a personal car, I'm not sure it's a good thing, in some ways. China now has some of the worst traffic jams in the world, especially during holidays. A friend of Pei's left Shanghai at midnight when the Spring Festival week began, and had still not left the city at dawn. Remember, this is in the winter, so dawn comes late. That's like 7 hours, and still had not left one city. Aya!

I mentioned earlier that after we got married, Pei and I drove back to Chengdu to see her family. I did most of the driving on the way there and back, and I did all of the driving around that city, even though I didn't have a Chinese license. Pei didn't want to drive because she said it was too crazy for her. I think Shanghai is nearly as bad, but they do tend to enforce regulations more, it seems to me. After that trip I typed up a list of things I learned by driving in China, and these many years later it still holds true:

- Other drivers and their cars are your enemies, so act accordingly.
- Follow way too closely or risk getting nosed out...getting there first is what it's all about.
- Left turn lanes are good for getting ahead of other traffic at intersections.
- No matter what size of vehicle you have, drive it like you would a bicycle.
- Always swear at other drivers, but never to their faces
- Don't take "No" for an answer. For that matter, don't take "Red" for an answer either.
- If that is where you want to go, just go there, even if it means turning right from the left hand lane.
- And speaking of lanes, they are an interesting concept, but not very practical.
- Turn signals are best used as an afterthought.
- Try to keep to the right of oncoming traffic, unless it's not convenient
- Don't run red lights, unless you really feel like doing it.
- Bicycles, pedestrians, and scooters are more fun when they try to escape your aim.
- Policemen directing traffic make nice street decorations. Just try not to hit them as they stand in the middle of the road making their funny hand movements.
- If you get a phone call or need to check directions, just stop or slow way down where you are, especially in mid-traffic.
- And finally...Green walk signals work well for luring pedestrians into a false sense of security that they can cross safely...but little do they know!!!
- If you don't know where to go, just stop and block traffic.
- Always cut in front of oncoming traffic when making left turns.
- Administrative offenses are more important than whether you drive well or not. (I added that one later after receiving a whole mass of tickets for the wrong license plate on the wrong road.)
- Read the "Art of War" before driving.

I laughed a lot while driving in China during that first trip. What else can you do in most situations? After I got my license and began driving regularly, I took to crying and shouting more. It's different when you have to get someplace, like work. Now that I'm retired, I've started laughing more again. My wife tells me it's much worse in India. Not sure I want to find out.

Getting my license was an interesting experience. At first it was difficult to figure out where we were actually supposed to do that. We tried several times and either the office listed on the website was closed or they said it was the wrong day for foreigners, or we needed to go elsewhere. On the third trip, we finally found someone to tell us that the office had moved. The new location was a much better organized and planned office than the one we had tried, and it really went pretty well. First I had to get my U.S. driver's license translated officially, which kept me from having to do driver school. They had a test available in English and gave me a list of 2000 possible questions to study, of which I would be tested on 100. Another foreigner who had been here longer than me said that a few years earlier the version of the test that was in English was nearly incomprehensible, but most of the questions made perfect sense on the new version. The biggest trouble for much of it was the pictures of the hand signals policemen made just didn't make much sense to me, but that didn't involve many questions. Two questions that particularly got me were:

- How and when to apply a tourniquet. I was an Emergency Medical Technician and I can tell you that tourniquets are for extreme situations where you expect the person to lose a limb. Are Chinese drivers getting told to put them on? I'm glad I haven't had to find that out yet.
- If your car is rolling down a hillside out of control, what should you do? The correct answer is to climb under the steering wheel by the pedals and hold onto the steering column. I'm 6 feet tall, and there's no way I'd fit under there unless I'm driving a truck.

Most of the questions were like those on any test I'd seen before, so I just focused on the ones that were new and different and passed with no problem. While driving was more convenient when we lived outside of the city areas, I'm not sure if overall it was the best thing to get my license, though. My dad fought against limiting and later ceasing driving in his old age. Sometimes I like driving, but I'd have to say after my experiences here in China, and given how much I've driven in my life, I look forward to someone else doing the driving for a change.

Food

There's a part of me that thinks I should write about food, but since the topic of Chinese food is so huge it can easily become a book in and of itself. I'll share a modified excerpt from a letter I wrote to my dad about food here, but suffice it to say that Chinese food is incredibly delicious and much more diverse than most people have any inkling about, from the rice and "we eat almost anything" of Cantonese, to the brown and slightly sweet sauces of Jiangnan (South of the Yangtze), to the wheat-based diet with beef and lamb of the north and west, to the spicy and numbing (mala) food of my wife's native Sichuan, to the varieties of hot pot, with Chonqing style most famous, to the thousands of pickled vegetables from every corner of the country, the dumplings and noodles of Shanxi, and so many, many more things than can be named. Chinese restaurants in many places I've traveled are frequently pretty good to even excellent from my experience, but they reflect only a small portion of what could be called "Chinese Food," and often quite different from what I've mostly eaten in the country of its origin. For one thing, fish and seafood are highly valued and commonly eaten in most of China, the western and northern deserts excepted. My wife nearly starts salivating if we talk of going out to eat fish head soup. (I'll let you in on something, the fish is really, really big, and there's a lot of meat on it. One head could be a main dish for 5-6 people.) A lot of Chinese food is spicy, not just that of Sichuan or Hunan. And as I mentioned, pickled and fermented foods are so very important to the diet for many people here, and based on a lot of traditional ideas of food from around the world as well as recent medical research, likely one of the healthiest aspects of the diet. So is the fact that food here is nearly always incredibly fresh. The vegetables were usually just picked and the chicken may have been running around, or at least alive, within the last few hours.

Along with all of this diversity of food, it only makes sense that you almost have to learn to eat again, and chopsticks are just the tip of the iceberg in that regard. I've seen people put a shrimp in their mouth, chew and swallow the meat, then spit out the shell, all of that done without the use of hands. I can't do it, and neither can my wife, but some of the coastal people are real artists at it. Shanghainese people are crazy about hairy crabs, and there's an art to eating them well, again one I've not mastered. Crab is OK with me, but too much work. When eating meat, you have to get used to having the bones, heads and other parts served with the meal. Eating pork ribs, among other items, can end up becoming painful as they just use a huge knife to cut them up bones and all. If you're not careful little bone pieces can crack a tooth thereby rendering the rest of the meal rather uncomfortable. I've had to have teeth fixed due to that very experience. It's just how it's done here, and for the most part, I wouldn't have it any other way.

As promised, here is a description that I gave to my dad when he asked about the food:

"The meals in Chinese restaurants are served family style in all but the rarest occasions, so we just order a bunch of dishes and everyone uses their chopsticks and digs in. So the food we ordered that night was…are you ready for this…are you sure you're ready? Well, it was:

For appetizers we had two cold dishes, one of steamed soybeans in the pod (called by the Japanese name "edamame" in the U.S.) and one of cut jellyfish with carrots, and a warm dish of steamed pieces of pumpkin, purple sweet potato, corn, taro, and more soybeans in the pod.

Next came the main dishes of
Stir-fried little squids with onions and chili peppers,
Fried taro balls
Eggplant in a garlic sauce with pork
Cut lettuce stalk in a soup with salted goose
Steamed wheat buns in the shape of little caps, with pickled vegetables and pork (you put the pork and pickled veggies in the little buns and eat it that way)
Stir-fried cabbage

Rice

and a huge bowl of rather spicy soup containing bean sprouts, pork slices, squids, and duck blood pudding

Then we also had a few drinks like a green bean drink and cold herb tea, as well as hot roasted barley tea

So I think that was all and it was quite good. The bill was 218 yuan, which is under $40 total for all four of us. I hope your mouth is watering, because it should be.

Tonight we ate at home and had a wonderful pork and squash soup, cold tofu (soybean curd) in sauce, stir-fried bean pods, stir-fried pork slices with young garlic stalks (yum), and rice.

The food is a little different than what I grew up eating, but I'm not at all complaining."

Food is important everywhere in the world, but seldom does it have the central part of culture that you find in China. This brief introduction will have to suffice for now. Almost every meal could be a story in itself and I will not torture you with all of those stories, all of those meals you can't have, unless you're here. Of course, if you're here, you would know all this.

Changes

Life is punctuated by new experiences that lend some variety to our day to day living. Oddly enough, while we remember those punctuated events, it's the mundane part of life which is usually the most important, that gives life it's long-term meaning. Vacations are great, but they lose meaning if we have no regular life to which we can return. Nonetheless, it's the new and different experiences that we often find most interesting and that are part of changes which lead us in new directions. In that spirit I offer a short list of some of the firsts I have experienced in China. I'll avoid those things which are obvious, like "first time to go to the Summer Palace," one of my favorite places to visit in northern China, or "first time to eat Chongqing hotpot." There are too many of those anyhow. So here is my list of notable firsts in China:

- Marriage - As I said before, I wanted to get married for a long time, but it was in China that I found my love. Well, on the internet first, then in China. I probably should have gone to China much sooner, as far as my love life is concerned, because women I've met have generally seemed to be more interested in me here than they were in other places I've lived, though I must admit such popularity could have been a problem for me as well. So maybe things happen the way they should sometimes.
- Buy a house or apartment - As an adult, I had always lived in apartments, dormitories, or cabins of various types, but only rented places. Technically I didn't buy a house in China either, as my name is not listed as an owner, but that's because it's just hard to do administratively. It made more sense for a number of reasons to list my wife and daughter as owners. Still it's a new house and it's mine as well as theirs. Then we traded in the house for two apartments, a long ways from each other, one in Shanghai and one in the far south.
- Have a child, see her down the aisle, have a grandchild - The first part of this was relatively easy. Yini was born in 1992, long before I knew her mother, but her father of birth passed away soon afterwards. She never really knew him. Pei raised her with the help of her parents until I came along when Yini was already 18, so most of the tough part had already passed me by. Still, she views me as her father, though I have no illusions that she sees me in the same light as someone who would have been there all those years earlier. I was surprised when she decided to get married and asked me to walk her down the "aisle," mainly because it's not part of a traditional Chinese wedding, though it has been adopted into many modern ceremonies. It was truly an honor to walk this wonderful girl, now become a beautiful woman, to the altar for her wedding. It showed me the level of acceptance they have accorded me into this family. My father passed away on April 13 of 2018, which didn't really surprise me, given how his condition had deteriorated, and he was 92 years old. My grief had quite a jolt when, within 24 hours of his passing, Yini gave birth to our first and, at this time, only grandson. How much more clearly can the cycle of life turn? Though I don't live near him, so I don't see him as often as I

would like, he is a true joy who brings me to tears frequently. After so many years of being on my own, I have a real family.
- Live in a non-western culture - If you've never lived in a place that has such contrast in language, the way of thinking, religion and so many other aspects of culture, then it's really hard to explain just how pervasive the differences can be. Living in Germany was certainly contrasting and eye-opening for me, even though I had come from a community of German and Danish American immigrants. Going there really gave me a much better idea of those things that define American culture, or should I say cultures. China added a whole other layer (or two or three) of complexity to that contrast. I hope some of the stories here have given a glimpse of those differences.
- Live in a non-christian culture - I consider it a relief to live in a place where I can have freedom FROM religion. I grew up with religion, with Christianity, with Wisconsin Synod Lutheranism, and I know the benefits of religion to society. The thing is, I was told that religion is needed for morality and for the connections that can hold society together, yet I see much of that still here in China, even though few have any real personal connection to religion. Confucianism, Buddhism, Taoism, and even Communism have all played big roles in the development of Chinese culture, but they are not pounded into you wherever you go. True, since the Reform and Opening period in China started in the late 1970s there has been a moral confusion, even a moral decline in many ways, but that can happen in any revolution or great change a nation experiences, and it is as much the influence of western capitalism and economic views that has affected this change as it is lack of religion or moral compass. Love it or not, capitalism, in its true nature, is not really moral in its fundamentals. I'm not saying if it's good or bad, just that it is not inherently moral, which leads us to the next point.
- Live in a communist country - In some ways when you are out on the streets here in China, it's hard to tell that we have such a contrasting style of government. It's an incredible mix, not only culturally, but also of communist and market ideals, really. Through my experiences living in and visiting many places, I've come to believe that almost

any type of government can work as long as the leaders, however they came to power, have the best interests of the people and the environment at heart. I'm not saying they always do that here, not by any means, but there are quite a few things that work well. And from my experience, they don't always do that in democracies either.

- Buy a new car and test drive a car without leaving the lot - Before coming to China I had only owned used cars, and even my first car here was used. That was the one where I test drove it on the lot. Traffic in that part of Shanghai was such that it was too crowded and hazardous to do anything but. Then I bought a new Volkswagen Cross Polo, a German car built right in Shanghai. It was a good car that I would still have were it not for retirement and us not needing two cars.
- First (and second) operation besides dental work - Before China I had never been in a hospital operating room before, only a dental office. I had the pleasure of experiencing bone spurs in my shoulder that I had to have removed. It went well. The doctor who did the operation had been trained in the United States and did on average 250 knee operations and 150 shoulder operations every year. If practice makes perfect, then he must be pretty damn good. And he was. Then a year or so later I had an emergency bowel obstruction that ended up needing surgery. Going into surgery, realizing that you will soon be unconscious and someone you don't really know will be cutting into your body, is a scary proposition. Add to that you hardly understanding anything they are saying, and it gets more so. But I lived and here I am.
- Live in a high rise apartment - Our first place where we lived was on the 29th floor and now in Jinghong we are on the 30th floor. I'm not crazy about living so high off of Mother Earth, but when you have so many people living in one country, there are not too many other viable options, so I deal with it. The group of buildings where we first lived in Shanghai probably had more people living in them as in all of Cave Junction, OR, just to put things in perspective.
- Live in a city over one million people - Not only that, it has more residents than any state where I've lived, except California, and it has

two thirds of their population as well. It boggles the mind.
- Teach middle school - It's a good age to teach, but a difficult one, what with them wanting to test the waters of adulthood and hormones kicking in and all. It's also a good age to teach in that they are still more active than high school and college, but more verbally communicative than grade school. I just wish it hadn't taken me so long to figure out how to include more active learning opportunities. I'm naturally a pretty good lecturer, but that doesn't get too far with 13 year olds. Still, I had some success, including some inspired to go on to do some really good things.
- Retirement - It's so nice not having to face the traffic anymore, but retirement still involves plenty of work when you have a spouse, dogs, a child, grandchild, a house, etc. I've done some tutoring and made an educational video, with the possibility of other videos in the future. We moved out of our house into two apartments. There's pretty much always plenty to do, and when not, you can write books.

Waiting in line a woman is holding her little girl who wears split crotch pants, while waiting to pay using her cell phone, to see a building that's 1000 years old. She wears a traditional qipao and carries an expensive European handbag, while her husband wears a Western-styled suit, but has the hands of a laborer. China is a place where the ancient mixes with the ultramodern and most people are caught somewhere in between. It's a nation of farmers living in some of the world's biggest cities. It's where communism mixes openly with capitalism in what is likely the fastest changing country the world has ever seen, undergoing the largest migration the world has ever seen, that from countryside to city. And then there's me, an aging former park ranger with limited language abilities trying to connect with Nature in massive urban sprawl. And while it often enough frustrates me as much as anybody, I'm glad to be here.

Searching

One of the silken threads that has woven itself through my life is that of seeking a relationship with the sacred, though over that time it has taken many different forms. I guess you could say I've always been sort of a "spiritual thrill seeker." I was raised a Christian, a Wisconsin Synod Lutheran to be exact. Of all the Lutherans, the Wisconsin synod are the most conservative and strict in their interpretation of the Bible and in the application of it to everyday life. People often look at Catholics as being strict and rigid, but our church considered the Catholics to be liberals with loose morals. While my parents weren't the type to talk a lot about the Bible in daily life, we still went to church every Sunday and holiday, prayed before every meal, and my sisters and I went to Lutheran schools through grade 12. I never thought of seeking other paths, because I knew no others.

The staid and narrow religion of my youth did not provide for personal experience of god, but that was what I sought in my own heart. The most emotional connections I had to a god from those youthful days were the holiday beauty, the decorations, the songs that touched my heart. One major contributor to those experiences was my Uncle Dick, who worked as a set manager for the local theater company, and who managed the decorations for the church's holiday programs. He poured his heart and soul into the lights, the flowers, the set pieces, and even the timing of how they all worked together to create a mood, to channel our emotions for the greatest effect. He was a true artist. I was often involved in the programs, but mostly in a musical sense, usually as a singer in the school classes and the youth choir. I loved singing and that's where I poured my heart for those presentations. That is, I did love singing in the church until one of the bigger boys a few grades above me decided that I looked ridiculous singing out the way I did and began to berate me, to make fun of me, to make me a laughingstock. I still sang, but began to temper my fervor. After I left grade school I became less involved, then even less as I reached my high school graduation.

I grew and I changed. My voice changed. My body changed. I began to broaden my horizons. When I caught the music bug again and began to study guitar, I sometimes performed classical pieces during our church programs. I didn't sing. At least not in church. I began singing in rock bands where looking funny was normal. In college studying geology I grew disillusioned with Christianity when the pastor at church gave me totally inadequate answers to questions I had about where geology and the Bible appear to conflict. I also was brushed aside by adults in the church for including anything remotely scientific in conversations about religious studies, even if it was in support of what they believed. I began to pull away and seek answers in other places.

That disillusionment with the religion of my youth really came to a head when my dear uncle, whose work had touched me so deeply, passed away. You see, Uncle Dick was gay, though at the time I didn't really know that. The church didn't think too much of gay people. Eventually I did know that, like his father, he drank a lot. In retrospect I'm sure he drank so much partly because of the influence of his dad, but also because he had great difficulty reconciling his homosexuality and his religion. He grew more distant from the family over time. His work suffered, though he still came up with great shows for church. His parents, my mom's parents and my grandparents, had passed away. Uncle Dick didn't leave home for many days on end and I think he ended up on public assistance. Then, when nobody had seen nor heard from him for several days, someone was sent to call on him. They found him lying dead from alcohol poisoning on the floor of the home in which he grew up. He was in his early 40s. I was living at the Grand Canyon then and my dad didn't even notify me until a week after it had happened. After all the work Uncle Dick had done for the church, I'm told that at his funeral the pastor said, "I wish there was something good I could say about Richard, about his life, some comfort I could give, but I cannot." The church didn't think much of gay people. That pastor never even knew my uncle. This experience sealed my separation from the church and religion of my youth. I went back a few times for my dad's sake and to say hello to people I knew and cared about, but the actual service had no meaning for me. Even my own dad blocked Uncle Dick from his mind. In 2008 I was doing some healing work and the subject of my lost uncle came up. I called dad and asked, "How old was Uncle Dick when he passed away?"

"Who?" he responded.

"Uncle Dick."

Pause. "I don't know who you're talking about.

"Uncle Richard, mom's youngest brother."

"Oh, him. I don't know, I think he was in his early 40s." My dad was 82 at the time, but his mind was still very sharp. Uncle Dick was just no longer on his list of people that mattered, but he mattered to me.

Studying the science of geology, studying about Nature, filled much of the void in my life for quite a while, but later, still feeling the need for something spiritual in my life, I began looking into other religions, including, but not limited to Buddhism, Taoism, Sufism, and Paganism. Paganism? Yes, Paganism, the old religion, the Nature religion, magic and witches and all that stuff. There are plenty of sources where you can read about it, so I'll not explain the religion as it's practiced today other than to say that it is a Nature religion where ceremonies are done to honor the spirits and cycles in Nature. There are parts of modern Paganism that I'm not so crazy about, but having a religion centered on Nature for someone like me who feels so close to the natural world is a logical fit. It's also one reason I like Taoism, which at its core is also a Nature-based religion. I read some about Paganism and attended a few ceremonies by a local Pagan group in my home state of Wisconsin.

One of those ceremonies was a naming ceremony for a baby born to a member of the group. We often hear in movies and stories of how evil witches are, but though this ceremony was conducted by a witch, it was one of the most loving and beautiful religious ceremonies I've ever experienced. The one that stood out in my mind, though, was a

Winter Solstice ceremony in Madison, Wisconsin, about 2 hours from my hometown. I had been in touch with the leader about this ceremony and they included me in their service in my capacity as a storyteller. I prepared a Norse tale about why we kiss under the mistletoe. That's a Christmas tradition, but it went back well before Christianity came to northern Europe, as the old Pagans there were very fond of the little plant. A winter storm was moving into the area, but I made it to Madison with no trouble. The venue was a meeting hall (the Old Synagogue?), one of the oldest buildings in town that sits near a large lake in the center of the city. I arrived early as instructed, but people were already filling the hall and drums began to vibrate the walls as we waited in the basement for our entrance. At the proper time we were ushered upstairs and walked through the crowd to the front of the hall. Outside was bitter cold and windy, but the hall was packed with people, the temperature soaring, the building vibrating with the beat of the drums and the feet of participants, and huge sticks of incense more than a meter tall filled the air with a musky aroma. At a hand movement of the woman leading the ceremony the drums stopped and all became quiet. She chanted, invoked the spirits, and welcomed the return of light after the period of growing darkness. One presenter did solstice songs, one talked of the meanings behind the ceremony, and then there was me, doing my dramatic best to weave a story of the Norse deities Balder, god of light, his mother Frigg, and the trickster Loki. It's a story that doesn't exactly stick to the original mythology, but it fit well in the ceremony. After the service ended around 10 p.m. I was so energized I could hardly contain my emotions, my energy. I thought of staying in Madison, but knew I wouldn't be able to sleep for a while, so instead I chose to face the blowing snow and try to make it home. I arrived sometime after midnight, still a bit energized, but starting to wane. When the adrenaline wore off I faded into the world of dreams.

In its truest essence, Buddhism is more of a philosophy than a religion, all due regards (??) to the Dalai Lama and other Buddhist leaders. I haven't read all of the Buddhist sutras, but from my readings and experience with Buddhists, the Buddha never said much about worship and god. I don't see anything really wrong with the concept of people practicing it as a religion if they want, not that anything I would say can change all of that, but in truth, the heart of Buddhism is meditation and in the attitude with which you approach life. That's probably why so many Christian monks have gotten away with adding some Buddhism to their religious practice, especially in the form of Zen meditation. So in its truest form it is spiritual, but not really religious, much the way I often am. I have read much about Buddhism and practiced many different forms of meditation in my life, including a lot of Buddhist meditation, but none was more intensive than the "Vipassana" retreat I attended. In the early 90s I traveled to a Goenka meditation center near Fresno, CA, at the urging of my Iyengar yoga teacher, Lisa. S.N. Goenka was a Burmese man who had become a successful businessman and then began developing serious migraines when in his 30s. He started practicing Vipassana meditation and eventually his migraines stopped. He began teaching the practice and became one of the most famous and successful promoters of Vipassana in the world, though far from the only one. Vipassana is part of the inspiration and basis for Eugene Gendlin's "Focusing," which has been a very successful method of personal growth for many people.

Upon arriving at the meditation center we were told the rules, the schedule and given a simple bed for our use, then the first evening had an introductory session. We were to stay at the center for the entire time and attend all of the sessions. Breakfast and lunch were provided, as was evening tea and fruit, but there was no dinner. We were awakened at 4 a.m. by the bell and started meditating, with the day's meditation totaling 8-10 hours. Getting up that early wasn't hard for me... I don't sleep much anyhow. Interspersed in the day's meditations were several videos we watched of Goenka talking about meditation and the theory behind it. He was a good speaker and very logical, somewhat scientific in his approach to the meditation. Goenka had a rather jovial and entertaining manner in his presentation, which made it the highlight of my days there. I recall one lesson where he discussed "craving and aversion" (basically what you want or don't want) and how they can lead to addictions. It makes perfect sense, actually, but the talk was amusing, as he would talk about these cravings/aversions and several times ended with wanting to say "and then you are an addict," but his accent was such that it sounded like "and then you are a dick." It's often true either way, but it provided chuckles for most of us in the class. The toughest rule for many was that of not talking during 9 days of the session, except in brief discussions with the facilitators, with whom I only spoke about 20 words in total. I actually had a pretty easy time with that and when, after the last day's morning meditation session we were allowed to begin speaking, found the sound of people's chatter rather annoying. The meditation itself, without going into too much detail, is basically one of scanning the body for sensations and just noticing them, not reacting, no cravings for pleasure nor aversions to displeasure. It sounds easier than it really is.

An experience like that retreat can affect a person in interesting ways. After it ended at about noon on the tenth day, I drove back home from Fresno to Flagstaff, AZ, including crossing the southern California desert. I remember stopping at a rest area and just sitting watching birds and people and wind through the trees in the sweltering summer afternoon heat. People's concerns, complaining and arguing all seemed so trivial and nonsensical to me, so superfluous to life. Of course, it wasn't long before I was back doing the same thing myself, but it felt good at the time to view it all in a different light. I continued doing the meditation fairly consistently for a few years afterwards, though not the 3 hours a day they suggested. Life has a way of altering our schedules. I can't say it cured me of anything, but I know it didn't hurt.

Soon after the time I did the Vipassana retreat I also began studying Kundalini yoga with a Sikh teacher. Sikhism is a religion based on both Hinduism and Islam, having started in India near the border with Pakistan. Of course, the geography teacher in me would be remiss not to remind you that Pakistan was part of India 500 years ago when it began, and the whole area was ruled by a Muslim caliphate. The American Sikhs I knew were pretty much all white folks who had adopted the religion, they almost exclusively dressed in white with turbans, and their last names were either Kaur (women) or Singh (men). Kundalini yoga often involves either repetitive motions or held positions, mostly not the slow movements of what we usually think of in yoga, with intense breathing exercises. Breath of fire, for instance, is a rapid movement of the diaphragm forcing breath out and in, usually through the nose. There are routines we would do that apparently had certain healing powers if you did them consistently over a long period of time. For instance, I once did an exercise for cleansing the liver that involved holding 9 different positions, each for three minutes, while doing breath of fire, 27 minutes of breath of fire in total. One position was seated on the floor with your left foot under your butt, hands on the ground behind you, and holding your right foot straight out at a 45 degree angle above the floor. You do that for 3 minutes while breathing rapidly in and out through your nose. Believe me, a session like that can really have you seeing life differently after a while. How? Try it. I studied with Mr. Singh for several months and continued doing some of the routines for years afterwards. I still occasionally do it, even if only the breath of fire, just for the thrill of it.

It was 1997 and I decided one Sunday to go to church, an Episcopal one to be exact. It had nothing to do with the religion so much as to do with the fact that my friend Jim wanted me to hear his choir, of which he was justifiably very proud. They sang like bluebirds on a lovely morning in May, which was interesting, because it was still the dead nuts of winter. Not only did I enjoy the music and the beauty of the Church building, which I had only seen once before in the dark, but that's another story, I also found the pastor's sermon to be one of the most inspiring I had ever heard. He didn't use a script nor even notes, unlike the pastors of my youth. The entire sermon was either memorized or improvised, and I suspected the latter, because it was so passionate and heartfelt, that I knew he wasn't just rattling off the words for rote. He talked of the real meaning of communion and of Jesus breaking bread with people, and it had nothing to do with formal ceremony, but with the importance of honoring the food and the people with you. I hadn't heard anything like it in a Christian setting before, and it greatly impressed me. I'd already been dabbling in other religions beside that of my birth for about 10 years, and various experiences had made me reconsider Christianity. I knew I still couldn't buy it hook, line, and sinker, but some of the basic tenets are still pretty valid, and it could be a method for healing as well as most others. After hearing the sermon I decided to give it a shot, and I started going to the Episcopal church near where I was living at the time near the Wisconsin Dells. The pastor was a woman and fairly liberal, from my experience, and I enjoyed the services she presented. She wasn't the same level as the other pastor I had heard that inspired me, but she did well. I decided to join and become a full member of the church, and after some formalities, I was sworn in by the regional bishop one Sunday morning. I did find, however, that in discussion groups, people were more open to other ideas than in the church of my birth, but still didn't quite get me. The pastor and I chatted about that a number of times, and she encouraged me to be patient, which is often good advice.

After several months living in the Wisconsin Dells, as the leaves of autumn faded and flakes started to fall, I once again changed my life plans and ended up moving to North Carolina to live with my sister Pat for a while. Along the way I made arrangements to spend several days in a monastery in New York state, the Hudson River Valley, to be exact. It was a wonderful location and a beautiful old complex of buildings. I went to services, shared meals with the monks, and even did some Zen meditation with one. I gave consideration to becoming a monk, but my sister was expecting me so I continued on to North Carolina, where I joined an Episcopal church in one of the oldest buildings in the area, dating to 1848. I became a full member there, and for that matter, I probably am still listed on their books as one. Anyhow, I enjoyed the people and the pomp and circumstance of their services. I got involved in their mediation group ... a lot of Buddhist thought once again ... though after time I once again began to fade in my interest for it. The same demons haunting me, I guess.

Can you hold two seemingly opposing ideas in your head simultaneously? It seems counter-intuitive, but people do it all the time. When traditional native tribes got together they would often share their creation stories, which were sometimes quite different from each other, yet they accepted each story as truth on some level. And look at some of those good Christians in church on Sunday, who go to work and screw their neighbors, both figuratively or literally during the week, not that Christians have any corner on that market by any means. I ask the question, because while in Chapel Hill I also got to be friends with a group of Sufis, members of the mystical sect of Islam. You know, whirling dervishes and all that! Even though I was going to the Episcopal church,

I began to spend some of my evenings joining the Sufi dhikr, a kind of religious practice. We had short stories or lectures by the teacher, Sherif Baba, who was from Turkey, and his translator Jem, also Turkish, and then we would sing songs, chant, and dance. I usually left before they finished, because they were drinking strong tea and stayed up past midnight and I had to work the next day, but it was good and I felt both at ease with and inspired by them. Watching dervishes spinning around in their traditional flowing coats is really a beautiful experience, flowers turning in the swirls of a mountain stream. I tried dancing like that and found it difficult, but intriguing. I spent New Years Eve with the Sufis dancing, feasting, and singing in the millennium, while outside drunken revelers were greeting the new year in a different way. It was a warm and beautiful evening on a cold night.

When I left Chapel Hill and moved to Oregon, after a few years I heard of a talk by the same Sufi teacher, Sherif Baba, and went to see him. He remembered me and we hugged. The talk he did involved something about a cave, and I told him I worked in a cave, which made him take a keen interest. I took him and his group of students through the cave a few days later, with me holding his hand, as he is partially paralyzed. I also went to see him a few months later when he came to Seattle and became friends with one of his students, a woman named Didar, which was her Sufi name. I rented a room in her place for a while after I left my permanent job at Oregon Caves in 2006. Funny how life connects! Baba is a very respected Sufi teacher, not only in North America, but also his native Turkey. He lives in Istanbul now, so I've read, but travels to the US and Canada a few times a year to do gatherings of the faithful. I doubt he will be coming to China anytime soon, though. I have a distinct fondness in my heart for Sufism, though little interest at all in becoming a Muslim for my own personal reasons (keep reading), and most of that fondness stems from my interest in the poet Rumi, whose works I often have found inspiring and comforting. Sherif Baba hailed from the tradition dating back to Rumi.

I'm not really sure how to approach the next part of this chapter, but it does behoove me to say something about my studies with Martin Prechtel. What's so difficult? For one, I don't think he would want me to say too much about what he does in his workshops, in his school, for that's between him and his students. I'll mention a few brief things, but the best thing I could say is to read his books, of which he currently has published six. That's really the only way to gain insight into this wonderful teacher. The other reason I would rather not say too much, is because I wouldn't want my descriptions to fail to live up to the beauty of what we experienced in those sessions together. Should I give an inadequate description, you might get the wrong impression of the good work he really does. I just wish more people could see the wisdom in it.

In the section on my storytelling, I mention that I went to Oaxaca, Mexico, to study with Jim May. Jim gave me a cassette tape (do they still use them?) of one of Martin's talks, a recording by him entitled "Grief and Praise." I listened to it so many times I wore it out. Then one night I heard an interview with him while driving through the dark, southern Oregon night, and it really hit home to me, so I noted where he was scheduled to present his talk and workshop in the area and made arrangements to attend. His talks are enthralling and his workshops are inspiring, cathartic, ridiculous, and absolutely wonderful, all rolled into one. Ridiculous? Yes, what could be more ridiculous than a bunch of mostly white people trying to perform a Mayan ritual in a public hall in the middle of a city! And yet, on many levels it works. So who is this guy? Martin is a Swiss-Irish/Native American half-breed who grew up on a reservation in New Mexico, his father a paleontologist (studies fossils), and his mother a school superintendent. As a young man he left there and wandered south into Mexico and then Guatemala, where he ended up nearly half dead in a Mayan village, and was taken in by a shaman. He learned the trade, became part of the village, and lived there for many years, before he had to leave during the country's civil war, when many of his friends were shot by American bullets, fired by Guatemalan soldiers, just for the crime of being indigenous people. He came back to America, where after some more trying times, he got his feet under him, began teaching, and eventually opened his own school, called "Bolad's Kitchen," among the pinion pines, junipers, rock cliffs, and big, azure skies of his native New Mexico. I highly recommend reading the story in his own words. While I see myself as a fairly normal guy living an exceptional story, he is an exceptional man living an amazing story. He's the most genuinely eloquent man I've ever heard. The heart of Martin's work is to help people reclaim their indigenous soul, indigenous in this case referring to having a culture deeply rooted in a meaningful connection to Mother Earth. Read that last sentence again carefully. Many people in the world are trying to do the same, but what makes Martin stand out from most, is his authenticity and how he has maintained it in spite of what he has lived through, his authenticity stemming from him being a fully-fledged member of a culture that maintained this connection for a seriously long time. Most such teachers are trying to build their own from scratch, but, even though they may have good things to offer, they often miss some of the subtle points that are vital to it really working, that can best be provided by an intact culture.

Anyhow, enough of a commercial. What did I do with all of this? First, I attended several of his weekend workshops and read his books. I loved his writing, so I attended his writing workshop in New Mexico one cold winter's week. My beloved Pedro had to sit tied to the tree outside due to the policy of the building we used, snow falling on him, watching the door for me to emerge. He loved all the attention he got from participants who came with me to pet him during breaks. When Martin started his school I considered attending, but believed I couldn't get the time off of work to go there for 10 days twice a year. It also scared me. I've never felt at all competent with my hands, and part of the Bolad's Kitchen experience is making things by hand. In his workshops we did a little of that, and my hand work always seemed totally inadequate to me, part of which was my own low opinion of myself and part was that in truth, it really wasn't as good as other handwork I saw, but I did it anyhow. One winter I heard they were putting the finishing touches on the construction of his school building, a magnificent, adobe structure behind the horse corral on his land, and they were asking for volunteers to come and help. I spent a week or so there doing whatever physical labor was needed, including mixing and applying adobe mud, and doing the same for the "slip" on the inside walls. Slip is a clay-based coating, sort of like paint, this one being made from a local clay that had little mica flakes in it that shimmer when they catch the light and glow with an earthy radiance. It's gorgeous stuff that really makes the walls come alive.

I finally got around to signing up for Martin's school and attended several sessions before I left for China. The school, as promised involved doing hand work, and I made some necessary tools out of natural materials like wood, stone, bone and cordage. I also made a couple of clay pots that turned out alright, and a pair of shoes made of elk skin and cowhide. Much of the time, though, is spent getting used to seeing the world through very different eyes than what we are used to, through the eyes of indigenous peoples. We looked at music, art, food, stories, clothing, and especially at history. Martin's work informs me even today, and at the time I'm writing this I'm also reading one of this books again. I now live in a very different place and culture than before and in spite of its problems, China's culture has its own lessons to teach, so my views have changed since that time 10 years ago, but I'm grateful to Martin for the different eyes I've been given to see culture here and all over the world in another light.

The truth be told, however, my work with Martin resonated with me because I had already been moving in at least one similar direction myself long before I met him. I just needed the voice of experience and tradition to help me along. This direction of which I speak is that of viewing all things as being alive and deserving of respect. I had begun thinking of what I call "animating the world," which isn't so much "animating" or "bringing to life," as it is recognizing the inherent life within all things, different though those lives may be. For a while in the early 1990s I was a vegetarian, but even then it often riled me when people would say things like, "we shouldn't eat anything that's alive." What? It's all alive! At a Thanksgiving potluck I attended several years before moving to China and just before working with Martin, the host, a local promoter of vegetarianism, told us in preparation for serving the meal that "All of the vegetarian dishes are on this side of the serving table, and all of the dead things on the other side." My response was, "I'm sure that broccoli and those mushrooms are overjoyed to have us devour them," or something to that effect. To his credit he smiled and thanked me for reminding us that it's all alive and to be grateful for their sacrifice. And that's the point. Everything we eat needs to be thanked and appreciated for giving their lives that we might live, and this gratitude extends not only to food, but to all things we use and all things around us. No, a pen is not alive in the same way that a tree or a toad are, but everything in the pen came from living things, the plastics from oil, which were the lives of creatures long ago, and the metals from the living mineral Earth that makes all of the nutrients we need for our existence. What's more, people's hands, ingenuity, and energy went into the making of that pen, and therefore they put their life into it. Living in a throw-away world becomes challenging when you see things this way. I'm not trying to preach, but that's just how I see things, and so do many of the truly indigenous peoples of the world, based on all my study. I think Martin would agree.

One area where my life and leading an indigenous life differ, is my tendency toward wanderlust. To truly live as an indigenous person you need to have a deep relationship with the Earth and those who live upon it. That implies also getting to know the plants, animals, fungi, and others who live around you. You can't know them for the entire Earth, it's best to learn those that live around you, and in order to do that you have to spend time with them. I mean REALLY spend time with them, observing them in different weather, different times of the day and year, over the course of their lives and yours. You can't move around the way I have and really come to that type of understanding. You need to learn what they eat, who they have relationships with, who they antagonize and who antagonizes them, what they do when it's cold or hot or raining or snowy or foggy, etc. etc. etc. In my vagabond life I have always tried to get to know the local characters as best I can, but more often than not I only learn what I can from books, and don't get enough from personal observation to truly understand who they are in the great scheme of things. Here in China I've learned many animals and plants around me. In fact, I often know the names of them better than my Chinese friends and colleagues, but I haven't been here long enough or done enough personal observation to really know them. Our lives all have give and take, plus and minus, benefits and detriments. So it goes.

Herman Hesse, in his book, *Siddhartha*, one of my all-time favorites, writes that a true seeker cannot follow a single path. I guess by that definition, I'm a true seeker. So where has all of this seeking over the years led me? Often confused, is the basic answer, but there's much more to it than that, and what's more, confusion isn't always a bad thing, if you work with it. After so many years of seeking I would have to say that I certainly am not actually searching as much as I used to. Part of that is because I've already looked deeply into most of the major religions of the world, though with Hinduism only cursorily. Even though I didn't mention Judaism in this writing, I have gone to synagogues and Jewish gatherings. And besides, if you are a Christian, which I was, you also have to know something about Judaism. Christianity could be called a sect of Judaism, in a way, though like every child it grew up to start its own family. I still do believe that all things are alive in their own way, so I guess you could say I'm an animist, but really, to be an animist or pantheist is to say that all things have their own god within them, and therefore we need to pray to and appease those gods. I don't exactly see it that way, unless you equate god with life, then OK. Another simple answer is that it depends on exactly when you ask me the question, for my ideas change often every day or even every hour. So then you could say I'm all of them, all of the religions I've studied as I do see the value in them all, but also the drawbacks of them. It's like the old story, probably originally from India, of the 6 blind men and an elephant. They all touched a part of the elephant and gave their descriptions. No one description was completely true for the elephant as a whole, but together they made a reasonable facsimile of one. So I think there's a lot of truth in the idea that all religions have a piece of the truth, but none has the whole truth. Hence the Hesse quote.

I will say this, that I see some value in religious experience, and by that I mean the experience of the ecstatic, which can be very cathartic. This includes things such as the Sufi dancing, intense chanting, meditation, deep breathing, etc. These things often happen when we push ourselves to the limits of our physical or mental extremes. The reality is, though, that these experiences are not really religious so much as physical and emotional. For example, I noticed in watching the Sufis chanting and dancing, that those who got into a state where they were shaking and to some degree losing control, was because of the movement, the breathing, or both, but you don't need to chant the name of Allah (or whoever) to do it, though I see nothing wrong in that either. Just the breathing and movement will suffice. I've found the same to be true in many other situations as well, such as hiking or climbing. The ecstatic effect is hard to explain, so all I can say is to just try it if you wish. If you go back to the chapter on my trip to Thailand I have a description of some breathing that can lead you to such a state. Some have promoted trying to achieve a constant state of ecstasy, but that's not a goal I wish to attain at this point, and in truth I don't think it's possible. It might be a beautiful experience, but such experiences, in my mind, are only valuable if you have a normal life to come back to, tempting as it is. Reality has its own meaning. A constant state of love? Now there's a much better goal I hope to someday reach. Constantly seeking these experiences, however, could be an addiction like any other: "And then you are a dick!" Apologies to Goenka.

Atheism frequently gets a bad rap, mostly because of the condescending way it's often promoted, since some atheist writers berate people for their religious beliefs. I know there are reasons for it when you look at the track records of so many religions. Remember the crusades, or the oppression of women and homosexuals by so many religious groups, the ungodly number of religious wars, pun intended, and on, and on, and on, and on, and on... Atheists are often criticized as being amoral, yet religions don't have a very good track record of morality either. Some religious peoples also wonder how can you NOT believe in god, and find it an incredulous concept, but that's just because it's so different from the way they were raised or have come to believe. As I mentioned before, one of the things I really like about living in China is freedom *from* religion. Many people here say they believe in a god, but that's about as far as it goes. In America, I grew really tired of people trying to shove it down my throat, and of course, it has to be THEIR religion, as according to them, there is no other truth. I was in Medford, OR, walking across a mostly empty parking lot one day, when a man asked me if he could ask me a question. (Well, you just DID ask me a question!). I said, "Sure." He said, "Have you accepted Jesus as your personal savior?" I said, "Sorry, I don't want to discuss that." He became irate and began shouting at me that I was doomed to burn in the fires of hell, that I was a horrible person and deserved eternal damnation. Good advertising. Sure makes me want to jump on board. I hadn't said I didn't believe, just that I didn't want to discuss it. I'd have to say that these days I believe in morality, I believe in ethics, but I don't always believe in god. It's just that when I look at history, at science, at Nature, at humans and their foibles, and at all the religions of the world, it's pretty hard to believe there is an intelligent, all-knowing being directing this bizarre tragicomedy. Or maybe it's just my self-effacing nature that keeps me from latching onto a religion. As Groucho Marx said, "I'd never join an organization that would have me as a member." I guess the best description to where I've landed with all of this is that of being an agnostic. I'm open to the possibilities, but I just can't say for certain. I'd like to, I might say I even long to, but I just can't.

Before I leave this, I feel compelled to add one more thing. Another aspect of life that probably caused me to search was my emotional relationship with myself and others. I mentioned earlier that I left music school partly due to anxiety. A word often connected with anxiety is depression. I know both of those ever so well, as they have demonized me nearly as long as I can remember, they and the physical difficulties they bring with them. They were with me as I stood gazing over the rim of the Grand Canyon and listening to wolves howl in Alaska, They sat on my shoulder whispering nasty comments as I flew to Germany, to Thailand, and to China. They bristled at the back of my neck while taking in a concert in the Thomaskirche in Leipzig and talks by Martin in New Mexico. They reared their fierce countenances into every friendship and intimate relationship I've ever had. Covering this subject with any useful adequacy would require another book to explain, one I've started writing and may someday finish, but it is not my intention to deal much with it here. What I will say is that it has had a serious impact on my life and pushed me to the brink of suicide numerous times over these last decades, not just the one I mentioned earlier with Pedro. I've tried a great many modes of treatment including one-on-one talk therapy, group therapy, isolationism, crystal healing, various forms of bodywork, homeopathy, herbs, and medications of various sorts. My spiritual seeking is likely born partly from the many dark nights of my soul. Suffice it for now to say that I'm in a much better place than I have been for a very long time. I'm sure most of those therapies I tried have helped in some ways. Nature has usually been a big help. Finding a good, patient, tolerant wife cannot be overstated in its importance. My searching goes on, but the hole in my soul doesn't seem to need quite as much filling. All I can say is that it is possible to lead a very full life in spite of, and maybe even because of, serious struggles with mental and physical health.

While I may not subscribe to a religion or follow a mainstream philosophy, all my wandering and experience has only confirmed to me that the Earth, all of Nature, is intensely beautiful and full of wonder, and I am ever so grateful to have had the opportunity to see and experience so much of it. From the flowering deserts, to the towering redwood forests, from the mighty expanse of oceans to the tiny, bioluminescent algae that float therein, from lush tropical forests to autumn, wine-red tundra. So, too, are the varieties of cultures on the Earth so fascinating and often magnificent in their own ways, from Hopi Buffalo Dances to classical ballet, from common street vendors in Thai marketplaces to European palaces, from Pagan chanting to Sufi dancing and church choirs, from rock and roll stages to Balinese gamelan, and ever so much more. Yes, there are awful things as well, and sometimes I focus too much on those, but they should not overshadow the wondrous beauties around us every day. What remains is for us to appreciate them and ensure they continue. For a start, we have only to really notice and appreciate, this moment and the next.

Afterthoughts and Acknowledgements

The good that I would, I do not;
the evil I would not, that I do.
—**Romans 7:19**

I imagine one main reason people write autobiographies is to answer the question "Who am I?", or for you as a reader to answer, "Who is this guy and why the hell should I read his book?" Of course, there are an infinite variety of ways to answer the question, and by now you have a pretty good idea of the answer based on the stories I've shared with you. Pop psychology and humanism would often have us respond to the question of "Who am I?" with ideas that tell us who we are not, such as: you are not your thoughts, you are not your feelings, the you that can be explained is not the real you, you are not your body, and other such esoteric pathways. I understand where they are going with that, trying to get at the "You" that underlies that which we perceive, but while there is value in such an approach, as I've gotten older I've often shied away from it in favor of a more practical approach. These days when I hear things like "You are not your thoughts" I am more inclined to respond, "Well, duh, of course I'm not my thoughts. How stupid do you think I am?" It's good to be reminded sometimes, though. We may not be our feelings or thoughts, but this person who lives in this world is partly defined by such things. They are a part of us and we should not trivialize them, even as we should not aggrandize them, but rather take them at face value and do what we can with them. I've come to believe that we are defined by what we do, what we say, what we feel and think, that which we hold dear, that which we dislike, and many other things. It's a complex and varied package deal and there is no simple answer and we do ourselves and the world a disservice in trying to make it simpler than it is. And this from a guy who likes the simple answers.

For now I just want to add a bit to what I've already revealed, and start by looking at the Bible quote above. The author apparently meant it to be taken in totality, which I certainly don't agree with, but it does offer food for thought. He was trying to make the point that we are all no good, "Our righteousness are as filthy rags," he later wrote. No wonder so many of us are screwed up and have no sense of self. The quote actually makes me feel a bit better about myself, since I'm obviously not the first person to feel this way, to find some truth in it. I've always, as long as I can recall, been a person who cares about doing the "right" thing, whatever that means. I've believed in values like tolerance, kindness, patience, humility, gratitude, good communication, and living with integrity and respect for all living things. To many people it may sound pretty good. Yet in trying to do those things, I've so often fallen on the opposite side of them that it boggles my mind.

Take respect, for instance. I've tried to live in respect for all people, all things, and yet so very many times in life I've done exactly the opposite, especially in my love life and close personal relationships. Things like showing up unannounced and 10:00 pm to a friend's dark house and knocking on the door without having called ahead, leaving a dear one standing for two hours with my dog while I got an acupuncture treatment, and degrading the wishes of a friend because I was blinded by my own fervent environmental beliefs and penny pinching ways. The list of such offenses could go on, and on, and on, ... well, you get the picture. I always TRY to respect people, but obviously fall flat on my face often enough. I've just met so many people along the way, that there was no possibility I could hold up to my own expectations, nor often those of my family and friends, in so many instances. I've tried, though.

I, and I think most of the people who know me, would consider me a reasonably intelligent person with a fair amount of common sense.

And yet I've made some of the most insane decisions and blunders you could imagine and often failed to learn from my mistakes. You might have gotten that impression just from some of the narratives above. One of the more ridiculous things I've done is when I lived in a three-story house on the north side of Chapel Hill, NC. My bedroom was on the third floor, the attic, if you will, with my kitchenette and bathroom on the second floor. I couldn't stand up straight in parts of the room. I rented it from a woman named Deborah, who tended to live life very grand and open. She had two children when I moved in and later a husband who was into computers. She wanted a washing machine and somehow got the idea to put it in the small bathroom I used on the second floor where there was no place for it to drain except through the toilet. So every time someone did laundry they would have to stick this big pipe into the toilet, otherwise it would dump all of the water draining from the machine onto the second floor. It's a crazy system, I know, but I'm sure you now know what I did. Yes, I put in laundry, then had to use the toilet and forgot to put the pipe back in the toilet. Her husband said, "Well, I'm sure you'll never do THAT again!" I thought to myself, "You don't know me, do you?" I started doing laundry back at the laundromat, though Deb always told me I didn't have to. Eventually I listened to her and did laundry in the house again. Before long I did the exact same thing and flooded part of the house. Rex's computer room was down below on the first floor. I never did laundry in the house again. And yet, when Deb's dear friend and our neighbor was having chemotherapy, I was the one who shaved my head in solidarity with her. Life is just so full of paradoxes, and I'm no exception.

Why do I tell you all of this? Why reveal my shortcomings? Partly it's because, in my self-effacing manner I didn't want readers to get the impression I think I'm perfect. It couldn't be further from the truth, actually. This is just how life has unfolded for me. But also and mainly, I want to take this opportunity to say to all the people I've disrespected or slighted, all those I've needlessly angered or hurt, that I know what I did, and I'm duly sorry for it. I don't expect that admission to just make things all better, but I hope it's a start. Just know that I'm the type of person who hasn't forgotten what I've done and I likely feel horrible about it, even though you probably have forgotten it or moved it to the back of your mind a long time ago. I hope that nothing I did has really hurt your life in any meaningful way, and that through it all I've done more good than harm to those I've encountered along the way.

Nobody truly does anything completely on their own, and along our varied roads in life we receive so many gifts that it's hard, impossible to offer thanks for them all. The best we can do is offer our thanks for the special gifts and make sure we pass on to others the goodness we receive. These stories couldn't have happened without the many people who have helped and supported me on my journey. In my seemingly never-ending travels I have slept on so many couches, spare beds, and floors, that I long ago lost count of them. I would stop and see friends and family, and rely on their hospitality, whether it was across the USA or in Europe. I have often tried to show my gratitude in whatever ways I could, but never felt that it was adequate, that I had done or given enough. Part of that was due to my relative poverty, caused not only by my lack of skills in making money, but also my choice of careers, which didn't lend themselves to having at all abundant financial resources. I never topped making $20,000 a year until I was 38 years old, when I finally realized it was not very much money, since I had to pay for heating oil in a very cold place and a house bigger than I'd ever had by myself, that in June Lake, CA. So to all of those people who gave me a place to lay my head for the night, or for many nights, all those who supported me physically or emotionally or both, for so many years, I want to say thank you with the fullness of my heart. I hope that something I've done for you has made it all worthwhile. And I wish you all well. If you didn't help me, hell with you. ;)

But seriously, now for those who did so much more than put me up for the night. I know I will forget someone, but I'll give this a try and say HUGE "Thank you's":

- To my parents and sisters for giving me the stable foundation of my early years on which to base the chaos that came after it.
- To my dear wife Pei for loving me, flaws included, and to all our Chinese family, for the stability to let me write this, and giving another bookend to the craziness in between.
- To Deb, Steve, Alan, Laurel, John, and all my southern Oregon and northern California friends, for their overwhelming support and love

through the years. If I ever move back to the US, that's likely where I'd end up again, seeming more like home than any other place in the country.
- To Garth for lending me more emotional support than I often deserved and being a good friend through it all.
- To Gerald, Yvette, and their entire family for introducing me to the Hopi way of life, for sharing with me the beauties of tradition, and for undying friendship, though thousands of miles separate us.
- To my good friends Lisa, Marianne, Brigitte, and Birgit in Europe for their more than generous hospitality, love, and abiding friendship wherever I've moved, traveled, lived in the world.
- To all my friends from SWFLMS, for giving me the chance to share my experiences with the next generation, and for the camaraderie of good colleagues.
- To all the teachers who pointed me in good directions, even when I didn't want to go there, including, but not at all limited to Martin Prechtel, Laura Simms, Jim May, Milbre Burch, Donald Davis, Ellis Richard, Gerald Fowler, and on, and on.
- To Pedro, for teaching me to love in a way no human could ever do.

Appendix

Here is a little timeline of how the stories, the parts of my life, all fit together:
- June 8, 1958 - born in Racine, WI.
- June 1971 - graduated from grade school.
- June 1971 - started working for my dad at Haumersen's in Racine, WI.
- June 1976 - graduated with honors from Racine Lutheran High School. During my final year there the old night janitor had a heart attack. My friend Herc was offered the job until a more suitable arrangement could be made, and he asked me to help. So even though we were students, we went in nearly every night and cleaned the school we were both attending. It's a good thing we weren't malicious individuals, but we did a little mischief. Just a little.
- September 1977-May 1978 - studied music at University of Wisconsin - Parkside, Kenosha, WI.
- September 1978 - December 1980 - studied music at Wisconsin Conservatory of Music in Milwaukee, WI.
- 1981-82 - Worked as a roadie for rock band Arroyo, while also working at my dad's store when we didn't have gigs.
- 1982-83 School year - returned to college and began geology studies.
- August 1984 - mother passed away suddenly after a family picnic.
- May 1986 - graduated Magna Cum Laude (GPA 3.0-3.5/4.0) from University of Wisconsin - Parkside with a B.A. in Geology.
- August-Nov. 1986 - Worked as a volunteer at Shenandoah National

- Park in Virginia for 3 months.
- January 1987 - moved to Tampa, Florida, to attend University of South Florida studying geology.
- May 1987 - Dropped out of graduate school.
- May-Nov. 1987 - moved to Grand Canyon National Park to work in a rock shop; also volunteered for the National Park Service (NPS) and got training as an Emergency Medical Technician (EMT).
- December 1987-Jan. 1988 - hired for a one month position as a ranger at Grand Canyon.
- January 1988 - returned to Racine to work as a night shift ambulance dispatcher - mostly boring as hell.
- May-Nov. 1988 - returned to Grand Canyon N.P. to resume position as ranger at Yavapai Museum.
- January-Sept. 1989 - worked at Yavapai Museum and Phantom Ranch as an interpretive ranger.
- October-Nov. 1989 - attended ranger law enforcement training at Santa Rosa Junior College.
- January-April 1990 - worked as a ranger at the Grand Canyon Visitor Center.
- April-September 1990 - worked as a law enforcement ranger at Phantom Ranch, Grand Canyon.
- September-Dec. 1990 - worked as L.E. ranger at Saguaro N.P. Tucson, AZ.
- January-April 1991 - L.E. Ranger at Indian Garden Ranger Station, Grand Canyon.
- May-Sept. 1991 - interpretive ranger at Denali N.P., Alaska.
- October 1991 - Feb. 92 - L.E. ranger at Grand Canyon N.P.
- May-Oct. 1992 & same months 1993 - interpretive ranger North Rim of Grand Canyon.
- January-May 1994 - interpretive ranger at Grand Canyon Visitor Center.
- July 1994-Feb. 1995 - Sales and Information Clerk at Flagstaff, AZ, Visitor Center.
- April-Oct. 1995 - environmental education intern in Nationalpark Hochharz, Germany.

- March 1996 - Feb. 1997 - Sales Manager at the Mono Lake Committee, Lee Vining, CA.
- Winter 1996-97 - Traveled to Thailand for 2+ weeks.
- April-Nov. 1997 - environmental educator at Upham Woods, Wisconsin Dells, WI.
- December 1997 - May 2001 - sales clerk at Wellspring Grocery, Chapel Hill, NC.
- June-Nov. 2001 - interpretive ranger at Oregon Caves N.M.
- December 2001 - April 2002 - interpretive ranger at Mesa Verde N.P.
- April 2002 - Dec. 2006 - Head Guide (ranger) at Oregon Caves N.M., Cave Junction, OR.
- July 2003 - met Pedro.
- December 2006 - Became a wanderer, freelance storyteller, freelance laborer, northern California and southern Oregon.
- 2007- April 2010 - Lived at the Frog Farm in Takilma, Oregon, and worked seasonally at Oregon Caves N.M.
- September 2009 - Met Wang Pei on the internet and began online dating.
- January-Feb. 2010 traveled to China and got married to the lovely Wang Pei.
- April 2010 - moved to China permanently.
- May-August 2010 - ESL Teacher for New Oriental Language School.
- August 2010 - began teaching geography and English at Shanghai World Foreign Language Middle School.
- April 2018 - father passed away at the age of 92, grandson born the next day.
- June 2018 - retired from teaching.
- January 2019 - moved to Jinghong, Xishuangbanna, Yunnan, China

www.ingramcontent.com/pod-product-compliance
Lightning Source LLC
Chambersburg PA
CBHW050310120526
44592CB00014B/1846